This book tells the extraordinary story of the Pinochet regime's economists, known as the "Chicago Boys." It explores the roots of their ideas and their sense of mission, following their training as economists at the Department of Economics at the University of Chicago. After their return to Chile, the "Chicago Boys" took advantage of the opportunity afforded them by the 1973 military coup to launch the first radical free market strategy implemented in a developing country. The ideological strength of their mission and the military authoritarianism of General Pinochet combined to transform an economy that, following the return to democracy, has stabilized and is now seen as a model for Latin America.

This book, written by a political scientist, examines the neo-liberal economists and their perspective on the market. It also narrates the history of the transfer of ideas from the industrialized world to a developing country, which will be of particular interest to economists.

Historical Perspectives on Modern Economics

PINOCHET'S ECONOMISTS

Historical Perspectives on Modern Economics

General Editor: Professor Craufurd D. Goodwin, Duke University

This series contains original works that challenge and enlighten historians of economics. For the profession as a whole it promotes better understanding of the origin and content of modern economics.

Other books in the series:

William J. Barber: *From New Era to New Deal: Herbert Hoover, the Economists, and American Economic Policy, 1921–1933**
M. June Flanders: *International Monetary Economics, 1870–1950*
Lars Jonung (ed.): *The Stockholm School of Economics Revisited*
Kyun Kim: *Equilibrium Business Cycle Theory in Historical Perspective*
Gerald M. Koot: *English Historical Economics, 1870–1926: The Rise of Economic History and Mercantilism*
Philip Mirowski: *More Heat than Light: Economics as Social Physics, Physics as Nature's Economics**
Mary S. Morgan: *The History of Econometric Ideas**
Takashi Negishi: *Economic Theories in a Non-Walrasian Tradition**
Malcolm Rutherford: *Institutions in Economics: The Old and the New Institutionalism*
Karen I. Vaughn: *Austrian Economics in America: The Migration of a Tradition*
E. Roy Weintraub: *Stabilizing Dynamics: Constructing Economic Knowledge*

Titles available in paperback are marked with an asterisk.

Pinochet's economists

THE CHICAGO SCHOOL IN CHILE

JUAN GABRIEL VALDÉS

CAMBRIDGE
UNIVERSITY PRESS

Published by the Press Syndicate of the University of Cambridge
The Pitt Building, Trumpington Street, Cambridge CB2 1RP
40 West 20th Street, New York, NY 10011–4211, USA
10 Stamford Road, Oakleigh, Melbourne 3166, Australia

First published 1995

Printed in Great Britain at the University Press, Cambridge

A catalogue record for this book is available from the British Library

Library of Congress cataloguing in publication data

Pinochet's economists: the Chicago School in Chile/Juan Gabriel Valdés.
     p.   cm. – (Historical Perspectives on Modern Economics)
Based on the author's thesis (doctoral) – Princeton.
ISBN 0 521 45146 9
1. Chile – Economic conditions – 1973–1988.
2. Chile – Economic policy.
3. Chicago School of Economics.
I. Title. II. Series.
HC192.V18   1995
338.983 – dc20   94–28011   CIP

ISBN 0 521 45146 9 hardback

CE

To Antonia

Contents

ix

Preface and acknowledgments

The research that has led to this book stems from a series of issues that have held a particular fascination for me throughout my intellectual development. The first of these concerns the generation, spread, and influence of ideas and ideologies. I probably became interested in this immense theme when, during my childhood, I was told that the notions underpinning our independence arrived on Chilean shores aboard ships bringing French wines and cloth. Books by Rousseau and Montesquieu were brought in clandestinely, hidden amongst candles and rigging, and subsequently passed from hand to hand along a growing, anonymous trail that eventually arrived at a collective sentiment. This tale stimulated my imagination, channeling it towards an issue that has been with me ever since. And it led, almost naturally, to curiosity about the groups formed around such concepts: namely, the ideas in people's minds, the goals, emotions, choices, insights, and all manner of projects that came to symbolize a collective identity – projects to transform society itself.

My generation yearned to eradicate all that had gone before and to secure a radically distinct starting point. The ideological phenomenon of the 1960s, once described as a "world time," knew no bounds of nationality. Across practically the entire globe, thousands of groups, enlightened by often contradictory ideas and vested with the convictions of the vanguard, embarked on a mission to change the established order. But how did these ideas and beliefs spread? How can we explain the surging ideological tides sweeping vertiginously through very different cultures, histories, and circumstances and advancing across frontiers – part of the always incomplete process of internationalization? The explanation is to be found in people, in the encounter between individuals across countries, in the creation of transnational networks of communication and in the casual or deliberate transfer of ideas.

Hence when, at the end of the 1970s, I chanced upon the "Chile Project Reports" among the archives of the Agency for International Development (AID) library in Washington DC, I immediately resolved to reconstruct the past. There, admirably detailed, lay the theoretical principles and the organizational details behind a deliberate process of transferring ideas from one country to another. But this was not the sole, nor even the main, reason for my interest in the affair. The documentation, dating from the late 1950s, described the transmittal of a well-known American tradition to a group of Chilean students. Remarkably, even as I read through the records, these very same students were using their posts as ministers and under-secretaries in a dictatorial regime to carry out the most radical change the Chilean economy has ever known.

Later on, once I had met the great names of the Chicago School of Economics and read Henry Simons and Frank Knight, I was able to pinpoint the roots of this economic vanguard's startling and all-encompassing discourse, which had provided the Pinochet regime with a revolutionary project. In truth the essentially political discourse of state, so much a part of Chilean democratic culture, had been replaced by an analytical matrix that propounded economic and market solutions for practically all problems in society. Shortly after returning to Chile in the early 1980s, I came to share the sense of confusion of a society – or at least of a social majority – which had felt its national identity to be linked to political democracy and to development defined as a form of social integration. The Chilean political elite felt itself stifled by an ideology that, shielded by the enforced silence of military repression, declared political activity irrelevant, heralded an individualism regulated only by free market forces and did not shrink from imposing, in the name of science, a penance for the historic errors of statism. It did so even though the poorest and least sheltered sectors of Chilean society might bear the brunt of the economic costs.

Isaiah Berlin has noted that not all forms of liberalism are pluralist. The type of neo-liberalism that emerged in Chile under military rule was intolerant, accepting neither the reconciliation of interests nor of values. This was an obsessive concept, dogmatically pursued. I am openly critical both of its social manifestations and of its imposition by an authoritarian state. Let me again seek sustenance in Berlin, who declared that the history of ideological stances can be correctly interpreted only by those who are themselves able to think in ideological terms and who are conscious of doing so. Now that democracy and tolerance have been restored in Chile, it is possible to sharpen the desire for reconciliation by looking back at the absolutist ideas which rose to the fore on both left and right during the 1960s and 1970s. In the new democratic framework economics cannot, as a science, be impervious to the ethical imperatives of a pluralist society. Economic practice must be guided by the force of argument, because the final determinant of its success lies in the political ability of society to reconcile creative and productive efforts.

This book originates in a doctoral thesis submitted to the Department of Political Science at Princeton University. I would therefore like to thank the department's professors, particularly Paul E. Sigmund for his constant encouragement to continue work on the manuscript during the quite extensive periods that I devoted to non-academic tasks motivated by the obligation to contribute to the restoration of democracy in my country.

Similarly, I wish to acknowledge all the remarks, criticisms, and comments that have enriched my work. Much of the actual research took place while the author belonged to the Latin American Institute for Transnational Studies (Instituto Latinoamericano de Estudios Transnacionales, ILET), based in Santiago, Chile. My friends Juan Somavía, Guillermo Campero, Héctor Vera, Alejandro Foxley Tapia, and Paulo Hidalgo contributed with their ideas or, more directly, with the results of their own research. Subsequently, in 1985, I was fortunate enough to receive an invitation from the Kellogg Institute of International Studies at the University of Notre Dame, which enabled me to continue the research and editing process in the excellent surroundings of its campus. The Ford Foundation in New York, the Rockefeller Foundation in Pocantico Hills, the AID Library in Washington DC, and the School of Economics at the Universidad Católica in Santiago, Chile, allowed me generous access to their archives, for which I am extremely grateful.

Many others deserve thanks for their cooperation and interest. Among them, my special appreciation to Ronald G. Hellman for unselfishly putting at my disposal his own research work on Chilean schools of economics. Similarly, I thank Paul E. Sigmund, Johan Galtung, Patricio Meller, Ricardo Ffrench-Davis, Alejandro Foxley, Aníbal Pinto, and Ignacio Walker, all of whom read and commented upon parts of the book or discussed with me the issues broached therein. Looking back on this extensive and interrupted research, perhaps the most enjoyable moments were my two long afternoons of conversation with Dr. Albert Hirschman. Like so many other Latin Americanists, I am indebted to him for his wisdom and ideas on economics and politics. While it is impossible to mention here all those who assisted with my work by granting personal interviews in Chile and the United States, I am grateful to all of them.

This edition, published by Cambridge University Press, would not have been possible without the interest and support of Professor Craufurd Goodwin, general editor of this economics studies series. I offer him my sincere thanks. Equally, I wish to express my appreciation to Professor Francis X. Sutton, the former director of the Bellagio Study and Conference Center of the Rockefeller Foundation, for indulging my desire for seclusion in this wonderful place. I thank the Bellagio Center and its current director, Pasquale Pesce, for the period of some weeks during which I was able to revise and rewrite important sections of the original text for the present edition. I cannot fail to mention, lastly, the enthusiasm and dedication of my secretary at the Embassy of Chile in Madrid, Magdalena Figueroa, who has managed to combine her work and our diplomatic agenda with the pendulum-like suspension and resumption of work on this book.

Chile: the outstanding example

Over the past twenty years, Chile has frequently been cited as a political and economic example for developing nations. Following the return to democracy, there has been unanimous approval of, and great regard for, the continued economic growth in Chile. The country has been held up as a model of balance, democratic prudence, and efficient economic management. There was a time, however, when the Chilean "example" attracted sharply divided opinions. Both the "revolution in freedom" of Christian Democrat president, Eduardo Frei (1964–70), and the "legal route to socialism" undertaken by President Salvador Allende (from 1970 to 1973) attracted a great deal of attention, albeit from distinct sets of people, at different times and in separate areas of the world. Both were championed as "models" to be imitated, or to be avoided. After the military takeover, and the abuse of human rights on a massive scale that it engendered, Chile retained the curiosity of diverse political and intellectual circles. The tragic example of a shattered democracy provided the spark for heated discussions and controversies in various countries. Chile's sudden shifts in orientation yielded a relentless supply of fascinating political and economic phenomena and fueled the wider debate on development, democracy, and social change. Luckily for Chileans, the recuperation of democracy rid the nation of its condition as a permanent laboratory. Henceforth, Chile's controversial recent history became more the stuff of historians and specialists. Even today, however, some continue to stress the exemplary nature of one particular experiment conducted in Chile's polemic past, which they see as an ideal model for other developing countries or nations in the process of modernizing their economies: the neo-liberal revolution implemented after General Pinochet seized power.

It will be recalled that, in September 1973, a military junta overthrew the socialist president of Chile, Salvador Allende, thereby provoking a worldwide wave of outrage at the destruction of Chile's longstanding democracy. General Pinochet and his brutal methods of government inspired near universal rejection. Nevertheless, and almost from the beginning, the economic transformation carried out in Chile acquired enormous prestige among international financial institutions, as well as in certain conservative academic circles whose economic (and social) views were, at the time, indistinctly termed "neo-conservative," "neo-liberal," or "neo-classical." From the mid-1970s onwards, the country enjoyed privileged treatment by the International Monetary Fund (IMF) and the commercial banks. Chile was doubtless the country most visited and commented upon by journalists from the international conservative press, as well as by a distinguished list of academics headed by the most prominent members of the Chicago School of Economics, including Milton Friedman himself. The reason for this interest is easy to comprehend: Chile had become the first and most famous example of applying the rules of economic orthodoxy to a developing country. Foreign trade was liberalized, prices were freed, state companies were privatized, the financial sector was deregulated, and state functions were drastically reduced.

Outside interest in Chile was sharpened by another element, which attracted both attention and a degree of professional solidarity. The group of economists appointed by General Pinochet to the main economic posts in his government had been known for some time in academic and business circles as the "Chicago Boys," since most of them had pursued postgraduate studies at that particular US university. Their status as former Chicago alumni apparently explains not just the audacity of their economic revolution, but also their limitless faith in economic science as the legitimizing basis for their draconian decisions, and in the market's ability to resolve the bulk of the problems faced by society. It was equally manifest in their complete and utter rejection of an active state role in the development process. The Chilean case thus became a model, a unique phenomenon that did not stem from any historical experience. Rather, it originated directly from what the Chicago Boys termed "economic science": a science to be found mostly in their textbooks.

These reforms and, to a certain extent, the drastic and radical fashion in which they were applied, continue to be regarded by some observers as the tough, but nonetheless admirable, groundwork underlying current Chilean success. The economic rigor to which Chile was subjected after Allende's failed experiment is thought to have laid the foundations for the free and balanced economy that, some twenty years later, distinguishes Chile's fledgling democracy. For several years, the IMF and other bodies closely linked to the financial heart of the industrialized world recommended the Chilean example as a model for the rest of Latin America. From the viewpoint of these organizations, for good or ill, Chile had stolen a march on a now universal current of economic liberalization, the privatization of public holdings and reduction of the state's social role as well as the rise in, and plight of, financial capitalism – a current that forced a change in course not just in the most developed nations, such as the United States and Great Britain, but also in the developing regions. In Latin America, Chile anticipated by over ten years the stabilization, adjustment, and liberalization processes that are now a generalized feature of the continent.[1] More remarkable still is that these ultra-liberal economic reforms came before analogous change in the United States and the United Kingdom. With a sense of anticipation that may perplex those who regard the developing world as mechanically dependent on events taking place in the central nations, Chilean economists appeared to foresee the final shift in the Keynesian era, as well as the rise to prominence of monetarist policies aimed at correcting the monetary imbalance fostered by "statism" during the preceding period. Their policies anticipated a fashion – financial abundance, assaults on the state, the denigration of government intervention, the celebration of rapid enrichment, the "yuppie" boom, and complete disregard for social policies – a fad that some neo-liberal intellectuals and especially economists felt would distinguish western "modernity" in the closing years of the century. It should therefore come as no surprise that the Chilean example has been cited as a prototype for the "shock therapies" that are to be used to combat productive chaos in the midst of uncontrolled inflation, such as in Russia or in parts of Eastern Europe. History is indeed capable of the strangest twists. These references to Chile seem to bow to the inevitability that, in such cases, the economic ills are so serious as to demand drastic remedies, even if they require draconian political strategies. As in Chile twenty years ago, some observers may be confusing the inevitable cost of economic normalization with the deliberate pursuit of ideological purifica-tion.[2]

It is precisely such controversial elements, however, that have sustained outside interest in the Chilean case during all these years. This, in fact, allows us to address a series of issues covering a vast area of concerns common to economists, political scientists, sociologists, and others in the social sciences. The economics profession has extracted copious quantities of data from Chile during its research into inflation, adjustment policies, and economic opening in developing nations. Nonetheless, discussion of the relationship between political authoritarianism and the structural economic change championed by neo-Liberals has been equally popular, and may even have eclipsed the strictly economic analysis of Chile. The Chilean case has frequently been cited by sceptics, who doubt that it is truly possible to combine democracy with neo-liberal economic adjustment. Structural reforms prescribed for Latin America by the cluster of public and private institutions that regulate international finance, which one author terms the "Washington consensus for developing countries," would seem to render impossible the preservation of personal freedoms.[3] Clearly, this whole question has been a principal argument of those opposed to the application of orthodox economic measures in the developing world. Indeed, this rationale is not restricted to these nations: the current, grave economic and social situation in Europe and North America has revived criticism of the impact of neo-liberalism on the domestic political and social order.

Something similar has befallen the issue of transforming the state through privatizations and the curtailment of its regulatory and distributive functions. As in all else, Chile in the 1970s seemed to be the most radical case: the state literally dismantled itself. Privatizations and the reduction of the state did not arise, as with later instances in Latin America, from IMF pressure. Nor did this process produce tension between the political sectors and economic specialists within the state. Rather, it served to illustrate the understanding between economists and the military to act together to change the type of state historically present in Chile. State emasculation in the economic and social arenas was conducted by its own institutions, backed by those who ran them.

From this stems, in turn, a further crucial point in the general debate: one stressing the negative impact of cuts in the state on the living conditions of the poorest in society. Chile also constitutes a very interesting case study in trying to assess the likely social costs of orthodox economic reforms in a developing context. Although large sectors were always marginalized from economic development and modernization, by the early 1970s Chilean society had become one of the most egalitarian in Latin America. The introduction of the neo-liberal model caused a significant fall in real wages, a dramatic rise in unemployment, and a decade-long deterioration in social services, particularly health and education. The huge gap driven between rich and poor during this period is today the most onerous legacy for democracy in Chile. That said, however, for many it remains an open question whether the current positive situation of the Chilean economy is really due to the radical reforms carried out in the early years of the Pinochet regime. The question could be posed roughly as follows: do the economic growth and the "liberal consensus" that characterize Chilean society today stem from the Chicago Boys' audacious and brutal imposition of market policies in the mid-1970s? Or, would it be more accurate to ascribe them to the more regulated and complex evolution of economic policy in the closing years of the dictatorship and during the first three years of democratic government? Some argue that the progressive economic stability and growth enjoyed by Chile could not have taken place without the initial reforms. They believe that these measures should be judged on their own merits and on their long term effects. For them, the Chicago Boys episode remains a positive and praiseworthy "example." Others, however, stress the catastrophic consequences of these policies and the dogmatic fashion in which the reforms were applied, despite the fact that they could have been accomplished in very different ways, with less costly results for the majority of the population. From this viewpoint, the Chicago Boys' measures are exactly the type of economic policy that must be avoided.

Obviously, then, there are no easy answers to the issues raised by the Chilean case. Such issues require a comparative approach and, more often than not, lead reflection down new paths and raise further questions. This is particularly true given that the issues of neo-liberalism and a market-regulated society are today matters of universal concern. Interest in the Chilean case no longer derives from its peculiarity, but because it contained elements of neo-liberal logic at its most extreme and paradigmatic. Many of the matters originally present in the Chilean process have reappeared in each of the subsequent neo-liberal experiences. For this reason, discussion of the Chilean case actually alludes in great measure to universal problems and ideological currents. These factors reflect a fresh mode of understanding society and economic development that rose to prominence in the 1980s and that is now present – in mild form – in many of the reasoning and decision-making processes in both developed and industrialized nations. It is not possible to refer here to each and every one of these factors, yet it is necessary for them to "filter through" as the central concern of this book unfolds. Let us now introduce the subject for the first time.

The most prominent aspect of the phenomenon that concerns us here was the neo-liberal ideological wave that inundated the United States, following the election of Ronald Reagan, and Great Britain, under the Thatcher government. It began in Chile in 1974 not simply as a set of economic measures, but rather as a broad, revolutionary ideology. In Chile, neo-liberal economic thought became an all-pervading framework of ideas. In a context of violent change in the political power structures, it was used by the new military rulers as the requisite substance for a radical transformation of the state. Those that proclaimed these ideas argued, persuasively, that the establishment of a free market necessitated an authoritarian regime. A "free society," regulated by the market, had to be forcefully imposed. The reasons were very simple: Chilean society had been molded over the previous half century by a powerful and interventionist state. Indeed this had been characteristic of Chile since its origins as an independent nation. Moreover, for fifty years, influential organizations – including political parties on the left and center as well as the Catholic church – promoted a political process and social climate marked by a pronounced egalitarian bent towards "social justice," the fight against social marginalization and support for national integration. The political democracy that formed part of Chile's very identity this century, moreover, seemed to have been built largely on the capacity of the state to distribute and to mediate between antagonistic social groups. It should not seem strange, then, that those who advocated a society regulated fundamentally, if not exclusively, by the market should decide that the only way to achieve this was by force, and in the briefest time period possible. This fateful decision, and the lucid blueprint adopted to carry it out, lead us to focus our analysis on the "revolutionary" elite – the group of economists – behind this experience.

They introduced into Chilean society ideas that were completely new, concepts entirely absent from the "ideas market" prior to the military coup. This elite posited, first and foremost, the concept of economic science – equivalent to the exact sciences – as the motor behind the organization of society. The Chicago Boys immediately converted a set of economic objectives into the sole determinant of all that was socially desirable. Economic analysis was subsequently extended to other areas of social activity, including a proposed ideal "modern individual": competitive and acquisitive, he was supposed to spawn a culture in tune with his own reproduction and the creation of a "nation of owners." The Chicago Boys introduced the concept of a minimal state, concerned solely with public order: in other words, a state limited to repressive duties and dealing with extreme poverty. Above all, they introduced into the "public debate" (which during the years of dictatorship became a mere monologue) a self-sustaining economic discourse, whose variables formed part of a theoretical framework that excluded ethical, cultural, political, or social considerations. Indeed, it did not even acknowledge the presence of such considerations. On the contrary, those who dared to criticize this logic once it was made public found themselves dismissed as persons ignorant of economic science and who, therefore, were incapable of understanding what was suitable for Chilean society.

Where did these ideas come from? To find out, we need to look at the economic training of the Chicago Boys, to explore the creation of this elite, the origin of their attitudes, and the way they defined their role as economists. This book deals with the story of an economic elite that attempted to utilize a military coup, and the extended period of political repression that accompanied the takeover, to carry out a neo-liberal revolution. In the remainder of this introduction, we will attempt to gain a better understanding of the truly revolutionary impact that these ideas had on Chilean society, and of the technical and political guidance exercised by this elite. It is useful, in so doing, to compare, albeit summarily, the revolutionary events of the *Unidad Popular* period under Salvador Allende with what followed, which we have termed the "neo-liberal revolution."

The two revolutions

In the course of a few brief and violent years, Chilean society was subjected to two completely contradictory projects. From 1970 to 1973, the Allende government implemented its "anti-imperialist, anti-oligarchical and antimonopolistic" program, deciding to nationalize the financial and productive sectors of Chile, to expropriate large chunks of rural property, and to replace the market with far-reaching price controls. From 1974 to 1978, the military regime of General Pinochet developed a radical economic liberalization program based on the indiscriminate use of market mechanisms, the dismantling and reduction of the state, deregulation of the financial sector, and a discourse that ascribed to market forces the ability to solve practically any problem in society. One extreme of radical ideology was immediately followed by its very opposite. Chilean society was twice called upon to begin its history from scratch. A brief comparison between these projects, as well as the attitudes of those that directed them, might prove useful as a more precise introduction to the objectives of this study. Let us now highlight the similarities and contrasts between the changes carried out and the elite that imposed them.

The first important affinity is that both projects intended to bring about radical reform. Socialists and neo-Liberals alike claimed that their principal aim was structural change, although in one case this referred to redistribution and economic reactivation and, in the other, to the battle against inflation. In the language of the Allende period, both wished to bring about "irreversible reform." Hence, if we include a reference to the anti-inflation goal in the quote below, then the conclusion reached by Larraín and Meller on the intentions of the *Unidad Popular* appears equally valid for the neo-liberal experiment: "there is no doubt," they say, "that the fundamental goal [of the *Unidad Popular*] was radical change and not simply better income distribution and higher economic growth."[4] For this very reason, both the Socialists and the neo-Liberals were prepared to carry through their reforms at any price and as rapidly as possible. One year after taking office, the *Unidad Popular* Treasury Minister could proudly announce: "the nationalization of the banking system is practically complete. The state now controls . . . 90 percent of all credit."[5] Four years after the military coup, Pinochet's Treasury Minister was able to solemnly declare that the "new economic order" based on the trilogy of economic opening, financial liberalization, and state privatization had been completed. His report on the state of public finances began: "virtually all fundamental measures in this respect have already been adopted."[6]

Secondly, for this same reason both experiments were comparable with respect to the magnitude of the change that they contemplated. Their discourse went far beyond normal measures, or the strictly economic. Rather, they posited an inclusive ideology that sought to modify the way that Chilean society was organized and functioned. The goal was nothing less than the transformation of the state, of customs, and of culture. In this sense, the "construction of socialism" and the military junta's proposed Declaration of

Principles – to bring about a "prolonged and profound operation to change Chilean mentality" – derive from an identical revolutionary purpose. Consequently, socialist and neo-liberal intellectuals proclaimed to their most receptive constituencies – workers for one, a new technocratic and business class for the other – two behavior "models" to be imitated: the "new man" popularized by "Ché Guevara" and the *homo economicus* present in the classical writings on economics. The former represented the ideals of solidarity and generosity, the fight for justice and equality; the latter stood for the cult of rationality and individual liberty, the quest for equal opportunities to compete in a free market.[7]

 Thirdly, both groups of "revolutionaries" were thus equally critical of Chile's past. Their diagnoses categorically condemned the type of state historically present, which historians have labeled the "mediatory state." This point requires a brief explanation. Since the great depression of 1929, Chilean development had revolved around expanding the state's role in the economy. The state carried out functions as the promoter of business activity in the private sector, as a major propellant of the industrialization process, and as an important economic agent in its own right. By the early 1960s, state intervention in, and management of, the economy had become traditional and was accepted to a greater or lesser degree by all economic actors, including private entrepreneurs. Business organizations participated in negotiating the complex web of regulations laid down by the administration to govern economic activity, competing to obtain the choicest share of state largesse. The state's role arose, however, from factors that were not strictly or exclusively economic. As with the welfare state developed in Europe under the influence of Keynesian theory, the "mediatory state" arose from the need to reformulate the dominant coalitions as a result of the process of incorporating the organized popular sectors, who acquired an important degree of influence in the political system through the political parties on the left. These groups, and those that represented the interests of the middle and upper segments of society, competed for shares in the power that the state was able to administer and distribute. Consequently, the state's role in the economy was a consubstantial element of the historic, if rather fragile, democratic political system that distinguished Chile from other countries in the region.

 The "mediatory state" model and its economic policies, however, declined into severe crisis at the end of the 1960s. The international crisis of those years imposed restrictions beyond the reach of national authorities. Moreover, Chile's import substitution policies tended to provoke severe distributive conflicts that, in turn, degenerated into recurrent inflationary crises, balance of payments difficulties, and intra-sectoral disputes. Towards the end of the Christian Democrat government of President Frei some economists warned that the cycle of industrial expansion through import substitution was exhausted, calling for a radical shift towards a strategy based on exports. By then, however, certain political problems were present. These would end by upsetting the balance of mutual confidence upon which the mediatory state had been established.

This was the state that both experiments tried to destroy, for reasons that were not wholly different. Some (the *Unidad Popular*) sought to do so because "the state role had always been to favor the basic interests of monopoly capitalism." Others (the neo-Liberals) believed that the state was, by definition, inefficient, favored monopolistic groups and, worst of all, hindered market freedoms. It was thus a major obstacle to the formation of a "free society." In the preceding decades, there had been increasingly frequent attacks on the state, its inefficiency and its penchant for interventionist and protectionist policies. Such assaults were launched from all ideological sectors, including the "structuralists" and the "monetarists," the two traditionally opposing economic groups. Yet, this current of criticism had never before reached the crescendo of the neo-Liberals and Socialists. For the first time, these groups considered the radical and definitive cancellation of the state in all its facets, including the political democracy that was an inseparable part of it. In effect, those responsible for these policies, both the Socialists and neo-Liberals, adopted a similar attitude of discredit and disdain towards what had hitherto constituted the country's democratic history. The democratic tradition that had distinguished Chile in Latin America was never deemed worthy of contributing to reform. Quite the contrary, it was rejected as a distorting element; an allegedly corrupt farce concealing either class domination or a political caste's use of the state for personal gain. In this manner, the intellectual authors of change were determined to reduce or simply to destroy the institutions they took to symbolize either "bourgeois democracy" or "statist political dabbling," as the case may be.

For a time, however, both sides were determined to exploit these same institutions. The ideologists of the *Unidad Popular* thought that the "bourgeois state" could be dismantled from within: its institutions would serve to foster greatly expanded democratic participation, to the point of altering the very nature of the institutional system and transforming bourgeois dominance into a true, popular democracy. The neo-Liberals employed the power of the state to cut it to a minimum. They believed, until the financial crisis of 1982, that the process was "irreversible"; that the state would never again interfere in the economy, and would restrict itself to enforcing the rules of the game and to caring for the most impoverished in society.

There was, however, a significant difference in the conduct of both groups when in control of state institutions, and this needs to be stressed. The attempt to construct a socialist economy was carried out in a framework of total respect for public liberties and democratic rights. Although, as stated above, most of the socialist ideologues cared very little for "bourgeois democracy," the fact is that the freedom of the press as well as the rights to assembly and expression (including the right to attack the government with practically any means at one's disposal) were more than meticulously preserved. The "end" objective for the Socialists of combining populist and socialist measures, which Allende referred to as "red wine and pies," was, despite the chaotic expropriation and nationalization policies, more present in the voluntarist ideological discourse of some of its architects and intellectuals than in reality. Socialism committed errors. It faced the opposition of business elements as well as of conservative political sectors, enjoying strong support outside Chile. The construction of socialism finally turned into a pitched battle. A politically exhausted government completely lost control over the economy and found itself devoured by the chaos that it had helped to create.

The neo-liberal revolution that followed was carried out quite differently. It went through two phases, clearly differentiated by the crisis and economic depression of 1982. The first period can be termed, in the words of one author, the "naive phase" of Chilean neo-liberalism. This was undoubtedly the most radical. The reforms faced neither criticism nor opposition since they were carried out in a framework of total deprivation of public liberties and citizen's rights. A military dictator set the context in which economic policy could advance regardless of the social costs incurred, or retrace its steps to correct apparent errors before resuming its path. The neo-liberal revolution was, in this sense, a true revolution. This elite conducted, organized, and exercised state power with great resolve: the group of "Chicago Boys" gradually occupied all the main state economic posts; it exercised increasing control over the intellectual reproduction process of its own theories, dispatching disciples to the various institutions of higher education for economics, thus imposing its particular view of "economic science" and marginalizing all others. The group built a system of links and personnel transfers between the public sector and Chile's main centers of financial and industrial power. It participated in an active press and television campaign to spread its own message on economic science and to reject views that had influenced the discussion on economic development in previous decades, including a radical critique of Chilean democratic traditions and the proposal for a "new, modern, authoritarian and technified" democracy.

A second phase followed the failure of economic adjustment in 1982, and the consequent departure of the most famous Chicago Boys from office. This period was distinguished by the "on the job training" of a second generation of Chicago-educated economists. They found themselves forced to conduct a process of state-led corrections to the economy that would finally yield positive results. During this second period, running from 1983 to the end of the military regime in 1989, the Chicago Boys continued to enjoy the advantages of decision-making conferred by twin control over both economic and political variables. In all, the Chicago Boys remained in government for almost seventeen years.

There is a further, vital distinction between the socialist and neo-liberal projects – the ability each showed when it came to stimulating Chilean economic growth. With the benefit of historical hindsight, the first project appeared fated to fail. The second, despite its limitations, was brave enough to incorporate the dominant world economic trends into the Chilean economy. Briefly put, the Allende government changed "pacted" state interventionism into a scheme whereby the state excessively appropriated all economic activity – a project that finally proved politically and economically unsustainable. The Chicago economists, on the other hand, radically altered the Chilean economic paradigm, bringing it into line not just with military self-interest in retaining control but also with the general tendencies of the world economy. Analysis of this point is a recurrent theme in the book. Suffice it to say here that the neo-liberal revolution contained certain basic elements which could have provided Chile with a viable pattern of development. But, due to the Chicago Boys' own dogmatism, these factors were rejected or postponed: they were condemned to await both less ideologically oriented economic policymakers and a stable democratic polity, without which the model could never acquire true legitimacy. The recent history of Chile demonstrates, then, that only flexibility and a combination of political and economic measures, based on consensus through persuasion, can result in a viable development model.

This is not, however, the main issue to be addressed here. Rather, we are most concerned with the ensemble of ideas and attitudes that defined the Chicago Boys as economists, and that appear definitive of their role in contemporary Chilean history. As we shall see, particularly in the final chapter of the book, *economic development* under the Chicago Boys can be judged in various and quite complex ways. Yet, their *behavior as economists* is surprising for its simplicity and transparency. By their own definition, this role is radically distinct from any notion of economics as an "art of persuasion." Far from accepting the plurality of economic viewpoints, or even the complexity of decision-making in matters affecting millions of people, the Chicago Boys conceived the economy in an entirely dogmatic fashion: as a science that needed to be imposed for the economy's own good and, therefore, for that of society. This issue renders the study of the Chicago Boys a relevant exercise and justifies reviewing the intellectual antecedents and behavioral patterns that contributed to their appearance.

Foreign ideas

General Pinochet's repeated rejection of "alien ideas" during his years in power, in reference to Marxist thought and, in general, to anything that smelled remotely of socialism, was rather paradoxical: the only concepts that had no known antecedent in Chilean political culture were precisely the neo-liberal viewpoints so enthusiastically embraced by his regime. It is clear that the ideas of Allende's *Unidad Popular*, for their part, had a long history of evolution in Chilean society. Their origin may go back to the introduction of Marxist socialism at the end of the last century and to the organization of Socialist Workers' parties between the early 1900s and the 1930s. Subsequently, the *Frente Popular* of 1936 – uniting in government the centrist *Partido Radical* with Communists and Socialists – prefigured the type of political alliance headed by Allende in the 1970s. The genealogy and trajectory of leftist ideas were thus easily recognizable in Chile. They formed part of national political culture and expressed themselves at all levels of social organization.

Something similar, albeit on a lesser scale, occurred with the conservative ideas representative of several of the more enthusiastic smaller groups that supported the military coup. In particular, the so-called *gremialistas* (young conservatives with pronounced corporatist and authoritarian tendencies) reflected a series of influences running from "Hispanism" and Spanish Francoism, to the conservative Catholic ideas of De Maistre and Bonald. It also included some of the Catholic church's traditional social thought, although it rejected Vatican II just as it rejected democratization in Chilean society and the socializing tendencies expressed, right from the beginning, by its major rival, the *Partido Demócrata Cristiano*. *Gremialista* thought, confined to the Universidad Católica de Chile during the period prior to Allende, was revitalized by the extremism of the socialist experience. Scant popular support for *gremialista* ideas should not, however, be taken to negate the movement's deep roots in national political culture. In reality, it reflected a conservative Catholic tradition going right back to the origins of the republic. Other conservative groups, seeing themselves principally as "nationalists," revered the role of the armed forces in Chilean history and showed vestiges of past sympathies for German nazism and Italian fascism. But even their ideas clearly derived from known itineraries in the ideological debates of recent decades. The same is true of liberal doctrines. Although divided into several broad currents, they retained a democratic and occasionally progressive bent, reflecting in part the influence and traditions of British liberalism. Chile's appetite for economic liberalism, in ascent at certain moments and in decline at others, was restricted to economic aspects: it absorbed neither from business discourse nor from the rightwing political parties any overall view of society that was antagonistic to democratization or to the pivotal role of the state. Finally, the military demonstrated, in addition to their professional, nationalist, and conservative nature, support for the principles of the National Security Doctrine and the hemisphere-wide defense strategy against communism – concepts that were only too well known even then.

In sharp contrast, the ensemble of neo-liberal ideas that evolved in Chile after 1975 had no antecedent in the nation's public life. As is well known, these concepts represented a radical break with the ideas of social change and distributive justice that had won a huge electoral majority in 1970. But, more importantly, they also differed from the ideology that had characterized Chilean capitalist classes and traditional rightwing sectors up until the Allende period. Indeed, such ideas had never appeared in the economic development programs presented by political parties, nor in the proposals of the main conservative economists during the thirty years prior to the *Unidad Popular* government. They definitely did not represent military ponderings on the economy. So where did these ideas come from?

The answer is to be found in the education of around one hundred Chilean economics students at the University of Chicago from 1957 to 1970. While not sufficient in itself, this training process was certainly a necessary condition for subsequent events. It constitutes a striking example of an organized transfer of ideology from the United States to a country within its direct sphere of influence. Unlike other processes involving the mere "culturalization" of local elites abroad, the education of these Chileans derived from a specific project designed in the 1950s to influence the development of Chilean economic thinking. Such thinking was regarded by a number of influential Americans as responsible for Chile's serious economic problems. This academic and political exercise clearly had an extraordinary impact on Chilean society. Its subsequent influence in Latin America, and indeed on the recent experiences in Eastern Europe, shows its particular relevance as a case of educational policy.

This book analyzes the organized transfer of economic ideas from the United States to Chile that culminated in the neo-liberal revolution of the Chicago Boys. It deals specifically with the origin and evolution of the agreements between the Universidad Católica de Chile and the University of Chicago; the cultural background of, and the belief transmitted to, the economists who trained under that program; and the way in which their perception of their own professional role evolved from the moment they finished their education at Chicago until the 1973 military coup. The book intends to show: (a) that a decisive element in the formation of the principles which later guided the economic team was the organized transfer of specific concepts, attitudes, values, and world-view;[8] (b) that this transfer resulted from a deliberate attempt by Chilean and US groups to combat the "nationalistic" and "structuralist" standpoints on the economy in vogue across Latin America both then and later; and (c) that the transferal or transmittal of concepts and attitudes was duplicated in the training provided to younger generations of economists at the Universidad Católica de Chile.

The historical reconstruction contained in the book is not an attempt to reveal a conspiracy. There was no such conspiracy. But this does not mean that the process through which economic concepts and world-view were transferred was accidental, nor that it lacked explicit goals. Quite the contrary, the transfer was implemented as part of a calculated bid to implant previously absent notions in the Chilean "ideological market" – concepts that, if they did exist, had long been discarded as impractical or politically inapplicable. This deliberate endeavor aimed, quite explicitly, to influence economic views and, potentially, to influence government decisions on the course of the economy. Nevertheless, it was an open and public process: the actors were convinced that they were engaged in a legitimate undertaking that they considered to be positive and extremely valuable for Chilean development. Hence, although the venture was a concerted and intentional act, it lacked an essential element of conspiracy: secrecy.

At first sight, the inter-university agreements seem to be similar to hundreds of other scientific and cultural accords between the United States and Chile, the sole apparent difference being the political impact that the agreement's implementation would produce fifteen years later. However, as we shall see further on, the subject (economics), the "issuing" entity (Chicago University), and the circumstances of the "recipients" (the Universidad Católica de Chile and Chilean rightwing economic circles) combined to mold the agreement into a veritable "mission." The process reflected efforts by a group of Chicago professors to defend true economic science (i.e. neo-classical orthodox theory) against contamination by Keynesianism or socialism. At that time, local capitalist groups were undergoing a profound hegemonic crisis. The transmittal of this "mission" gave Chicago-trained Chilean economists the strength to undertake the revolutionary assignments that they felt compelled to undertake.

From this standpoint, the study also analyzes, in more generic terms, the part played by technocratic, modernizing elites in developing countries. More specifically, it assesses the role of economists acting as conveyors for a theory that seeks preeminence over political and moral issues, which they dismiss as mere "ideological factors." In doing so, the book begs a series of questions concerning the ability of our political democracies to withstand the inevitable onslaught of transnational cultural, financial, and political forces. In their quest for "modernity," these forces harness a range of ideologies, all coated with the veneer of science, and cherish above all else the advantages supposedly inherent to the "application of science," regardless of the means and whatever the cost.

The book is divided into an initial chapter, which describes the rise to prominence of the Chicago Boys in the Pinochet government, and three longer sections. Section one, covering chapters 2 to 5, deals with ideological transfer – the process and the actors involved. It begins by offering certain theoretical considerations on the transfer of ideas. Chapter 3 defines and evaluates the "Chicago tradition of economics." The following chapter addresses the actors who conceived and promoted the university agreements, looking at their interests and motivations: the US government's International Cooperation Administration (ICA), Chicago University, and the Universidad Católica de Chile. Chapter 5 gives a detailed account of the background to the agreements signed by the two universities.

Section two, comprising chapters 6 to 8, deals first with the training of Chilean students at the University of Chicago. Chapter 7 covers the implantation of the Chicago School in Chile and, finally, chapter 8 examines the export of the Chicago tradition to other Latin American countries.

The third and last section, containing chapters 9 to 11, considers what might be termed the "radicalization" of the Chilean context and the creation of power opportunities for the Chicago Boys. It commences by describing the reform process in Chilean universities and the dangers this entailed for the Chicago Boys based at the Escuela de Economía of the Universidad Católica de Chile. Chapter 10 analyzes the radicalization of business and rightwing sectors in general, in reaction to the increasingly threatening clouds on the political horizon. Section three ends by looking at the Chicago front-line and the business world: their role during the Allende administration and in drawing up an alternative economic program for an eventual military government. The book's conclusion addresses events following the 1982 crisis: the Chicago Boys' second phase in power, progress towards a stable economy, and the return to democracy.

CHAPTER 1

Authoritarians without a project

The junta of generals and admirals that seized power in Chile in 1973 lacked a definite government project.[1] The national security doctrine to which the junta constantly referred was but a mere "substitute for a political project or model." It could not provide the blueprint for an efficient relationship between the state and "civil society."[2] The Chilean armed forces lacked experience in government and they acted compelled, not by a predetermined plan to impose a military administration on the state, but rather in reaction to something they regarded as a grave threat to national security and to their own institutional survival – the Allende administration and the ever more radical political and social situation.

The military's decision to overthrow the constitutional government, moreover, had initially enjoyed support from a vast, transient coalition, made up of groups, trade unions, and political organizations representing very diverse social interests, which professed varying degrees of sympathy and enthusiasm for the military intervention. The major conservative party, the National Party (*Partido Nacional*, PN), extreme rightwing groups, business associations, and the newspaper *El Mercurio* (probably far more influential than the others mentioned) welcomed the new government enthusiastically and without reservations. The majority, centre-oriented Christian Democratic Party (*Partido Demócrata Cristiano*, PDC) offered lukewarm support for the coup. However, a group of noted PDC leaders distanced themselves from the bulk of their fellow party members, condemning the overthrow of the constitutional president and regretting his death. The persecution, assassination, incarceration, and/or disappearance of leftwing party leaders immediately after the coup quickly prompted the concern of the Catholic church and, subsequently, of the PDC. It soon became apparent, however, that the military did not feel the need for political advice before making decisions. Above all, the armed forces wished to demonstrate their independence from any political grouping. This desire for autonomy, and the variety of the support they received, made the situation much more complex: it became difficult for the junta to adopt a unified and coherent strategy for the type of regime that should replace the one that had just been overthrown.

This deficiency was particularly evident in the field of economics. The navy, which initially took charge of the economy, shared the general awareness of the gravity of the situation. Indices of wholesale prices showed that inflation exceeded 800 percent; goods were in short supply and industry was paralyzed as a result of prolonged social conflict. The new authorities, however, lacked a technical background in economics. Prior to the military coup, moreover, they had not established political links with any specific Chilean interest group that might then have led them to select a given group of economists. Naturally, this does not mean that they did not have an overall ideological position. Given their middle- and upper-class roots and conservative traditions, Chilean naval officers instinctively favored liberal economic policies and loathed the socialist project represented by the Popular Unity (*Unidad Popular*, UP) administration.

Thus, one of the first steps taken by the new economic authorities was to attempt to form an emergency economic team, consisting of those they considered to be technical experts. Sergio Molina, Minister of Finance in President Eduardo Frei's PDC administration (1964–1970), was among the first to be approached. Admiral Gotuzzo, the newly appointed Minister of Finance, offered him the post of Undersecretary for Finance. Molina declined the offer.[3] Gotuzzo then approached other experts linked to the PDC, including Carlos Massad, president of the Chilean Central Bank under Frei. Massad, who had a PhD from Chicago University, was then with the World Bank. Raul Sáez, another minister in the Frei government, was also approached. Sáez possessed great prestige in international financial circles and subsequently joined the regime as Minister of Finance and the Economy.

Links to figures connected with the PDC soon abated, ending completely when the party conditioned its participation – in a political or technical capacity – on the fulfilment of certain political and human rights criteria. The final break in relations was hastened by the military regime's decision to opt for a political strategy more in tune with the aspirations of the most radical rightwing groups. In fact, immediately following the coup, the debate on economic policy became closely linked to the dilemma surrounding the new regime's self-definition: a choice between a "restoration" scheme, which merely required "repressive pacification," or a "foundational scheme," which implied the need for a revolution.[4] The first option presupposed that the armed forces, having restored constitutional rule and public order, would provide a bridge to the next civilian administration. The "foundational" approach implied that the military junta would direct a transformation project. As stated in the military government's Declaration of Principles, this required nothing less than "profound and prolonged actions to change Chilean mentality."[5]

The arrival of the Chicago Boys

One of these naval "probes" would be decisive in defining the initial debate mentioned above, and would provide the regime with its "revolutionary" credentials – the contacts with Hernán Cubillos, then president of the advisory board of *El Mercurio*, Chile's most influential newspaper. *El Mercurio* commanded the respect of the military as one of the main actors in the campaign against the UP government. Cubillos was trusted by the navy, with which he was connected through family ties. Cubillos and Roberto Kelly, a newspaper employee and former naval officer, were fully aware of a plan secretly devised since 1972 by a group of economists, mostly from the Universidad Católica de Chile in preparation for possible military intervention. The plan, and the economic team behind it, were warmly recommended to the naval authorities by the newspaper's executive staff.[6]

The program prepared by the team formed part of an overall strategy aimed at destabilizing and overthrowing the leftist regime.[7] The semi-clandestine work undertaken during 1972 intended to provide opponents of Allende particularly in Congress with the information and economic guidance they needed. But it also entailed a program to be applied if the UP administration were overthrown. The team received generous funding from Chilean business organizations themselves financially backed by Latin American business groups. At least part of the monies channeled to Chile came from the US Central Intelligence Agency (CIA).[8]

Rolf Luders, a prominent member of the Chicago group, but who was not in the country at that time, described this technical "shadow team" as follows:

the work group's existence and success was probably made possible by their common educational background. In the mid-fifties, Chicago University and the Universidad Católica de Chile initiated a program for educational exchange. Under this agreement, Chicago University sent professors to Chile to do research and accepted Chilean graduate students. Through this program and in combination with supplementary scholarships, approximately one hundred students had completed graduate studies at Chicago University by the early seventies . . . Up to 1973, on their return to Chile, many of these economists became professors at local universities. Others worked for the government, particularly during Frei's administration. The rest joined the main firms in Chile. But they all formed a single community – incremented annually by new generations of economists graduating from Chilean universities – sharing the same technical language, a rationalistic approach to problem solving and the eagerness to contribute, through their efforts, to creating a prosperous, fair and free society. Most of these economists are currently known – whether they like it or not – as Chicago Boys.[9]

The group's principal figures were: Sergio de Castro, a former dean of the School of Economics at the Universidad Católica, whose strong personality made him the natural leader of the group; Pablo Baraona, ex-director of the same economics faculty; Sergio Undurraga, also an economist with the Universidad Católica; Emilio Sanfuentes, Manuel Cruzat, and Juan Braun, linked to business groups; Alvaro Bardón, J. L. Zabala, Andrés Sanfuentes, and Juan Villarzú, economists from the Universidad de Chile who had studied at Chicago and were linked to the PDC.

Approximately two years later, Sergio de Castro, Pablo Baraona and Alvaro Bardón, together with Rolf Luders, Miguel Kast (who in 1973 was studying in Chicago), and Sergio de la Cuadra, would become the main figures in what *El Mercurio* labeled the "Chilean economic revolution." Sergio de Castro was Minister of the Economy from April 1975 to December 1976, at which time he was appointed Finance Minister – a portfolio he held until April 1982. Pablo Baraona was Minister of the Economy from December 1976 to December 1978, a position later held by Rolf Luders (August 1982–February 1983). Alvaro Bardón became Undersecretary for the Economy under Baraona while Miguel Kast was Minister of Planning from April to August 1982. Other lesser known Chicagoans occupied various posts at the Central Bank, the Budget Office and in the government planning divisions. They included Juan Carlos Méndez, Alvaro Donoso, Ernesto Silva Bafalluy, Jorge Selume, Alvaro Saieh, etc. The Chicago group's ideological positions were shared by other prestigious economists previously connected to the Christian Democrats. Among them, the most notable were: Jorge Cauas, who headed, as Finance Minister, the group just mentioned, and under whose authority "shock" treatment was applied to the economy; and José Piñera, who as Labor Minister carried out the labor plan and several other social reforms, collectively known as the modernizations. However, the latter were not Chicago alumni. Cauas took graduate courses at Columbia University and Piñera at Harvard.

Acquiring power

From the beginning, the Chicago team had to struggle for control in a "coalition" of economists that did not necessarily agree with their views on the content and timing of the measures to be taken. More importantly, the remainder of the coalition did not share their radical, neo-liberal views, which advocated structural change to drastically alter Chile's existing pattern of development. In fact, right from the start, it was clear that the Chicago Boys "preferred a liberal economic organization." In this early phase, however, "economic policy focused mainly on correcting the imbalances created during the previous period."[10] Thus, military personnel in charge of the economy saw their main task as balancing the budget and curbing inflation. They supported the measures suggested by the *técnicos* (as they were called by the High Command). Later on, the first predominantly civilian economic team reiterated that its intention was to "gradually curtail inflation" through moderate cuts in fiscal spending, fearing that "drastic solutions would produce catastrophic results."[11] In July 1974, almost a year after the coup, the newly appointed and prestigious Finance Minister, Jorge Cauas, reaffirmed that the goal was to create "a modern, mixed economy" and to reestablish order, given the severe disequilibria inherited from the previous regime. Official declarations stipulated that market laws should determine the allocation of productive resources, although accompanied by "adequate general guidance provided by government in order to increment its social scope."[12] Therefore, initial measures "did not aim, not even implicitly, at producing radical changes in the economic system that Chile had had up to the 1970s, but only attempted to 'normalize' its operation and introduce gradual reforms in parts of the system."[13]

In fact, official declarations, added to some spectacular measures against inflation, obscured the implementation of discreet, but nonetheless radical, structural reforms by the vast number of Chicago economists appointed to official posts by Sergio de Castro. From 1975 onwards, as Minister of the Economy (a post he assumed at the same time as former Christian Democrat Jorge Cauas became Minister of Finance), de Castro intensified the attempt to bring about profound structural change in the Chilean economy. He acted with the liberty furnished by a traditionally subordinate post, under the protection of a man like Cauas who was more flexible and receptive to publicity than he was. The prevalence of the Chicago team was simultaneous to the introduction of "shock" treatment. Carrying on the anti-inflation policy begun in 1974 with the elimination of price controls (except for wage rises, which remained tightly restricted), the group of economists decided in 1975 to attack the public deficit through "fiscal shock" measures. After a controversial period in which the Chicago Boys flaunted their academic qualifications and contacts with well-known US economists, supporters of a "gradual" anti-inflation strategy were defeated. The Chicago group proceeded to bring about a drastic cut in public spending through the reduction of state employment and the elimination of agricultural subsidies. The result was a 12.9 percent drop in GDP. In a single year, these economists had managed to restore Chile's historical level of fiscal deficit. Control of inflation, however, was an elusive goal: in the first year of military rule, and in spite of the above measures, inflation declined only slightly, from 376 percent to 340 percent.

The objectives of shock treatment were, however, wider than the mere fight against inflation. As Arnold Harberger stated in an article published a year later: "public debate has focused so intensely on the twin problems of inflation and unemployment that important structural changes introduced into economic policy have gone practically unrecognized."[14] Thus, almost imperceptibly, the most profound transformation of the Chilean economy this century had begun. At first, Chilean public opinion failed to comprehend the reasons underlying such change. *El Mercurio* stated, during the four-year period, that Chile and its economy were governed "by a small and select team that seldom explains its reasons and . . . does not communicate its decisions in advance."[15]

The economic measures

Table 1, developed by Meller, shows exactly which structural changes were introduced during the first phase of the Chicago Boys' command over the Chilean economy.[16] The measures that characterized the economic model can be classified into three general areas: "liberalization of the price system and the market; an open regime on foreign trade and external financing operations; and reduced government involvement in the economy."[17] These measures corresponded to a theoretical model that "might be defined as a capitalist model of private firms, operating under laissez faire and completely integrated into the world economy; i.e. a private economic system of free markets, trade and capital movements, along with neutral rules and automatic mechanisms that supposedly resolved any economic problem."[18] Let us first briefly examine the measures adopted.

From 1973 to 1980, virtually all government controls on retail prices were eliminated. As of 1974, the internal capital market was liberalized and private financing companies other than banks were authorized to operate. This was followed by the return to the private sector of banks nationalized by the previous administration. In 1975, once the neo-liberal economic team gained control of economic policy, the State Corporation for the Promotion of Production (*Corporación de Fomento de la Producción*, CORFO) transferred 86 percent of its bank stock to private citizens.[19]

The labor market, however, was kept "under strict restrictions and control" during the regime's first six years in power. This control was justified as necessary to avoid cost-push pressures.[20] It was only in 1979, and due mainly to international pressure coordinated by the AFL–CIO (the American Federation of Labor) and the US Department, that a "labor plan" was devised. Although it authorized collective bargaining between workers and management in each firm so that workers could improve their salaries, it also imposed a restrictive framework carefully defined by the government.

The process of "opening the market" to foreign operations was equally swift. Almost from the start, the regime tended to ease restrictions on the import of foodstuffs. Average import duties were successively reduced, first

Table 1: *Structural change under the Chicago Boys (first phase)*

	Situation in 1972–73	Post-1973
1. Prices	Generalized price control	Freed prices (excluding wages and the exchange rates)
2. Privatization	The state controls over 500 firms and banks	In 1980, twenty-five companies (including a bank) belong to the public sector
3. Trade regime	Multiple exchange rates; import quotas and bans; high tariffs (average of 94 percent, maximum of 220 percent); prior deposits on imports (10,000 percent)	Unified exchange rate; uniform tariff of 10 percent; no other barriers to trade
4. Fiscal regime	Taxes on buying and selling; swollen public employment; high fiscal deficit	Value added tax (20 percent); cuts in public employment; fiscal surplus (1979–81)
5. Domestic capital market	Controls on interest rates; nationalization of the banking sector; credit controls	Market-set interest rates; privatization of the banks; liberalization of the capital market
6. Capital account	Absolute control on capital movements; the government is the main external debtor	Gradual liberalization of capital movements; the private sector is the main external debtor
7. Labor regime	Powerful unions with strong bargaining power; law of permanence; obligatory salary increases; high proportion of non-salary labor costs (40 percent equivalent of salaries)	Atomized unions with no bargaining power; simple dismissal procedure; drastic fall in real salaries; low proportion of non-salary labor costs (3 percent equivalent of salaries)

Source: Meller, Patricio, "Revisión del proceso de ajuste chileno de la década del 80," *Colección de Estudios CIEPLAN* 30, December 1990, Santiago de Chile, p. 7.

from 92 percent to 52 percent and then seeing even more drastic reductions after 1975. From 1975 to 1977, they fell from 52 percent to 22 percent, finally levelling off at 10 percent in 1977.[21] Together with reductions in customs duties and tariffs, all import restrictions were eliminated in late 1976, following negotiations undertaken by the Finance Minister (although this task formally corresponded to the Foreign Ministry). Chile withdrew from the Andean Pact. The Pact had hitherto formed part of the foundations for Chile's future industrial development. The schedule of customs duties for member states and the restrictions imposed by the Cartagena Agreement on foreign investments in the subregional integration area were incompatible with the modernization of the economy.[22] Chile's new foreign investment regime, approved as soon as it had left the Pact, gave "national treatment" to foreign capital operating in any economic sector.[23]

Mechanisms regulating foreign capital movements were also modified.

Foreign investors were authorized to bring capital into Chile without restrictions and, should they decide to withdraw, were given guaranteed access to foreign exchange. Further, banks were authorized to borrow directly from abroad and regulations on offering loans in local currency based on such foreign borrowing were gradually relaxed.[24]

Nevertheless, the overall goal of this policy was to reduce and reorient government involvement in the economy. There were three main objectives: "to reduce the magnitude of the public sector; to minimize the government's regulatory influence on the economy; and to eliminate the role played by the government in direct production and as a body charged with promoting development."[25] Government spending was reduced from 40 percent to 26 percent of GDP from 1973 to 1979. These reductions, aimed at cutting the fiscal deficit and inflation, were continued even when the deficit had been eliminated. Government employment fell by almost 20 percent in less than four years, the total number of civil servants declining from 360,000 (1974) to 290,000 (1978).

At the same time, government mechanisms for regulating the economy were discarded. As already mentioned, price controls (excluding those on wages) were eliminated, together with all other administrative measures which regulated certain economic activities. It became mandatory for public firms and other state organizations (such as universities and TV channels) to be self-supporting.

However, the most radical change was the elimination of the government's role as a producer. In this respect the radical thrust of the Chicago team was most intense: in 1975 alone, CORFO transferred to private hands the stocks and rights of more than 110 firms and 86 percent of its bank holdings.[26]

It is estimated that, from a total of more than 400 government-owned companies, which were up for bids or had been returned to their prior owners up to 1978, the sale of only forty-five firms (including four banks) represented a patrimonial transfer in excess of $730 million in 1978. This amount is equivalent to two-thirds of gross geographical investment for that year. Land reform was also reversed. In the first quarter of 1979, around 30 percent of expropriated land had been returned to its previous owners. Although an additional 35 percent was distributed to 35,000 individual peasants, it is estimated that by the end of the decade almost half of this land had to be sold or rented out because the peasants lacked government support enabling them to became small farmers.

In the financial services and banking sectors, of nineteen banks in which the government was the major stockholder in 1973, only four were still held by CORFO in 1977 and by early 1981, only two remained.[27]

Denationalization affected all productive activities, including mineral deposits, urban property owned by public utilities, and even companies that had been set up at government initiative some thirty or more years previously, for example, the Pacific Steel Company (*Compañia de Acero del Pacífico*, CAP). These activities were turned over to the private sector, which would become the main and eventually (this was the end objective) sole producer. Import substitution industrialization was condemned as "exhausted" and" artificial." The Chilean economy would henceforth concentrate on activities which offered "comparative advantages" in the world market. Therefore, industrialization was rejected in favor of activities such as mining, agriculture, forestry, and fishing.[28] Government officials declared that, "within the scope of economic activities which exist in Chile, none are forbidden to private enterprise; conversely the government is precluded from participation in almost all productive activities."[29]

CORFO gradually reduced its involvement in promoting economic activity, to the detriment of small and medium scale mining, agriculture, and industrial companies. Thus, the government was now confined to dealing with "extreme poverty," the sole sector that the Chicago "model" considered to be a government responsibility. In this respect, a budget line was set aside for specific mother–infant programs, covering nutrition and maternal education, as well as an increase in the number of homes with running water and proper drainage systems. These programs, far from diminishing the enormous social cost of the whole experience, provided a group of young people linked to rightwing groups (including members of the "second generation" of Chicago Boys) with a degree of political notoriety.[30]

In de Castro's January 1978 report on the "state of public finances" – termed the "new economic order" – he introduced the second section stating that "virtually all fundamental measures in this respect have already been adopted." This categorical phrase was charged with connotations, the consequences of which few Chileans understood at the time. Together with the measures indicated above, the economic team had decided to retain the nominal fixed exchange rate ($39/US$) in force from July 1979 until June 1982. This was not a measure without importance, as Meller points out: "this fixed nominal exchange rate was not regarded as an instrument, but rather as an economic goal; it was the nominal anchor of the entire economic system and the symbol of the success, confidence in, and continuity of the model." The principle of a fixed dollar parity, adopted by the Chicago Boys as part of their support for the so-called "monetary approach to the balance of payments," was totally backed by the entire military government, to the point that General Pinochet categorically stated that "to devaluate would be suicide."[31] The fixed exchange rate was the principal factor behind the catastrophic conclusion to the Chicago Boys' "naive phase" in economic power: in 1982 the "model" was confronted by the foreign debt shock. Before that, and without yet trying to evaluate the model, let us briefly consider the overall economic and social impact of the reforms.

The economic and social impact

As already indicated, the main stated aim behind the transformation of the Chilean economy was to defeat inflation. The measures adopted in this regard yielded paltry results. In 1980, seven years after the reforms began, inflation still stood at 35.1 percent. Only in 1981 did the rise in prices fall below 10 percent. To achieve the anti-inflation goal, the Chicago Boys first eliminated price controls, then reduced the fiscal deficit, and later introduced a trade opening, arguing that once the Chilean economy functioned at international prices, inflation would cease. Finally, in 1979, financial liberalization began. It induced a massive influx of foreign credit, permitting the exchange rate to be fixed at $39 to the US dollar. Through this mechanism, the Chicago economists managed to repress – or, rather, to disguise – inflationary pressures and to reduce the level of price increases to international levels (9.5 percent). The debacle of 1982, which would force a devaluation, led to a fresh outbreak of inflation.

A number of Chilean economists have noted with surprise that an economic team as extraordinarily well prepared as the Chicago Boys should have taken eight years to reduce inflation to acceptable levels. Pinto[32] has underlined the unprecedented advantages enjoyed by the regime's economic team: strict control over salaries; a tight grip on fiscal and monetary policy; complete freedom to manipulate the exchange rate; being able to safely ignore rising unemployment; the complete suppression of union and political pressures; and, a total monopoly on political power, as well as absolute control over the compilation of official statistics on the economy. However, it failed to achieve something that, even for a less powerful economic team, should not have been so difficult. As Meller has indicated, "the Chicago Boys' team had the power not solely to act on the most important variables, but also influence directly or indirectly other variables in the *ceteris paribus*."[33] The most obvious question is, then, why did it take so long to control inflation? Foxley[34] and Tironi[35] have argued that the explanation resides in the fact that the Chicago group actually sought to stress *not* the fight against inflation, but rather to carry out structural reforms that, in tune with a preconceived theoretical framework, were considered essential under any circumstances. In this way, the neo-liberal and monetarist economists became the new "structuralists": any economic measure required a transformation in the organizational basis of the Chilean economy. The fight against inflation thus became simply a very useful pretext for a project with goals well beyond the economic growth required of a new economy, which, in turn, necessitated a new form of social organization – one that put individual economic freedom at the heart of social activity.

Economic growth during this phase of the military regime was subject to great ups and downs. The huge inflows of foreign capital at the end of the 1970s permitted high growth rates, reaching 8 percent in 1977 and 1979. Yet, there were also great falls, such as 17 percent in 1975. Hence, average GDP growth for the 1974–81 period was barely 2.6 percent. As stressed by Ffrench-Davis, the reason for scant economic growth must be sought in the low level of investment – under 15 percent – during these years.[36]

However, the effects of the decisions made by the Chicago Boys had their most immediate impact, and long term consequences, in the treatment of the state and its reduction. We have referred to the cuts in state spending. The magnitude of these decisions can be appreciated if one considers that the 1975 fiscal shock redressed in only a year the fiscal deficit inherited from the Allende government, cutting it from 10.5 percent of the GDP in 1974 to 2.6 percent in 1975. In 1980, public spending on health had decreased by 17.6 percent compared to 1970, and education by 11.3 percent. Salary levels in 1980 were 16.7 percent below those of a decade previously. Family benefits collapsed by over 30 percent from 1973 to 1983, well above the 6 percent average for the 1960s. Clearly, then, the Chicago model had a regressive impact and significantly widened the existing gap between rich and poor in Chile.

Similarly, the privatization process carried out in the first phase demonstrated the economic team's indifference to a greater concentration of ownership. From 1974 to 1978, state shares in 197 companies were sold. The conditions of sale were extremely favorable, since only a minimal part of the purchase price had to be paid in cash (10–20 percent). The remainder could be provided through long term credits at real interest rates of 8–12 percent. Buyers were even allowed to use shares in the firms they purchased as collateral.[37] Obviously, public enterprises were in a dreadful state following the Allende period and urgently needed substantive reform. Nevertheless, the sell-offs took place amidst recession in the private sector – with a distinct lack of government interest – and thus led to serious losses for the Chilean state. Foxley estimated the implicit subsidy at around 30 percent of the firms' book value.[38] According to Muñoz, most serious of all was the fact that these sales "facilitated the creation of extremely concentrated financial groups, through indebtedness, without sufficient guarantees and sheltered by the financial liberalization then being implemented." None of this seemed to be discerned at the time. The "economic groups" established close ties with the government through the transfer of personnel in either direction, particularly young economists, followers of de Castro and Baraona, who were mostly former Chicago students.[39]

Again, the underlying intention was not to generate business for the state, nor to provide a set of rules for the behavior of the new, private groups. In Meller's analysis, there were to be only three basic rules governing the private sector. First, a "Darwinian" law: producers had to be efficient and to compete. Only efficient firms would remain in the market. Uncompetitive enterprises would disappear; indeed it was healthy for the economy that they went to the wall. Second, the profits and the losses of companies would be "private": under no circumstances would the state come to the rescue of private firms in financial difficulties. Finally, the private sector could take on as much debt as it wished, domestically and abroad, since this was the exclusive responsibility of the borrower. When, and for what purpose, should the state intervene? "If a private enterprise borrowed abroad, it knew what it was doing, and had incorporated the cost of the credit into its calculations on the yield of the investment to be financed by the loan. Thus, external indebtedness in the private sector was not a matter for preoccupation. Rather, it was concrete evidence of the great number of viable projects in Chile, which Chilean businesses were now exploiting."[40]

The brief and decisive story of the 1982 Chilean economic crisis was not simply a tale of the impact of international economic contraction on a developing nation. It was also the result of an ideological adventure undertaken by the Chicago team that, draped in supposedly scientific criteria, stood on nothing more than the simple logic expounded above. The crisis seemed to be preceded by a process of recovery in the macro-economic order. From 1976 to 1981, GDP rose by an annual 7.2 percent and there was even some optimism over inflation. The fixing of the dollar at 39 pesos stabilized the price of imported inputs and products, arriving in massive quantities and which, according to the economic authorities, had a positive impact in obliging domestic firms to compete at these prices. To the government's mind, the public accounts were kept in order. There was a fiscal surplus and a positive balance in the non-financial public sector. Besides, until 1981, the state sector (including state firms) had very restricted access to external financing. For this reason, the public external debt rose (in current dollars) only from $5.2 billion to $5.6 billion during 1978–81. In the meantime, however, private debt rocketed from under $2 billion in 1978 to over $10 billion by 1981, and some $14 billion in 1982. Measured in GDP terms, the sums on the current account and in term deposits rose from 9.3 percent in 1974 to a peak of 25.7 percent in 1982. This situation was deemed to be the exclusive responsibility of the private sector. The government made no judgments and neither was it to intervene.

In 1981 there were clear signs of an approaching international recession. The Chicago Boys "explicitly made clear that a 'do nothing' policy was the best choice, since: (1) the international recession would be short; and (2), all the basic problems had been taken care of."[41] Such passivity derived from a dogmatic, theoretical concept – the monetarist approach to the balance of payments, which was used to argue that the Chilean economy possessed an automatic adjustment mechanism – the interest rate.[42] In 1982, Chile plunged into crisis. The contraction in the world economy hurt Chilean exports. Copper prices collapsed from 99 US cents per pound in 1980 to 67 cents in 1982. The deterioration in the trade balance was unsustainable. In consequence, GDP fell 15 percent; industry and construction contracted by over 20 percent (in 1982). Effective unemployment hit 30 percent (in 1983). Bankruptcies tripled in 1982 alone. The private financial system suffered losses of, on average, twice its capital. The Central Bank lost over 45 percent of its international reserves. Chile had gone into its worst recession since the 1930s. On 16 April 1982, General Pinochet invited de Castro to resign, marking the end of the Chicago Boys' "naive" phase in power.

Ideological expansion

From 1976 onwards, the ideological basis for the technical measures described above began to become more explicit.[43] The model seemed to be working, and this was apparently enough to be able to proclaim an "economic miracle." The economists in charge of the process spoke plainly of their theoretical beliefs. They granted interviews, contributed to newspaper columns and magazine articles, as well as many of El Mercurio's editorials. In all these writings, they demonstrated a shared, coherent ideology – which was also evident in their manner of speech and in their actions. Thanks to the media publicity they received, and the triumphant discourse surrounding them, from that point on, the economists became the regime's central protagonists. They also acquired mythical status for a dominant social sector, which desperately needed an ideology capable of helping them come to terms with the trauma of the Allende administration.[44] The group's loyalty to Pinochet was total and their influence on the ruling military team's discourse notorious. Thus, the shape of an "alliance between the military and the economists," later trumpeted by El Mercurio, began to emerge. According to the newspaper, the military were charged with ensuring "order, security and confidence" while the economists provided "the new ideas needed to lift Chile from its current dejection and to liberate the energy needed to begin the swift course towards economic growth."[45]

The following section includes a brief outline of various aspects of the group's ideological discourse, wherever possible in their own words – the acceptance of, and adherence to, political authoritarianism as a necessary condition, the use of science to legitimate power thus acquired, and the attempt to replace politics with technology.

Firstly, the Chicago Boys undertook a radical and critical examination of Chilean history over the preceding half century, reducing it to the UP period. According to the economists, the economic advances made over the past four to five decades were not worth preserving, not even in part. Their disapproval focused mainly on the economy: "a detailed analysis of that three-year administration," said de Castro, "leads us to conclude that economic policies prevailing at the time were not actually modified, but rather that existing policies were merely applied more intensely. This led to the full development of a crisis that had been brewing for half a century."[46] Enlarging on this criticism, El Mercurio considered that in order to make Chile a modern nation, it was necessary to move away from a paternalistic, dirigiste, and slightly feudal economy towards a market-oriented economy, open to foreign exchange flows and free from unnecessary government interference.[47] Thus, attacks on the previous decades were finally and unambiguously extended to the political field. In 1978, Pablo Baraona reached the conclusion that inefficient and corruptive growth was ultimately due to a malady masked by the government and which fed on statism: namely, politics. The most prominent features of the forty-year period prior to 1973, he said, were "the quest for power for its own sake and increasingly unrestrained demagogy."[48] This explained the eagerness to nationalize and was the ultimate reason for state expansion, since "whoever struggles to gain power, and is successful, becomes an ardent supporter of the irresistible urge to nationalize, favors ever greater and wider powers, promotes the creation of as many public companies as possible because this creates electoral, political and economic power of, quite simply, prestige." In this way, politicians, as a class, were necessarily statist and interventionist, since these tendencies were imbued into their very nature. It followed that no type of social organization built on a "political" base was of any value. Thus, in Alvaro Bardón's words, Chile had only a "pseudo-democracy", a "perverted" system laced with "undemocratic features"; a democracy that, "thanks to excessive economic centralization," became a "mere formula."[49] Further, Chilean democracy was indistinguishable from dictatorship: "former members of Parliament were exempt from responsibility and, in fact, political majorities in Congress exercised an absolute, un-restrained dictatorship, and were not held accountable for their acts."[50]

Therefore, the fact that Chile was now under an authoritarian regime should not have come as a surprise. On the contrary, it was a positive and necessary situation. It allowed the historic vices of statism to be corrected, without attention to the social cost this implied. The economists and their media apologists did not hesitate to admit that it was precisely the authoritarian nature of the regime that allowed the reforms to take place. As El Mercurio acknowledged, "the current experience would not have been feasible if exceptional conditions had not existed in politics and in labor."[51] In an earlier editorial the newspaper had stated that the regime "firstly, has the virtue of being long-lasting; secondly, it can confer on the authorities an efficiency denied to deliberative democratic systems; and thirdly, it can enforce a model conceived by experts, without yielding nor attending to – at least for a period of time – the social reactions produced by its implementation."[52] For some of the economists, however, authoritarianism was not simply a circumstantial characteristic that was convenient for a given period of time. On the contrary, they openly considered it to be an ideal regime, guaranteeing the market's neutrality: "because an authoritarian government is a strong government which defends equal standards for all," declared Bardón.[53] De Castro was even more explicit: "A person's actual freedom can only be ensured through an authoritarian regime that exercises power by implementing equal rules for everyone."[54]

Authoritarianism in Chile, however, was not a simple executive mechanism through which the demands of interest groups were denied. For almost a decade, it constituted a system of institutionalized terror, directed against the traditional parties of the left, the unions, social organizations, and the opposition in general. Proof of this resides in the disappearance of over 2,000 people, whose whereabouts remain unknown even today, the forced exile of hundreds of thousands of Chileans, as well as the frequent and massive arrest of people who were then subjected to brutal torture, in secret camps. The defenselessness of citizens hauled before courts that shamefully refused to grant the right to *habeas corpus*, brutal police repression of protest marches, espionage networks, and intimidation campaigns directed against moderate political leaders: these were the true characteristics of the Chilean authoritarian regime. It was not the authoritarianism of which the Chicago Boys spoke so enthusiastically. They, along with many of those with "technical" roles during the military regime, tried to draw a distinction between an authoritarianism that they regarded as necessary – "technical firmness in decision-making" – and that which the opposition and human rights organizations showed to be taking place in Chile. The Chicago Boys labeled the latter type as "inevitable," "unfortunate," and restricted only to isolated abuses, for which they were anyway not responsible. State terrorism – which has been fully documented since Chile's return to democracy – served to unify and make coherent both "mild" and "severe" authoritarianism. Scientific and technical authoritarianism was protected by physical force and wholesale intimidation of the population. The authoritarian system refused either to discuss the measures if implemented, or to amend them in line with their cost, while physically threatening all those who tried to organize protest or demand their rights. Seen in this light, authoritarianism was indeed an efficient mechanism for the drastic transformation of the Chilean economy.

Neo-liberal groups supported this style of regime not simply, as has sometimes been suggested, in reaction to the socialist threat of Allende, who anyway perished in the early hours of the 1973 coup. The underlying motive resided in the historical value attached by neo-liberals to economic reform and to state transformation. These were seen as sufficiently important to warrant their imposition, even if this meant deploying the entire repressive power of the state military apparatus. The objective of the Chicago Boys and their sympathizers in Chilean society was to create a "free society," and this involved nothing less than the forging of liberty, particularly the sole type that really mattered to them – economic liberty. Spreading this precept to the Chilean people, and holding it in place until it bore fruit, required the protection of "strong government." Thus, the authoritarian project was vital in securing military acceptance of free market principles. Thus, the principle which held that personal liberty and a free market were synonymous became, together with the military's anti-communist "National Security Doctrine," the regime's major ideological concept. From this it followed that, in the absence of individual economic freedom, there could be no political liberty. "The market is the economic manifestation of freedom and the impersonality of authority," Baraona emphasized.[55] It was also "a neutral, technical mechanism, which did not have ideological connotations," according to Bardón.[56] As such, the market was not only the main place to exercise liberty but also the "locus" for science. For the Chicago Boys, the market combined freedom's normative principles with the neutral and objective practice of economic science.

The authority of economic science was the principal argument put forward by the group. Alternatives were neither independently chosen nor depended on the government's authority. They were determined, instead, by science in accordance with the rules of nature: "social justice cannot be built separately from the real world," declared José Piñera to *The Economist* in apparently Marxist terminology. "The laws of economic science merely unearth and reveal objective aspects of reality, a reality which cannot be ignored because it is known that to act against nature is counter-productive and self-deceiving."[57] People who resist and criticize the measures adopted by a group that has the necessary scientific knowledge do so because they represent "sectoral and group interests," "moral judgments," "ideological positions," or mere ignorance, and resemble people who, in the Middle Ages, tried to impede scientific progress for dogmatic reasons.[58] The mere use of "economic science" increases liberty because, "if we acknowledge economics as a science," says Bardón, "this immediately implies less power for government or the political structure, since both lose responsibility for making such decisions" and thus decision-making returns to the individual and the technicians.[59] Through their scientific knowledge, the economists gave back to society and to economic laws the liberty inherent to nature: "we are so monetarist that we have reached a position whereby the Central Bank is hardly in control of the money supply any longer. It controls itself," Sergio de la Cuadra told *The Economist*.[60]

Thus, the Chicago economists had discovered that in Chile, "there were two different worlds, with separate analytical capacities and public responsibilities"; one incorporating the professional economists, who possessed overwhelming methodological weaponry, and another represented by the "intellectually unqualified and improvised statements issued by trade unions, politicians, and . . . Church leaders, submerged in a pre-modern world alien to science."[61] Society's transformation not only demanded the political interdiction of that a-scientific and pre-modern world but also required "constructive proselytizing by professional economists on the fundamental laws of science."[62] Through *El Mercurio* and *Qué Pasa* (a conservative weekly magazine), a systematic indoctrination was carried out in the style needed to spread a dogma. Allusions to the objective and scientific nature of such decisions were repeated to exhaustion: "ODEPLAN's positions on income distribution are based on the teachings of economic science,"[63] claimed *El Mercurio*, referring to the government planning office, in one of its frequent editorials on the subject. With respect to the limited wage negotiations which the dictatorship was forced to accept in 1979, under pressure from the US government and American trade unions, *Qué Pasa* reassured its readers, arguing that "the native economic model" required "a high and increasing dose of freedom," adding that "the economist's cold reasoning considers adequate prices in the capital market (interest rates), and in foreign exchange (foreign currency parities) just as imperative as adequate labor prices (wages)."[64]

The fundamental intention was to replace politics with technology and politicians with economists. As Pilar Vergara pointed out, the Chicago Boys considered that collective decisions which contained value judgments, even when made by political authorities, should be "highly technical and scientific." They should be implemented by experts and based on technical efficiency criteria. Therefore, priorities should be established by "experts who would also determine the coherence and compatibility of different evaluative decisions."[65] The ideological construction developed by the group and its supporters further maintained that decisions pertaining exclusively to the desires of citizens should be "informed" decisions. Citizens should be aware of the consequences of their decisions and the necessary information should be provided, once again, by the technicians and experts on economic science. "Science," therefore, should be absolutely dominant over "ideologies" and "individual peculiarities."

The economists were equal to the task. Economic and political structures nurture each other and economic science has advanced more than other social sciences. "This explains the economists' growing interest in the [political] issues," declared Baraona, adding that, "Adam Smith was the first of those that can be considered politicians."[66] The economists were therefore the best suited to establish the conditions for legitimating the regime's decisions and for defining the desired "democratic" project. Piñera declared that the military government was based on two forms of legitimacy: "a redeeming legitimacy, for rescuing us from communism and rebuilding Chile . . . and a revolutionary legitimacy . . . enabling it to undertake profound transformations to ensure that the cycle that ended with the Marxist regime will not be repeated." Alluding to the impossibility of proceeding using democratic methods, he justified the understanding that "many Chileans" have shown for the regime's authoritarian traits. "It is well known that these reforms cannot be undertaken within traditional political frameworks; therefore most Chileans have given their support to the government enabling it to . . . achieve these goals."[67] Baraona described the "new democracy," which Pinochet's regime would create, in the following terms:

The new democracy, imbued with true nationalism, will have to be *authoritarian*, in the sense that the rules needed for the system's stability cannot be subject to political processes, and that compliance with these measures can be guaranteed by our armed forces; *impersonal*, in the sense that the regulations apply equally to everyone; *libertarian* in the sense that subsidiarity is an essential principle for achieving the common good; *technified*, in the sense that political bodies should not decide technical issues but restrict themselves to evaluating results, leaving to the technocracy the responsibility of using logical procedures for resolving problems or offering alternative solutions.[68]

The economic growth registered in 1979 seemed to encourage the modernization project and gave rise to limitless triumphalism. The victory of the military regime in the 1980 plebiscite – in which the citizenry had to decide for or against a new constitution, but without democratic guarantees and with no electoral roll – changed optimism into euphoria.

After 1978, the Pinochet government perceived that the social and economic conditions not only permitted, but demanded, a process of institutionalization. It was thought that the time had come to bolster the regime's initial legitimacy – based on the containment of socialism – with a fresh claim to legitimacy so as to revitalize, this time in the political and institutional field, the basic definition of the economic model. The challenge of this institutional construction, moreover, would help to reduce political tension inside the regime between groups of "hard-liners" and "moderates." The self-styled "nationalist" sectors lacked social roots and found themselves cornered by the success of the Chicago model. Yet they continued to seek support for Pinochet in a manner reminiscent of fascism and not entirely devoid of populist traits. General Pinochet's excessive and unregulated power, and the eventual personalization of his regime, led the most powerful economic groups and their allies inside the government – especially the economists – to seek institutionalization in order to secure the continuity of authoritarianism and the neo-liberal model.

The two opposing sides tended to accept the constitution. On the one hand, the constitution laid down, via a series of articles, that authoritarianism was to be maintained intact and posited a long term transition to ensure the prolonged exclusion of political activity. The document thereby satisfied the supporters of both militarism and "national Pinochetism." On the other hand, the constitution confirmed the permanence of the economic model, thus raising its main features to constitutional status. It reinforced and ratified, thereby, the role of the main actors in the economic transformation model – the large economic groups and the economists. The landslide victory in the plebiscite (67 percent voted "Yes") does not simply reflect "moral fraud," as alleged by the fragile opposition, but also the fact that economic, political, and social initiative now lay entirely in the hands of the government bloc. Opposition was non-existent.

It was in this context that the Chicago Boys launched their program of "modernizations," with which they sought radically to change the way society functioned. Reforms in the public health, education, and social security systems, as well as the revision of labor legislation and the structure of guilds and professional associations, aimed to lay the ground for a new model of society. This model was meant to be able to expand and to regulate itself, relying on little more than the free play of the market. The reforms clearly had immediate, practical aims. They were partly intended to fortify the business sector and allow it to accumulate capital. Thus, the social security and health reforms injected into the market significant quantities of cash that had hitherto been publicly administered. Moreover, these changes sought to create a new organization of society able to prevent social conflict, limit the amalgamation of interests, and impede social mobilization. The regime's labor legislation aimed to dismantle and fragment the old union apparatus. A series of measures were adopted, which effectively handed labor relations over to a single regulator – the market. Similarly, the reform of higher education weakened the largest universities – institutions that propagated middle-class culture and served as a base for the political center. Instead, the regime facilitated the rise of small "factories" turning out professionals. Laws were passed abolishing the obligation to join professional associations, in an attempt to eliminate both public and private control over the exercise of such professions.

Clearly, then, this package of reforms installed an institutionality under which the amalgamation of interests and social mobilization were heavily regulated and restricted.[69] But this did not stem solely or principally from a defensive standpoint on the model and the political regime. Rather, it arose fundamentally from an ideology that regarded the market as a competitive space needing to be freed from the monopolistic bodies that impeded and regulated individual liberty. The unions, the trade guilds, and the public health system all belonged to this species, preventing the consumer from freely choosing the form of health care he wanted, or the type of university at which he wished to study.

The period from 1980 to 1981 was probably the high point of the military regime and, therefore, of the Chicago Boys. In a period of abundant consumption and optimistic economic indicators, the modernizing euphoria reached its maximum intensity and the economist's discourse knew no limits. Chile had changed for ever.

The conservative magazine *Qué Pasa* described the period as follows:

These were the years of sweet money. Expansion was not limited just to the economic groups. In the same way as large conglomerates based their growth on credit, people turned to the banks and finance houses to satisfy their most expensive desires. With lower tariffs and a cheap dollar, cars ceased to be a luxury reserved for the few. Consumer electronics found their way into even the most humble of homes. American whisky replaced local *pisco* . . . and foreign holidays became fashionable among the wealthiest sectors. The government itself propagated such triumphalism. On the 11th of September 1980, President Pinochet described his goals: "to create a million new jobs, build 900,000 homes, enable one Chilean in every seven to own a car, one in every five to watch his own television, and one in every seven to install a telephone."[70]

Chicago: a reference point for external legitimacy

The election, in 1980, of Ronald Reagan as president of the United States, verified the military government's belief that their famous Chicago Boys had anticipated the global spread of neo-liberal economic principles. At the same time, it confirmed the suspicions of many in Chile, namely that the economists were the main public link between the Chilean dictatorship and the outside world. As we said in the introduction, concepts such as the "Chicago economic model" and the "Chicago ideology" – indeed, the term "Chicago" itself – acquired precise meanings for most Chileans, since they came into common usage. Depending on the particular way in which Chileans viewed the group, the image projected by the economists – of authority or of power abuse, of modernity or quasi-religious dogmatism, the virtual inevitability or ideological/arbitrary nature of their decisions, and the apparently inescapable processes stemming from each such characteristic – became as strong as, or even stronger than, the image projected by the military. A key element in this characterization was the Chicago Boys' capacity for external action. They were seen as part of an international movement and, at the same time, as people offering new and distinct ideas superior to those of politicians and economists in the past. The economists, in fact, did their best to foster this image. To do so, they turned to their point of common identity, their *alma mater*.

The University of Chicago was the image chosen by most Chicago Boys in order to reaffirm the group's scientific prestige, to stress its homogeneity, and what one author has described as "the interweaving of their relationships and personal trajectories." Chicago was the "force which nurtured the myth of self-identification."[71] The following introductory description in a press interview constitutes a good example of the group's attitudes towards the university: "he speaks of the years spent at Chicago with true inspiration, as if he had entered into a total commitment with society, as if a model which extends beyond economics was being created there, one which offers answers to a wide range of existential issues," wrote the reporter.[72] Another economist, consulted on the main features of "Chicago," believed it to be characterized by "absolute respect for rationality and empiricism as applied to the study of economic science and also to the policies it recommends . . . I would add that in Chile we are trying to apply to a very specific political context the principles established by the Department of Economics at Chicago University."[73]

This identification with a specific school of thought was further corroborated by the considerable international backing provided for the model by conservative US circles, not least the principal figures from the "Chicago School." The local impact of such praise was extremely significant. While the military regime was universally spurned for violating human rights and ending Chile's democratic tradition, the economic model was heavily praised by some as an astonishing and admirable experiment. Economists, bankers, philosophers, and political scientists even visited Chile – a country isolated in all other political and cultural respects – to personally honor this experiment in "freedom." Frederick von Hayek, Milton Friedman, and Arnold Harberger visited Santiago in the glare of tremendous publicity. Von Hayek was made honorary president of the Center for Public Studies (Centro de Estudios Públicos, CEP), dedicated to promoting conservative ideas; Friedman appeared on state-controlled television to give a master lecture. Harberger, a frequent visitor, debated in various public fora with his former pupils. There was also a visit by Gordon Tullock, the chief representative of the "Virginia School," or "school of public choice," of political science.[74] Moreover, the ultra-conservative Société Mont Pélérin held its 1978 annual convention in Viña del Mar. From 1976 to 1980, there was endless praise for the "model" in *El Mercurio* and on television, by bankers, foreign businessmen, conservative journalists, US officials and monetarist economists. According to *Barrons* – a conservative US magazine – the Chilean reforms "were the most important modifications implemented in the developing world in recent times." Chile was a unique model of economic rationality. "Economic treatises [in the United States] hold that this is the way the world should work, but it is another country that is putting it into effect."[75]

Where did these ideas come from? As *Barrons* explained, they emerged partly from textbooks, such as those employed at the Economics Department of the Universidad Católica de Chile by Chicago-trained economists. Yet textbooks were only one aspect, and never the most important one, of an organized cultural transfer implemented by Chicago University professors in the United States and later by their disciples in Santiago over a period of more than fifteen years. This was the main source for the ideological equipment used by Pinochet's economic team.

Ideological transfer could have been confined to the academic and relatively marginal framework that characterized it for over a decade. For this transfer to become a social project, certain changes in Chilean society were required. Political and ideological developments which severely altered the evolution of society during the previous period were a necessary condition. In other words, it required a crisis within the political system. It was precisely this predicament – including the severe identity crisis that began to afflict Chilean power groups at the end of the Frei administration and during Allende's period in government – which allowed these previously unfeasible ideas to become a revolutionary project supported by a sector of the Chilean bourgeoisie.

In the next chapter, we discuss the transfer and implantation of beliefs and ideological behavior in a more conceptual manner.

CHAPTER 2

Ideological transfer

What does the transfer of ideas consist of? How can we conceptualize a deliberate process of ideological transfer? Such questions occur naturally to anyone who assumes the intellectual task of constructing a biography of an ideological elite that, originating in one country, is transferred to another in the expectation that it will apply the principles with which it has been imbued. In the brief notes dedicated here to this theoretical issue, we attempt first to identify what we mean by ideological transfer. We then refer to theoretical evaluations of these issues made in the fields of political and sociological studies.

The subject of "formulated bodies of thought passing from one cultural orbit to another" may be approached from different perspectives. As Goodwin and Holley have pointed out, it is, first and foremost, a question of communications in which the theory or science of communications has something to say.[1] Cybernetics and its circular concept of communication, in which feedback by the receiver affects the original flow; its concepts of entropy and "noise," in which the former is the amount of chance or lack of organization included in the communication and the latter is the amount of useful information included in the transfer; are useful concepts for studying these situations.[2] As the authors point out:

The capacity of a noiseless channel, meaning the maximum rate at which useful information can be transmitted over a channel, the coding process, the disturbing effects of noise, and the use of redundancy to overcome uncertainty in communication are all factors which the historian, in the same way as the communications technician, should examine in any system he studies.[3]

In this respect, psychology also offers a series of equally useful concepts. These refer especially to the affective context that surrounds the transfer, the expectations of the actors involved, the perception of roles by emitters and receivers of the "message," the active orientation or task orientation that forms part of the message transferred to the receiver, as well as other subjective factors that condition behavior and are included – consciously or unconsciously – in the transfer. Finally, perhaps over and above other approaches, the study of culture, semiology, and the symbolic structures that provide the context for behavior, are aspects that cannot be avoided in an in-depth exploration of these processes.[4] It is evident, therefore, that the theoretical analysis of the transfer of ideas can be a highly complex matter.[5]

In this case, however, we are more concerned with developing a methodological framework for our history rather than with investigating the general theory of this type of process. Therefore, we shall only outline the fundamental elements that constitute a transfer of ideas. The first thing that needs to be pointed out is that any transfer of ideas from one cultural context to another involves at least two parties: a *transmitter* and a *receiver*, and it also requires a *product* or *message*. This process necessarily takes place in a *specific situation*. Furthermore, there may also be an intermediary or coordinator, who is in charge of establishing the actual relationship.

By "transmitter" and "receiver" we mean the "actors involved in the transfer." The emitter possesses a system of relatively structured symbols and the necessary mechanisms required to transfer the symbols to a consignee or receiver who participates, voluntarily or involuntarily, in the acquisition of these symbols.

The characteristics of the actors involved in the transfer may be highly different in nature and several alternatives are possible: (a) the actors may be individuals, institutions or complex organizations ; (b) the transfer may be organized – in one extreme – by a specialized structure specifically dedicated to this purpose or – on the other extreme – it may be the outcome of involuntary individual or group situations, a mere chance result; (c) the actors may, knowingly or unknowingly, participate in the process in a voluntary or involuntary manner;[6] (d) all transfers inevitably imply a lack of power balance, as far as influence is concerned, that may or may not be acknowledged explicitly. In the case of an organized transfer, the individuals, institutions, or organizations that transfer ideas and inculcate concepts will be considered by the receivers as possessors of influence and authority. This will provide the legitimacy referent regarding the validity of the messages transmitted.

The analysis of the message leads us to even greater complexities that can be dealt with only briefly here. In the first place, what is a message? In general terms, a message is any symbolic construction transmitted between one cognitive point and another. More specifically, this symbolic construction may be: (a) not highly formalized or systematic, in which case we shall be referring to arbitrary or accidental phenomena that, at most, are capable of producing "cultural contamination"; or (b) a more formal and systematic symbolic construction, in which case we may speak of a "cultural product" that can, in the extreme, require a high degree of logical correspondence between its component parts. These categories are also related to the time demands employed to communicate the message and to the degree of redundancy required to clarify their meaning.

Using Clifford Geertz's approach, a message, like all other "interworked systems of construable signs," must be imagined as a symbolic "context" that contains the beliefs, behaviors and identity standards that are transferred. From the perspective of this "symbolic context" they become intelligible and significant.[7] The analysis of the message – as a "context" – gives specific meaning to the affective elements necessarily included in the message. The same is valid for the task or action orientation of the receiver that is included, explicitly or implicitly, in that "context."[8] The approach used by Geertz must be emphasized because he explicitly states that the transfer is not confined to ideas. We shall return to this fundamental point later.[9]

The situation – the space in which the transfer itself takes place – includes the limited sphere of the relationship established between transmitter and receiver as well as the broader level established by the period and the historical context in which the transfer of ideas takes place. On the first level, namely, the relationship between the actors in the transfer, the interesting aspect is the degree of functionality of the situation with respect to the message. In this case, the adequate question is: does the situation under which the transfer takes place ease the way or does it impede the transfer? And, in what way is the transfer determined by the situation?

The second, broader level leads us to the issue of the transfer of ideas within relationships of power and influence between societies and the circulation of substantial cultural flows between them. This aspect is related to the structural level or the "scenario" in which the transfer takes place. Transfers of ideas are engendered by a homogenizing drive in the cultural sphere. The direction of this trend to achieve uniformity usually corresponds to the patterns that predominate in the society that is considered more developed. These processes have usually tended, in the last analysis, to reduce the resistance of the weaker society *vis-à-vis* the homogenizing efforts exerted by the stronger society in other fields of activity, such as the economic or political. Therefore, although ideas do circulate in both directions between interdependent societies with varying degrees of power and influence,[10] it seems more important to point out that, historically, powerful empires and nations have transmitted – sometimes by simply organizing their influence – their values, beliefs, and forms of organization. And in every case, specific elites located in the power structures of these powerful nations have understood the political value of these transfers and have tried to find the best way to organize them into a permanent flow. We will return to this matter later on; for now, it is sufficient to emphasize the importance of the historical context in which the transfer takes place.

A final observation on this conceptual level is the question of the "effectiveness" of the transfer process. There is a measure of "effectiveness" involved in the message and its transfer. It seems appropriate, therefore, to introduce the concepts of *implantation* and *operationalization*. By implantation we mean the process through which the receiver definitely appropriates the concepts that were transferred. By operationalization we mean the actor's capacity to remodel his social environment on the basis of the appropriated concepts that were, initially, the object of the transfer. In other words, in the case of an organized transfer of a formal cultural product, such as the one that concerns us, the transfer does not actually take place or become a volatile and therefore irrelevant event unless *the product is appropriated by a specialized group that must fulfill the same function as the transmitter and that is determined to reproduce the transferred product and to spread it throughout society.* This appropriation signals the success of the transfer process.

Finally, the possibility of making these concepts operational as standards that serve to organize social practices will vary according to the social influence achieved by the groups who appropriated the transferred concepts. The success or failure of the operationalization will naturally depend on existing social and political conditions in the receiving society.

Modernization and dependency: two possible approaches

It seems appropriate, at this point, to situate this conceptual reference in the framework provided by the concepts of *modernization* and *dependency*. What is the usefulness of these approaches for analyzing the subject that concerns us? Apparently, one of the most notable differences between the theories on "modernization" and those on "dependency" is the fact that the former is more concerned with the "microsociological" aspects whereas the latter tends toward a "structural" type of approach.[11] In general, most perspectives of "modernization":

tend to be behavioral and microsociological; the primary focus is on individuals, their values, attitudes and beliefs. The dependency perspective, by contrast, is structural or macrosociological. Its focus is on the mode of production, patterns of international trade, political and economic linkages between elites in peripheral and central countries, group and class alliances and conflicts, and so on.[12]

From this point of view, the transfer of ideas could, theoretically, be situated in a middle point between studies on modernization and those related to dependency. This subject necessarily entails analyzing the actors, interests, motivations, ideas and beliefs involved. Simultaneously, the necessary analysis of the historical situation under which these phenomena develop leads us to power relations (and therefore to economic and political structures) that operate in the relationships between elites in the central countries and elites of the "peripheral" society. It is surprising, however, that neither of these two approaches considers that the organized transfer of ideas from one society to another is a subject worth studying. Actually, dependency theories do attempt to define the structural framework and the pertinent relationships between groups from the "center" and the "periphery." However, they are either solely interested in economic aspects, thus relegating ideological phenomena to a second or third derived level, or else they do not explore the specific forms and channels through which these links are established and developed. Studies on modernization, in turn, focus their attention on the modernizing revolution and on the elites that conduct them on a political, ideological, and technical level, but consider that the way in which these elites acquire their behavior patterns is not an important aspect. The channels are hinted at: it is assumed that they exist but they are considered unintentional and, therefore, are merely mentioned in passing, as if this were an accidental situation produced by contagion.

Both approaches clearly devote different measures of attention to ideological phenomena. Dependency is defined as "a situation in which the rate and direction of accumulation are externally conditioned."[13] In fact, this theory has little to say about ideological processes, unless we consider that reductionist statements that perceive ideological phenomena as mere reflections of the economic structure constitute an analysis of the subject. Certain analyses from the dependency point of view have frequently tended toward this approach. Although it would be unfair to say that all the literature on dependency is marked by this trend, a great number of these studies tend to consider that the actor's behavior is a mere consequence derived from the objective position of the social classes in the structure of production. This approach or, worse still, approaches that implicitly relegate these processes to the sphere of unimportant issues, engender an inability to understand ideological phenomena and are simultaneously incapable of perceiving the complexity of the relationships inherent in dependency, which they reduce to a simple economic subordination.[14]

Instead, the scholars who developed the concepts of modernization have approached the subject of the "leadership of modernization" very directly. One of their main subjects, particularly with regard to "political modernization," has been the process through which "modernizing" political and technocratic elites are formed, their role in developing countries, and the ideological elements that conform their identity. This approach views modernization essentially as a mass phenomenon that takes place within the national setting. Modernization, by definition, implies mass mobilization.[15] Increased literacy, exposure to mass media, industrialization, and demands for economic, social, and political participation produce a "legitimacy crisis" that requires the presence of elites capable of establishing institutions and of confronting archaic or traditional patterns. In the elites that arise from that mobilization, intellectuals come to play a privileged role as "bearers of modernity." They criticize social institutions and traditional value systems that hinder development, and thus contribute to their elimination.[16]

The attention given to ideological phenomena in the theory of modernization is therefore derived from the basic assumptions of the approach. As David Apter has said, the "reality" to be observed "lies between that revealed by structural and behavioral analyses of any given social system," and to know it "we need to screen individuals in their roles, identify congeries of roles in which individuals act, understand the mechanisms by means of which the regulation of roles takes place, and be aware of the symbols by which unities and disunities in roles are articulated."[17] Ideology thus becomes crucially important for understanding the process itself: a "modernizing revolution . . . has no subject matter other than that provided by its interpreters and its thinkers, its writers and pamphleteers, its orators and proclaimers" – says Apter – and "in creating this public meaning and identifying the interconnections and directions of change, the intellectuals play a critical role." Their role is a "key indicator of the nature of the polity during modernization" he adds.[18]

Apter's thoughts on technicians and their role is pertinent to our discussion. In the first place, it is assumed that technicians possess "many of the characteristics of professionality, including lengthy periods of education and training, a guildlike organization, a standard or performance and a sphere of competence."[19] The technician is in touch with science, an essential element in the modernizing process. "At its widest limits," says Apter, "the modernization process is the confrontation of the ideologue and the scientist, not because their respective ethics are antagonistic, but because of the changes that occur in the modernization process itself."[20] Thus, the introduction of science has great repercussions on politics and decision-making processes. Politics increasingly becomes a field in which technicians operate, and the formulation of government policies on crucial subjects related to economic and social development tend to resemble a scientific enterprise. Finally, "politics declines as it becomes the property of a technical career role. At the same time . . . the technical role becomes political."[21]

These views on the "technification" of politics and its decline in relation to the role played by science is important, not because it describes an actual situation in developing societies, but because it reflects the perspective of people who wrote about the subject in the United States during the 1960s. As we shall see, these views were also very important in relation to the training offered to technicians in international cooperation sent by the United States to developing countries during the 1950s.[22] It is a well-known fact that studies on modernization actually reflected the interest not just of political science but of governmental circles in the United States regarding phenomena engendered by the incorporation to the international world of societies that were not highly developed in socio-economic terms and whose political institutions were in an even more incipient state of development.[23] Societies in Africa and Asia were the principal models that most scholars devoted to these subjects had in mind when they reflected on the way in which elites develop, and the role played by technicians and science. The establishment of political order and the factors that determined the foundation of nation-states were among the main concerns that prompted them to pursue these studies. Thus, the modernization that took place in societies which were just beginning to establish rudimentary political institutions in tribal contexts was compared to processes of modernization that turned into a revolution in societies marked by complex and sophisticated cultures and imperial pasts. These authors considered that the interesting aspect lay in the discovery of general patterns and, with that goal in mind, highly different phenomena were considered as representing "modernization," and societies with enormous historical differences were included in the same category. For example, Gabriel Almond included Chile in the category of non-occidental societies.[24] And Parsons defined as the first common feature of Latin American societies their inclusion in the "particularistic-ascriptive pattern" "focused around kinship and local community, and de-emphasizing the need for powerful and legitimate large centers of authority such as the state" which was exactly the opposite of what had taken place in the development of Chilean society, where the state had occupied a central role since the nineteenth century.[25] The emphasis placed on the changes brought by modernization occasionally obscured the fact that developing countries were not starting from zero.

At the same time, the subject under analysis – modernization – was correctly considered to be a universal process. The type of development studied by theories of modernization was undoubtedly a widespread process and took place in dissimilar societies and cultures and the outcome was the transformation and alteration of their social and political systems in varying degrees. The inability to perceive certain essential aspects of modernization was actually due to the theoretical approaches employed to study these phenomena – from the tendency to create "models for modernization" rather than from the lack of identity of the processes that had been detected.

One such limitation was the tendency to study *national societies solely,* or at least principally, as isolated analytical units. In fact, it was not enough to acknowledge, as Reinhard Bendix did, that "all conceptions of modernizing processes necessarily take off from the Western European experience, because that is where the commercial–industrial and national revolution originated."[26] As Theda Skocpol pointed out, the point is that, in general, structural–functional evolutionism considers modernization as a "dynamic internal to a nation," when in fact the case is precisely the opposite: "from the start, international relations have intersected with preexisting class and political structures to promote and shape divergent as well as similar changes in various countries."[27] By considering modernization as a phenomenon encapsulated within national boundaries it was impossible to perceive that it is in fact a national phenomenon but that it always develops within the context of transnational structures that respond to a historical course of development, both in economic and ideological terms.

A second comment, related to the preceding one, is that scholars that formulated the theories on modernization considered this as a social process or final model rather than a deliberate project undertaken by some groups who had specific interests in mind at a given moment.[28] The process was usually considered as a mass phenomenon, whether the issue was mass mobilization, urbanization, participation, demands made upon the state, or democratization. In this respect, and according to these theoretical perspectives, modernizing elites interpreted – even in their more authoritarian versions – the course of development of universal processes within the framework of the specific society to which they belonged. The possibility of engendering modernizing elites in "modern" countries and their exportation or re-importation to countries in the process of modernization, does not seem to have been considered important. Apparently, the possibility of importing an organized set of ideas that did not predominate in the central country nor in the country "in the process of modernization" was not contemplated. In the literature of the 1950s and 1960s on the subject of modernization the issue was presented very differently. Nationalism, industrialization, and even socialism were seen as the most typical concerns of intellectuals and modernizing elites in general. These were positive signs of modernization that, it was thought, were more easily found among "those who have had direct contact with the west, particularly through education abroad or under western auspices at home."[29] Nationalism could serve to move intellectuals, who were more aware of the disadvantages *vis-à-vis* the international world, to exert pressure in favor of industrialization. However, descriptions of the characteristics of modernizing elites did not deal with the transfer of ideas, nor did they consider important the mechanisms through which the elites became "infected" with western ideas that made them proceed to unleash processes of modernization. *The possibility that modernization was a process purposefully "promoted" from abroad, by the international power centers, was also not considered.*

Another limitation of these approaches stems quite naturally from this situation. These theories seem to consider modernization as a neutral or objective process. In the first place, modernization is seen as a course followed by developing societies toward a state or situation basically outlined by industrially developed societies.[30] It is the consequence that results from the differentiation of social functions, and the rest of the processes that take place from "the actual transformation of individuals through their assimilation of modern values."[31] However, this assimilation is not explained. *It is assumed that it is due exclusively to a natural or inevitable reverberation of the more powerful societies upon less developed societies.* Local elites, it is said, have been "exposed" to western values and they find in those values the inspiration and the strength for their modernizing endeavors. There is no precise attempt to verify the reasons why some concepts and not others reverberate among the elites in developing countries, nor how these reflections are transmitted. But, more importantly, the underlying interests, the power factors, and the domination involved are also not analyzed. The picture offered by the visions of modernization seem to be lacking in power interests and motivations, and cultural "exposure" takes place in a context in which the motivations and impulses worth studying are only those that belong to the society that is in the process of modernization but never those that take place in the modern society that induces and promotes that process.

Although the theories of modernization do approach issues related to the ideologies of change and the modernizing elites, and have the virtue of emphasizing the massive social nature inherent in modernizing processes, they are nevertheless limited by their concentration on national aspects and by the difficulty of integrating factors related to international power that promote the process. Consequently, they also fail to pay attention to the transfer process, through which the various ideas on modernization circulate and become established in developing countries.

Studies on dependency have apparently reacted to this approach that leaves in the background the linkages that help to transmit the cultural products and their original motivations. Cardoso and Faletto have stated that "there is no such thing as a metaphysical relation of dependency between one nation and another, one state and another. Such relations are made concrete possibilities through the existence of a network of interests and interactions which link certain social groups to other social groups, certain social classes to other classes."[32] Dependency is described – in the more elaborate versions of this approach – as a complex network of relationships and associations in which the importance of external aspects is crucial in varying degrees and in which internal variables can help to reinforce or discourage external linkages.[33] However, as we indicated before, this approach stays within the limits of a structural view and the studies do not furnish empirical data on the linkage patterns between specific actors in a given historical period. This information would be needed to go beyond the level of mere hypotheses to which the theory of dependency has been confined.

However, some studies undertaken by the so-called "linkage theory" seem more useful for the subject that concerns us.[34] This approach goes beyond the purely structural aspects and explores, on the basis of empirical data, the relationship between identifiable groups. At the same time, it analyzes power relations and external influences – aspects that the theories of modernization do not usually take into account. More specifically, studies like those undertaken by James N. Rosenau adequately serve to conceptualize relationships such as the one that gave rise to the Chicago Boys. Rosenau does not confine his work to formulating concepts. Instead, he assigns special significance to cooperational development programs on the understanding that, in contemporary societies, cooperation for development constitutes a highly important instance of the "transfer of modernity" from one society to another. "Linkages" are defined by this author as "any recurrent sequence of behavior that originates in one system and is reacted to in another."[35] According to Rosenau, organized efforts in "technical assistance" offered by the United States and the type of situations that it creates constitute a typical example of these processes. Thus, technical assistance is a "direct policy output" "designed to bring about a response in another system." It is "a penetrative process" in which "members of one polity serve as participants in the political process of another." Technical assistance is based upon an agreement between emitter and receiver, through which the emitters "share with those in the penetrated polity the authority to allocate its values."[36]

Douglas A. Chalmers, who adopts the same conceptual approach to the study of Latin America, refers in even more explicit terms to the transfer of ideas between the United States and Latin America promoted by international cooperation institutions. The text quoted below begins to link the theoretical and conceptual subject analyzed so far with the historical characteristics acquired by the transfer of economic ideas from Chicago.

Looking at the overall linkage pattern . . . it is clear that generally construed as the transfer of ideas, technical assistance constitutes by now a very broad movement, and this cannot fail to have an effect on the approaches that decision makers take to the problems they face . . . Although it is a highly explosive topic, it is also unquestionable that the content of much of the advice that comes from abroad has the effect of perpetuating certain kinds of arrangements and ties and particularly the power of certain linkage groups. Given the dominance of the United States in the flow of ideas and resources, it is not surprising that much advice, along with sometimes subtle and sometimes blatant pressure to take such advice, tends to influence the system in the direction of approximating North American ideas about the organization of society and economy, and more particularly, to protect North American interests in Latin America. The policy of urging Latin American elites to define communism as a chief internal threat, or the austerity program for combating inflation urged by the International Monetary Fund, or the recommendations on the importance of encouraging foreign investment as a basic development strategy are all obvious cases in point.[37]

As we can see, the merit of this approach is that it illustrates that there is a "major category of purposeful behavior that is often overlooked . . . namely those recurrent activities that private persons or groups undertake with the intention of preserving or altering one or more aspects of the policy's external environment."[38] It also suggests that each transfer process forms part of a multiple series of transferred ideas that are not necessarily consistent but that tend rather to be contrasting.[39] In this sense, the different types of linkages express the complexity of the emitting and receiving societies.

The factors related to the effectiveness of the transfer, that we defined above as "implantation" and "operationalization," have been labeled as "reactive" and "emulative" processes by Rosenau. By a "reactive" process he means the response of those who experience ideological output and, logically, he labels "emulative" the capacity demonstrated by the receiver to imitate behaviors originated in the other system. The appealing aspect of these concepts is that they suggest an element that has to be added to the concepts of implantation and operationalization: namely, that the message reproduced will be marked by traits that belong to the receiver. Once the cultural product has been appropriated by the receiver, it will never be identical to the one existing prior to the transfer. Disciples will imitate their masters but they will use the transferred ideology differently.

The hypotheses in this study

The concepts discussed above make it possible to outline the features of the process of ideological transfer between the United States and Chile that is the subject of this study. In the first place, we are referring to a deliberate, organized, and systematic transfer undertaken by specialized institutions. This feature evidently makes it easier to study the process.

In fact, unlike other processes of transfer of ideas, in which linkages become diluted, mysterious, and casual, scattered through time, and products of individual initiative that are almost impossible to trace, in this case, there is a transparency and a peculiar simplicity. Transfer appears here as a deliberate and planned event organized around three key actors, who participated both in the conception and the concretion of the initiative: the government of the United States and its foreign programs; the Department of Economics of the University of Chicago and the group forming it, who represented the "Chicago tradition"; and the Universidad Católica de Chile, together with the conservative group of businessmen who sought to revive free market ideas in Chile during the mid-1950s.

To analyze these actors we must examine their roles in the process, their interests and motivations. Furthermore, it is necessary to analyze the context and the specific situation under which the transfer took place. Finally – and this is the main point – it is necessary to analyze the message transmitted and received when the linkage was being established. The hypotheses outlined below summarize the approach to the process that will be discussed in the remaining chapters.

1. The ideological transfer of ideas from the School of Economics of the University of Chicago to Chile was originally promoted, in 1955, by the International Cooperation Administration (ICA) of the United States government. This specialized entity established the connection and promoted the contacts between the emitter, Chicago University, and the receiver, the Universidad Católica de Chile. By following general guide-lines recommending the promotion of agreements between universities in the United States and in developing countries, and based on ICA's experience in other countries in the region and on its own ideological perspective, ICA representatives in Chile sought an interlocutor who would permit them to start an "experiment" that involved inserting in Chile the most conservative economic ideas regarding a free market economy that were being proposed in the United States. The explicit goal was to foster pluralism in the economic theories that were taught in Chile at the time. The implicit goal was to combat what was perceived as "socialist ideology" in Chilean economics and to change things in such a way as to transform the country's economic administration within a decade. Therefore, right from the start, the process being discussed was a deliberate and programmed attempt to transfer ideas, an effort that was backed by a specialized structure – Chicago University – and was based on an intermediary who had the adequate means – particularly the financial resources – to make the operation viable.

2. The transmitter of the message – Chicago University – was a highly reputed and specialized institution well known to produce a specific type of professional. This fact determined ICA's decision to stipulate that Chicago University should be the compulsory counterpart in the agreements offered to the Chilean universities that were approached – the Universidad de Chile and the Universidad Católica de Chile. The interest of the University of Chicago was based on two factors: first, the quest by a group of economists from that university to oppose the influence in the region of development theories, which had been proposed by the United Nations Economic Commission for Latin America (ECLA); and second, the on-site experimentation with theories on human capital that, engendered by the Economics Department of that university, were shared by the heads of the foreign assistance programs of the United States government.

3. The entity receiving the transfer – the Universidad Católica de Chile – presented a vacant space in the field that constituted the object of the

transfer – economics. Its weakness in this area was total and it was greatly interested in establishing a department of economic studies that could be competitive and capable of serving the business class. However, the university's capacity to resist and/or select the contents of the message transferred was virtually non-existent.

4. The immediate circumstances of the transfer were based on a careful organization of the space within which the message was delivered. By sending to Chicago students who had been previously selected by professors from that university, and through the surveillance of research studies carried out in Chile, it was possible to ensure a minimum of distortion in the socialization process, an adequate period for the transfer, and a convenient degree of redundancy in the messages transferred. On a broader level, the circumstances under which the cultural product was transferred were marked by social and political developments in Chile that openly contradicted the fundamental assumptions of the message. In a country that was going through a series of socializing transformations, the ideological isolation of the product, rather than helping to weaken its effect, contributed to its strength as the expression of "science persecuted for political reasons" and also helped to strengthen the role of Chicago University as the sole legitimacy referent for these imported ideas.

5. The message or "system of interactive symbols" subject to transfer included a series of regulatory propositions and several policy recommendations derived from the two aspects mentioned above. The mechanisms used for the transfer incorporated elements that were not distinguishable from the intellectual aspects of the theory. They included creating emotional and affective attitudes with regard to the doctrine and its propagators as well as a strong disposition to act.

6. The process of implanting the transferred concepts took place among a specific team of students and intellectuals at the Universidad Católica de Chile in Santiago. The team expressed the appropriation of the transferred concepts not only by reproducing them in the teaching and research conducted at the Universidad Católica but also by a transfer of roles between professors from Chicago University and their students. This materialized when the latter, acting as representatives of Chicago University, initiated programs of ideological transfer in other Latin American countries such as Argentina and Colombia.

7. The capacity to "make the transfer operational," that is, to remodel the social environment according to the ideas that were transferred, was initially confined, in this case, to the School of Economics at the Universidad Católica. The "macro-social" possibilities for making the transfer operational were severely restricted by the structural characteristics of Chilean society, its democratic political system, and the ideological

traditions that formed part of the country's political culture. The imported product was a foreign element. It was an alien element for the entrepreneurs, the economists, and the traditional political class. It was not possible to make it operate under the "state of compromise" which characterized Chilean democracy. Furthermore, the socializing trends that prevailed in Chile during the 1960s, made it an esoteric product. The implementation of the transferred model required, therefore, a full revolution with regard to the political circumstances in Chile.

8. The intensification of the socializing trends that took place under the administration of Frei and Allende, and the concurrent ideological and political polarization, gradually created the possibility for the receiving group to spread its influence and provided the takeoff point for the group when the crisis that put an end to Chilean democracy became generalized and opened the way for authoritarian reaction.

9. In the framework provided by this crisis and the establishment of authoritarian rule, the possibility of making the transfer operational – the remodeling of the social environment on the basis of a product transferred eighteen years previously – began to seem feasible. As of 1974, ideological transfer began to be implemented through the power of the state, thus initiating an attempt to radically transform Chile's economy and culture.

CHAPTER 3

The Chicago School of Economics

This chapter intends to show how the general ideological model explicit in the programs of Pinochet's economists was inscribed in a particular intellectual tradition and in a very specific "school" of economic thought. We shall examine briefly what has become known as the "Chicago Economic Tradition." The purpose is to observe not only how a doctrine and its main constitutive theoretical elements are formed, but, more importantly, how the ideological traits that make Chicago a subculture were personalized in a handful of individuals who transmitted their vision of the world and their science inside and outside of Chicago to their disciples.

This analysis requires insight from a historical viewpoint. We must focus on the personalities and their relationships, on their ideas, and the way in which they converged or diverged in their historical context and the turning points in the shaping of a school of economic thought. This historical description, however, must avoid simplifications. It must, particularly, avoid the tendency to identify the Chicago School of Economics with the entire University of Chicago or, for that matter, at least before the 1950s, with its Department of Economics. The fact that the ideological outlook described as "Chicago" became predominant in the Economics Department after the meeting of Milton Friedman and other economists did not affect the character of a university endowed, in general terms, with a liberal reputation. Moreover, not all the economists from the department, not even those who could be described as conservative, participated in the School.

However the history of the "normative science" characterizing the School does not commence with Milton Friedman's influence at the department. The influence of Friedman's thought and, more generally, the constitution of the School itself, must be seen in the light of a tradition inaugurated by other economists, such as Frank Knight, Jacob Viner, and Henry Simons, and of the emergence of a conservative reaction to the "Keynesian revolution" and the growth of state interventionism. This reaction was expressed by some, but not all, influential economists from the department, as well as members of other university departments, such as Frederick Hayek. These caveats constitute a synthesis of the topics we intend to develop in the following pages: first, a historical perspective of the School and of its adherents; second, an analysis of its main ideas and their elaboration. The reaction of the School *vis-à-vis* the new "economic development doctrines" will be discussed in another chapter.   *which ?*

The Chicago tradition: conservatism and polemics

The existence or non-existence of a particular orientation, tradition, or school of economic thought, which can be ascribed to Chicago, seems to be a discussion totally mastered by common usage and acknowledgment. As Milton Friedman has said: "the term is used sometimes as an epithet, sometimes as an accolade, but always with a fairly definite though by no means single-valued meaning."[1] Common usage does not mean, in fact, agreement over concise definitions, and when H. L. Miller wrote in a 1962 issue of the *Journal of Political Economy*, published by the University of Chicago, that "Chicagoans do, in fact, form an interconnected group with a set of common attitudes and interests which distinguishes them from the rest of the academic progression," and attempted to present these attitudes in a systematic way, an immediate skeptical, if not negative, reaction arose within Chicago ranks. George Stigler, a distinguished member of the School, in the same journal, objected that Miller had not described "either a unifying ethical or political philosophy or an articulate and reasonably specific policy program." And another Chicagoan, M. Bronfenbrenner, who also entered the discussion, confessed his initial "visceral reaction" against a term which, most of the time, was used pejoratively, and his concession *vis-à-vis* the evidence of "distinctive Chicago policy and methodological propositions, formerly associated most emphatically with Henry Simons and currently with Milton Friedman." Hence, there were, as Bronfenbrenner argued, not one, but two Chicago Schools; "the departure of Jacob Viner and the passing of Henry Simons" marked the watershed between them.[2]

The discussion had struck not only a theoretical, but also a historical chord. If such a school did exist, there had to be a history of it and perhaps not a short one after all. If its conservatism and economic orthodoxy were its hallmarks, its origins could well be traced back to the very creation of the University of Chicago in 1892.

The most relevant academic event, the founding of the University of Chicago, was tainted, however, from its inception with a conservative, pro-business reputation, to the extent that, in A. W. Coats' words, "John D. Rockefeller's munificent donations bestowed upon the new institution the opprobrious title of The Standard Oil University."[3] Perhaps more than other universities in the country, Chicago reflected in its origins – what Barry D.

Karl has described as "the extraordinary level of agreement on a wide range of fundamentals between those industrial leaders who used their vast personal resources to build a modern system of higher education in America and the trained academics who assisted them and were assisted by them."[4]

In fact, this conservative and pro-business reputation was completely confirmed by the appointment of J. Lawrence Laughlin as the first director of the Chicago Department of Economics. His traits, as described by Coats, seem to raise the possibility of a hypothetical historical consistency in the reproduction of those attitudes which now identify Chicago economists. Laughlin "was a dogmatic theorist and a vigorous controversialist whose insistence upon the need to separate 'what is' from 'what ought to be' did not prevent him from engaging in downright partisan advocacy of his favorite policy proposals." Laughlin, one of the nation's most conservative economists, acted during most of his career in disharmony with the prevailing mood of American economists, who preferred to shun incorporation into polemic causes whose ideological nature threatened the efforts made to consolidate the scientific reputation of the profession. It was not without reason, therefore, that the Chicago Department of Economics acquired, during the 1890s and early 1900s, "an unenviable reputation as a center of doctrinal orthodoxy and extreme conservatism in matters of policy." But this was, in perspective, an unjust reputation. As Coats argues, the department was neither solidly conservative, nor unduly under Laughlin's influence, and, by the time he retired in 1916 after twenty-four years of directorship, Chicago was one of the nation's leading centers of academic economics and widely regarded as such until Friedman's arrival. Traditions are persistent, however, and even if in Laughlin's times there was nothing resembling the present conceptions of the Chicago School, the mental reflex which now equates Chicago economics with a conservative academic clique might well inherit reverberations from the beginning of the century.[5]

"When giants walked the earth"

The formative period of the "Chicago tradition" has been traced, less speculatively, to Jacob Viner's integration in 1916 and even more precisely to the constitution of a group of brilliant conservative economists during the pre-war years. It was during the 1930s that the "founding fathers" of Chicago economics established their influence in the department: Frank Knight, Jacob Viner, Henry Simons, and Lloyd Mints initiated the golden age of Chicago economics and gave birth to the "subculture."

The 1930s were, in fact, a golden age for the University of Chicago, both for the development of conservative thought emanating from different western sources and in the advancement of social science teaching and research. Adler and Thomism were in fashion and, while Leo Strauss taught political philosophy, Charles Merriam, the leading exponent of the empirical study of political behavior, published his work, *Political Power*, in 1934.

Some of these powerful intellectual figures developed a strong influence at the university. The most remarkable case was that of Leo Strauss, whose elitist philosophy had an extraordinary influence on the intellectual climate of students from the politics and philosophy departments. Straussianism, as a school of thought, may have had an important ideological impact on the configuration of the "economist's philosopher," entrusted with the mission of defending the true principles of classical political economy that would begin to appear in this same period at the Chicago Economics Department.[6]

During the 1930s, however, Chicago economics was characterized by a substantial degree of doctrinal diversity. A socialist such as Oscar Lange, quantitative economists such as Paul Douglas, Henry Schultz, and Lange again, and institutionalists like John U. Nef and Chester Wright were members of the faculty. Even among the "founding fathers" differences were not negligible. As Stigler recalls, "Knight was a great philosopher and theoretician, almost in a Marxian sense; Viner was steadfastly non-dogmatic on policy views; Mints was a close historical student of money and restricted himself to that field; Simons was the utopian."[7]

Since the arrival of Frank Knight and his disciple, Henry Simons, however, some changes could be noticed in the relationships between teachers and students. Reder argues that, before that time, it would have been hard to identify a particular intellectual style among Chicago PhDs.[8] The influence exerted by Knight and Simons seems to have been, therefore, the originating force behind "the School." What were the characteristics of these men?

Frank Knight has been described variously by his students as "a sage and an oracle" (Reder), "a gentle cynic" (Patinkin), or an intellectual approaching the category of "a near saint of scholarship" (Stigler). His influence was not oriented towards "the reproduction of influence over the professional mechanisms of that academic community to assure their own continued research and production," as Karl described the role of a contemporary Chicagoan, Charles Merriam, but toward the formation and the transformation of his students' minds. Knight, rather than initiating research programs which did not interest him, or promoting statistical studies in which he did not believe or policy recommendations of which he was skeptical, imbued his students with clear, definite, if not dogmatic principles ("If you don't learn anything else from me, then learn this ..."), wherein an emphasis was placed on individual freedom as being the most basic value. Endowed with a trait best expressed in a saying he liked to quote – "an irrational passion for dispassionate rationality" – he rejected what he considered to be the "irrationality of religion," particularly in its clerical and Catholic expressions, but was simultaneously "deeply skeptical of the extent to which rational discussion could solve social problems." As Patinkin observes, his view of human society involved a deep contradiction:

on the one hand he regarded individual freedom as a basic value, and recognized that representative democracy was the only way in which a large society of free individuals could govern itself; on the other, he had the basic misgivings about the actual workings of the democratic process – and was accordingly deeply pessimistic about its future. So much so that on some occasions he predicted the natural disintegration of democracy and its replacement by dictatorship."[9]

Simons, who taught price theory and public finance, was, in Stigler's words, "the Crown Prince of this theoretical Kingdom, the Chicago School of Economics." His famous pamphlet, *A Positive Program for Laissez Faire*, published in 1934, contained all the major ideas on which he would elaborate in the following decade. "Completed in the trough of the deepest depression of modern times, it had an urgency which never left his work: western society was near the point of no return."[10] What Simons' "manifesto" carried to its extreme was his central philosophical point: for the preservation of personal freedom it is essential to have a large sector of economic life organized privately and competitively.[11] Patinkin's recollection of Simons' lectures and of his impact on his students are worth reproducing in detail. They show the admiration and reverence Chicago students developed towards these men, feelings which, as we shall see, were maintained and reproduced in later generations of students. They also single out the essential characteristics of a style of teaching and, as Stigler would say, of "preaching about economics" which would be classic in the Chicago tradition. In *A Propos of A Positive Program for Laissez Faire*, Patinkin writes:

I still remember my esthetic enjoyment of its clean and incisive style (Mozart, not Beethoven – he once told us – was the music for him), and my intellectual enjoyment of its trenchant argument. What was particularly exciting were the same qualities that made Marxism so appealing to many other young people at the same time: simplicity together with apparent logical completeness: idealism combined with radicalism. For Simons carried out his approach to its logical extreme, with the unshaken conviction of a world reformer that life would be better if only his policy recommendations were carried out. Market competition was to be assured by opposing with equal vigor all forms of monopoly, business as well as labor unions; a high degree of equality was to be achieved by a progressive income tax, applied to receipts of any kind – not only of ordinary income, but capital gains, inheritances and gifts as well; the instability of the banking system was to be solved by requiring 100 percent reserves; and, of course, mass unemployment – with the waste and suffering that it represented – was to be prevented by a contracyclical policy of varying the quantity of money so as to stabilize the price level ... Simons' intellectual impact was such that we all left his classroom "simonized" to some extent or other.[12]

Perhaps more than Viner and Mints, Knight and Simons, therefore, were the initiators of a group endowed not only with powerful theoretical notions, but also with a conception of the role of the economist as a crusader, whose job it was "to divest people of prejudices, to have them see the questions as they are."[13] They did this not only with the strength of their personalities and the brilliance of their intellects but, also, and this is a relevant factor, through the creation of strong bonds of affection with their students and protégés, a kind of relationship which, as Reder remarks, they did not have with colleagues of their own generation. By the mid-1930s, then, Knight and Simons had established an affinity group of brilliant students whose principal figures were Milton Friedman, Rose Director Friedman, George Stigler, Allen Wallis, and Aaron Director.

The war period: change and consolidation

The war years were the final years of the traditional Chicago School. In 1938–9, the old Chicago department experienced a series of jolts resulting from the death of several of its members (including Henry Schultz), the election to public office of others (including Paul Douglas), and a sense of losing track with theory developments. At the same time, Oscar Lange played a leading role in the rebuilding of the department. However, in 1945, he left the country and abandoned academic life for his native Poland. The following year, Jacob Viner moved to Princeton and Henry Simons died, thus marking the watershed between the old and the new Chicago Schools. At this time, T. W. Schultz joined the department and soon became its chairman, providing the leadership that had long been missing. In this role, "he mediated among contending factions while pursuing his own research programs."[14] Also, in 1946, Milton Friedman returned to Chicago (where he had completed his MA degree in 1933), at which time he began a career that would make him the formidable baton passer of Chicago free market economic ideology.[15]

Transition between the old and the new Chicago Schools was not, however, a short one. Reder says:

In retrospect, the key to the development and eventual dominance of the "Chicago view" was to unite Friedman, Stigler, and Wallis on the Chicago Faculty. This took 13 years to accomplish: Stigler was appointed to the Wallgreen Professorship in the Graduate School of Business with a joint appointment in the Economics Department in 1958; the other two were appointed in 1946 – Wallis to the Business School, where he became Dean in 1955, and Friedman to the Economics Department.[16]

From the 1950s, however, a certain hegemony of the "Chicago view" became apparent and was mentioned by outsiders and insiders as a distinctive feature of the Chicago Faculty. The existence of a Chicago School was not only inferred from the predominance of a particular doctrinal perspective within the faculty, but also from tendencies towards a "politics of ideas," that is, from the attitudes and behavior of economists who were "committed to the development of certain ideological positions which they sought to establish within the academic community" and society as a whole. A letter from Jacob Viner to Don Patinkin depicts, in a somewhat irritated but transparent manner, the feelings that the new era invoked among members of the old guard. It deserves to be quoted in full.

It was not until after I left Chicago in 1946 that I began to hear rumors about a "Chicago School" which was engaged in organized battle for laissez faire and the "quantity theory of money" and against "imperfect competition" theorizing and "Keynesianism." I remained skeptical about this until I attended a conference sponsored by the University of Chicago professors in 1951. The invited participants were a varied lot of academics, bureaucrats, businessmen, etc., but the program for discussion, the selection of chairmen, and everything about the conference except the unscheduled statements and protests from individual participants were so patiently and rigidly structured, so loaded, that I got more amusement from the conference than from any other I ever attended. Even the source of the financing of the conference, as I found out later, was ideologically loaded. There is a published account of the proceedings of the conference, but it does not include the program, etc., as presented to the participants to direct their discussion. From then on I was willing to consider the existence of a "Chicago School" (but one not confined to the Economics Department and not embracing all of the department) and that this "School" has been in operation, and had won many able disciples, for years before I left Chicago. But at no time was I consciously a member of it, and it is my vague impression that if there was such a school it did not regard me as a member, or at least as a loyal and qualified member. In any case, I am not well informed about the past or the present of such a "school," and therefore I have nothing to contribute to the recent inquirers about the intellectual history of this putative school.[17]

Viner was referring, in fact, to the most controversial aspect of the School, its sectarianism, a feature which invites, as Stigler complains, "a slovenly stereotype of the men's thinking," which had led, according to Bronfenbrenner's ironic assertion, to the caricature of Chicago as "Pangloss plus Gradgrind, with touches of Peachum, Torquemada, and the Marquis de Sade thrown in as 'insulter's surplus.' "[18] Whatever the complaints were, however, Viner's was an important point, because it put a finger on an element which, notwithstanding the seriousness of Chicago University economics, had begun to stand out as a central lineament of its practitioners.

What were the reasons for the development of this mentality? An attempt to answer this question demands more than simple reference to personalities; it requires a brief observation of the impact and reactions that their ideas had on the ideological establishment of economics prevailing at the time.

Revolution and counterrevolution in economic theory: the roots of the School

The revolution of the 1930s in economic theory was the Keynesian revolution. Keynes' *The General Theory of Interest, Money and Employment*, published in 1936, constituted an onslaught on Say's Law, the argument that, in the long run, the "real forces" of the economic system would naturally tend toward full employment equilibrium.[19]

Keynes' work criticized the policies of deflation to control economic depression advocated until that time. Assuming full employment as being objectively preeminent for economic policy, he rejected the classical perspective that the state had to limit its functions at the economic level to the satisfaction of basic social needs, affirming that the state had to guarantee a volume of global demand allowing for the full employment objective.

It has often been remarked that Keynes' assault on "classical theory" expanded with astonishing speed. In fact, as Daniel Bell has noted, one of the reasons for this was the fall of neo-classical theory to a rather low level of esteem during the first three decades of this century, particularly in the United States. "It was regarded as 'academic' (in the pejorative sense of the word), as theoretical (again pejorative), abstract, ahistorical, hypothetical-deductive, etc."[20] Keynesianism, therefore, made a leap forward, devoid of major theoretical opposition, confirming that, as Henry Johnson has suggested,

by far the most helpful circumstance for the rapid propagation of a new and revolutionary theory is the existence of an established orthodoxy which is clearly inconsistent with the most salient facts of reality, and yet is sufficiently confident of its intellectual power to attempt to explain these facts, and its efforts to do so expose its incompetence in a ludicrous fashion.[21]

After decades of mass unemployment in Britain and the other leading capitalist countries, Keynes' theory offered not only a convincing explanation of the nature of the problem, but also a set of policy prescriptions based on that explanation, which were to become, during the war and, indeed, in the decades that followed, the accepted economic wisdom, both at the governmental policy level and in the principal centers of academic economics.

Keynesian economics proved essential to wartime economic management and then became the official government orientation in both Britain and the United States. In the US, this dominance continued throughout the Kennedy and Johnson years. But also, which is perhaps more important to our subject, Keynesianism came to command the most prestigious economics departments (Oxford and Cambridge in Britain, Harvard in the United States), generating the rebellion of a young generation who could then "escape from the slow and soul-destroying process of acquiring wisdom by osmosis from the elders" and occupy, through their command of the "New Economics," the leading positions in a field which was experiencing a rapid process of professionalization. Through successive generations of undergraduates, Keynesian economics became "part of the intellectual culture of the elite and eventually of common culture. Through successive generations of graduate students, who became academic teachers and economic civil servants, it gradually conquered academic economics and became the orthodoxy of the macroeconomics side of economics."[22]

Facing this new orthodoxy was "a University of Chicago oral tradition" that kept alive the "understanding of the fundamental truth among a small band of the initiate through the dark ages of the Keynesian despotism."[23] Milton Friedman has written, describing the 1950s:

It is hard for persons who were then active, let alone for the more than half of the current population who were then less than ten years old or had not yet been born, to reconstruct the intellectual climate of the time. Those of us who were deeply concerned about the danger to freedom and prosperity from the growth of government, from the triumph of welfare state and Keynesian ideas, were a small beleaguered minority regarded as eccentrics by the great majority of our fellow intellectuals.[24]

It was from the spirit of a "small beleaguered minority" that a number of behavior patterns were to develop: ego involvement, professional identity, political preference and, *inter alia*, the debater of adversary mentality, all of which were to form the character of a "rational sect" adopted by the "Chicago School."[25] The defeat of "the collectivist drive" required the organization of a determined group of intellectuals, who could reverse the "road to serfdom" that Hayek had so vigorously denounced, through the cultivation and advancement of the teaching of classical economists.

This was not, of course, a simple or mechanical process, nor should it be seen as more conspiratorial than that normally required to promote ideas which conflict with an established orthodoxy. As Viner suggested in his letter to Patinkin, the "School" did not include the entire Chicago Department of Economics, nor was it reduced to it. Its expansion, both inside and outside the walls of Chicago, implied the gradual recruitment of adherents, "acolytes, sympathizers, and kindred spirits," both conscious and unconscious, on a scale that varied from total adherence to irreducible liberalism to a powerful attraction by Chicago economic logic and policy alternatives.

By the 1950s, it was recognized, as we have already seen, as a doctrinal "school," endowed with relatively homogeneous views on fundamental questions, including what is considered to be important, forming a fairly coherent philosophy or position on relevant issues which differed somewhat from most others.[26] Its road to influence and success was not a short one, and the primacy of its views constitutes, in the United States and other leading industrialized countries, a fairly recent phenomenon. The reasons for this development are twofold and we can deal with them only very succinctly.

The first one was the erosion of the Keynesian consensus. Since the end of the 1940s, the new orthodoxy established by Lord Keynes and his followers began to experience fissures and shortcomings, adopting the same type of critical evolution previously ascribed to "classical" economics. What was realized by then was that the corollary of the Keynesian view regarding the primacy of the unemployment problem had been a pronounced tendency to play down the adverse economic consequences of inflation. The result was that, by the mid-1940s, the new established orthodoxy had become ripe for attack in the same way that Keynes had assaulted "classical economics" in the 1930s. As Johnson describes it, the New Economics had become vulnerable on two fronts: its inability to prescribe for what had come to be seen as a major social problem – inflation, in contrast to the unemployment of Keynes' times – and a "dependence on the authority and prestige of senior scholars which is oppressive to the young."[27] Monetarism began to stand out as a' major counterrevolution, which concentrated on convincing the profession and the public that inflation was an important issue, and that monetarism could provide an explanation and a policy, whereas Keynesianism could not.

The second factor of success was the existence of the Chicago School and the leadership role assumed by the most distinguished of its members, Milton Friedman. During the 1950s Friedman published the three works, which (notwithstanding the "oppressive" intellectual ambience, as he saw it) would establish the basis for the monetarist counterrevolution. *The Quantity Theory of Money: A Restatement* (1956) and the *Program for Monetary Stability* (1959) provided the central elements for a "theoretical resuscitation of money" (Bell). His *Capitalism and Freedom*, first edited in 1962 as a collection of lectures delivered in 1957, became the manifesto of the economic philosophy and the ideological tenets which gave strength to the School. As Friedman recognized in the preface to the book, he owed the philosophy and "much of the detail in it" to many teachers, colleagues, and friends and, above all, he wrote,

to a distinguished group I have been privileged to be associated with at the University of Chicago: Frank Knight, Henry C. Simons, Lloyd Mints, Aaron Director, Friedrich A. Hayek, George J. Stigler. I ask their pardon for my failure to acknowledge specifically the many ideas of theirs which they will find expressed in this book. I have learned so much from them and what I have learned has become so much a part of my own thought, that I would not know how to select points to footnote.[28]

What were the ideas which Friedman was acknowledging and which have become the essence of the Chicago School? We will now elaborate upon them in greater detail.

The ideas

The discussion of the ideas included in the Chicago tradition requires a brief observation regarding what is now known as the science of economics. In fact, economics as a science includes, along with the methodological and analytical notions most specifically linked to the discipline, a vast and complex list of ingredients which have been described by most economists as either ideological or metaphysical, philosophical or simply political. We refer to assumptions about man and society expressed in concepts, such as "general equilibrium" or "rational utility maximizing individual," for example. We also refer to "policy-oriented" conclusions, that is, conservations of governmental behavior and recommendations to political authorities. It is to these aspects that we shall turn our attention.

The function of economics as an apologia for capitalist society and the market system, or the inclusion of "moral judgments" in economic discourse, is obviously not an exclusive feature of any particular "school of thought," but has constituted an integral part of the western economic tradition.[29] We want to argue here, however, that within this tradition, Chicago represents (a) *a particularly coherent and forceful articulation of ideological and positive economics, bestowed with an instrumentalist methodology which, in the end, locates the validation of its hypothesis in the area of social and political activity*. We hope to show further that, (b) *inheriting a long tradition of economic mistrust and contempt for politics, Chicago constitutes the "extreme vanguard" of the process of contemporary penetration of economics into political thought*.

The development of this discussion needs to take into consideration the following two observations. The first is that this doctrine focused as a "pattern of interworking meaning," to use Geertz's expression, constitutes a product in itself, whose power as an intellectual artefact has to be observed without respect to "externalities" or the social determinations which are at its origin.[30] At the same time, however, Chicago as an idea system is composed both of elements which reaffirm classical or neo-classical notions of economic thought and of elements which are innovations or express a particular emphasis on ideas which were not stressed as being crucial previously. The observation of the product itself must, therefore, incorporate both dimensions: Chicago as a legacy and Chicago as a new or different recomposition of economic ideas. We will state first the central Chicago view and then proceed to trace the inherited elements which give Chicago what we consider to be its main thrust as a doctrine: its nature as a vanguard of neo-classicism and of the penetration of economic notions into political thought.

This analysis has been facilitated by the discussion developed, particularly since the 1970s, among economists in the United States, on the basic elements distinguishing Chicago economics from other schools of economic thought, and Chicago economists from other economists in western societies. The discussion has been intense and, as Samuels has indicated, has confronted difficulties in avoiding stereotypes and simplifications for several reasons: (1) the size and complexity of the subject matter; (2) the emotional content, that is, the heavy ideological element; (3) the (inevitably) limited space; and, *inter alia*, (4) the ease with which the Chicago School position can, in fact, be reduced to a stereotype, partly due to the self-admitted and intentional propaganda role of Chicago spokesmen.[31] Yet the discussion also shows, with some minor, though not negligible, exceptions, an important level of agreement between Chicago and non-Chicago economists on the elements which concur in defining the specificity of the Chicago School economist.[32] More interested in characterizing the Chicago School of thought than in discussing the validity of its assumptions and conclusions, we plan to continue this discussion by organizing it into two topical hypotheses devised to sustain the theme of our main argument. In utilizing them, we plan to develop a summary of Chicago ideas and attitudes, along with the most relevant features observed by their critics and opponents. These hypotheses are conceived at the same time as a gradual approximation to the subject of the political significance of the School and its ideas.

The first of these topical hypotheses is synthesized in the assertion that Chicago economics is a "normative science," that is, an ideas system whose internal articulation attempts no demarcation of its scientific elements from its normative rules and political precepts. The second is that "Chicago" carries with it *an attitude framework of knowledge, a conception of the economist as "a radical reformer," or a pattern of "polar attitudes"* which had to be considered *as the vanguard of "economic penetration" into political thought.* One of our aims is descriptive: we attempt to draw a complete picture of the ideas and attitudes portraying the School. Another is analytical: the understanding of the "power" of the ideological product, a goal which is the main link with the discussion that will follow with regard to the impact of the Chicago ideas in Chile.

A normative science?

The first problem to be mentioned refers to the traditionally tense relationship between "metaphysics," to use Joan Robinson's characterization of ideological or normative principles, and science in the history of economic thought.

In fact, the exigencies of a neutral economic science and the need for a distinction between the "political" and economic aspects of political economy can be traced back a long way. Writers such as John S. Mill, Senior, and Cairnes, to name only three, insisted upon the view that economic science had to restrict its scope to the study of the factual and the probable. Cairnes wrote that the aim of political economy "is not to attain tangible results, not to prove any definite thesis, not to advocate any practical plan, but simply to give light, to reveal laws of nature, to tell us what phenomena are found together, what effects will follow from what causes."[33]

Yet, as Gunnar Myrdal has pointed out, in spite of the apparent general agreement in the economics profession with regard to these principles, it is the contrary that has prevailed.

We are only too well aware that throughout the past century economists, speaking in the name of their science, have been airing views on what they considered to be socially imperative. They have proceeded to calculate immediately, on the basis of their scientific findings, the course of action which is economically "desirable" or "right," just as they have also opposed certain policies on the grounds that their realization would decrease the general "welfare" or imply the "neglect" (or even the "infringement") of economic laws.[34]

The need for a precise boundary between what is scientific practice and what is rational politics cannot establish as its origin, however, the work of Adam Smith or the physiocrats. Their first objective was the study of the "natural state": an ideal type model of the society which actually existed and concurrently a definition of the society which they felt should exist. As a consequence, one of the central functions of theoretical analysis was, in their view, the formulation of normative rules. As we shall see, this is exactly the tradition from which the Chicago School developed its approach to economics as a discipline.[35]

But, in general terms, what became the official position in scientific economics was the establishment of a conceptual boundary between what was scientific and what was rational politics, not to prevent the venturing beyond the frontier line, which was seen as both natural and even highly desirable, but to make it clear that, when they did, "they then no longer practiced economic theory in the narrow sense but became the superimposed science of 'moral philosophy.' "[36]

Thus, while J. S. Mill developed the distinction between "science" and "art," which, in his view, differed in the same way as comprehension is distinguishable from volition, or as Pigou asserts, the "positive" and the "normative," meaning the distinction between what is and what ought to be in the economic organizations of society,[37] Milton Friedman and the Chicago School has opted, as we shall see, for the distinction between "economic science" and "economic policy," which implicitly suggests not a difference in quality between what is and what ought to be, but a necessary link between them.

From our standpoint, however, these efforts to distinguish between what is and what ought to be – for the most part futile, as Myrdal shows in his work – are less important than the linkage that each economic doctrine has established between them. For it is in the way in which such links and articulations have been constructed that the main specificity of a doctrine and of a particular school of economic thought can establish its foundation.

To formulate the same idea in a more positive way, what we want to stress here is that, if we consider the science of economics as formed at its most basic level by (1) assumptions or fundamental premises; (2) a nucleus of positive theoretical accumulation including methodology; and (3) policy conclusions, these elements admit different forms of articulation or combination, of which there are two that seem crucial to the determination of the characteristics of a "school of economic thought": (a) the degree of cohesiveness – tight or diffuse – given to the conforming elements and (b) the degree of instrumentality, or the way in which the number of logical steps between the ultimate formal premises and the specific final conclusions are treated as mediations for the support and strengthening of such conclusions.[38]

Our first contention is very simple: the more an economic doctrine adheres to a tight articulation between its fundamental premises and its (positive) body of theoretical accumulation, and the more instrumentalist its methodology, the more incorporated, as an indissoluble and explicit part, into the formulation and operationalization of its ideas system a body of normative assumptions and precepts becomes. Tightness and instrumentality demand explicit adherence to a set of normative principles as a necessary condition, for reasons we hope will become obvious in the next section.

Let us present, for the discussion of this problem, the central element characterizing the Chicago School doctrine, as seen by its practitioners and critics. Milton Friedman's own definition provides a good point of departure. Friedman has stated that:

In discussion of economic policy, Chicago stands for belief in the efficacy of the free market as a means of organizing resources, for skepticism about government intervention into economic affairs, and for emphasis on the quality of money as a key factor in producing inflation. In discussions of economic science, "Chicago" stands for an approach that takes seriously the use of economic theory as a tool for analyzing a startlingly wide range of concrete problems, rather than as an abstract mathematical structure of great beauty but little power; for an approach that insists on empirical testing of theoretical generalizations and rejects alike facts without theory and theory without facts.[39]

This definition could be criticized as both insufficient and excessive; excessive because most non-Chicago economists in the United States can be included within it, insufficient because Chicago characterizations must consider the degree of ideological adherence with which these values are held. In the first sense, George Stigler has argued that there are economists who have a strong preference for a private, competitive organization of economic activity (and, for that matter, accept the relevance of price theory to substantive problems), but he doubts "that 1 per cent of the economist 'members' of this school have any connection with Chicago, it being true that there are many economists who share this view at Chicago and perhaps no more at any other single institution."[40] H. Laurence Miller's line of argument, on the contrary, could make Friedman's definition seem insufficient for, in his view, the Chicago economist is characterized mainly by attitudes, among others, the following:

1. a polar position as advocate of an individualistic market economy;
2. the emphasis he puts on the "usefulness and relevance of neo-classical economic theory";
3. the way in which he equates the actual and the ideal market;
4. the way in which he sees and applies economics in and to every nook and cranny of life;
5. the emphasis that he puts on hypothesis testing as a neglected element in the development of positive economics.[41]

Samuels has emphasized similar points, concentrating on the idea that Chicago constitutes

the extreme vanguard of neo-classicism. It is the foremost ideological extension of that area of economics, representing its most conservative tendency, manifest, in part, in its emphasis upon Pareto optimality. It is characterized by a greater than average belief in the neo-classical analysis and, therefore, by its substantial efforts to push that analysis into newer applications. In comparison with general neo-classicism, however, the work of the Chicago School comes closer to institutional economics in its attention to the problem of organization and control of the economic system.[42]

David Wall has put Chicago traits succinctly: "First, that theory is of fundamental importance; second, that theory is irrelevant unless set in a definite empirical context, and third, that in absence of evidence to the contrary, the market works."[43]

If we leave adjectives aside for the moment and defer the discussion of what we shall term "the attitudinal framework" of knowledge in Chicago economists, we can perceive a certain degree of agreement on the basic elements included in Friedman's definition. Chicago implies emphasis on theory – neo-classical theory – set in an empirical context, along with the belief that it can be extended to the analysis of a "startlingly wide range of concrete problems." Chicago adheres to an unrestricted defense of the individual free market systems and to limited government. Yet, the questions that must be posed are what is, first, the meaning given to market and government in the Chicago view, and, second, what is the relationship which these meanings or significances establish between the "policy matters" and scientific accumulation? It is on these matters that the discussion has been concentrated, for it is here that the crucial elements characterizing Chicago economics as an ideological product are found.

In the following pages we shall briefly examine the notions of market and government in the Chicago view, as well as what has become its central contemporary contention regarding macro-economics: the quantity theory of money or monetarism. We shall then move on to the question of the relationship of the normative and the positive approach to economics professed by the Chicago School: its vision of economics as a science that requires a normative setting.

The market

The notion of market, in the Chicago view, incorporates or is at the base of three ideological paradigms:

1. the market as the framework of free and informed individual exchange;
2. the market as the paradigm of freedom or of a free and non-coercive social organization;
3. the market as the focus and the objective of economic scientific accumulation.

These ideological paradigms are mainly – as we shall develop more extensively later – nothing more than reflections or legacies of the classical notions of economic theory as expounded by Adam Smith and others. In fact, the first thing which is remarkable about them is the faithfulness with which classical and neo-classical beliefs, the themes and concepts, are received, reaffirmed, and, in some cases, driven to an extreme.[44]

It is well known that the neo-classical notion of market is indissolubly linked to a conception of the individual. As classical economists saw it, the fact of scarcity creates a necessity for choice and a careful comparing of alternatives. Accordingly, a new view of human nature came into focus. "The rational, calculating human emerges clearly in the pages of ... most of the works of neo-classical writers."[45] It also constitutes an article of faith for Chicago economists. George Stigler states flatly, "We believe that man is a utility maximizing animal – apparently pigeons and rats are also – and to date we have not found it informative to carve out a section of his life in which he invokes a different goal or behavior."[46]

It is the action of this utility maximizing individual which gives rise to economic activity. Through the exercise of his free will, he enacts "the elementary, yet frequently denied, proposition that both parties to an economic transaction benefit from it provided the transaction is bilaterally voluntary and informed," writes Friedman.[47] Or as Stigler puts it, it is because market transactions are voluntary that they must benefit at least one party and not injure the other.[48] Each individual uses his own means to achieve his own ends. The advantage of this association is derived from his ability to use another individual as a means, under the principle of free mutual consent.

Belief in the Pareto optimality theorem, the trade-off theory of neo-classical economics, appears, therefore, at the basis of the notion of market.[49] It subsists in the hedonist psychology which gave rise to utilitarianism and projects from a utilitarianism encounter with natural law theory, the idea of a "general equilibrium," a state of social harmony based on individual exchange. Suffice it to say that given those logically ideal conditions, the perfect market achieves efficiency in the use of resources, as economists have demonstrated in their models of static general equilibrium.

From this basic individual exchange, the simple and most efficient form of society is produced: a number of independent households, a collection of Robinson Crusoes, as it were. Friedman echoes Adam Smith when saying:

Each household uses the resources it controls to produce goods and services that it exchanges for goods and services produced by other households, on terms mutually acceptable to the two parties to the bargain ... since the household always has the alternative of producing directly for itself, it need not enter into any exchange unless it benefits from it. Hence, no exchange will take place unless both parties do benefit from it. Cooperation is thereby achieved without coercion.[50]

This basic structure, whatever the complexities introduced by modern society (enterprises, division of labor, and money, among others), represents the central feature of market technique.

As in that simple model, so in the complex enterprise and money exchange economy, cooperation is strictly individual and voluntary provided: a) that enterprises are private so that the ultimate contracting parties are individuals and b) that individuals are effectively free to enter or not to enter into any particular exchange, so that every transaction is strictly voluntary.[51]

A rational optimizing individual is, thus, the basis of the market vision held by the Chicago view. The market involves, above everything else, profit-seeking behaviour, for "individuals can be counted upon to pursue constrained maximization or calculation advantage adjustments within the extent opportunity sets as market conditions."[52] The market becomes, therefore, an individual, behavioral, and rationalistic assumption which is justified on the basis that it promotes a free economic order. "The idea of a purely individualistic order," wrote Frank Knight, "is a logical device, necessary to separate for study the tendencies of individualism from those of socialism."[53] In this, Knight went even further than the utilitarians. As a "libertarian moralist," he rejected the utilitarian treatment of freedom as a means to an end: his commitment was not to "maximum satisfaction" but to "maximum freedom." The perfect market is "ideal," because it is the "embodiment of complete freedom." It makes it possible for everyone to be "free as Crusoe was free."[54]

The defense of the market conceived as the defense of freedom becomes, then, the main theme of Chicago "normative" literature. The idea that the "market works" constitutes, as a result, an affirmation of the possibility of freedom. Freedom is possible because the market works. Institutionally, this means the convergence of three features: (1) the private ownership of capital or productive assets; (2) the private management of economic enterprise; and (3) competitive enterprise.[55] This convergence can be referred to as a competitive private enterprise economy, or – as Friedman calls it – "a free private enterprise exchange." The existence of this system guarantees a minimum of coercion in the development of social activity. As Friedman puts it:

It prevents one person from interfering with another in respect of most of its activities. The consumer is protected from coercion by the seller because of the presence of other sellers from whom he can deal. The seller is protected from coercion by the consumer because of other consumers to whom he can sell. The employee is protected from coercion by the employer because of other employers for whom he can work, and so on. And the market does this impersonally and without centralized authority.[56]

This does not mean, obviously, that the need for a government is eliminated. The government must exist as a forum for determining the "rules of the game" and as an umpire to interpret and enforce the rules enacted. Friedman then continues:

What the market does is to reduce greatly the range of issues that must be decided through political means, and thereby to minimize the extent to which government needs to participate directly in the game. The characteristic feature of action through political channels is that it tends to require or enforce conformity. The great advantage of the market, on the other hand, is that it permits wide diversity. It is, in political terms, a system of proportional representation. Each man can vote, as it were, for the color of tie he wants and get it; he does not have to see what color the majority wants and then, if he is in the minority, submit.[57]

He concludes by saying: "By removing the organization of economic activity from the control of political authority, the market eliminates this source of coercive power."[58]

The market is, therefore, the mechanism which reduces coercion to a minimum, and coercion is equated with government and, in the last analysis, with politics as such.[59]

The government

Following a long tradition, Chicago School economists have seen the government as a form of monopoly that "inhibits effective freedom by denying individuals alternatives to the particular exchange."[60] This perspective, which also dates back to Adam Smith, considers that the importance of private monopolies has been largely exaggerated by critics of the market system. Frank Knight wrote, "I still think [that] Adam Smith is largely right; if the government would keep its hands clean of encouraging monopolies, much of the problem would largely take care of itself."[61]

An exception to this line of thinking was formulated by Henry Simons, who, in his *Program for Laissez Faire*, demanded "an outright dismantling of our gigantic corporations" and "persistent prosecution of producers who organize . . . for price maintenance and output limitation,"[62] but tradition has been reimposed by Friedman and Becker, among others. In Gary Becker's view, "it may be preferable not to regulate economic monopolies and to suffer their bad effects; rather than to regulate them and suffer the effects of political imperfections."[63] Friedman acknowledges the polemics and states his view by saying:

> When technical conditions make a monopoly the natural outcome of competitive market forces, there are only three alternatives that seem available: private monopoly, public monopoly, or public regulations. All those are bad so we must choose among evils. Henry Simons, observing public regulation of monopoly in the United States, found the results so distasteful that he concluded public monopoly would be a lesser evil. Walter Eucken, a noted German Liberal, observing public monopoly in German railroads, found the results so distasteful that he concluded public regulations would be a lesser evil. Having learned from both, I reluctantly conclude that, if tolerable, private monopoly may be the least of evils.[64]

"The role that the government should play in a society dedicated to freedom and relying primarily on the market to organize economic activity," as Friedman puts it, has constituted, therefore, one of the major themes of his ideological production. In order not to behave as a monopolistic force, the government must adhere to three roles: "to provide a means whereby we can modify the rules, to mediate differences among us on the meaning of the rules, and to enforce compliance with the rules on the part of those few who would otherwise not play the game."[65]

Therefore, what becomes important is not the government but the rules, those central conditions, "unintended outcomes of custom-accepted thinking," which result from men's voluntary agreement.[66] In brief,

the organization of economic activity through voluntary exchange presumes that we have provided through government for the maintenance of law and order to prevent coercion of one individual by another, the enforcement of contracts voluntarily entered into, the definition of the meaning of property rights, the interpretation and enforcement of such rights and the provision of a monetary framework.[67]

Friedman's preaching on the subject of government abstinence is long standing. As Reder reports:

Soon after coming to Chicago, Friedman began to combine economic research with advocacy of specific proposals for socio-economic reform (negative income tax, substitution of publicly subsidized private schools for public schools, making participation in social security voluntary, abolishing licensure for doctors, volunteer army in lieu of the draft). All of these reform proposals involved either increased use of the price system, substitution of private for public production, replacement of legal compulsion by voluntary, financially-induced private cooperation or a mixture of all three. In an important sense, they reflected the spirit of [Simons'] *A Positive Program* [*for Laissez Faire*]; most Chicago economists did and still do agree with most of them, and they have become identified – both to the profession and to the general public – as the Chicago view on economic policy.[68]

Monetarism

The second characteristic of Chicago doctrine identified with the School has been monetarism or, as Friedman would prefer to describe it, an adherence to the quantity theory of money.

The principal tenet of monetarism is that inflation is at all times and everywhere a monetary phenomenon. Its principal corollary is that only a slow and steady rate of increase in the money supply – one in line with the real growth of the economy – can ensure price stability.[69]

The confrontation with the idea that money does not matter has been a battle waged since John Locke's times by those who argue, on the contrary, that money can only reflect or distort real relationships. The basic framework of the argument has been that, if the total quantity of money is kept steady, the general price level will not rise because individual prices will adjust to each other as demand shifts. The idea that the private sector is self-stabilizing, which was a fundamental premise of pre-Keynesian economics, was reassumed by Henry Simons and developed later by Milton Friedman. The corollary was, again, that "real world instability results primarily from the fiscal, monetary, and regulatory actions of government."[70]

Since the publication of his monumental *Monetary History of the United States*, Friedman led a "monetarist" movement, first from his Chicago workshops on monetary theory and then from different public stands, with the dedication – as he once said – of "an old-fashioned preacher delivering a Sunday sermon" whose text for each talk is, *cherchez la monnaie*.[71] The enemy against which huge amounts of data and arguments were amassed was, of course, Keynesian doctrine – more precisely, its basic proposition that variations in government spending, taxes, and the national debt could stabilize both the price level and the real economy.

The battle, waged now for almost fifty years, has long since moved into the policy area. As Macesich argues, "the critics of monetarism declare that the proposed monetarist cure for inflation can work only by imposing excessive burdens of huge losses in real output and prolonged output losses in the economy. The monetarists answered that the burden must be borne because there is no other way to restore the economy to price or economic stability."[72]

What is behind this strict adherence to the quantity theory of money is again the basic assumption of a general equilibrium of the economy, which ensures price stability and which can only be hampered by government monetary intervention. The basic assumptions of general equilibrium, and of individual models of market exchange, over which positive, scientific accumulation can be developed, are thus reaffirmed.

For Chicago economists, economics is hence the science of the market, a science which concentrates on the choice of households and firms expressed primarily through the market, a rational system which has logic behind it responding rationally to changes in the alternatives of choice. Its proposition concerning society is that this rational system has to be left free and unhampered if stability is to be assumed. Thus, writes Buchanan, "when non-individualistic norms are introduced, the domain of economics as I define the discipline is abandoned,"[73] and he adds elsewhere: "Order replaces chaos through the spontaneous coordination of the market, that is, of course, the central message of economic theory, from Adam Smith onwards, and it is, in fact, about all there is to economics."[74] As Samuels states:

the paradigm governs positive and normative considerations, including the definition of the discipline "A question will be deemed economic only if it can be formulated in terms of the dominant paradigm." It is the goal of the Chicago School to establish a framework of economic thought and policy which would consider on its own terms and channel in its approved direction all economic analysis and policy.[75]

What is, however, this central paradigm and what methodological assumptions constitute the steps leading to economic analysis and policy? This question directs us to the second part of Friedman's description of the School, which can be summarized in the idea that "theory matters."

A tight paradigm

"To take seriously the use of economic theory" is, in Friedman's own definition, the first and most fundamental characteristic of Chicago economics. It encompasses the series of logical steps, from the theory's assumptions to the hypothesis drawn from it, which have to be empirically tested.

Melvin Reder has located the essence of this theoretical perspective in what he terms the "Tight Prior Equilibrium" theory. This is rooted, he says, in the hypothesis "that decision-makers so allocate the resources under their control that there is no alternative allocation such that any one decision-maker could have his expected utility increased without a reduction occurring in the expected utility of at least one other decision-maker."

As Reder argues, this is a definition of Pareto optimality – that point when no person would be less well off and at least one person would be better off – acceptable to most economists but "which may or may not be associated with a model that yields particular testable hypotheses, depending upon whether certain further assumptions are made. Chicago economists typically make these assumptions, while others often refuse to do so."[76]

It is through this set of further assumptions directly derived from Pareto's initial principle that the Chicago view arrives at the construction of "a stochastic analogue of the exact (non-stochastic) competitive general equilibrium model" which has the following property:

if for all commodities, expected price and expected quantity are treated as proxies for the corresponding price and quantity in the exact model, all propositions concerning partial derivatives of prices with respect to quantities (and of quantities with respect to prices) in the exact model will hold for the stochastic model as well, provided that we substitute "expected price" and "expected quanitty" for "price" and "quantity," respectively.[77]

What this means is a proportion of reality as strictly dependent on an abstract model; moreover, on a model that, from its basic Walrasian general equilibrium origins, developed through the work of Arrow, Debreu, Koopmans, and others into "a jeweled set of movements," a "celestial clockwork," as Bell has vividly depicted it, "a work of art so compelling that one thinks of the celebrated pictures of Appelles, who painted a cluster of grapes so realistic that the birds would come and pick at them."[78] It means, in the end, an adherence to a basic principle of neo-classic economics that, beneath the surface, there is an underlying structure of reality. For the Chicago School of Economics the question of whether the general equilibrium, defined in theory as a fiction or a normative standard, is the description of how economic exchange (if unhampered) takes place in accordance with the "laws" of economics, received an affirmative response.[79] Theory, in the Chicago view, does model reality. The conclusion of this chain of reasoning appears clearly stated in the belief that "there are no stable empirical relationships among prices, quantities and disturbances other than those with the aforementioned analogues in the exact equilibrium model," which also means that the paradigm or mode of observing reality set by the analog model is "the only valid proposition of economic theory."[80]

The consequences of this tightness between the model and reality are multiple. They particularly reflect the transmission of the philosophical assumptions behind Pareto's optimality to the construction of the conceptual structure around which theory is built, which leads to the view of the market we have discussed. Tightness implies, at the same time, however, a particular approach to empirical research. Reder presents this relationship in the following way:

As I perceive them, Chicago economists tend strongly to appraise their own research and that of others by a standard which requires (inter alia) that the findings of empirical research be consistent with the implications of standard price theory (as described above). Any apparent inconsistency of empirical findings with implications of the theory, or report of behavior not implied by the theory, is interpreted as anomalous and requiring one of the following actions: (i) re-examinations of the data to reverse anomalous findings; (ii) redefinition and/or augmentation of the variables in the model; (iii) alteration of the theory to accommodate behavior inconsistent with the postulates of rationality (constrained optimization) by one or more decision makers (resource owners); (iv) placing the finding on the research agenda as a researchable anomaly.

The "Chicago" tendency is to shun the modification of theoretical principles. The subject matter of the tight prior is the adequacy of this approach to theory as an explanation of whatever behavior is considered as economic ... It is not appropriate to characterize this prior as "dogmatic," it suffices to say that [Tight Prior Equilibrium] adherents – with variation among individuals – focus attention upon (i) and (ii) and, failing a quick resolution of the anomaly, move to (iv) but pay little attention to (iii).[81]

If this is what "to take seriously the use of economic theory" means, let us move now to the rest of Friedman's statement. He states that theory has to be considered as "a tool for analyzing a startlingly wide range of concrete problems, rather than as an abstract mathematical structure of great beauty but little power"; as an approach "that insists on the empirical testing of theoretical generalizations and *rejects alike facts without theory and theory without facts.*"[82] Leaving aside, for the moment, the question of the extension of the model to the explanation of all sorts of human behavior, we want to concentrate instead on the last part of Friedman's idea, the instrumentalist approach to economic theory. It is here that we find the logical steps leading to policy predictions.

Instrumentalism

The idea that theory has to be taken not as an abstract structure, but as a powerful instrument for the analysis of concrete problems, whose validation process arises from its empirical testing, represents the main subject of Milton Friedman's methodological propositions contained, particularly, in his *Essays on Positive Economics*.[83] With it Friedman departed radically from Frank H. Knight's tradition of mistrust and indifference towards empirical economics, although, as we shall see, he gave a methodological base to another of Knight's most fundamental tenets, the necessary relationship between normative principles and economic theory.

Friedman has considered as "entirely correct" the description of his methodology as "an instrumental argument for instrumentalism."[84] Instrumentalism is defined here as the belief that "the purpose of economic theory is prediction for purposes of testing and evaluating alternative policies."[85] "It is predictive success and not descriptive accuracy which constitutes a theory, except by the conformity of its prediction to observations."[86]

Friedman's most relevant argument runs as follows:

A hypothesis is important if it "explains" much by little, that is, if it abstracts the common and crucial elements from the mass of complex and detailed circumstances surrounding the phenomena to be explained and permits valid predictions on the basis of them alone. To be important, therefore, a hypothesis must be descriptively false in its assumptions; it takes account of none of the many other attendant circumstances, since its very success shows them to be irrelevant for the phenomena to be explained.

To put this point less paradoxically, the relevant question to ask about the "assumptions" of a theory is not whether they are descriptively "realistic," for they never are, but whether they are sufficiently good approximations for the purpose at hand. And this question can be answered only by seeing whether the theory works, which means whether it yields sufficiently accurate predictions. The two supposedly independent tests thus reduce to one test.

As Frazer and Boland argue, Friedman was rejecting logical positivism, "the conventional view in the economics of the time . . . that conclusions could be derived from assumptions and that the truth or falsity of derived statements would follow from the truth or falsity of assumptions."[87] Yet, in opposing this notion, Friedman has also compacted the steps leading from the ultimate assumptions to the policy prescriptions and their testing at the empirical level. Moreover, he has led economic theory to a testing process which needs to "take on a more general form of public debate and possible acceptance (or rejection) in the national policy sphere."[88]

That the hallmark of science is prediction is derived from a well-known tradition in the philosophy of science, developed especially in the work of Karl Popper; what Friedman does, however, is to unite the first step, which ties the ultimate assumptions with the hypothesis and the construction of a model, to the second, which develops predictions and tests them in the policy-making sphere. In Popper's terms, he develops predictions from "unconditional hypotheses" – "those which can be described as well isolated, stationary, and recurrent" – which become, in this case, a logical operation derived from the basic tight relationship established between the model of general equilibrium and the analog model we have already described, and then tests them in an empirical setting. This process has, in Friedman's view, a scientific status similar to that of the physical sciences. As Rose Friedman has said:

His position is that the social sciences do not differ . . . from the physical sciences and that those who contend otherwise largely do so because they misconstrue the nature of the physical sciences. No science can generate meaningful hypotheses that are "true" in any other sense than they are provisionally accepted because no hypothesis generating more accurate (or less costly) predictions has been discovered.[89]

As viewed by Friedman, then, the logic of scientific discovery can be summarized as follows: a set of premises – necessarily false because they cannot but simplify and distort reality – give origin to and find themselves closely articulated with a set of hypotheses, a model, which is "unconditional" in the sense that it constructs an isolated, stationary, and recurrent universe, endowed with the same scientific validity as that of the physical sciences.

This analog model gives rise to predictions which can only be verified in an empirical context, which implies for economics their introduction into the sphere of public debate and public policy.

A new classic paradigm

In his work on ideology, Geertz argues that the difference between science and ideology has to be sought "in the sorts of symbolic strategy for encompassing situations that they represent." Science, he says,

names the structure of situations in such a way that the attitude contained towards them is out of disinterestedness. Its style is restrained, spare, resolutely analytic: by shunning the semantic devices that most effectively formulate moral sentiment, it seeks to maximize intellectual clarity. But ideology names the structure of situations in such a way that the attitude contained towards them is one of commitment. Its style is ornate, vivid, deliberately suggestive. By objectifying moral sentiment through the same devices that science shuns, it seeks to motivate action.[90]

The criteria proposed by Geertz easily lead us to classify much of the most characteristic output of the Chicago School as ideological. The School's insistence on the key role of the market and its categorical rejection of state intervention testifies to an "ornate, vivid and deliberately suggestive" style. The aim of Milton Friedman's theoretical treatise in defense of the bond between market freedom and individual liberty is to motivate action. These are not, however, the only criteria that allow us to focus on the ideological aspects of the Chicago School. Another characteristic derived from the

School's instrumental methodology, already mentioned above, is its attempt to adjust the real world to its working hypothesis and models. The notion can be summarized in the following way: the basic need to protect the initial relationship between the analog model and its ultimate premises, invested with explicit ideological elements, forces the concurrence with the verification process of a whole set of normative principles, whose social existence is necessary for the process of scientific verification and, thus, for the validity of the model itself. Leonard Rapping, in reference to Friedman's recognition of the inevitable flaws in the initial hypothesis, adds:

it is in the nature of human beings, and the Chicago students prove this point, to forget after a time that the assumptions may be false. You start thinking that it describes reality. Repetition not only makes perfect, it makes believers. Many Chicago people would agree that the world is, in fact, competitive. They tend to believe their own pragmatic myth.[91]

Lastly, there is a third perspective on the ideological character of some of the Chicago School's output. This refers to the tendency to apply economics "to every nook and cranny of life." Karl Brunner has explained this tendency with his usual conciseness and precision: "our fundamental point," he declared, "is that price theory is the crucial paradigm – as a matter of fact, the only paradigm – that economists have. You can use this paradigm to explain the whole range of social phenomena."[92] Economics *is*, in fact, the price theory and also constitutes the only scientific paradigm for the analysis of social phenomena. Brunner and other members of the Chicago School, such as Friedman or Allan Meltzer, tend to rule out the value of sociology, history, or political science as instruments able to improve our understanding of any social phenomenon. Only economics and, specifically, economics based on the price theory, are of analytical value in social matters.

In explaining his differences with Keynesian economists like Tobin and Modigliani, Brunner declared that:

the disputes about the role of government and the range of political institutions as social coordinating devices involve more than ideology . . . Two very substantive views of the world determine the nature of the conflict. Keynesians are prone to approach non-market situations and social institutions in terms of an essentially sociological perception . . . We reject an escape into sociology which offers no relevant analytical framework. We maintain that socio-political institutions are the proper subject of economic analysis. This entails an entirely different view of political institutions and their operation. The sociological view typically supports the goodwill theory of government and yields conclusions favoring a large and unlimited government. An application of economic analysis, in contrast, alerts us to the fact that politicians and bureaucrats are entrepreneurs in the political market. They pursue their own interest and try to find optimal strategies attending to their interests. And what is optimal for them is hardly ever optimal for the "public interest."[93]

It is not necessary to delve further into the Chicago School's attitude towards politicians and the functions they perform in western democracies, implied in this paragraph. It is no surprise that an appreciation of the democratic process does not figure among the priorities of the School's disciples. Their bias against politics and the negation of its relative autonomy – as a separate, specific sphere of problems and field of analysis – implies an economic reductionism, which is probably the most potent ideological element affecting the Chicago School.

To develop its predictive function, science requires, therefore, a normative order which the scientist himself must promote. He has to adopt, along with the standards of rigor and technicality associated with his discipline, the role of a propagandist for the values which science requires to be in existence. A global and encompassing vision of man in society becomes, in the last analysis, the condition for the functioning of the economic system. With his methodological constructions, Friedman made operational one of Frank Knight's most essential tenets: "reality is not what is logical but what it suits our purposes to treat as real."[94] From it stems a line of reasoning in which the notions of the utility maximizing individual, the market, society, and politics become articulated by a paradigm which reunites indissolubly positive and normative considerations.

This doctrinal constitution of Chicago doctrine explains therefore not only its internal strength as a powerful ideology, but also the attitudinal framework which surrounds the professional practice of Chicago economists and has been singled out as one of the most distinguishing features of the School.

The economist as a priest and a preacher

The attitudes about economics as a science and the role of the economist as educator and propagandist are an intrinsic part of the characterization of the Chicago School. As we suggested before, the conception of economics as an apologia for the market system is not an exclusive feature of Chicago economists, but acquires, in their case, a polar nature expressed mainly and most evidently by the fact that it has been publicly recognized and explicitly adopted by the School's principal figures. As Samuels has extensively argued, the business of economics is, in the Chicago view, to explain the system in a favorable light. Frank Knight put it very explicitly:

Assuming that men have a right to want and strive to get whatever they do want, and to have the tasted and "higher" values they do have, as long as their conduct does not infringe the equal rights of others, the business of the economics of principle, of utility, and through buying [and] selling enables everyone to do whatever he tries to do (whether rational or not, as judged by anyone else) many times more effectively than would be possible if each used his own means in a self-sufficient economic life.[95]

The socialization function includes, however, the selection of what has to be considered and what has to be avoided and omitted, because the main purpose is the internalization of the norms of the system:

Likemindedness in belief and ideas regarding itself is the really important thing in society, and to produce and maintain it is the really important function of education in the social field. That the unanimity has to do with symbols, and that a part of the task is to keep people from asking what these symbolize in a concrete sense, is mere corollary; for nothing is more obvious than that any such questioning would turn the likemindedness into universal enmity and conflict. The teaching of social science on any considerable scale must be of this sort and inevitably will be, and there is simply no problem.[96]

The modern student of history and social process soon learns that societies have lived in a state of relative peace and order by not raising problems they cannot solve and discussions of which would only stir up antagonism and probably lead to conflict if not to a social nervous breakdown.[97]

This has a practical consequence for the teaching of economics: "Certainly the large courses should be prevented from raising any question about objectivity, but should assume the objectivity of the slogans they inculcate as a sacred feature of the system."[98] "For a vitally important fact which is almost systematically ignored by the critics of economic theory . . . is that the subject as expounded in modern times has been developed with definite reference to the practical needs of a free society."[99]

The sacred principles of economics are basic to the maintenance of "the free society" and this gives them a religious nature.

The principles by which a society or group lives in tolerable harmony are essentially religious [and their] essential nature is that not merely is it immoral to oppose them, but to ask what it is, is morally identical with denial and attack.

"There must be ultimates" and they must be religious, in economics as anywhere else, if one has anything to say touching conduct or social policy in a practical way. Man is a believing animal and to the few, if any, it is given to criticize the foundations of belief and to believe "intelligently."

To inquire into the ultimates behind accepted group values is obscene and sacrilegious; objective inquiry is an attempt to uncover the nakedness of man, his soul as well as his body, his needs, his culture, and his very goods.[100]

It was obviously on the basis of this vision of the essentials of economics that the economist as practitioner was raised to the stature of a high priest, having access not only, as Myrdal has put it, "to a sphere of values which are both objective and observable,"[101] but also to the sacred principles regulating social harmony. And this belief had to be enforced with particular strength when the introduction of error and confusion was the sign of the times. Simons wrote in his *Program for Laissez Faire*: "The precious measure of political and economic freedom which has been won through the centuries may soon be lost irreparably, and it falls properly to economists, as custodians of the great liberal tradition out of which their discipline arose, to point the escape from the chaos of political and economic thought which warns of what impends."[102] The community of economists risen to a Platonic category as "the scientific community" was also seen in Knight's writings as the appropriate model for the "free society."

The Chicago School, then, developed a vision of itself as the community of true economists, "having the gift of faith, steadfast witnesses to the social glory and redemptive power of the market system."[103] More than economists in the restricted sense, they became social or moral philosophers; they tended to form – to use a Weberian concept – "a rational sect."

CHAPTER 4

The actors of ideological transfer

American foreign assistance: its context and motivations

The transfer of the complex ideological tradition we have just described was, as we argued in the first chapter, a deliberate and planned event built around three key actors who participated both in the conception and the concretion of the initiative. They were the government of the United States and its foreign aid programs; the Department of Economics of the University of Chicago and the group forming it who best represented the "Chicago tradition," and the Universidad Católica de Chile, together with the conservative group of businessmen who sought to revive free market ideas in Chile during the mid-1950s.

In this chapter we will examine the main interests and motivations behind the initiative. What gave to the United States government foreign assistance programs the idea of generating in Chile a group of economists imbued by the Chicago tradition? The answer to this question requires a brief discussion on the history of American foreign aid. The subject is of interest to us here from a very specific angle: that of the conscious efforts of the United States to export its "modernity," through the transfer of knowledge and technology that seemingly would help the developing countries to improve their quality of life, social organization, and economic growth potential. One of the most important initiatives within this effort was the promotion of "university agreements" between US universities and universities in the developing world.

A historical overview

It would appear to be possible to distinguish two periods in the development of the cooperation programs of the US government. The first was initiated with President Franklin Roosevelt at the outbreak of the Second World War. The second one gained strength at the end of that war during the Truman administration. While the former was inspired basically by the need to cooperate with Latin America, required by the US military effort in its preparation for the war, the latter was located within the context of the cold war and the politics of opposition to communism in the region and, in general, in the developing world. The most important difference between the two periods is the outcome of the dissimilar ideological climates that reigned within them and was expressed particularly in the attitudes and ideas of the one person who was called upon to perform a central role in the development of these projects: *the technical assistance expert*. We shall now look at these issues in greater detail.

The history of American technical assistance begins in 1939, when the United States government, compelled by the outbreak of the Second World War, initiated cooperation programs with Latin America. This concept had been contemplated during the previous decade, but never put into practice. Since Roosevelt's proclamation of the Good Neighbor Policy in his 1933 inaugural speech, discussion with regard to technical cooperation had intensified. The probability of an American involvement in the war had led to a growing awareness of hemispheric interdependence and, as Glick has written, "overnight the oft-discussed importance of strengthening the friendly relations between the United States and Latin America seemed to become a matter of immediate urgency."[1] In fact, the Good Neighbor Policy, from the time of its announcement, paved the way for an improvement in relations. Roosevelt's new policy was an attitude more than a practice, however, and some time passed before concrete proposals for action were produced. It led first – although indirectly – to the establishment of the Export–Import Bank in the mid-1930s, which represented the United States' first small steps toward an aid program. The outbreak of the Second World War, marking a dramatic turning point in the evolution of international relations, uncovered very concrete needs which indicated the convenience of responding favorably to the increasing requests for technical and economic assistance coming from Latin America. The war proved that magnanimity and self-interest can be combined, and influence through aid was a good alternative to the historic extremes of sheer domination and utter neglect. It was through Roosevelt's initiative that, in 1939, "the first organized and systematic intergovernmental technical cooperation program" with Latin America came into being. The program was set up as two parallel operations: the work of the Interdepartmental Committee on Scientific and Cultural Cooperation and the activities of the Institute of Inter-American Affairs (IIAA).

The first of these organizations was the result of a decision adopted by Congress, authorizing the president to deploy "for temporary service and not exceeding one year at a time, any person in the employ of the United States to give advice and assistance on request to the government of any American nation." The United States government could respond to the requests by Latin

American governments for short term technicians in different areas. That same year, 1939, Congress expanded its authorization, allowing the president "to use the services of any government department to carry into effect the reciprocal undertaking and cooperative purposes enunciated in the treaties, resolutions, declarations, and recommendations" signed by the American republics in different hemispheric conferences during the previous decades. Under these statutes, the government could launch a broad program, sending American technicians and administrators "to give technical advice and assistance to the Latin American governments in a broad range of activities." That program was organized by the Interdepartmental Committee on Scientific and Cultural Cooperation. From that point on, as Glick writes, "the Latin American governments asked for and received assistance in a broad spectrum of cultural, technological, and scientific fields, ranging from archival science to zoology. Most of the projects were in agriculture, geological investigation, civil aviation, child welfare, and the improvement of statistical services."[2] In 1942 Roosevelt opened a new line in cooperation programs with the organization of the Institute of Inter-American Affairs, whose first coordinator, named by the president, was Nelson Rockefeller. The key objective behind this initiative was that of strengthening US military capability in the face of the inevitability of its involvement in the world conflict. The defense of the hemisphere required the emplacement of troops in unhealthy places and the production and shipping of raw materials, which Latin American governments were in no condition to carry out.[3] The IIAA then was established "as a United States corporation attached to the Department of State," authorized at first to conduct cooperative programs with the Latin American governments in the fields of public health, agricultural development and, later, in elementary and vocational education. From 1942 on, it began to send its representatives to most of the countries in the area.

World War II shifted attention away from the less developed countries to the allies, who were provided with civilian goods and military supplies through lendlease programs.[4] With the war ended, foreign aid was concentrated on European reconstruction. In 1948 Congress approved the first general foreign assistance law, "The European Recovery Program," better known as the Marshall Plan. Based on this, one year later President Truman would launch his initiative called Point Four: *"a bold new program for making the benefits of our scientific advances and industrial progress available for the improvement and growth of underdeveloped areas."*[5] As a result, the transfer of modernity became a governmental policy. In 1950 Congress would proclaim "The Act for International Development":

It is declared to be the policy of the United States to aid the efforts of economically underdeveloped areas to develop their resources and improve their working and living conditions by encouraging the exchange of technical knowledge and skills and the flow of investment capital.[6]

Thus, an official sanction for a wave of inter-American cooperation with Latin America was extended. US technicians were sent to the countries of the south and professionals and students from Latin America would travel to training centers and higher education institutions in the United States. Missions, advisory teams, instructors, and professors would be sent to the region to transfer ideas and knowledge under the optimistic hypothesis that with the production of more food, "more clothing, more material for housing, and more mechanical power, the United States would contribute to 'freedom and democracy,' 'prosperity,' 'dignity,' 'international understanding and goodwill,' 'world peace,' and other vaguely defined good things."[7]

The motivations that inspired these decisions have received extensive treatment in the literature about the subject. We shall limit ourselves here to outlining their most basic components.

The motivations of foreign aid

The conceptions orienting aid policies and the notions of modernity that must be transmitted to its recipients in Latin America were certainly not the outcome of bureaucratic maturation existing in the government offices of Washington. They originated from, in the last instance, beliefs and ideas for progress refined in American political culture, derived essentially from a vision of its own national history. As we shall see, they were also developed on the basis of its own aid and cooperation experiences that different kinds of American "experts" had developed and would continue to develop based upon direct contact with other societies. They were conditioned, ultimately, by the ideological climate determined by the general conditions of the international system. We shall have a brief look at these three dimensions.

Tocqueville had already observed that "the spirit of Americans is averse to general ideas; it does not seek theoretical discoveries. Neither politics nor manufactures direct them to such speculations."[8] This structure of American mentality – essentially pragmatic and conservative – would mark strongly the focus of economic and political development experiences. It would be expressed more concretely in a view of economic and political development that, as R. Packenham has argued, rested upon what a school of historians from that country has called "the exceptionality of historical development of the United States." This historical process, perceived as singular and relatively smooth, established the framework that was possible and desirable for the development of other countries. It produced, according to this author, the following essential beliefs:

1. Change and development are easy.
2. All good things go together.
3. Radicalism and revolutions are bad.
4. Distributing power is more important than accumulating power.[9] *Packenham*

Belief in the smoothness and inevitability of change and development, mostly on the basis of the American demonstration effect; confidence in the direct relationship between capitalist development and political democracy; rejection of radicalism and revolution; and mistrust of the state as a political and economic organizer of society, were certainly central elements in the formation of the American vision of developing countries. They also gave shape to, implicitly or explicitly, some of the objectives that American foreign aid administrators hoped to achieve in the countries of the Latin American region. Economic assistance and technical cooperation aspired to develop confidence in the ways of capitalist organization of the economy as a necessary corollary of a democratic political organization and to reduce, at the same time, the tendencies favoring radical political change in the society. The one to define these ideas in practice through his role as "the implementor" of cooperation programs was the technical adviser. The observation of this role throws some light on the various important aspects of the American ideology of cooperation. This role has been defined historically by two antecessors of American technical and ideological expansion in the world: the missionaries of American religious groups, located in different regions of the globe since the end of the nineteenth century, and the agents of American enterprises that appeared on a massive basis in the region at that same time. They had been inspired by and transmitted simultaneously "the venerable ideal of an American mission throughout the globe."[10] This ideal, traced by American historians to the American Revolution and to the geographical and economic expansion of the nineteenth century, had, as one author has written, "an aggressive adolescence at the turn of the century," "attained a somewhat subdued maturity since 1900," and continues to operate, giving strength "to the feeling that America can effect an uplifting of the quality of life in foreign nations."[11] The new role created by the foreign aid programs had, as Glick noted, "no matter how fine the motives with which it was offered . . . the inescapable danger of arrogance latent in the very premises of the program."[12] But it was based on the hypothesis that "the international transfer of knowledge – a highly mobile resource – from rich countries to the poorer ones tends to diminish the differences in the material conditions of life among peoples of different countries."[13] It assumed, nevertheless, that "The American way of life – however variously that may be defined – could be exported to the advantage of other nations." Its basis of ideological support was a perception of the United States as a "unique combination of economic power, intellectual and practical genius, and moral rigor."[14]

The logic behind the technical assistance role determined, aside from this ideological characteristic, another that was derived from the technocratic nature of its function. In virtue of this, development always appeared as a parceled phenomenon, divided into functional compartments: health, agriculture, education, etc. By definition, the outside adviser was unable to observe the phenomenon of development or modernization as a multifaceted process in which cultural, economic, and political elements were linked. Furthermore, this last factor was precluded, not only because of its "delicate" and "conflictive" nature, but also because it was often observed as a fact that complicated and impeded the success of technical programs.[15]

The views that the administrators of cooperation for development had of both Latin America and their own role were often, however, highly conditioned by more global ideological situations that characterized the US perception of the international system and the world political situation. The first pioneering and organizational period of foreign aid allowed certain creative and more liberal orientations towards social change which would later fade, under the strength of a more defensive approach introduced by the perceived threat of communism. That first stage in the training of the foreign technician and of the technical assistance programs was characterized by a certain naive enthusiasm: the sensation that all was possible and that it was enough to merely introduce rational, modern patterns of conduct in certain elites in order to attain economic development objectives. The fight against communism would also be added to this style afterwards, not only as an addendum, but also as a central axis. The objective of contention granted not only an organizer and rationalizer principle, but also served as a mechanism to explain the obstacles that were erected in relation to the modernizing task: communist agitation, Marxist ideas and socialist tendencies were more than a threat for American interests, they were one of the principal internal factors explaining the difficulties in making progress. In parallel, the social development and economic growth of these countries became an urgent task. They were, definitely, the best defense in the face of the communist offensive.

Joan Nelson has put this point with great clarity. She noted:

the concern for the peace and pattern of internal economic and political evolution in the developing countries is fed, to various degrees at different times . . . by humanitarian desire to ease and ultimately conquer poverty; by Cold War-stimulated fear of successive Communist takeovers in the less developed world; and by the recognition that even in the absence of the Communist threat, the tensions caused by rising expectations, populations growth, and economic and social change already underway would pose a threat to internal progress and international stability throughout the underdeveloped world, hence to the emergence of an international community in which the States can live in peace and prosperity.[16]

R. Packenham has recognized two general lines of thought regarding the economic and political objectives of American aid during the period prior to the Alliance for Progress. The first, known as the "economic approach," essentially sought to promote economic development. "Aid would contribute to economic development; and economic development would contribute to a host of good things – political stability, non-communism, democracy, pro-American attitudes and foreign policies, international understanding, world community, peace." The second, the "cold war approach," stressed political stability, the strengthening of non-communist forces, and "other narrowly defined security purposes." "The theory was that aid could promote non-communism, pro-Americanism, and stability, which were viewed as conducive to American security in the context of the cold war."[17]

As we shall see further on, these two lines of thought are interlaced in the motivations that led to the university agreements, which are the theme of this work.

Elites and education: university agreements

The transfer of knowledge and the organization of institutions of higher education had a long history in the private initiatives for development aid by the United States and would also have a predominant place in government technical cooperation programs. American high schools and universities had developed initiatives abroad since the end of the last century. American religious groups had founded high schools, reproducing to the letter the organizational structures of their original institutions.[18]

In the ideological framework of American foreign aid programs, the role of the local elites in the development of their own countries was defined from the beginning as a decisive subject. Cooperation in the processes of modernization and formation of "responsible" elites, with "technical capability," held high priority; they were located in the essence of the cooperation programs.[19]

A fundamental area of these efforts was found in the governmental teams. The idea was to train, following a rigidly functionalist approach, specialists in agriculture, health, education, and other areas, on the basis of personalized contact between American technicians and Latin American functionaries. As Glick says: "the essential nature of these activities may be summed up in the statement that they were joint operations . . . conducted on the theory of 'let's do the job together.'"[20] This joint operation was called a *servicio*. Separate *servicios* were organized for the separate fields of agriculture, health, and education. They encouraged "intimate, daily cooperation between United States technicians and host technicians." This was based on the belief "that a serious shortage of competent technicians and administrators in Latin American countries made it imperative that the technicians and administrators sent to Latin America by IIAA be able to go well beyond the giving of advice and the conduct of demonstration projects."[21] The technicians must educate and train people to be able to assume the tasks of modernization.

It was undoubtedly this perception of the insufficient training of Latin American teams that, along with the tradition of American university exportation, produced an awareness of the need for an action policy in the area of the universities. In 1953 the International Cooperation Administration initiated a program promoting these agreements. In October of that year, Director Harold Stassen called upon American universities to cooperate in the Foreign Assistance Program. In two years, seventy-eight contracts were accorded with American universities for programs all over the world.[22]

The importance granted to these agreements by the formulators of American foreign cooperation policy cannot be overemphasized. In 1955 US Senator William Benton wrote, after his visit to Chile, that he knew "*of few ways to contribute to the well-being of mankind that can match the needed development of Latin America's universities . . . no single area of action open to the United States . . . is more promising per dollar than the effort to lift the level of its higher education.*"[23] The importance of these agreements was not limited only to the terrain of intellectual development. They were seen, moreover, as a factor that could become determinant in the economic and political orientations of those countries.[24]

In this context, the role that American universities performed was fundamental. They had to become interested in these agreements and actively participate, making their best academics available to the cooperation programs. In 1955 the National Public Association Special Policy Committee on Technical Cooperation recommended "*university cooperation as having much greater promise than direct cooperation with the host government.*"[25] The report, coordinated by T. W. Schultz, chairman of the Economics Department of the University of Chicago, outlined the advantages and requisites of this form of cooperation. It affirmed that "curricula and types of training now available in most Latin American universities are not adequate to transmit the knowledge and teach the specialists."[26] The American contribution could thus be tremendously effective: in many cases, it could practically start from zero. On the other hand, those who go to teach would have a series of advantages: "they will learn at first hand much about the host country in which they work – about the characteristics and customs of the people, the organization and administration of the government, and the institutions with which they are cooperating."[27] And, it added, "the US universities should not yield to the temptation to keep all their best talent on the home campus and send their mediocre faculty members abroad."[28] In sum, the academic, along with the technical adviser, must take his role as a missionary of American modernity seriously.

Within the promotion of the university agreements, economics or the study of economics did not occupy a predominant role at the beginning. As we shall see, the incorporation of this discipline was requested by the American technicians who had to implement assistance programs in countries where there were either no economists or the existing ones did not fill the criteria for quality desired by the US functionaries. From the mid-1950s, however, the evaluations of the technical cooperation programs carried out by both ICA technicians and evaluation teams visiting the region – as was the case of NPA – agreed that, besides technical advice in specific areas, attention needed to be directed toward the more global issue of economic development. The operators of technical assistance programs discovered that it was necessary not only to produce economists in the Latin American countries, but also to study the problems of economic growth, about which there was still very little knowledge in the United States.

Two ideological factors performed a very important role in the shaping of this perspective: the cold war, on the one hand, and faith in market mechanisms in the organization of the economy on the other. The following quote by Theodore Schultz summarizes clearly a view in which these ideological elements are intermingled. As Schultz declared at a conference held immediately after his Latin American tour where he headed an evaluation mission for NPA:

The Soviet Union is making a series of new moves to enlarge its role and strengthen its position in poor countries. It is bringing new and important economic measures into play. We, however, have been slow to perceive that these moves are under way. Our eyes are so fixed on the atomic queens in this chess game of power, that we have all but lost sight of the bishops and knights. It is these lesser pieces that are being maneuvered into position against us, while all powerful queens stand poised. *The Soviet Union with its bold new moves has already gained much freedom of action, while we stand by, burdened with inflexibility. The United States must take stock of its economic programs abroad . . . we want [the poor countries] to work out their economic salvation by relating themselves to us and by using our way of achieving their economic development.*[29]

This last passage makes explicit the fundamental pillar upon which the visit of American technical assistance programs would be based with regards to the economic development of Latin America. The economic growth of the region was possible to the extent that their economies were associated with the American one and they followed the economic organization guidelines that had allowed the development of the United States. The coincidence of economic interests between the United States and Latin America was seen as being evident. The perception of the communist threat added the element of urgency for action. What was needed was to identify, in the first place, those elements that had been determinant in American development and establish the way to transfer them to the Latin American region; and to confront, in the second place, those characteristics of the Latin American economies that impeded growth. In principle, these were none other than the ones which were clearly different or contrary to the characteristics of the organization of American economics, the ones that, for whatever reason, departed from the model which had already proved successful in shaping the United States.

We will move on now to the examination of the development of these perspectives in Chile. The observations with regard to its economy and the importance that university agreements could have for those perspectives were disclosed with clarity in the reports sent to the American Congress by the program for Chile of the International Cooperation Administration.

Chile from embassy windows

The different reports submitted to Congress by the Mutual Security Program, Regional and Country Program Detail for Latin America during the years 1955 and 1956–61 detail the objectives of that program in Chile and include an assessment of the basic economic problems of the country, along with the measures proposed to confront them. They reflect the growing interest in the teaching of a "free market" economics.

The 1955 report includes a first mention of the establishment "probably through a US university contract with the University of Chile, of a course in public administration and management."[30] The 1956 report contains a description of the current situation in the following terms:

Chile is a democratic country with a long record of friendly cooperation with the US. Inflation is Chile's major economic problem. Although not chronic, inflation has been accelerating rapidly during the past few years and in 1954 the cost of living increased 70 percent over 1953. Despite favorable copper prices, Chile is confronted with a substantial balance of payments problem.[31]

And in another section, the 1956 report informs:

Chile has recently requested a university to university contract in the field of general resources management. Chile desires to establish an Institute or permanent group of persons who will concern themselves with an objective analysis of the conditions that have brought about the present economic situation and who will propose suitable measures to surmount the problems involved. This constructive Chilean approach to its problems is encouraging. It is planned to implement the requested university contract in the F.Y. 1956 Program.[32]

The 1957 MSP report to Congress includes a "General Narrative Statement" outlining the objectives of the Mutual Security Program for Chile:

1. Assist Chile in maintaining the economic, social, and political stability necessary for sound economic and social development.
2. To encourage and assist Chile *in resisting Marxist influences in economic and political institutions* and countering communist subversion and propaganda.
3. To encourage and assist Chile in making her maximum contribution to inter-American security and solidarity.
4. To assure continued production and availability of copper and other strategic materials.
5. To promote an appreciation among Chileans of the real benefits and advantages of achieving economic progress through methods of economic and political freedom rather than through totalitarian techniques.
6. To encourage Chileans to promote an atmosphere favorable to foreign investment.[33]

A different section headed "confidential" states that:

Chile's economic plight is characterized by continuing uncontrolled inflation, and a declining foreign exchange situation, the government has not dealt effectively with problems of national housekeeping, principally because political instability has inhibited firm corrective action in matters of fiscal and economic policy. Political factionalization, with continuously shifting alliances among twenty political parties is at the root of the political immobility. Government intervention in the matter of wages and prices, the creation of increasing obstacles to foreign and domestic investment and trade, and the adoption of increasingly expansive welfare programs have all tended to impede sound national development and have added to the complexity of Chile's problems.[34]

The 1959 Mutual Security Program objectives point in a more direct manner to the question of the ideological conditions for development. In fact, after a first general consideration on the advantages of cooperation, the report lists:

(a) To aid Chile in conquering her longstanding inflation.
(b) *To give increasing support from every possible side to the Chilean movement toward free enterprise capitalism.*
(c) *To develop and improve Chilean educational institutions so that they can provide effective technological, economic, and management training to Chileans.*[35]

These official assessments and objectives constituted the policy framework wherein the university-to-university contracts were to be established. The allusions to the internal economic situation of the country and the strong emphasis on the need to give "increasing support" from every possible side to "the Chilean movement toward free trade" found in the 1959 report are clarified when observing other official or unofficial statements on the characteristics of the Chilean economists and the universities of the period.

In October 1955, during a visit to Chile by the Subcommittee on

International Operations of the House of Representatives concerned with US technical assistance and related activities in Latin America, a United States Information Service report manifested the ideological purpose of university agreements:

Our efforts are specifically directed toward the discouraging of the Communist and demagogic practices of blaming the United States government and United States companies for Chile's ills; to explaining the benefits of the free enterprise system to any nation and to Chile by implication; and particularly to point out the beneficial role that foreign capital has played in the development of other nations including the United States itself.

. . . Recently, the United States signed a Fulbright agreement with Chile which is the first of this kind in this hemisphere. When this program gets under way, *it will assist particularly in our economic objectives through closer relations with the various universities* here and will help us get into the important student organizations which have in the past been traditionally infiltrated with communist and pro-communist thinking.[36]

In a subsequent part of the report, an appendix prepared by the embassy summed up the political conditions of the country by saying:

From 1938 until 1952, Chile's government was controlled by the left center Radical party. During that period, it was "fashionable" to be leftist, with the result that a heritage of Marxist–Socialist thinking has accumulated over recent years. *In general, this tends to be more evident in the economic than in the political sphere.*[37]

A scenario of this nature required particular attention. The university agreements permitted this situation to be confronted and they fully responded to the interests of the United States as a nation. The 1961 Congressional Presentation of the ICA List of Active Projects contained a general outline of the ICA contract with the University of Chicago and a list of the "specific goals and end-products" of the project. The document concludes with the indication that "*this project will contribute directly or indirectly to the achievement of all Mutual Security Program objectives.*"[38]

What these quotes show clearly, therefore, is that what was decisive in the promotion and making of the university contracts in Chile was the US government's official perception that: first, Chilean economists and universities were "leftist," characterized by socialist or statist tendencies; second, the most important factor impeding Chilean development was inflation and this factor was not confronted, precisely because these statist or socialist tendencies were predominant; and third, with promotion of free trade and free market as being an inseparable part of US interests, US aid should confront these local tendencies by helping in the training of economists imbued with the values of American economics.

The Chicago School and Latin America

Let us now observe the motivations behind the decision taken by the University of Chicago or, more precisely, by the specific group of economists included in the Chicago tradition to participate in the agreement with the Universidad Católica de Chile. A first point to be addressed refers to the attitudes and positions of these economists with respect to the discussion on Latin American economic development. The emergence of the economic development theories originating in the region during the mid-1950s became, in the Chicago perspective, an ideological challenge that had to be confronted.[39] This was the main motivating force behind the Chicago interest in Latin America, a thrust that generated not only the impetus for action, but also the creation of theoretical perspectives – such as the ideas of Theodore Schultz regarding human capital – as well as the need for a specific place for empirical experimentation. The university agreements and technical cooperation policies of the American government provided precisely the possibility to experiment with economic growth theories that did not stray away from the dictates of economic science, but that found in that science their support base.

Development economics and the Chicago School

Since the 1950s, the Department of Economics of the University of Chicago had begun to reflect – as we have argued previously – a hegemony of the views held by George Stigler and Milton Friedman. The 1950s and 1960s were also the decades of development theories. The process of decolonization, the building of new traditions, the impact of the great depression on the economies of developing societies, the expansion of the new Keynesian orthodoxy and the cold war were all factors behind the upsurge of new theories and proposals for economic growth.

These ideas, which began to take the shape of proposals at the beginning of the 1950s, were solidified into their most definite and articulated version in the publications of the *Economic Commission for Latin America of the United Nations* and from the work of Raul Prebisch, its first executive secretary. Some of the initial points discussed in ECLA documents with respect to Latin American development were the following:

1. A criticism of the traditional theories of international trade, more specifically of the nature of the relationship between the center and the periphery.
2. The reasons favoring industrialization and the analysis of its principal problems in the region.
3. Planning as an imperative for development.

4. The appropriate forms that external financing should adopt in order to promote development.

5. Regional integration as another imperative for development.

6. The "structural" nature of inflation in Latin America and a critique of conventional stabilization policies.

7. The" social dimension" of economic development. The analysis of the social factors behind it and the effects on the structure of employment in different social sectors.

8. Situations and positions of Latin America *vis-à-vis* international trade policies and the exchange between "developing economies" and industrialized nations.

9. A global, integrated vision of development problems in the region and of the "structural changes" needed to promote a more dynamic development and a more equitable distribution of resources.[40]

This schematic summary of ECLA's ideas, postulated both before and after the founding of the institution as presented in two seminal works by Prebisch – *The Economic Development of Latin America and its Principal Problems* (1945) and *Measures for the Economic Development of Underdeveloped Countries* (1951) – suffices to show what the two main points were on which to concentrate the discussion. The first was the premise of an unequal distribution of the gains from trade between the center and the periphery; the second, the inadequacy of market mechanisms in allocating resources for development.

These assertions, to which some economists in the industrialized countries would soon adhere,[41] caused a "psychic spur" in the more orthodox economic circles in the west. They "fell like a bomb" and were considered "an affront" and a blasphemy.[42] It was on the basis of this abhorrence of "the mischievous fantasies of protectionists, central planners," "development enthusiasts," and "millennial minded economists," as they would call the new theorists, that conservative economists, among them some of the most distinguished members of the Chicago School, decided to enter the discussion.[43]

From their perspective, the first and most general point to be opposed was the idea that a new body of theory was needed for the economic analysis of poorer countries undergoing transition processes. This was, of course, another expression of their rejection of Keynesianism. It was Keynes, after all, who had argued in favor of resisting the action of global forces attempting to establish a system of equilibrium, based on the "ideal" principles of laissez faire capitalism. He had made the original call to become, during the period of transition, "our own masters," "as free as we can from the pressures of the outside world."[44] Yet, what they were witnessing now was an extension of these notions to limits that were simply outrageous. Ideas, such as those of

Gunnar Myrdal, who believed that "the price system as a part of a very irrational whole, namely the economy of a backward country, can hardly have any great claim to rationality to begin with,"[45] were indeed shocking for economists who thought that "economics was economics whether in London, Delhi, Tokyo, or the moon."[46] From their point of view, "only the classical body of thought was relevant to show that market interest rates would raise and deploy capital in an optimal manner, that flexible exchange rates would solve balance of payments problems, that inflation and planning are bad, and competitive profits are good."[47]

In different moments and facing different problems in the development field, irritation would surface from the Chicago ranks in response to these "new ideas." Jacob Viner reacted typically when writing that he doubted that Prebisch had "the slightest acquaintance with the actual writings of the English classical school."[48] Harry Johnson would denounce the transfer of ideas made by Central European intellectuals into the Anglo-Saxon tradition, arguing that this "infiltration" had "implanted the habit of thinking in nationalist rather than cosmopolitan terms," "a habit which was easily adopted by new states."[49] Friedman would conclude in his classical style that:

What is required in the underdeveloped countries is the release of the energies of millions of able, active and vigorous people . . . an atmosphere of freedom, of maximum opportunity for individuals to experiment and of incentives for them to do so in an environment in which there are objective tests of success and failure – in short, a vigorous free capitalistic market.[50]

Chicago economists devoted their attention mainly to three specific policy areas: international trade, foreign aid, and the cultivation of market institutions. There was, in parallel, a theoretical contribution to the discussion on development that is of much greater importance to our analysis: the theory of human capital developed by Theodore W. Schultz. We shall briefly survey the propositions on these policy areas and then concentrate on Schultz's ideas.

Opposition to protectionism was an important, although not original, reaction rising from Chicago ranks. The first and main point raised by Jacob Viner centered on the industrialization thesis promoted by ECLA. Viner read in Prebisch's thesis of the deterioration of the terms of trade "a dogmatic identification of agriculture with poverty." Without necessarily advising against industrialization, he predicted that concentration on industry would lead to misallocation of resources.[51] T. W. Schultz would also rebuff "the economic thinking based on two central ideas, disguised unemployment and industrialization" as a "crude rule of thumb having little to recommend it either as a good economic policy or as a useful theory."[52]

In 1954, Milton Friedman criticized compulsory stabilization schemes for primary producers,[53] and Harry Johnson, in a variety of essays, criticized tariffs and analyzed the costs of their use to correct imbalances in markets.[54] These two economists also wrote extensively on the advantages of foreign direct investment, assuming that it brought about technology training and reinvestment of profits "more or less automatically."

Foreign aid was also an object of attack, yet the subject found the School at odds. While Friedman thought that economic aid "can only have disastrous consequences for our country and our way of life," affirming that "I do not believe that the world needs a redistribution of wealth. I think that is wrong." Others, like Arnold Harberger and T. W. Schultz, would call upon the United States "to do much more than it is doing presently to reduce the inequalities of income among the peoples of the world."[55]

On this matter, there was an area of agreement, however, which should be underlined, for it brings us to the theme of human capital. While maintaining his opposition to foreign aid, in 1955 Friedman advised the International Cooperation Administration not

to take it for granted that there is a rigid and mechanical ratio between the amount of investment and additions to output . . . At one extreme output can increase even without investment . . . the form and distribution of investment are at least as important as its sheer magnitudes. *The danger is that concentration on it may lead to policies that increase physical investment at the expense of investment in human capital.*[56]

Friedman was echoing what Schultz had written in reference to American aid to developing countries and this reflected the profound influence that Schultz's work on economic growth exerted at the time on his colleagues at Chicago and elsewhere.

Human capital: the Chicago approach to development

Schultz's ideas on human capital are essential to the understanding of the history of the Chicago School expedition to Latin America. They constitute the most interesting contribution that the Chicago School made to the debate on development in Latin America during the 1950s. Their influence, moreover, was not limited to the academic field. They had a lasting impact on the perspective of the United States government aid programs and on the work developed by American foundations in the area. From our viewpoint, these ideas provided the intellectual drive for the establishment of the operational network leading to the university contracts in Chile and to the design of the "experiment," which would be launched at the Universidad Católica.

The concept of human capital was not in itself a new idea. It can be traced back to Adam Smith. Moreover it was fully in line with classical traditions since, as Peter Bauer noted, the classical writers "closely related capital accumulations as an engine of development to the activities of particular groups, organizations and classes . . . to social attitudes, relationships, and institutions and to changes in these."[57]

What Schultz did was to give to one of these factors, education, the main role as the unexplained factor of development in the United States.

His ideas were derived most directly from the studies of Solomon Fabricant and Moses Abramowitz about national income in the United States. These economists had determined, based on historical surveys of relevant data, that an increase in GNP was not only related to an increase in capital and labor intensity, but principally to technology management administration and through a knowledge of economics.[58] Based on these studies, Schultz concluded that the economic growth that mattered was "the rise in production where the additional output exceeds the additional inputs of the conventional type" and this rise in output comes, in fact, from "two neglected variables: the development of the quality of people as productive agents and the raising of the level of productive arts."[59] He wrote:

We in America do not really understand our own economic growth and how it was achieved [for] we have omitted a part of wealth, and my thesis is that this omission is represented by the additions that have been made in the stock of human wealth. This human wealth consists of improvements in human effectiveness arising from the fact that man has developed capacities that result from investment in man.[60]

One of these "omitted inputs" could be represented as "the return on the investment" that had been going on in education, in high schools, colleges, and graduate schools in the United States.[61]

These considerations resulted in important consequences for poor countries and for the attitudes that the United States should adopt vis-à-vis the development dilemma. On the first point, Schultz's thesis was that "the more available resources that a poor country has committed or will commit to these two neglected classes of inputs, the greater has been or will be its economic growth."[62] This thesis, Schultz added, "carried radical implications for our thinking about the rest of the world." It implies that "fewer steel mills and other big plants should be built in the underdeveloped countries and more invested in the people of those countries, as we have invested in ourselves." He recommended that

whether it be in Point Four technical assistance programs; in activities like the Rockefeller Foundation work . . . in the work of church groups operating through some sixteen hundred mission projects in agriculture, education, and health in Latin America and elsewhere, or through private business, the transfer and development of new knowledge, new abilities and capacities are the most important contributions we can make.[63]

Schultz's propositions were immediately successful in attracting the interest of the economic professions and of individuals and organizations concerned with development problems. The success of his ideas in academic circles came mainly from the originality of its approach. As economists saw it, it treated education not simply as a form of consumption, but rather as a productive investment. The approach had, as Karabel and Halsey have remarked, a "distinctly pro-capitalist ideological sentiment" and, more importantly, an ability "to align itself with the increasingly powerful interests of the higher education industry," doubtless an important factor in its attractiveness.[64] From our point of view, the ability to address problems which were essentially non-economic from an exclusively economic perspective was equally important. The human capital approach presented the array of sociological and political factors suggested by the new theories as causes of underdevelopment with a rigorously economic response. "Non-economic" factors like "social and political elites unreceptive to change, gross deficiencies of the technical skills and capacities required by modernization, markets that are poorly organized and whose proper functioning is further impaired by ill-conceived public policies"[65] could be addressed by economists without having, as Schultz put it, "*to sell economic analysis short, recurring to theories based on cultural, social, and political considerations.*"[66] Poverty in underdeveloped nations was not attributable to the structure of international economic relations, but to "internal characteristics," most notably their lack of human capital. The remedy to these internal deficiencies did not lie in "structural changes," but in the redressing or creation of human resources, in the education of individuals. And this was, more than anything else, an economic process whose value for underdeveloped nations had been proved by economic development in the United States.[67]

The reactions of Chicago in response to the development theories and ideas regarding human capital expressed by Schultz explain, to a great extent, the interest of the School in the subjects of economic growth of Latin America,[68] because human capital was the banner under which the group of American economists undertook the experiment in Chile. The redefinition of teachings in economics and the creation of an elite of economists in an underdeveloped country represented the probational empirical exercise of the validity of this approach. Through this, the "technical perversions" preached by ECLA and its economists would be expanded, not only in Chile, but in other Latin American countries, as we shall mention further on. This would be, in fact, a response to the ideological challenge engendered by developmentalism, which would go much further and be much more sophisticated than the pure and simple initial reaction of disqualification expressed by conservative economists upon encountering the ideas of Prebisch.

The interest of the University of Chicago in the Latin American venture went further than the ideological factors inspiring some of its professors. There were also elements of an extra-ideological nature that also gave thrust to this initiative.

During the 1950s, Chicago had serious difficulties in competing with eastern establishment universities in obtaining the best economics students. They preferred to choose Harvard, Yale, MIT, or Princeton. During the period prior to the development of the policy of university agreements promoted by government foreign aid programs, Chicago obtained the majority of its students from the Hebrew University of Jerusalem and the City University in New York. The contracts with ICA and later the Agency for International Development were the third source of student recruitment. These contracts were vital for two reasons: first, because the experience in training foreign students – starting with the agreement with the Universidad Católica de Chile – produced excellent academic results (many of the Latin American students were good students), and second, because Chicago needed the funds from government cooperation programs to finance its graduate program. Funds to maintain students were scarce and private foundations tended to grant their backing to students who carried out doctoral work in leading universities.[69]

The prestige factor played, therefore, an important role in the gestation of the Chilean initiative of Chicago. The development of training programs for Latin American students and the success of many of them, in both academic and labor fields, upon returning to their own countries, was also a factor that led to the renovation of sources of financing and opened the doors of foundations, such as the Rockefeller and Ford Foundations. We shall look at this subject further on.

Chile: economy and society during the 1950s

In the previous pages we have attempted to ascertain the motivations and the interests inducing the United States government programs of foreign aid and the University of Chicago to participate in the "Chile Project." The attitudes of the "transmitter" and the characteristics of the "ideological product" of the transference have been thoroughly discussed. We should now turn to the receiving end of the message: what were the conditions for the *implantation* and the *operationalization* of the product in the society to which the product was being transferred?

In this last section of the present chapter, the discussion will be centered around two topics. The first one addresses the characteristics of the evolution of Chilean society since the 1930s. What it shows is that any discussion, even if superficial, of Chile's development leads to the conclusion that Chicago as a doctrine and as a set of economic policies utterly contradicted the social, economic, and political basis on which this development had been built. The second point, more restricted, refers to the characteristics of a particular sector of the Chilean dominant classes – *la Derecha Económica* (the "economic right") – by which we mean the group concentrating economic and social power in society. It is within this sector that, during the mid-1950s, a demand for orthodox remedies to Chilean economic ills began to develop.

The state and the industrial consensus

It seems like a paradox that Chicago ideas came to land in Chile, which has rightly been called "the fatherland of the state."[70] A central factor in the country's political and economic organization during the nineteenth century,[71] the state was pushed by the depression to the forefront of economic activity.[72] Already by the end of the 1950s, state intervention and management of the economy constituted a historical phenomenon.

In 1938 the creation of the Corporación de Fomento de la Producción (CORFO) prompted a qualitative transformation in the responsibilities of the state toward the economic management of the country.[73] The state had become both an entrepreneur, creating public enterprises and regulating institutions, and a planning agency, which "defined a horizon and provided the means – from projects to external and internal financing, including all sorts of incentives – for the development of private enterprise."[74]

As most authors have argued, the appearance of this entrepreneurial state cannot be seen as stemming only from the harsh economic conditions imposed by the depression. The new model of state initiative was also, and foremost, a political answer. It has to be seen, as Muñoz has affirmed, as "a new institutional framework which expressed the changes in operation at the level of the power groups and their mutual relations."[75] The most important include the diversification of the oligarchical sectors, deepened by the strengthening of an entrepreneurial class, and the consolidation of social and political organizations representing the middle sectors and the working class with a clear awareness of their interests. It was a state, therefore, which pursued and sometimes achieved the representation of a wide consensus based on the acceptance, the demand, or the toleration of its role as the director of industrialization and development, as a social modernizer, and a regulator of class conflict.

This was particularly clear in the case of industrialization. While, from the viewpoint of the entrepreneurial sectors, state protection and incentives constituted – as we shall see next – a necessity without which industrial progress could not be achieved, from the perspective of the working-class organizations and the political parties representing them, industrialization was also an imperative not merely due to economic considerations; the development of a national bourgeoisie was seen as a requisite in order to confront feudal agrarian structures and imperialism.[76] Therefore, the years between 1938 and 1947 represented a foundational period in Chile. They marked the following decades with a predominant ideological thrust in favor of a central state role.[77]

Industrialists and the state

Corporate entrepreneurial behavior during the decade of the consolidation of state-oriented development and up until the mid-1960s was characterized by a well-known paradox. While accepting the central role of the state in the management of the economy and demanding its protection and incentives, the industrialist organizations kept a predominantly free market discourse and adhered politically to the traditional oligarchical parties, those most staunchly opposing economic modernization and reform. At the same time, they tended systematically to identify economic development with the achievement of their most immediate interests and were, thus, unable to project themselves beyond their corporate dimensions. While, on the one hand, they would be fearful of and resist any state concession to working-class demands, describing that possibility as a threat to stability and to trust in the economy, they would accept orthodox attempts at economic stabilization only to the extent that they would not include measures affecting their immediate interests. At the prospect of "shared sacrifices," they would mobilize their organizations and the political parties of the right, denouncing these policies as "out of touch with reality."[78]

The reasons for this ambiguity, which is by no means exclusive to the Chilean entrepreneurial class, are complex and can be discussed here only at a level of generality. The first point to be stressed is that the attitudes of industrialists toward the state stemmed most directly from their realization that "increased levels of protection and substantial state economic support could turn hitherto unattractive ventures into profitable businesses, no matter how inefficient they might happen to be, if an international scale of comparison was applied."[79] But this immediate class interest must be placed within the framework formed by two other elements, one structural and the other political. The industrialist demand for state protection originated after the depression, from "the radical reduction of the amount of foreign exchange that could be spent in buying manufacturing goods," coupled during the war years "with a parallel and drastic reduction of the goods that industrialized countries were prepared to sell the countries that usually provided them with raw materials."[80]

Their commitment to the endeavor was fostered by "the catalyzing function" performed by a group of "technico-political specialists," as

Cavarozzi calls them, who filled strategic positions in different public agencies, particularly in CORFO, and had the very important role of generating a "state ideology" of industrialization and of providing entrepreneurs with an "industrializing ethos."[81]

What stood out rather clearly, therefore, during the period of the consolidation of the style of development, was the coincidence of interests of the industrialists and the state, the convergence of the entrepreneurial belief that protection was a necessity, essential for the development of industry, and the push by state technocrats (and politicians) to direct the process of development from the state apparatus. The ideology of industrialization provided "a rallying point for those who were advocating, and those others who would benefit from, a transformation of the country's economic structures."[82]

So, as Muñoz has stated, it was not in relation to the objectives of production growth induced by the state that conflicts with the industrialists existed during that period, nor can an explanation for their conservative political options be grounded there. Conflicts developed, rather, at the level of the social relations between industry owners and the workers and around the role the state had to play in them.[83]

Development and democracy

The crux of the problem has been well summarized by Moulian:

the industrialization process was developed in an ideological and political framework of democratization, which, although limited, was to create permanent tensions between the logic of accumulation demanded by capital and the logic of legitimization demanded by the functioning of a democratic regime, which politically integrated the working class into its party system.[84]

Industrialization, as the main element of a capitalist modernization of society, had begun quite paradoxically, in fact, under center-left governmental coalitions composed of the predominant center party, representing the middle classes – the Radical Party – and the socialists with the support, either externally or, as in 1946, as full participants, of the Communist Party.[85] State intervention in fostering industrialization, protecting the internal market, and expanding internal demand during recessive periods operated also in the control of prices, the development of social legislation, the creation of health, education, and housing programs, the restrictions imposed on monopolies and speculations, etc. These last interventionist policies received resistance from the dominant groups. From the point of view of the state, however, they reflected the growing strength of the working-class organizations and of the different popular sectors which had incorporated themselves into the political system.[86]

In fact, the different governments were forced to dedicate a growing amount of resources to the satisfaction of basic needs and the demands coming from groups that had become incorporated into society, or which had assumed a larger relative importance within the system. But, the economy appeared to be incapable of expanding at a sufficiently fast rate and thus was unable to respond to these demands adequately and opportunely. What surfaced, therefore, was a complex and tight interrelation between the socio-political and economic spheres making it difficult to disentangle "what was the cause and what was the effect of both the increasing socio-political participation and the insufficient economic growth."[87] The end result would be a gradual radicalization of political conflicts.

The entrepreneurs and the conservative parties

Therefore, it was the perception of a "class threat" involved in the evolution of the socio-political setting that constitutes the first reason explaining the support given by the entrepreneurial classes to the traditional conservative and liberal parties. A threat that tended to reinforce the sociological trait described by Enzo Faletto as the "abourgeoisement" of the landowning class and the "aristocratization" of the industrial bourgeoisie,[88] a class cohesion which gave these parties their source of permanent electoral support, but which limited their degree of political maneuverability.[89] In fact, they could not transcend their base with a program reaching a "national" social majority and form with the majority centrist parties (first the Radicals, later the Christian Democrats) a coalition capable of both pushing for a capitalist modernization of society and politically excluding the left. This inability to compete at a national level was shown by the fact that the right lost four successive presidential elections between 1938 and 1952.[90]

Yet, these electoral defeats did not signify a loss of social or economic power for the dominant classes; what they basically demonstrated was, as Moulian and Torres indicated, that domination does not pertain exclusively to the political level. They expressed the incapacity of these sectors to accommodate a complex social structure and to lead the tasks required for capitalist growth, but were not an indication of social or economic subordination. The principal lesson learned as a result of these defeats was that the right had to negotiate and had to make the most of its political capabilities. In fact, the substantial degree of electoral support it maintained until 1965 preserved its capacity for negotiation, neutralization, and even for veto in certain matters.[91] It was mainly for its own use in this political setting that the right and the main social sectors linked to it professed a rhetorical but nonetheless passionate adherence to the basic principles of liberal economics.

Ideology and identity in the Chilean right

To understand the role that free market ideas played in the context which has just been described, the notion of "misplaced ideas" seems quite useful. Market principles were normative statements for which "the reality test was not decisive." Free market ideas "could not be practiced but were at the same time indispensable."[92]

The right, in general, adhered to them, even obsessively, more as an identity device and as an instrument for political defense than as a set of policy recommendations. A quotation from one of Jorge Alessandri's speeches to businessmen is quite useful to illustrate this point.

The intervention of politics – and I use the expression in its noblest sense – in economic activities makes it now quite dangerous for men devoted to business practices not to have some well-grounded basic [economic] orientations. It is necessary that they have principles and that even if they have to sacrifice brilliant commercial expectations, they adhere to these principles . . . [for their forgetfulness] creates precedents that could turn against us.[93]

State support and protection, since Alessandri was referring to these, were not able to attract the entrepreneurs to such an extent that they forgot free market principles. These principles were a safeguard in a world shaped by the intervention of politics "in its noblest sense." But, the pretence that they shape society or the economy did not exist.

What Alessandri and the entrepreneurs rejected was not the direction that the state exercised over the economy, but the arbitrariness in the management of the economic instruments controlled by the state. In the same speech he argued in favor of the principle that "a regime of political freedom can only subsist within a regime of economic freedom" and that the affirmation of this principle "*did not mean in any way disregarding the attributions that correspond to the state in the economic orientation of our country.*" "But please note," he continued, "that to give the state *the faculty to intervene and orient economic life* does not mean to endow the big and small functionaries with excessive discretional faculties, because this would simply mean making economic life impossible."[94]

In sum, with his carefully worded language, Alessandri recognized "state intervention in the economy as [being] necessary and irreplaceable"; recommending the concept of "private enterprise" over that of "free enterprise," "for it carries implicitly the idea of a legitimate action of state control."[95] As Pinto has noted, he conceived the relation between the state and private enterprise as "some sort of quid pro quo between the support given by the first to private initiative and the obligation of the latter to

increase its productivity and competitiveness *vis-à-vis* external production."[96]
This was undoubtedly the ideological orientation guiding the mainstream of
the business class.

The mid-1950s: crisis and the Klein Saks mission

From the beginning of the 1950s a crisis within the model of industrial
development began to unfold. This crisis, shown principally by an uncontrollable level of inflation, generated a passionate economic discussion among the
economic and intellectual elites and the revitalization of liberal economic
ideas within the "economic right." The nature of the inflationary phenomenon was hotly debated between two "schools" of economic analysis: the
estructuralistas, represented mainly by ECLA and the University of Chile
economists in Santiago, and the *monetaristas* whose best advocate was the
newspaper *El Mercurio,* but whose most relevant expression was an American
economic team hired by the Chilean government to control inflation: the
Klein Saks mission.

The development of this polemic and the relative failure of this mission to
control inflation, created the setting for the ICA proposal to bring Chicago
economists to Chile and begin the training of Chilean economists in the neo-
classical tradition.

In 1953, as a result of the expansionist policies of the Ibáñez government,
inflation reached 80 percent. The crisis led to orthodox remedies and
conservative doctors: in July 1955, the government hired the services of a
United States private consulting firm headed by Dr. Julius Klein, to make a
study and issue recommendations on inflation. As Aníbal Pinto wrote at the
time, this governmental decision was guided by "a gradual and subtle
variation in ideas [based] on the following premises: a contraction of the
activity and influence of the state on all fronts; an emphasis on 'free
competition' as the factor of economic orientation including that of imported
goods and national products; an accent on the decisive role of private foreign
investment." Pinto attributed this change in ideas to the fatigue produced by
state interventionism which, in his opinion, had lost all semblance of
rationality, and to "the powerful fan of ideas and practices which has its point
of irradiation in the United States."[97]

The Klein Saks mission stayed in Chile for three years and, through the
application of monetary measures, decreased inflation to 38 percent in 1956
and 17 percent in 1957. Yet, the mission could not be called an unqualified
success, particularly considering the sacrifice of the salaried classes with
respect to their purchasing power, unemployment, and a general slowdown in
productive activity.[98] In fact, it appeared as being "defeated" by the
combined opposition of political parties in Congress, the Confederación de la

Producción y el Comercio, the Sociedad de Fomento Fabril, and working-class mobilization and strikes.[99] Entrepreneurs, politicians, and Chilean economists alike criticized the emphasis placed by the mission on monetary reasons (money supply and credits to the private sector) as the main factor behind inflation.[100]

Alone, as defender of the mission, stood *El Mercurio*. The newspaper gave sanctuary to a group that, although in a minority within the business sector, nurtured positions of much greater faithfulness to free market principles and was, in that position, an instrument of formidable influence. Agustín Edwards, the owner, as well as other persons linked to the so-called "Edwards group" such as Carlos Urenda, had close business contacts with United States interest groups and recognized the influence of liberal thinkers, particularly von Hayek and von Mises.[101] The group represented, both in its economic and intellectual dimension, the most internationalized sector of the Chilean economy, composed not only of entrepreneurs, but also of lawyers of foreign enterprises. In the discussion generated by the Klein Saks mission *El Mercurio* stood in opposition to the attitudes of the Confederación de la Producción y el Comercio and the Sociedad de Fomento Fabril, the main business associations. Yet, the newspaper editorials did not hesitate in unleashing a bitter campaign of denunciation against the critics of the mission:

all opposition voices joined the campaign to defeat the anti-inflationary policy. The infinite number of interests affected have been expressed, some with virulence, others with justice; some affected by the damage caused to their business activities, others to gain advantage from the possible collapse of the walls built against inflation.[102]

The discussion concerning the mission led, as has been stated before, to the establishment of two theoretical positions *vis-à-vis* inflation and economic development. The so-called "structuralist" perspective of inflation included most members of the technical teams that had transformed the role of the state, had participated in the foundation and management of the state enterprises of CORFO, and had organized the economic studies in the Universidad de Chile. In their view, economics necessarily incorporated social and political factors and its role as a science reunited both technical service to the state and industry, and the theoretical analysis of development problems. A good example of their view is provided by the contemporary topics selected for study by the Economics Institute of the Universidad de Chile. These topics included:

1. the low level of the average income and the great inequality of income distribution;
2. the dangerous dependency of the Chilean economy on copper and nitrate exports;

3. the low proportion of these exports returning to the country;
4. the low percentage of national income allocated to reproductive investment;
5. the need to increase the economic independence of the country by expanding its industrial activity and the technological capacity of agriculture and by inducing foreign companies to invest in areas other than mining, as well as to require the purchase of their inputs and replacement parts in Chile, etc.[103]

With respect to inflation, the essence of the structuralists' argument was that price stability could be attained only through economic growth. The basic forces of inflation, they thought, are structural in nature. Financial factors might be important, but only as factors propagating inflation and not originating it. "Monetary policies could be easily managed and have relatively quick effects, but they attack only the symptoms and therefore cannot cure."[104]

These perceptions of the role of economic science and of the nature of the economic problems of Chilean society led to two consequences: the first was the economists' espousal of propositions favoring structural changes, particularly agrarian reform, which would, in their view, modernize the economy and stimulate the industrialization process. Secondly, the predominance of this vision among economists left no room in Chile for an economic perspective among educated circles which did not take into consideration the social and political factors expressing the structure of society.

Vis-à-vis the hegemony of these perspectives and of the economists who supported them, the sectors adhering to the classical ideas of economic liberalism could only resort to the assistance of "foreign missions." With the visit of the Klein Saks mission to Chile, the concept of a foreign mission as a solution became a custom among different governments.[105] From the viewpoint of those who recommended them:

the bringing of these foreign experts is not because we do not have true capabilities in financial matters but rather because these experts are backed by an international reputation that makes their proposals less controvertible. Besides, their recommendations inspire a greater guarantee since they are neutral in an excessively distrustful environment such as ours. This is very important. Frankly, these members of foreign economic missions cannot be attributed with any given political interest and there is a greater possibility that their advice will be heeded.[106]

With the arrival of the Klein Saks mission, *El Mercurio* reiterated these arguments, adding, moreover, an incisive condemnation of local economists. In its editorials, the newspaper recognized that these foreign economists would be criticized because they would not be able to comprehend all aspects of economic policy and its social or other implications. But, based upon "their long experience," these economists knew that to begin by changing the social and juridical regime amounts to putting "the coach before the horse." If the local technicians "were allowed to carry out their task as sociologists and not as economists," the newspaper argued, "we should put into practice the socialist populist plan which includes the agrarian reform, the nationalization of mines, the organization of workers' and technicians' committees in industries and the control by the state of all basic industries." The process would finally lead "to the establishment of the dictatorship of the party."[107]

It was within the framework provided by this discussion that the offer of the International Cooperation Administration to bring to Chile a group of American professors to train economists in the perspectives of orthodox economics was received. The offer could not have been better accepted by those sectors that shared the dark vision of national development that foreboded, from their point of view, the predominance of structuralists, planners, and statists. It combined the virtuous characteristics of the foreign mission, backed by the prestige and image of neutrality existing in all the ideas and teams coming from other more developed countries, with the promise of a transfer of that prestige to a Chilean group. The new economists would subsequently intervene in the national discussion, defending the viewpoints of private enterprise with attributes very similar to those of the external mission: the prestige of an American university and the presumption of the neutrality of science.

CHAPTER 5

The contracts between ICA, Chicago, and the Universidad Católica

The foreign assistance technician

We shall examine in this chapter the history of the contracts between the University of Chicago and the Catholic University of Santiago and the number of different events that led to that academic exchange known in Chicago as the "Chile Project." The motivations and interests we have described in the previous chapter were expressed by a group of individuals in whose interaction there was a considerable amount of calculation but also of chance. How did these individuals come to meet each other? Why did they commit themselves in this initiative? These are the main questions we shall address in the description of the circumstances leading to the contracts. In the following pages we shall address the predominant role played by three persons: Mr. Albion Patterson, Mr. T. W. Schultz, and Mr. Julio Chaná. They can rightly be called the "fathers" of the contracts. As we shall argue later, the title of "father" of the Chicago Boys must be given in all justice to Dr. Arnold Harberger. Later in the development of the group's history, two other men would adopt the father role: Mr. Agustín Edwards and Mr. Augusto Pinochet.

Born in Massachusetts in 1904, Albion W. Patterson graduated from Princeton University and later studied at the University of California and Middlebury College. A teacher and school administrator for twelve years, he was later employed by the federal government on agricultural marketing programs before joining the Institute of Inter-American Affairs in 1942, as an agricultural expert. That same year Patterson went to Paraguay on his first mission abroad. During the 1950s and 60s, he became, as Glick notes, a name that appeared on every list as one of the most capable administrators in the US technical assistance service; with "imagination and insight, competence and devotion," Patterson showed, moreover, a strong sense of leadership.[1]

Patterson's relationship with economics and, more specifically, with the teaching of economics, is paramount, not just because it led to his initiative to introduce Chicago economics into Chile, but also because it reflects very clearly the evolution of a particular "ideology of development" instituted by an administrator of cooperation programs on the basis of his working experience, more than his own intellectual formation in the application of official policy directives. In fact, the origin of Patterson's interest in economics can be traced back to his experience during his first years of service in Paraguay. He had been initially hired by the IIAA to help the Paraguayan government increase food production but, in searching for background information at the Ministry of Agriculture, the only data that he and his team were able to uncover pertained to climatic conditions. Upon this discovery, they decided to take an agricultural census, for which they had to train, with the assistance of an economist from Cornell, 1,300 Paraguayan census takers. The development of these activities within the framework of the *servicio* manifested the need to increase the technical level of local functionaries participating in the projects. Indeed, after the first tentative experiences were concluded, and when more ambitious projects came to the fore, the lack of more and better prepared technicians – particularly in economics – became one of the principal obstacles to cooperation. Patterson reported that, by 1945, the *servicio* programs in the agricultural sector were having an impact on the areas of health and sanitation, education, and food supply. This was so much so, in fact, that the ministers of the Paraguayan government began to rely on Patterson for facts and information about their own country. However, he was very often unable to fulfill all the requests he received from the government due to the lack of adequate personnel trained in economics. When he asked Washington for "a general purpose economist," he received no answer. Says Patterson, "in 1945, economics had not been discovered by Washington." As there were no economists as such in any of the *servicios* in Latin America, Patterson decided to recruit his own economists from the Universidad de Asuncion.[2]

This experience came to be decisive in establishing his interest in the field of economics and in his understanding of the political and social elements involved in the training of economists in Latin American societies. In fact, as he described them, these economists had the advantage of having a middle-class background. They did not share landowners' conservative values and were, therefore, keen for modernization in agriculture. Unfortunately, they were very poorly trained, with five years of courses in accounting. Furthermore, they were – in Patterson's own words – "pink," leftwing and politically active; most of them were exiles from Argentina and Brazil. He said, "I made a pact with them. I told them to stop making fiery speeches and work with me: 'I'll give you tenure, you'll learn well, have fun, and make studies for your country.' It was in doing this that I got interested in economics."[3]

This initiative responded to two interrelated concerns. The first and most immediate one was the need for economists. Assistance could not function without economists and other well-trained technicians, to make decisions at government level. The second concern was for the stability of the programs. In fact, the first observation that US technicians made about the countries in which they were working was the irritating and destructive character of political activity. Faced with strikes and civil wars, coups and ministerial instability, diplomats and technicians attempted to find ways to give permanence to the projects in which they were engaged, and to the local staff involved in them. After the first decade of operation, it was possible to report that the *servicios* had introduced a certain degree of stability into the local political system. "When governments have changed, either by peaceful or by violent methods," an official document asserted, "*servicios* have never ceased operations. In this respect, they are making a fundamental contribution to the solution of one of the serious problems of Latin America – instability of governments and lack of continuity in government programs."[4]

Stability demanded the creation of a truly modernized technocracy preserved in isolation from the turmoils of active politics. Economists, in particular, had to remain above political conflict, for they would be effective only if they acted as a national reservoir of excellence and objectivity. This was precisely what Patterson attempted to do with the Paraguayan economists. He hoped that, instead of assuming an activist role in politics, they would exert their influence through a kind of unofficial planning board, which they accomplished by performing fiscal studies for the Minister of Finance, production studies for the Ministry of Economics, etc.

Therefore, training, education, and instruction attempted not only to introduce specific material techniques for a particular field of economic activity, but to affect behavior, to inculcate and disseminate new attitudes. In fact, aid and technological assistance for development and modernization could only mean the infusion of certain "techniques of social organization," which, having shown an enormous degree of success in the development of the social and economic organization of the United States, were necessarily and almost by definition the best technology that Americans could export. This was the fundamental thrust of the American missionary spirit. It was endowed – at least during the first years of the experience – with a rather candid belief in the feasibility of this endeavor. As Patterson stated, US missions in Latin America were characterized by a spirit of invincibility, by a "we could accomplish anything we set out to do" attitude.[5] Naïveté is perhaps one of the most typical historical characteristics of missionaries of all sorts: cunning, however, is also, and in this case the efforts of the imagination of real individuals deeply committed to transferring development, along with the awareness of the tremendous vigor of American expansionism, converged to recreate this perennial combination of power maneuvering and humane candor. The conviction that Latin Americans had to recognize, after all, the undeniable superiority of American civilization gave profound strength to the efforts in cultural transformation.[6]

It was in Paraguay that Patterson established his first contact with Theodore W. Schultz, Dean of the Department of Economics of Chicago. As a result of his sudden interest in studying economics, he bought a library, concentrating on the subjects of agriculture and development. There were at that time, he recalls, other important figures in the field. He turned instead to Schultz's work because it seemed "more modern" and he soon established active correspondence with him. Schultz's work on agricultural economics had an important impact on his ideas and was to become a valuable source of inspiration for the biggest project with which Patterson was involved during his career, the *Plan Chillán*, a plan conducted in cooperation with the government of Chile.

In 1953 Patterson went to Chile as director of AID "Point Four" programs in that country. With him, and also from Paraguay, came a new US ambassador to Santiago, Willard L. Beaulac, a diplomat with longstanding Latin American experience, who had established, during his period as ambassador in Asuncion, a close working relationship with Patterson and who shared his passion for technical cooperation.

Patterson and the US aid mission in Chile: 1953

Patterson recalls that his transfer to Chile was due to Washington's concern for the recently created agricultural *servicio*, where the American director had been accused of arrogance by his Chilean counterparts. The Asociación de Ingenieros Agrónomos was said to have petitioned the Chilean government to declare the American *persona non grata*.[7] Therefore, as soon as he arrived, Patterson proposed to the government of General Ibañez an agricultural development plan designed to prove that "he meant business." "With a lot of luck and some good management, sixty odd days after my arrival in Chile," Patterson said, "it was possible to pull all the ends together – and those ends concerned four Chilean ministries, and the Chilean Development Corporation – and sign up what is now known as the *Plan Chillán*. This was in early July of 1953."[8] The *Plan Chillán* was an agricultural development scheme designed for one region of the country, which included not only agriculture in the broadest sense, but also health and sanitation, housing, industrial development, and transportation. The success of this initiative – the first the United States had promoted somewhere other than a capital city in Latin America – helped Patterson to gain support from Washington for the continuation of other experiments in foreign assistance. His contacts with Chilean authorities and with about eighty local technicians helped him to draw a picture of the country and allowed him to put forward his principal concern: education in economics.

In fact, the idea to conduct an experiment in this field had occurred to him as soon as he came to Santiago. He recalls that, after a couple of weeks in his new post, he had raised the matter with the ambassador. He told Beaulac: "In Paraguay, we had nothing but weather records, we had to begin with agricultural experimentation, establishing institutions and the basic stuff. This is a different situation: Chile is a sophisticated country; we do not need to show these basic things. What we need to do is to change the formation of the men, to influence the education, which is very bad." Beaulac agreed, but after discussing what they could do with the universities, they concluded that they did not know where to start.[9]

T. W. Schultz and the human capital theory

It was at this time that Patterson met the person and found the intellectual construction that provided both an institutional backing and a rationale for his drive to educate. "Then, one day, late in 1953," Patterson remembers, "T. W. Schultz walked into my office." Schultz, on leave from Chicago, was heading a National Planning Association mission which, under financing from the Ford Foundation, had been studying Latin America for two years. In June 1956 the NPA would issue a report entitled, "Recommendations for the Future," with more than 100 recommendations on policies and methods designed to help public agencies, private groups, and the governments and peoples of Latin America, through more orderly and effective technical cooperation to speed economic and social development.[10] Schultz had, as director of research, organized the plan of study and selected the research staff. The group of more than fifty associates had done fieldwork in all twenty Latin American countries, where they made surveys, examined records, and consulted persons concerned with technical cooperation programs. One of Schultz's associates was Simon Rottenberg, a Chicago professor who would be later appointed by Schultz as the first director of the Chicago-Universidad Católica contract, the "Chile Project."

Patterson and Schultz met every day for a period of two weeks. Schultz needed information for his mission in Chile, which "concentrated primarily on aspects of education."[11] They extended their discussions to all sorts of subjects from agricultural development to education in Latin America. It was during one of these conversations that Schultz told Patterson about his studies on human capital.

Patterson describes this conversation as "opening my eyes" and "changing my whole attitude of being a director of technical cooperation." Schultz provided, at last, a "scientific" base for his old convictions regarding the importance of education; he gave a new light to traditional economics which – Patterson felt – had "grossly underestimated the role of education in economic growth." From that point on, Patterson devised and became dedicated to a plan to develop Latin American higher education in "the strategic fields of economics, agricultural technology, engineering, business administration, industrial engineering, and public administration." This plan, which – in his design – should become a major project under Point Four, would be channeled through "a series of regional universities . . . in Latin America, each of which would seek to develop instruction in at least one of the major fields."[12]

The first contacts with Chilean universities: failure and success

It is understandable that these ideas had an enormous impact on the way Patterson perceived his chances of promoting the initiatives he had been planning since his days in Paraguay. Schultz was the dean of one of the most prestigious centers of economic studies in the US, and he had an imposing personality. He was an expert on development problems and had conducted a two-year study in Latin America. More important, perhaps, Schultz reacted favorably to Patterson's ideas of pushing for a university contract with Chile in the field of economics; he immediately agreed to discuss participation with his colleagues in Chicago. In the meantime, Patterson would explore the subject with the authorities of the Universidad de Chile and he would keep Schultz informed on developments.

Patterson recalls that he had developed a good personal relationship with Juan Gómez Millas, who was the rector of the national university, the most important in the country. Gómez Millas was dedicated to a program involving the modernization of his institution and had established contacts with European and American universities to exchange professors and organize scholarship programs.[13] He was, therefore, interested in cooperation schemes with the US aid mission in Santiago. Patterson went to see him and proposed his plan. The US government could finance a university contract between the Universidad de Chile and the University of Chicago wherein Chicago professors would conduct the "modernization" of the studies of economics at the Universidad de Chile and a program of scholarships at Chicago would be established for Universidad de Chile graduates in economics.

The rector discussed the idea, but ultimately rejected it. According to Patterson, "he showed a lot of fears," and finally informed him that "he wanted to run," but that he could not control the leftwing economists, who were in control of the Faculty of Economics. They would clearly oppose the initiative, due to the conservative reputation of Chicago economists and the official US support for the contract. Patterson's version is contradicted, however, by Gómez Millas' recollections of the episode. According to him, Patterson's negotiations were conducted exclusively with Rafael Correa, who was then the dean of the faculty of the Universidad de Chile, and with Jorge Bande, a professor of that same faculty. From their perspective, while the university was interested in establishing contacts with American universities through Point Four offices, it had no reason to restrict this kind of contract to a particular US institution. Patterson insisted that the contract had to be made with Chicago, and was adamant about this condition.[14]

At the end of 1953, Correa traveled to the United States, where he visited Harvard and Columbia. In New York he met Dr. Joseph Grunwald, an economics professor at Columbia, and invited him to come to Chile to organize the Department of Economics at the national university. Grunwald, reluctant at the beginning, became convinced and enthusiastic about the idea after meeting with Flavian Levine, a professor at the Universidad de Chile, who impressed him greatly.[15] He decided to accept the invitation for one year, starting in January 1954. He stayed in Chile for seven years, during which time he taught and wrote extensively, actively participating in the discussion about Chilean and Latin American development during the period of the rise of development economics.

Grunwald's experience, as well as different initiatives undertaken by the authorities of the Universidad de Chile to establish links with American universities, tends to disprove Patterson's perception of the reasons behind the opposition by Gómez Millas to his plan.[16] If there was, indeed, an ideological factor for the negative response from the Universidad de Chile to Albion Patterson, it was not based on Point Four or American participation in the plan, but on the perception of inadequacy which the type of economics identified with the University of Chicago elicited in a school where development economics and structuralism were the mainstream. In addition, and more importantly perhaps, one cannot but conclude that it did not require leftwing tendencies to oppose the sort of agreement which granted an American university exclusive tuition over a school of economics which had influence and prestige not only in its own country, but in the Latin American region in general.

It was in 1954 that Monsignor Alfredo Silva Santiago, rector of the Pontificia Universidad Católica de Chile approached Patterson for help. Silva Santiago, Patterson recalls, took him to a "fundo," "where peasants wearing *ojotas* and white gloves" served them a delightful lunch. "Do a program with the UC [Universidad Católica], Mr. Patterson," the rector requested. He wanted help, more specifically for the Agricultural Department, which had traditionally been an important part of the university. Patterson, however, was not interested. He had learned in Paraguay that he could not make changes in agriculture through *dueños de fundo* (landowners), and knew that most of the upper-class students of the school from that particular university were sons and heirs of landowners. "Let us forget agriculture," he told the bishop, "let's work together in economics."[17]

Less than a year later, the details of the contract with the Universidad Católica had been accorded.[18] Patterson had been informing Schultz throughout these negotiations and he could now telephone him in triumph. He recalls the moment: "We were all excited, this was a great thing for the country, the introduction of economics at the graduate level to strike a balance in the economic thought in the country. There it was, the best free market group to come and help. We were giving an alternative."[19]

Patterson's perspective is well expressed in a book written by Senator William Benton, *The Voice of Latin America*, whose section on education was prepared entirely on the basis of Patterson's memos. After celebrating the "project in the field of economics between the Catholic University in Santiago and the University of Chicago," the senator included the following footnote:

One observer reported to us that a grave problem in Chile has been posed by the Marxist, leftwing oriented economists who have come from the university economics departments and who have infiltrated into the Chilean government and economy. Another close student of Latin America reports that University of Chile economists have been followers of Keynes and Prebisch more than of Marx, and that the Chicago influence at the Catholic University will introduce a third basic viewpoint, that of contemporary "market economics." All these reports show the importance of university training applied to a country's political as well as its economic orientation.[20]

Albion Patterson, the "close student of Latin America" mentioned by Senator Benton, was, in fact, fully aware that the type of "modernization" of economic studies which the United States government should promote in Chile could not be organized by giving the local aid recipient the opportunity to shop around and select the university or universities to acquire the contract and the type of program it felt most suitable to its own needs. What Chile required was "to right the balance of its economics," and what was lacking, Patterson thought, was the best economics available – good American free market economics. That explains his adamant position of imposing Chicago as a condition, as well as the dimensions given to the contract – the details of which we shall discuss later – which was conceived not as some form of "external cooperation" with an established institution, but as a real appropriation, in practice, of an institution – a very weak institution, as was the Faculty of Economics of the Universidad Católica – in order to redefine its programs and its purposes as an academic center. Education was – as he said – a good way "to transplant things from one country to another. It sounds indirect, but it is not. And this strategic approach constitutes a legitimate form of influencing one country's development."[21]

This perspective was couched in very different terms – deeper and more sophisticated – than those used to define the approach held by most of the embassy staff with respect to economic ideology in Chile. That vision was that of a "red cell" of economists with whom no contact was possible. Joseph Grunwald reports that, on his first visit to the embassy in Santiago, Ambassador Beaulac warned him that he was about to enter into a "communist nest," meaning the Faculty of Economics of the Universidad de Chile. According to Dr. Grunwald, Beaulac's embassy "was out of touch with the intellectual community of the country," which was not surprising given embassy viewpoints and the fact – as Grunwald puts it – that "all the intelligent people [in the economics profession] were structuralists."[22]

Who then were the counterparts that Patterson found at the Catholic University?

The Universidad Católica de Chile

In one sense, it could be argued that the study of economics began at the Universidad Católica with the signing of the contracts with the University of Chicago. In fact, before 1955, the university had only a School of Commerce, imparting the principles of accounting, administration, and mathematics, but not economics. From another viewpoint, however, the Universidad Católica had also been influenced by the world crisis and its impact on the Chilean economy. The increase in the activities of the public sector, which resulted from it, led people such as President Aguirre Cerda, who had been the founder and first dean of the Faculty of Economics of the Universidad de Chile; Guillermo del Pedregal, who would become the first head of CORFO, the state corporation promoting industrial development; and others, like economist and planner Alberto Baltra, to promote the study of economics, creating the degree of *Ingeniero Comercial* (commercial engineer) at the Universidad de Chile. In the Universidad Católica, an "Academy of Economic and Commercial Sciences" had existed since the 1920s, where landowners and entrepreneurs linked to the church met once or twice a year to discuss, from the Catholic doctrine perspective, the situation of the agricultural and commercial sectors in the country. Yet the development of economic studies at the national university exerted a certain influence on its Catholic counterpart, and in the 1940s a school also granting the degree of commercial engineer began to function. According to a student, the school was inferior and underdeveloped, and the educational level did not meet university standards. Professors were old, most of them were lawyers with very little knowledge of economics, and full-time professors did not exist. The library was poor. Most students left the school after the first year and the others used their free time, which was abundant, to study mathematics, the only well-taught course in the school. Yet they did not know what to do with it and most had to take other jobs after completing their education.[23]

This precarious situation contrasted with that at the Universidad de Chile, where a group of brilliant economists – Herman Max and Flavian Levine, among others – besides being involved in state planning and development activities, cultivated an intellectual influence in their faculty, which extended beyond Chilean frontiers to make the Universidad de Chile a leading center of economic studies in the Latin American region.

The conference of faculties of economic sciences

In November 1953 the Union of Latin American universities organized in Santiago a congress of Latin American universities, one of whose main events was a conference of faculties of economic sciences. The initiative and its origin are a useful device whereby one can observe the type of ideological approach towards economics prevailing at the time, not only in Chile, but in the whole of Latin America. As we shall see, the conference is also one of the antecedents of the contracts between the Universidad Católica and the University of Chicago.[24]

The purpose of the conference was in itself indicative of the spirit of the times. Following a proposal made by Raúl Prebisch, executive secretary of the Economic Commission for Latin America (ECLA), created six years earlier in Santiago, the conference had as its main point of discussion the design of a "model or pilot school" for the study of economics in the region. This idea shows, in fact, one of the most distinctive traits of the approach followed by the majority of Latin American economists of the period: the need for a regional economics or for a particular Latin American approach to economic theory and development.

The expansion of this perspective throughout Latin America is clearly shown in the abundant literature of the 1940s and 1950s of *El Trimestre Económico*, the most important economic journal in the region. It was enthusiastically supported by the Faculty of Economics of the Universidad de Chile. The Dean, Luis Escobar, in a speech to students and members of the faculty made some years after the events we are discussing here, summarized this point of view very explicitly:

The Latin American countries do not have a national theory of economic development. They tend to base their policies on a diagnosis or interpretation made, basically, within the model prevailing during the thirties in which classical theory continues to show important remnants of its powerful influence . . . the task of present social scientists is precisely to discover those characteristics, which I call "interior" and which are basically "national."

I believe that each zone has its own development problems which have to be interpreted in the light of the political, social, historical, cultural, and economic variables which define them in particular ... To accept this principle implies recognizing that a general theory of development valid for all regions cannot be formulated. One has to find as many interpretations as there are situations, some can be similar, others can have very little in common.[25]

These ideas were obviously one of the most important tenets of the development theories originated in the writings of Raúl Prebisch and established in Latin America since the end of the 1930s, and particularly since the foundation of ECLA. The central point under attack was the validity of "economic science" as a universal paradigm applicable in any period and everywhere. Developmentalists or structuralists opposed the need for a specific theory for developing countries, a notion which – as we have seen – was easily inserted into the Keynesian orthodoxy prevailing in the economic and political spheres of the most developed countries at that time. The corollary for developmentalists was, as Prebisch wrote, the need to confront "the traditional propensity to introduce from abroad remedies which are strange and in discordance with the requisites of the situation in Latin America."[26]

It was only logical, therefore, that an initiative to give more homogeneity to the studies of economics in the region would appear as the central issue of a conference of economic faculties of the region. The event was inaugurated by Dean Rafael Correa of the Universidad de Chile, conference organizer, with a speech in which he stated that:

The individualism of the nineteenth century has given way to [a process by which] the main subject of economic, social, and political activities is not the isolated man, but the collectivity, which, organized or not, gives its character and orientation to the whole of society.[27]

He further underlined the following as being the first fundamental orientation of the proceedings:

The activity of teaching and research in Faculties and Schools [of economics] has to have as its primary objective, in the first place, the study and knowledge of the economics of the countries to which they belong, and secondly, of the peoples who are passing through a similar stage of economic evolution, with a particular emphasis on those of Latin America.[28]

These notions were related to a second basic premise of this approach to economic studies, the premise that one of the main objectives (if not the main purpose) of the training of economists was to provide the state with skilled individuals who could perform the new activities developed by the public sector.

In fact, this had been the fundamental motivation in the organization of the faculty of the Universidad de Chile, where – as Luis Escobar mentioned in his speech to the conference – the increase of state intervention in the economy had produced a lasting impact, "determining changes and reforms of an institutional type [in the university] conducive to endowing those individuals being trained with new characteristics, so that they could respond efficiently to the new predominant conditions."[29]

These general tendencies towards economics as a profession were to appear in their clearest expression in the "projects of agreement," adopted by the different commissions into which the conference was subdivided. The first sub-commission recommended that the faculties, schools, and institutes of economics in Latin America adopt a general principle which would establish that the fundamental goals of their educational activity would be:

The adapting of the well-known instruments and techniques of analysis to the peculiar conditions of our economies and, if possible, the finding of others especially suited to their study and the training of economists not only invested with advanced scientific preparation, but also convinced that their primary duty as professionals consists of their contribution to both the elimination of social injustice and the increase of the general well-being, material and cultural progress, and the economic independence of the societies to which they belong.[30]

The commissions expressed the desire that more consideration be given to teaching, establishing full-time professorships in the basic courses. They particularly hoped that schools of economics at the university level would become "the spiritual centers of the economic and social transformation under way in Latin America." It was finally recommended that the schools and faculties dedicate particular attention to the development of those courses impinging on the question of industrialization in the area.[31]

What remained to be discussed was the proposal made by Prebisch and taken up by the Unión de Universidades Latinoamericanas regarding the creation of a "model school" of economics for the region. The Unión, through some of its directors, had suggested that, "given the excellent conditions of the teaching of economics in the School of Economics of the Universidad de Chile and the fact that such important organizations as ECLA and the Centro de Investigaciones Estadísticas y Financieras and others function in Santiago," the Universidad de Chile should take charge of the study and, if possible, of the direction of this initiative.[32]

The university accepted the proposal and named a commission, which issued a report on the creation of a Latin American School of Economic Sciences, recommending the organization of a postgraduate course   in economics at the Universidad de Chile. The conference of faculties approved the motion almost by unanimous vote, yet the congress of universities ultimately rejected it on the technicality that the Unión de Universidades Latinoamericanas, being merely a coordinating entity with no authority over academic organization, should not have made the initial proposition. The true reasons for the rejection of this motion, however, return us again to the subject of the Universidad Católica.

The Universidad Católica participated in the conference with a delegation, formed by the dean, Rafael Luis Castillo; the director, Lukas Bakovic; and other professors, most of whom were lawyers, including Julio Chaná Cariola, Hugo Hanisch, and Carlos Vial Espantoso. The most important figure in the delegation was, however, Julio Chaná. A successful lawyer with important ties with business organizations and a professor of the School of Law, he had been called in during the period prior to the conference by the rector, Monsignor Alfredo Silva Santiago, who assumed the mission of preventing the approval of the motion establishing the "model school of economics" at the Universidad de Chile.

In fact, the Superior Council of the Universidad Católica had viewed this proposal with great alarm. In the first place, it feared that this initiative would set limitations on the autonomy of its own school of economics, whose weakness was a painful reality for the council. More importantly, it felt that the need to preserve the Catholic perspective of economics, expressed in the social teachings of the church, as recorded in various papal encyclicals, demanded an overt remoteness from a university where freemason, Marxist, and other materialistic orientations predominated.

Chaná's mission was not easy. It was difficult to openly oppose a distinction bestowed upon the most important Chilean university. As he recalls, in order to prevent unanimity he profited from the rivalry of Mexican delegates with regard to the central role offered to the Universidad de Chile. He then organized a "parliamentary operation," which resulted in the rejection of the motion by the congress. Consequently, Rector Silva Santiago requested that he accept the position of dean of the Faculty of Economics and proceed in its reorganization.[33]

Dean Chaná and the Chicago contract

Upon his appointment, Julio Chaná attempted to initiate a modernization of his faculty. As El Mercurio reported on 14 April 1955, under the direct action of the dean, Julio Chaná, Alberto Neumann and Hugo Hanisch, director and secretary of the faculty, new departments of economic research and business organization and administration were established, headed by Ricardo Cox Balmaceda and Domingo Arteaga Infante, respectively. The program of studies was extensive and incorporated courses of pure economics and applied economics, philosophy, sociology, ethics, and business organization and administration, as well as some essential technical matters, such as accounting, pure and applied mathematics, law, and foreign languages. A new group of professionals – lawyers, commercial engineers, civil engineers, educators, and business leaders – were integrated into the faculty, who, through their doctrinal and technical capacities, transmitted the practical experience they had acquired in their private (business) activities. *El Mercurio* affirmed that this new organization had been praised by Chilean and foreign academics and that "the representatives of the organizations of aid and cultural exchange of the United States maintain close contacts with the faculty."[34]

Chaná soon came to the conclusion, however, that with the team he had, he could not produce the "modern" Faculty of Economics that the university desired. He felt he needed foreign professors who could stay for some time, probably years, and could assume the tasks of teaching and helping in the organization of a new curriculum. He then visited European universities in Switzerland and Belgium (Louvain), with whom the university had traditional relations. He received interested responses, offers of short term visiting professors, but not the solution he was seeking.[35]

Back in Santiago, however, he was visited by Patricio Ugarte Hudson, a professor at the faculty who worked as a Chilean counterpart in one of the *servicios* of the Point Four office in Santiago. Ugarte and other professors, such as Washington Cañas, belonged to the first generation of "commercial engineers" of the Universidad Católica and had completed postgraduate courses with scholarships provided by CORFO in different universities in the United States. Ugarte had been at the Massachusetts Institute of Technology (MIT) and had worked at the US Department of Labor; Cañas had done graduate work at Stanford. Upon their return to Chile, these men formed an alumni association with the purpose of assisting in the development of the faculty at the Universidad Católica. Their main activity was to teach courses on an *ad honorem* basis. Ugarte had been recruited by the Point Four program in Santiago, where he was the Director of SCTI (Servicio de Cooperacion Técnico Industrial).[36]

It was through Ugarte that Dean Chaná first encountered the possibility of obtaining support from official US sources for a modernization program of the Faculty of Economics. Ugarte, an ardent defender of the importance of foreign investment in Chilean development, had already discussed with Patterson, the aid director, the idea of supporting the creation of an "institute for the study and promotion of foreign investment" at the Universidad Católica. He tried to convince Chaná to visit Patterson and to initiate the negotiations.

Chaná, who was reluctant, took the matter to the faculty council, where –

as Ugarte reports – the idea met outright rejection from a group of professors, including the most conservative in the faculty, who opposed the promotion of foreign investment as a sell-out of the country and had serious misgivings toward American support of any kind. In a situation where the most conservative groups were profoundly influenced by *hispanismo*, and the most progressive by the social teachings of the Catholic church, the Universidad Católica had no room for the liberal-pragmatic approach which, in their view, characterized American education. European academia, with scholastic overtones, plus the difficult digestion of the new social doctrines of the church, created, particularly at the higher authority levels of the Universidad Católica, an ideological climate where any intellectual influence coming from the United States could only be eyed with suspicion, if not outright antipathy.

But Ugarte did not concede defeat and he, along with other professors, encouraged Chaná to visit Patterson and, at least, discuss the idea with him. Chaná finally accepted and the meeting was a complete success.[37] A series of meetings followed in which the terms of the initiative were thoroughly discussed. The men from the Universidad Católica proposed to Patterson the creation of an "institute for the study and promotion of foreign investment," which would essentially be oriented toward fostering foreign (i.e., American) investment in Chile. This institute would be located at the Faculty of Economics of the Universidad Católica and would give it a "specificity," permitting visits by and participation of American professors and businessmen.

Patterson received the idea with caution. He stated that he was enthusiastic in studying the possibilities of a contract with the Universidad Católica. He did not conceal, however, that, given the low standard of development of economic studies at that faculty, there would be a need to add some other basis of support in order to interest an American university and convince the US government that the project was worth funding. Furthermore, he added that, if there were a contract, it had to be signed with the University of Chicago.

On 6 January 1955, Patterson and some of his aides, including Ugarte, were solemnly received at the Universidad Católica by the rector, the dean of the Faculty of Economics, the dean of the Faculty of Law, and a group of ten professors. Speeches were made in which the plans of the faculty were outlined and Patterson presented his audience with the new facts, showing the role of education in the development of the United States.[38] After the meeting, Monsignor Silva Santiago invited Patterson to spend the weekend at the university "fundo."

In a letter prepared by Ugarte and sent by Dean Chaná to Albion Patterson on 27 January 1955, the Universidad Católica explained the philosophy and the terms of the contract it was seeking to establish through US aid.[39]

We are convinced that national economic development should be realized essentially through the initiative of private capital. We are not, therefore, in favor of planning policies of the country's economic resources which suppose a unique direction, but of a systematic study of our conditions and resources in order to give efficacy to private capital investment.

To get to our objective we are lacking an element which is indispensable: we lack those experts or leaders who can provide the necessary orientation to obtain the maximum promotion of our national economy through the application of private resources.

It is our desire to obtain, through the cooperation of your institute, an agreement between our university and a university from the United States – which according to our information could be the University of Chicago or the Massachusetts Institute of Technology (MIT) – for the joint creation of an institute for the study of the economic resources of Chile and the best way to develop them through the application of private technology and capital.[40]

After indicating the resources the Universidad Católica was prepared to contribute to this task, the letter included a paragraph designed to overcome the fears expressed by Patterson in their previous conversation:

We can add that we have conducted preliminary conversations with most of the directors of agricultural, mining, industrial, and commercial enterprises, the stock exchange, and the banking sector and we have met with a most enthusiastic reaction to this idea. They have expressed to us their desire to collaborate in the most efficient manner possible for them and have already suggested the idea of creating an advisory council with the most representative individuals in each field.

In view of these facts, we respectfully request the institute under your direction to execute an agreement between this university and the University of Chicago or with other university institutions deemed adequate in this respect for the above mentioned purposes. Our wish is that the Institute of Study and Promotion of Investment, which would function in Santiago in connection with our university, through the Faculty of Economic Sciences, be able to utilize the services of a small and select group of North American professors. As indicated in previous conversations, the concrete support we expect from the institute under your direction would include, among others, the financing of the participation of these professors.[41]

Patterson called Schultz to inform him of the success of the operation. Schultz responded that he would organize a delegation and travel to Santiago for a first-hand view of the situation.

At this point, two small problems had to be solved. The first one was the opposition by some members of the Superior Council of the Universidad Católica to Chicago. Monsignor Manuel Larraín, a powerful figure in the Chilean and Latin American church and a leading representative of its most progressive wing, called Chaná to express his concern with regard to this agreement with a university which adhered to "a brand of conservative economics where social justice considerations do not exist." Similar complaints came from other members of the council, like Carlos Vial Espantoso.[42] Chaná transmitted these concerns to Patterson, who placated him, saying that Schultz's leadership of the project constituted a guarantee that those aspects worrying the Universidad Católica would not surface in the development of the project.[43]

The subject of the Catholic disposition of the university also constituted a subject for concern for North American professors. As Professor Gregg Lewis reported, "there was among the faculty people some concern because of the religious character of the institution with which Patterson had made the agreement. They feared that religious doctrine would interfere with the teaching of economics. At the same time, they were surprised to know that most of the Faculty of Economics at the Universidad Católica were not religious people and that most of them were people involved in business."[44] These matters would be clarified during the negotiations in which Chaná would offer assurances that no type of ideological criterion would interfere in the teaching of the science. During these negotiations, the most rigid aspects of the presentation of Chicago economic thought would be restrained by the personality of T. W. Schultz. As Chaná said, "we were fascinated by him."[45]

A second matter referred to the US government's formal participation in the contracts. As Patterson had told the rector and Chaná, the project needed the participation and backing of Chilean personalities who were representative of free market positions in the country. He specifically asked the rector to organize a meeting of twenty individuals, who were on a list provided by Patterson, including the most prestigious graduates in finance and economics of the Universidad Católica, former finance ministers, and leaders from business associations. Some days later, the rector introduced Patterson to a host of personalities, among them Jorge Alessandri, president of the Confederación del Comercio y de la Producción; Walter Muller, president of the Banking Association; Domingo Arteaga, president of the Sociedad Nacional de Agricultura; and Javier Echeverría Alessandri, a lawyer also linked to important business circles. Patterson explained the content of the project, mentioning "the tremendous opportunity to introduce a free market group, highly unlike what you have here now," and explaining "the struggle that it would be, the excitement and the disappointments, but also the great things this program could produce, in a ten-year period, for the future of the country." "You have to back it to the end," he told his audience, who applauded enthusiastically.[46]

Following Patterson's advice, some of these people visited Ambassador

Beaulac, at which time they backed the idea and consequently secured the official approval of the embassy.

On 19 April 1955, the rector of the Universidad Católica officially asked the Chilean Foreign Affairs minister to request the approval of the embassy of the United States for the participation of the Institute of Inter-American Affairs in an agreement with the Universidad Católica for the purpose of "bringing to the country a group of professors from some university of the United States of America in order to establish a center of postgraduate economic studies related to the planning of natural and human resources in Chile."[47] On 26 April 1955, the embassy answered the Chilean ministry petition:

The government of the United States is agreeable to the initiation of such a worthy project and accordingly the Director of the United States' Operation Mission to Chile has been authorized to enter into an agreement in the name of the Institute of Inter-American Affairs with the Catholic University of Chile to initiate such a project in conformance with provisions set forth in the Basic Agreement (for Technical Assistance) of January 16, 1951.[48]

On 27 June the mission headed by Dr. Theodore Schultz, chairman of the Department of Economics of the University of Chicago, arrived in Santiago. It consisted of Professor Earl Hamilton, who had done extensive research on the economic history of Spain; Professor Simon Rottenberg who, as we have seen, had been one of the principal members of the NPA mission headed by Schultz, research director at the University of Puerto Rico, and had spent a good deal of time in Latin American countries; and Professor Arnold Harberger from the University of Chicago. These professors remained in Chile for a week, during which time they carried out detailed discussions about the agreement with the rector of the Universidad Católica, with other people from university administration, and with members of the Faculty of Economics. They also held a series of meetings with members of the "cooperating committee," composed of well-known businessmen and public figures.[49]

In the course of that week the visitors agreed upon the responsibilities that both universities and the Point Four program would have. The latter would supply initially $350,000 to the University of Chicago and would participate in overseeing the organization of the operations.

The professors from Chicago returned to their university where they obtained approval of the terms agreed upon in their department. On 29 and 30 March 1956, the final contracts were signed, whereby a three-year project was established.

CHAPTER 6

The Chile Project and the birth of the Chicago Boys

The Chicago reports

The contract between the University of Chicago, the Universidad Católica de Chile, and the International Cooperation Administration (later known as the Agency for International Development, AID) was originally planned to have a duration of three years, expiring in the spring of 1959. By that date, however, an extension until 1961 was accorded, followed by another with an expiry date of June 1964. As a result, the contracts lasted for a period of approximately eight years, although not all of their component parts had a similar life span.[1] During that period, a group of twenty-six Chilean economists were trained at Chicago. Some of them were hired, upon their return to Chile, as full professors at the Universidad Católica, where, with the guidance of the Chicago professors, they carried out a complete transformation of the Faculty of Economics. In 1964, when the Chilean students gained control of the faculty and succeeded in electing one of their professors as dean, the relationship with the Department of Economics of the University of Chicago or, more specifically, with some of its professors, became a permanent feature of economics and economists at the Universidad Católica.

The period of organization and development of the contracts between the two universities was described in a careful and detailed manner in the reports sent by the Chicago staff to the American government aid program. These reports, a total of fourteen, covering the period between July 1956 and June 1964, are one of the sources which enable us to reconstruct the history of the "Chile Project," as it was aptly called, from its inception up until the moment when the "Chicago Boys" forced the resignation of Dean Julio Chaná. Other documents obtained from the archives of the Ford and Rockefeller Foundations serve to complete the picture of the training of the Chicago Boys.

The Chicago reports are not a mere bureaucratic or academic curiosity. They constitute a remarkable account of a systematic and well-organized process of institutional and ideological transfer, oriented by the concept of the creation of human capital. They are a rigorous example of what was understood to be modernization at that time and demonstrate the ways of and the difficulties encountered in creating an elite in one particular ideological setting and then implanting it into a different one. It is the account of this last process, emerging in different sections and during the various periods covered by the reports, that gives them their ultimate interest. For what they show is the way in which externally induced modernization occurs and formally organized ideologies are transferred: not as unilateral conspiracies, nor as well-woven plots consciously conceived to brainwash and dominate, as some simplistic descriptions of dependency would seem to imply, nor as inevitable, unintentional, neutral processes of acculturation, as the seminal literature on modernization and change intended.[2] What the reports show is a purposeful, deliberate, concerted action adopted by carefully selected actors who had at their disposal the means, the influence, and specialization required to implement it. Even if they were to describe in a very favorable light an operation which has, as other documents show, a series of shortcomings and internal conflicts which are not mentioned in these reports, the Chicago papers adequately portray an organized effort to infuse systematic knowledge, induce attitudes related to that knowledge, and promote particular types of behavior in a group which, installed in a pre-arranged setting, would be able to change not just some beliefs prevailing in their most immediate environment – the professional circles – but also the ideas and decisions that organize that particular society. The hypothesis was twofold: first, that these scientific and professional orientations would necessarily put into obsolescence certain ideas prevailing in that society, which were seen as prejudices resulting from ignorance or "ideology"; second, that the mere displacement of these ideas and the application of the scientific principles and methods being introduced into the sphere of policy decisions alone would foster development.

Before entering into the content of the reports themselves, it would be useful to develop some of these points. But, first, we should make it clear that the reports were written for the consideration of the American government. Their objective was, therefore, to impress upon the authorities of the governmental development agency the need to continue support for the project. The reports tend, as a result, to avoid descriptions of mistakes, conflicts, or outside criticisms of their endeavor. With the exception of the description of the conflict with Julio Chaná, the reports follow an idyllic tendency, particularly with respect to the relationship between the American professors and their perspectives of the project. Other papers obtained from the Rockefeller archives show that this was not a true picture and that some strong criticisms toward the project emerged from within the ranks of the visiting professors. Most of these discussions refer to the development of the project in Santiago *after* the return of the students from Chicago. We shall refer to them in the next chapter. It should be pointed out at the same time that the reports show in a very open way the planning and development of an enterprise that its organizers thought to be perfectly honest, correct, and desirable.

Yet, the reports also show that this was not an exclusively academic operation, designed, as Albion Patterson, its godfather, insistently argued, "to right the balance of university economics in Chile," to introduce pluralism into the profession. While the academic elements were central to the Chile Project and the academic role that the Chilean students of Chicago would perform upon their return to Santiago was the most salient purpose of the endeavor, the project was based on an underlying hypothesis full of political and ideological meaning: the economic difficulties of Chile are due basically to bad economic decisions. In other words, if Chile remained under-developed, it was because its economics and its economists were bad, they ignored the core principles of economics and did not follow the right standards of professionalism. These economists were influential, nonetheless, and their decisions had produced that enormous amount of government control which prevented market mechanisms from functioning and, therefore, development from unfolding. Consequently, the Chile Project could not define its sole objective as being the creation of a well-trained group of university professors and academic researchers, but the breeding of a particular type of economist, endowed with a mission: to do research that would serve and influence the "dynamic" and "modern" sectors of Chilean society, what the reports call "the Chilean community," and, guided by "the core principles of economics," to make decisions that would shift Chile away from the wrong course it was following.

This was, of course, in the best Chicago tradition and was primarily the reason that the University of Chicago had been the only choice offered by ICA to the Chilean universities. The Chileans trained there would be given not only a solid curriculum and rigorous instruction, but also a sense of mission, the mission of the economist who, as the new philosopher, transmits science and modernism to society, teaches the layman to defend his freedom and multiply his options, and offers the politician the privilege of being guided by science in the adoption of his decisions on economic matters and of being able to rationalize his general vision of society. The reports indicate the conditions that the economists being trained would have to fulfill in order to perform that role. They refer, in the first place, to the exacting training in the core principles, and to the ways in which research would apply the abstract models to Chilean economic reality, but they also expand upon the characteristics the economist would have to acquire in order to sustain his objective and scientific posture. These principles of "professionalism" are not, as exposed in the reports, simply rules for objective research. They demand from the economist a rejection of politics and of party membership; they proclaim the need for independence from any "vested interest"; they reflect, in particular, a deliberate remoteness that the experiment maintains and strives to maintain from certain characteristics of Chilean society which, as we shall discuss later in more detail, were central to its political culture. We refer, specifically, to the way in which elites related politics and economics during public discussion and public decision-making. These characteristics are presented as obstacles to the project, to the application of scientific methods to economic decisions, and thus to development. And, as no possible accommodation with these characteristics and with the people and the institutions that represented them was seen as being possible, the reports show a gradual process of introspection in the experiment, which ends with a note of preoccupation with regard to the isolation experienced by the Chicago Boys in the local academic and economic environment.

The reports also show that a related purpose of the project, no less important than the one already described, was to treat Chile as a "laboratory" for the study and research of certain topics which were material both to the Chicago professors and to the developing world. The project itself was an experiment in human capital creation, the subject on which T. W. Schultz and Gary Becker were working. But Chile was also a country with a serious and peculiar problem of inflation, which was another area into which the monetarist approaches developed by Friedman and others could be put into practice. Questions like agricultural development and social security, which could be well explored in Chile, were also themes of interest for the Chicago faculty. These were, obviously, also important subjects for Chilean development. Thus, as is commonly seen in academic ventures conducted overseas, individual research topics and important national problems tended to coincide.

Last, but not least, the content of the reports is important in the sense of what is omitted. A first aspect refers to the perception they reflect of Chilean society and their understanding of it. As was typical of neo-classical economists in the early 1960s, the role of history in determining development possibilities was completely ignored. There is not a single mention of social problems or culture lags intervening in the research topics being selected, and conflict in Chilean society is seen as non-existent. It is assumed that the introduction of scientific economics and its application to policy-making will impel a process of modernization and development in the interests of all groups in society. There is, therefore, a presupposition of a normative consensus of individual and societal goals.[3]

But there was another subject of a totally different nature that the reports imply, both by reference and by omission. This was the attitude of the recipient, the Universidad Católica and, therefore, the type of relationship established among the different actors in the project. As has been accurately pointed out, there is, in some studies on educational transfer, an assumption of passivity on the part of the recipient – "their participation in decision making processes is regarded as minimal, given their enthusiasm for institutional innovation in their academic systems."[4] What the reports seem to show is that, in this case, Universidad Católica authorities were active only with respect to the protection given to the project from outside attacks and criticisms, and in response to administrative requirements or financial initiatives suggested by the Chicago staff. They seem to have been passive, however, in every other aspect referring to the actual content of the project, as well as in all important decisions regarding organization. This conclusion stems, however, not from any explicit statement in the reports, but precisely from the absence of any mention of initiatives or proposals coming from the Universidad Católica in this regard. What the reports repeatedly state is the gratitude of the Chicago staff towards the authorities of the Universidad Católica, who maintained their enthusiasm for the project and permitted the American professors to do their job in absolute freedom.

Finally, the reports overlook the fact that the prevailing economic ideas in Chile constituted a school of thought that had become dominant throughout the region and had as its most relevant expression the work of the Economic Commission on Latin America. Criticisms of their viewpoints, when mentioned in the reports, are considered to be the result of "group interests," deficient economic formation, or simple ignorance. The fact that there was a conflict of views, which later achieved public notoriety as polemics between structuralists and monetarists, is not recognized by the documents. Yet, as we shall see, the conflictive character of the experiment being developed by the Chicago staff surfaces in many ways during the period documented in the reports.

One final introductory observation: these documents are also striking as an expression of a gradual process of learning about a country and of a commitment to a cause by a group of American professors. Prepared by Professor Gregg Lewis, who was the project coordinator for the entire period covered by the contracts, the papers give evidence of the initial inhibitions that certain traits of Chilean society generated within the group of Americans organizing the Research Center in Santiago, as well as of a cautious and exploratory attitude *vis-à-vis* the role they should perform as modernizers. However, as the project developed, naiveté and caution gave way to an increasingly decided and protagonistic conception of their role, along with a remarkable degree of professional devotion and emotional involvement with the project and the students participating in it.

We shall come back to the discussion of most of these subjects at the end of this chapter. At that point, we plan to approach the most important question raised by the examination of the Chicago reports: to what extent can the behavior and the ideas of the economists who conducted the economic policy of Chile during the Pinochet regime be attributed to their training at Chicago?

Let us now address the reports themselves. We have organized the discussion of them in relation to three topics which, although not structured in the same way in the papers themselves, facilitate the analysis of the operation they describe. Two of the topics are merely descriptive: the organization of the project and the development and organization of the instruction. The third is mainly analytical and initiates the discussion along the lines of the problem of the transmission of the normative science giving shape to the Chicago tradition the configuration of the professional attitudes of the Chilean Chicago Boys. These three points form the principal elements of the documents and are present, explicitly or implicitly, in the definition of the purposes of the Chile Project.

The first and most explicit definition of the Chile Project is included in the third report. It states that:

From the beginning, the University of Chicago has viewed the central purpose of the project as that of training a core of Chileans to a high level of professional competence as economists who would devote their careers to fulltime teaching and research in economics and who would become the intellectual leaders in economic affairs in Chile. The achievement of this goal involves several ingredients: (1) the discovery of native Chileans with high promise as economists; (2) the training of those Chileans both in Santiago and in Chicago; (3) the demonstration to these trainees and to others in Chile of high standards of research and teaching; (4) the establishment at the Catholic University of Chile of an organization in which trained Chilean economists may devote their full time to teaching and research, and (5) the financing of this organization by the Chilean community on a permanent basis.[5]

These are, simply summarized, the methodological elements conforming the process of institutional and ideological transfer. These purposes required an important organizational effort. We shall now turn our attention to that effort.

Organization of the "Chile Project"

The strategy of organizing institutions and particularly educational institutions abroad designed by American missionaries in China, Japan, and the Near East since the nineteenth century, has exerted, as Frank Bowles has argued, an indelible influence on American university thinking about foreign students until the present time. The formula was quite simple: "the institutions that were formed were American, built with American money, staffed with American teachers, using American programs, methods, and standards. Only the students were foreign, and the best of these were selected for further training in the United States."[6] This was exactly the concept applied by the University of Chicago to the Chile Project.

There was a difference, however, for the institution created – the Research Center – would be Chilean, if not in the sense of its activities – economic science needs no nationality – then due to the fact that it was located at a Chilean university. This presented the advantage of having to deal with an academic institution as a counterpart and not with a government, as was usual in other contracts of this sort. This factor allowed Chicago to exert an influence on its counterpart, wherein national differences appeared to be an asset more than a hindrance. In fact, Chicago enjoyed complete freedom in the execution of the project and could pay careful attention to the selection and training of the people. T. W. Schultz was quite aware of this advantage. In a summary of an interview with Schultz, Montague Yudelman of the Rockefeller Foundation stated that "the Catholic University is worthy of support, as he [Schultz] is quite positive in his view that the best research into problems of this kind could be done only at institutions which have no link with the government. In Chile, the Catholic University would be free from pressure in studying these delicate problems, while the National University would be subject to quite a degree of control because of its government sponsorship."[7]

It was common at the same time that many universities entering these types of contracts left their regular staff and organization untouched, sending to their overseas operations persons recruited strictly for this purpose.[8] As we shall see later some of the professors Chicago committed to the project were criticized as inadequate or uninterested. In this case, however, the difference was made by some project members, more specifically by Arnold Harberger, who became a very decisive factor in the success of the experience.

What seems to be important about the organization of the project is, therefore, that it was based on three "principles": Chicago had complete freedom and power to make decisions about the execution of the project and the naming of the staff; it could select carefully the students to be trained without real external intervention; and, finally, it would propose the formulas for financing, which would be executed in conjunction with or by the Universidad Católica on its own. We shall turn now to each of these aspects.

Appointment of staff

While planning for the project began in Chicago before the contracts were even signed, the first report indicates that the three months that followed the agreements were devoted to the selection and appointment of staff both in Santiago and in Chicago.[9] Planning of the research enterprises and the training process to be conducted under the project were also developed during that period. Chicago appointed three faculty members for a two-year stint in Chile. These were senior economist Simon Rottenberg, who was named representative of the University of Chicago and who was responsible, along with the dean of the Universidad Católica, Julio Chaná, for the general supervision of the project; agricultural economist James O. Bray; and professor Tom E. Davis. Rottenberg came to Santiago in May 1956 and the other two in August and November of that year.

Two other professors were sent to Chile for a shorter period of time – Martin Bailey, who came for ten months, and Arnold Harberger, who stayed for only thirty days at the outset of the project. With time, Harberger would become the most decisive figure in the project and in the constitution of the group of Chilean economists. Harberger and Bailey had, as their main function, however, the coordination of their work, with the research conducted by the "home staff" at Chicago.

The report indicates that at Chicago the Department of Economics gave top priority to the project.[10] Professor Gregg Lewis was designated project coordinator, "responsible for coordination and directing the University of Chicago support to the staff in Chile and for research and training programs at the University of Chicago." John Deaver and Siegfried Marks were named assistants to Lewis, while Professor Bert Hoselitz, director of the Research Center in Economic Development and Cultural Exchange, was asked to be a consultant.[11] Professor Theodore Schultz, as the highest authority in the department, performed a role of general supervision and, as we shall see, had active participation in the training aspects of the program.

Research and training were organized in the Research Group in Economic Development in the Department of Economics. This was one of several "workshops" in the department and received partial financing from the Ford Foundation.[12] The project was located in the Social Science Building at the University of Chicago.

The Universidad Católica, for its part, appointed two research assistants and a secretary for the project. They were Ernesto Fontaine, a fifth-year student, Pedro Jeftanovic, a graduate, and Juana Subercaseaux, a secretary. According to the first report, Rottenberg and Chaná discussed at length the organization of the project with faculty members and students at the Universidad Católica. They also established an advisory committee. This committee, which had been provided by the agreement, included Chaná, Rottenberg, and two other representatives from each university, Professor Joseph Grunwald, Director of the Institute of Economics at the Universidad de Chile, Dr. José Mayobre, a member of the Economic Commission for Latin America, and Professor D. Brownlee of the staff of the Institute of Inter-

American Affairs. The advisory committee had its first and, as far as the
reports show, its only meeting on 4 July 1956.

The establishment of this committee seems to show an initial openness *vis-à-vis* other academic or international institutions in Santiago which adhered to a
different vision of economics and the teaching of the discipline. Yet the
initiative appears to have been more a diplomatic move than a real attempt to
create a permanent advisory group. Dr. Grunwald recalls that, in his first
meeting with Professor Schultz, he referred to the opportunities for cooperation between the Universidad de Chile and the Universidad Católica, opened
up by the agreement with Chicago, to which Dr. Schultz replied: "we came
here to compete, not to collaborate."[13]

As later reports show, the staffing of the project continued almost intact
during its first phase, ending in 1959. There were obviously some changes in
personnel at the research assistant level, but the main figures from Chicago
remained the same. In September 1957, Mario Ballesteros, an economics
instructor at Chicago, was sent to Santiago to participate in the training of the
research assistants attached to the Economic Research Center. In the same
period, and with the assistance of a grant from the Rockefeller Foundation,
the Universidad Católica added several other assistants to those already in the
project.

Besides these assistants and Dean Chaná, who held a formal, but
nonetheless important, role as the local authority participating in the
decision-making of the project, the reports do not mention the names of
any other Chileans at the professorship level participating in consultations
or in any other capacity in the project's organization and development.
However, relations between the institutions remained excellent. The first
report describes the Universidad Católica authorities as "extremely
cooperative," adding that "the enthusiasm of the university for the project
which the representatives of the University of Chicago found in their
exploratory visit in the summer of 1955 is unabated." The fourth report,
dated February 1958, confirms that "the [Catholic] University's general
administration and its Faculty of Economics have been remarkably flexible
and the Chicago group has encountered no vested interests which have
impeded its work."

In the spring of 1957, after a trip by Dean Julio Chaná to Chicago, in
which he also visited other American universities, the Universidad Católica
requested from ICA an extension of the arrangement with Chicago. In
August, Professor Schultz, acting as chairman of the Department of
Economics, made an inspection visit of the project in Santiago. The
authorities at the Universidad Católica "gave him firm assurance of their
determination to make the work in economics developed under the contract
an integral and major part of its educational program." Upon his return to

Chicago, Schultz's report was discussed by the department faculty, which agreed upon an extension of the contract until 1961.[14]

During the period from 1959 to 1961, and then again until 1964, a transition process began in the project's organization. Most of the roles assumed initially by the Chicago professors were transferred, as planned, to the Chilean students returning from their Chicago training. A schedule of shorter visits and residence periods in Santiago by the Chicago staff then became the rule. Eventually, Professors Reuben Kessel, Zvi Griliches, H. G. Lewis, Larry Sjaastad, Mary Jean Bowman, and, of course, Arnold Harberger spent some time in Santiago. After 1961 the reports show a routinization in the relationship between the two universities. Organizational matters are seldom mentioned and the participation of the Chicago professors in decisions both at the Center of Economic Research and at the Faculty of Economics of the Universidad Católica seems to have been a normal and fully accepted activity. This would become a more sensitive question, however, during the critical period prior to the resignation of Julio Chaná as Dean of the Faculty, a matter we shall discuss further on. Let us now turn to the organization of training.

Selection of students

Between September and December 1956, the first three "promising young Chileans" left for Chicago to study for a minimal period of one year. They were Sergio de Castro, a fifth-year student in economics at the Universidad Católica, Carlos Massad, assistant to the director of the Institute of Economics at the Universidad de Chile, and Ernesto Fontaine, who had already been appointed research assistant in the Economics Research Center at the Universidad Católica. This initial group was later joined by two other students: Luis Arturo Fuenzalida and Pedro Jeftanovic and, by January 1958, three others had been added to the initial list: Raul Yver, Mario Albornoz, and Alberto Valdés. The number increased to twenty-six students in 1961.[15] What was the methodology used in the selection of these people?

According to the contract, the students had to be selected jointly by the dean of the Faculty of Economics of the Universidad Católica and by the Chicago staff. Candidates were obtained from graduates of the Economics and Agronomy Faculties of the Universidad Católica and the Institute of Economics of the Universidad de Chile. In the majority of the cases, there seems to have been no process of submitting applications, but rather specific individuals were invited to participate.

The reports indicate that "the primary criteria for choosing among candidates are capacity for rational intelligence, quality of prior training in economics, and command of English."[16] In the light of certain previous experiences with Latin American students, the Chicago staff had concluded that "in certain respects training in economics in Latin American countries prepares students inadequately for the rigorous instruction in economics at the University of Chicago."[17] It was recommended, therefore, that selection be based on a "special detailed interview." At the beginning of the project, this interview was conducted exclusively by the Chicago professors. Later, upon their return from their training at Chicago, the first Chilean students also participated in the process. Dean Chaná was rarely present at these interviews, although he suggested names and was in a position to influence the final decision in favor of or against a particular student.[18]

Initially, the pattern of selection seems to have been less structured than later in the project. As there were not enough candidates from the Universidad Católica to fill the number of trainee positions established in the agreement for the first year, an invitation was extended to some students from the Universidad de Chile. Accordingly, the first two graduates selected from the university, Carlos Massad and Luis Arturo Fuenzalida, had to pass a written and an oral examination along with the interview.[19]

The interview centered exclusively on knowledge of economics and price theory. Price theory was added after the return of the first trainees and the course (taught by Ernesto Fontaine) was introduced into the faculty's curriculum. No ideological or social criteria were apparent in the selection of candidates.

There was, however, one element which became an important, if not the most determinant factor involved in the selection of candidates, which allowed the Chicago professors to evaluate the intellectual, vocational, and personal characteristics and attitudes of each student considered for training at Chicago in a more thorough manner than could be established by a mere interview. As the reports indicate, evaluation was done "by selecting talented students in their fifth and final year . . . and observing them while they work with the Chicago staff as research assistants."[20] This meant, in Arnold Harberger's more abrasive language, "picking the best students for fellowships by 'living with them.' "[21] The fact that nearly two-thirds of all those selected were engaged, at some time, as assistants in research projects conducted by the Chicago professors or by returning Chicago trainees, constituted both a strong socializing element in Chicago economics and a good criterion for judgment for those making the decisions with regard to the adequacy of the candidates. Research assistants were normally trained before their departure for Chicago by the staff of the project and were subjected, therefore, to special treatment in the faculty. As the second report indicates: "some Chilean students, who were appointed as research assistants, were given classes by the Chicago staff and were exempted from normal requirements [at the Catholic University]."

There was another factor included in the selection process, which reinforced the tendency to form a "privileged circle" among the "chosen few." It had important consequences in reproducing the characteristics that would distinguish the "Chicago Boys" in future generations and, therefore, in reproducing the group itself. This evolved into a procedure whereby trainees at the University of Chicago would recommend new candidates.[22] This practice allowed sectarian criteria to develop at a later date, when only Chileans were involved in the selection process; those who were seen as academically fit to attend the University of Chicago tended always to coincide with those who had similar ideological tendencies with the Universidad Católica professors who selected them.

Hence, the selection process had the advantage of guaranteeing the intellectual capacity of candidates, while tending to reinforce, simultaneously, the ideological homogeneity of the group, which was in itself conditioned – as has been mentioned elsewhere – by the social characteristics of the Universidad Católica. The tendency towards ideological homogeneity with time became the rule without exception due to the fact that non-conservative students at the Faculty of Economics of the Universidad Católica were inclined to seek other alternatives for postgraduate training and had no interest in an option which they identified with the most conservative professors in their faculty.[23]

Financing the project

The considerations made in the reports about the financing of the project indicate that the Chicago professors gave high priority to the long term financing perspectives of the initiative, which were expected to emanate basically from backing by "the Chilean community."

This is an important point because it conditioned some of the strategies followed in the organization of the project, particularly with respect to the impact that it should have had from the outset in certain sectors of Chilean society. The reports make clear that the project had no reason to be concerned about its immediate financial future. The initial sum provided by ICA amounted to $375,000 dollars. In 1964, the AID contributions equalled $812,300, and from 1956 on the project was receiving contributions from other sources, the primary source being a Rockefeller Foundation grant of $19,000, dedicated mainly to the research projects conducted in Santiago by the Chicago staff.[24] Yet the reports insist on the requirement that the project be organized in such a way as to establish links with potential local contributors. In fact, the idea is included in the definition of the project itself. The first report states the goal of the project is "to put into business in Chile at the Catholic University an Economics Research Center, with a full-time staff of trained economists, that will serve the Chilean community so well with high quality economic research that the community will provide the support to continue the Center as a permanent part of the University."[25] The third report further adds that, while the selection of students, their training, and the demonstration of high standards of teaching and research are largely the responsibility of the University of Chicago, the future financing of the project is mainly a responsibility of the Chilean community and, most particularly, of the Universidad Católica: "we view it as vital to the ultimate success of the joint undertaking of the two universities." "The University of Chicago is pleased," the report says, "to have information through Rottenberg that the Catholic University has started a fundraising campaign on behalf of the Economic Research Center and the Faculty of Economic Sciences at the university."[26]

As a decision designed to help in this direction, the Chicago staff initiated a "series on popular economic education," that would hopefully make the Center known to the general public. These publications, described as "simply written," brief popular bulletins in economics, would have a distribution of 5,000 to 10,000 copies to the Chilean community with the dual objective of "disseminating rather widely elementary principles of economics and of making the existence of the Center known."[27] The second report goes on to say: "The Chicago staff is preparing one on money and inflation; the working of the monetary mechanisms; the interest rate as an instrument of monetary policy, and an empirical paper on the magnitude and the incidence of the inflation tax in Chile."[28] The production of these papers was the "subject of most discussion both in Chicago and in Chile." James O. Bray, who succeeded Rottenberg as project director, thought that they did more harm than good. The idea was dropped after the first three pamphlets had been issued.[29]

The idea to produce them was important, however, because it showed once more the broader and more ambitious intentions of the project and, more than that, because it was the initial effort to make the Research Center and the Chilean economists who were employed there "an organic intellectual elite" of the local entrepreneurial class.[30] Given the linkages established during the 1960s between most of these economists and the Chilean economic groups, in particular the Agustin Edwards group, this idea, promoted from the beginning by Albion Patterson and the Chicago professors, seems to have been one of the most significant elements of the "Chile Project." It began, as we have already mentioned, with the invitation, extended by Dean Julio Chaná, of twenty-six leaders of entrepreneurial organizations, at the time of the signing of the contracts, to participate in an advisory committee which, in fact, did not function.

In 1956, by the time the Chicago staff were organizing the project, Dean

Chaná and Washington Cañas, an alumnus of the Faculty of Economics of the Universidad Católica, founded the Fundación Facultad de Ciencias Económicas de la Universidad Católica de Chile, which revitalized the alumni organization of the faculty, which had been in existence since the 1940s, with the intention of promoting fundraising activities for the Center and the faculty.[31] The initiative, duly celebrated, as we have seen in the reports, did not appear in the beginning to have much success. In 1959, the seventh report expresses alarm at the fact that "the Chilean community does not [seem to] appreciate the full potential value it can derive from the discovery of new knowledge about its economy," adding that "the next two years will be the critical ones." After publications had been made, it remained to be seen if the Chilean community would react or not, "and will be persuaded to give long run support to the research efforts of the young Chilean economists in the Economics Research Center."[32]

"Reaction" began to be manifested in 1965, when Sergio de Castro, the new dean of the faculty, invited Carlos Urenda, one of the leading members of the Agustín Edwards group, to conduct a fundraising effort oriented toward acquiring a new building for the faculty. Whatever the success of this effort, the Universidad Católica, like all other Chilean universities, continued to depend on state support, a characteristic maintained even during the reign of the Chicago Boys over the Chilean economy. The idea of financing universities through business contributions simply did not work in Chile. But we shall discuss these events in more detail in the following chapters. Let us turn now to the training process and its organization in Chicago and in Santiago.

Training of Chileans in Chicago and in Santiago

The most outstanding aspects of the organization and development of training at Chicago were the extraordinary attention devoted to the students by the Chicago faculty, the emphasis placed on the "core principles of economics" in the program of study, and the excellent academic performance of the Chilean students. These three aspects would have an enormous influence on the lasting effects of the project on the group of economists trained and at the Universidad Católica. Let us review them briefly.

The dedication of the Chicago staff to the preparation of the students selected for training both before and after their arrival at Chicago was indeed noteworthy. The second report explains that:

It was expected that the participants would differ . . . in their command of English, in their preparation in economics, and in their intellectual power and that, therefore, the participants could not follow a single plan of course instruction. Accordingly, the staff in Chile was asked to give the participants an "orientation" to the University of

Chicago graduate program . . . before their departure from Chile. Each participant . . . was given counsel on a suitable program for his first academic quarter . . . his counsel was reviewed by the Project Coordinator upon the arrival of the participants and a tentative program laid out . . . the participants reviewed at frequent intervals their progress in their courses . . . with Professor Lewis and where mistakes were discovered, course programs were amended. In addition, members of the home staff quite frequently were called upon to give individual tutoring to the participants.[33]

Chileans were given special attention by the staff beyond that normally accorded the other economics students. They were provided with desk space; in short, they were "more closely guided and counseled than other students."[34] As we shall see later, this close attention would not merely have academic results, it would become, in fact, one of the factors behind the close personal relations established between some professors and students, which later would allow a permanent exchange between the Department of Economics of Chicago and the Faculty of Economics of the Universidad Católica.

On the basis of this feature of the project, the Chicago staff decided, in 1957, to change the original policy of a one-year training period. The third report states: "we have found that almost without exception the trainees, though clearly men of substantial promise, have had insufficient training in Chile, including the period of training there with our staff, to reach high levels of competence with only one year of training at Chicago." Indeed, the report adds, even two years will not suffice in order to gain research experience. "We have, therefore, decided that, in general, the training period will be at least two years long."[35]

Training at the Universidad Católica had been particularly weak in matters that were central to any modern perspective of economics, but which were especially crucial to the Chicago standpoint: price theory, national analysis, and the "core principles." Therefore, the program of instruction had to place a "very heavy emphasis" – the report says – "upon achieving a really solid command of the basic principles of economics; price theory and resource allocation and monetary theory." Some of the participants would also be given training in statistical inference, because of the importance of this tool to economic research.

Preference for this program did not stem from a work plan that would lead the participants to an advanced degree. The goal was "solely that of giving [the students] the best training we can in terms of their ultimate usefulness to the Chilean economy."[36] The ninth report reiterates this idea, stating that:

the experience of the Department of Economics has demonstrated that students who come from relatively low income countries, and who are expected to return there to teach, or engage in scholarly research, or advise on policy for economic growth, or to serve in some other capacity requiring the use of economics, need to be trained to command the core of economics. This means they must have a firm understanding of microeconomics – or price theory – and of theory of income and employment. They must also have some considerable proficiency in the handling of tool subjects, such as mathematics and statistics.[37]

The report added flatly: "the Department believes that students who master these fields will communicate correct knowledge and make correct decisions, when they return, and that those who do not master them will teach wrong things and make wrong decisions."[38] Specialization, therefore, could only be achieved after the course on core principles had been mastered. If a student went directly into content fields like agricultural economics, international trade, or economic growth without first "having achieved a mastery of the tools and the core of economics," he would be "badly trained, will give bad advice, and will produce shoddy research."[39]

After the first tentative experiences in "mapping out" a study program tailored to each student's needs were accomplished, the typical course program imparted to Chileans was, as could be expected, very similar, if not identical, to the normal graduate course in the department:

FIRST YEAR

First quarter
Intermediate economic theory
Mathematics for economists
Monetary theory

Second quarter
Price theory
Theory of income and employment
Introduction to statistical inference

Third quarter
Price theory
History of economic thought

Monetary and fiscal policy

Fourth quarter
Statistical inference
Field examination or research paper

SECOND YEAR

First, second and third quarters
Three courses in statistical inference
Three courses in a problem field (agricultural economics, labor economics, international economics, public finance, etc.)
Three courses in a second problem field or the undertaking of a research project in one of the research workshops.

Fourth quarter
Field examinations
Completion of a research paper for MA degree.[40]

The reports emphasize that instruction was not only delivered in classrooms, formal courses, or informal meetings with advisors. A similiar emphasis was devoted to a series of workshops.[41] As in the course program, insistence on the core principles of economics was also the hallmark of the workshops. They were perhaps the most characteristic organization of the Chicago Department of Economics. Rather than simple student discussion groups, the workshops were places where – as Reder says – faculty members of all ranks and visitors discussed their work with students, where "issues on current research are debated by leaders of the field immediately concerned and of adjacent fields as well."[42] As in the course program, workshops were also directed to the inculcation of principles, but now not as mere theoretical notions, but as tools to be employed for the understanding of concrete realities. The purpose of the workshops, therefore, was, as described in the reports, "to drive home by repeated application to the experience of Chile, the fundamental principles of economics and to create an attitude towards economics as a highly useful problem solving discipline rather than as a set of articles of faith to be memorized."[43]

The "Chile Workshop" was organized as soon as the first group of students came to Chicago. Aside from the home staff and the Chilean students, Latin American graduates and other advanced students in the department, plus some postdoctoral fellows, participated regularly. More importantly, Professors T. W. Schultz, Arnold Harberger, and Clifford Hardin were permanent members. After some time, Chilean students were offered the opportunity to chair the meetings, and the workshops grew to incorporate Chilean students in other economics departments in the United States.[44]

One of the main workshop activities was to discuss the research being done by the Chicago staff and their assistants in Santiago. This was indeed an essential part of the participation of the Chileans in the project. It developed their critical capacity, exposed them to research practice and methodology, and oriented them in the perception of the principal problems of Chile.

The third report contains a thorough and explicit definition of the purposes of research in the Chile Project, which deserves to be quoted extensively:

The research undertaken by our staff in Chile and in Chicago is directly related to the central purpose of the Chile Project in two ways and related to somewhat broader purposes of the Point IV program in still another way. There is, first of all, a "demonstration effect"; the showing to the Chilean trainees, to the Catholic University and, indeed, to the larger Chilean community in general that economic research can be conducted in a rational – that is scientific – manner, and that when it is so conducted, it can lead to a high payoff in terms of understanding, and thus solving, basic social economic problems. Secondly, the research projects undertaken by our staff provide an opportunity to draw the Chilean trainees as research apprentices, giving them actual research experience under the close supervision of experienced research workers.

Our purposes in research, however, are not entirely pedagogic. The research projects which our staff have undertaken have substantial relevance, we believe, to Chilean economic affairs and we hope our research findings will contribute to the solution of Chile's basic economic problems.[45]

An even broader purpose was finally mentioned: Chile may be viewed "as a laboratory" in the study of problems of the economic development of the less developed parts of the world.[46]

The main areas of research had been stated both in the agreement and the contract. They included the problems of inflation, of improving the rate of agricultural development and the use of existing resources, and of expanding these resources through domestic and foreign investment.[47] The first research projects outlined in Santiago and in Chicago were thus on: (a) inflation and the demand for and supply of money; (b) inflation and resource use; (c) multiple exchange rates, trade controls, and the external trading position of Chile; (d) the Chilean security system; and (e) problems of agricultural development, inflation, trade, and agriculture.[48]

These research projects and those which followed later involved an increasing number of Chilean students in their development, first as research assistants and candidates for training in Chicago, then, upon their return, as researchers at the Research Center at the Universidad Católica.

These were then, in essential terms, the main elements of the training of Chileans at Chicago and in Santiago. Now, what were the academic results? In fact, they turned out to be excellent. In 1960, of a total of nineteen Chilean students, only three had not done sufficiently well in their first year to be able to continue on for the second year of study. The reports show that the average performance of the Chilean students had been substantially better than that of other "self-selected" foreign students enrolled in the Department of Economics, and only somewhat less than that of US students.[49]

Some of the Chilean students had records that were much better than those of US students, and they received a good deal of praise in the reports. Carlos Massad, the second report says, "has a performance record to date on a par with the very best students in our Department. Massad's capacity obviously is superior."[50] Another report indicates that the performance level of de Castro, Fontaine, and Fuenzalida had been "a pleasant surprise to the Faculty at Chicago."[51]

On the basis of this successful performance, some of the students were kept at Chicago for a third year of training[52] and were encouraged to pursue academic degrees at the Department of Economics, an objective which was not necessarily contemplated in the project at its inception. Another factor in this decision was the consideration that the earning of an advanced degree is viewed in Chile as a mark of such great prestige that, without the degree, the participants would command less respect than was due them.[53]

The good performance of the initial group of Chilean participants in the project was repeated by the following generations and Chileans in Chicago became known as good and serious students. The reports characteristically saw these results as "demonstrating clearly that our assumption regarding the availability of local talent was well founded." The project would produce, as expected, "a reservoir of skills which the Chilean community will be able to draw upon for many years to come," "a human capital asset that is uncommon in the world's low income countries," whose yields "can be expected to be very high."[54] This optimistic prediction would be disputed later by some of the Chicago professors who were in Santiago at the time the students came back to teach at the Universidad Católica. We shall refer to that point in the next chapter.

Let us turn now to the elements of professionalization that were transmitted through the Chile Project. By that we mean the attitudes and practices which had to be adopted by the students as a constitutive element of the role of the economist or, more precisely, of the "new economist" role they were expected to perform in Chile. It should be remarked from the outset of this discussion that the point leads us necessarily to an analysis of the transmission of those characteristics which we have described in an earlier chapter as the Chicago tradition. It was exactly this tradition that was perceived as the decisive element defining professional behavior by those orienting the Chilean students. Yet what interests us here is not the model of the economist à la Friedman, Simons, or Knight, but the more specific aspects which were imprinted upon the Chileans, the way in which the students received the message, and particularly the way in which they related it to their role as "new economists," practitioners of a "new profession," or at least of a newly defined profession in their own country.

Transmission of professional values

In the preceding pages, we have merely described, in a relatively detailed manner, two formal processes: the organization of the process of institutional transfer and the central program orientations guiding the instruction of the project's participants. What we will attempt to show now is that these formal elements of organization and instruction pointed to the reproduction of an ideological pattern identifying adherence to the beliefs and methodological approaches of the Chicago School of Economics. This pattern, impressed upon the Chile Project, stemmed from the notion of science and of scientific validation, which was basic to the study program. The latter was not the only source of professional notions, however. There were other norms, explicitly mentioned in the reports, which referred to the "external" attitudes – those orientations which should be maintained towards society and politics as rules of scientific objectivity. The reports, moreover, contain certain ideas about Chilean economic problems, Chilean economists, and the "mission" expected of the Chilean trainees, which are important in comprehending the general framework within which professionalization came to be understood in the project.

Let us turn first to the course program and its utilization in the transmission of the "normative science" tradition of the Chicago School.

The course program

As we have seen, the course program selected and emphasized certain subjects that were considered to be "core principles": price theory and monetary theory, which were taught to the students as being the rigorous and systematic framework from which all economic analyses should start. Knowledge of these principles and their application to concrete situations constituted the specific difference distinguishing the professional economist from any other professional (and, in fact, from any other human being), as well as distinguishing professional economic activity from any other specialized activity. Moreover, their knowledge and their use was the measure that allowed the identification of a "real" economist from a "fake," a "good" from a "bad" professional. In fact, the more these principles were used to analyze not only economic activities, but also all sorts of other social actions, the more "economist" and professionally identified was the practitioner of the science. And, of course, the more they were used, the more this economist would adhere to the neo-classical, philosophical notions about man and society, which were the "correct" general and rational orientations he should develop to confront "externalities."

The process of identifying the profession with neo-classicist price and monetary notions included a necessary side effect: it deemphasized or left in total obscurity those elements of knowledge which were not included in the initial definition of professional activity. Thus, historical, cultural, structural, or psychological considerations were excluded, deemed at best to be knowledge belonging to other disciplines or, at worst, to be pure" ideology." This was a relevant fact from the viewpoint of the Chileans, because some of these elements, particularly those referring to history and the development of social and economic structures, were deeply embedded in the vision of economics held by the mainstream of economists in Latin America in that period. The adoption of the Chicago perspective of professionalism led, as a result, not only to the conclusion that they were bad economists, but to the more drastic consideration that they were not economists at all, at least not in a modern and scientific sense.

The course program was essential, therefore, in transmitting the Chicago oral tradition. Even the Chicago economists have recognized this. Reder has indicated that the crucial factor in the preservation of the oral tradition has been the structure of the PhD program – more specifically, the central role attached to the examinations in price theory and monetary economics in the PhD program, demanding a strong concentration on the graduate price theory sequence.[55] He argues that the PhD theory courses constitute *"an acculturation process . . . whose end result is an economist with the Chicago style of thought."* The power to imbue its students with this distinctive approach is based, Reder conjectures, *on its rigid standards for a doctorate . . . and in the correlatively high failure rate."* "To obtain a Chicago PhD," he concludes, *"one must learn to do certain specific and fairly difficult things quite well, and the learning process inculcates distinctive habits of thought."*[56]

There is no reason to think that this "acculturation process," as described by Reder, did not operate in the case of the Chilean trainees. One might conceive, on the contrary, of at least two reasons why the process might have been deeper in their instance than in that of the American graduates. The first is obviously the degree of attention dedicated by the Chicago professors to the Chilean students, particularly, as we have seen, to their training in these fields. The second, looking now at the problem from the perspective of the recipient, was his awareness of the absence of previous training in these subjects but, more importantly, his perception that his concentrating on them would open up a theoretical and methodological world, putting him in a simultaneously adversarial and "superior" condition with respect to the Chilean economists of that time.[57]

The most significant fact demonstrating that this transmission was effective is the curriculum adopted by the Faculty of Economics of the Universidad Católica. Organized at first by the Chicago professors, the curriculum was maintained by the Chicago disciples once they were back, along with the same emphasis and identical reading lists. Concentration on price theory and monetary theory went hand in hand – at the Universidad Católica – also with the identification between professionalism in economics and "the tendency to apply economics to every nook and cranny of life." The Universidad Católica became a subsidiary of Chicago, reproducing the "oral tradition" as best it could. However, let us put aside this question for the moment and turn instead to the role of the research training in the formation of the professional function.[58]

Research training

Research operated along the same lines as the course program: principles not only had to be believed, they had to be applied. This was the basic premise upon which normative science was based. The reports give a clear example of the way in which professionalism and the principles were linked through research. The initial endeavor required of research assistants in Santiago by their Chicago professors was "the collection and processing of price data." The report adds: "the prevalence in Chile of the notion that prices play a fairly insignificant role as a guide to resource allocation in Chile has suggested the usefulness of demonstrating to Chilean economists some simple but important relations between prices and resource use in some of our papers."[59]

Hence, all the research projects conducted along strict monetary lines were conceived as models showing the essential rules of professional activity. In Chicago, John Deaver led the discussion on inflation and the quantity of money in the Chilean economy; J. Bray in Santiago conducted research on the economic problems of Chilean agriculture, with the opening hypothesis that "agricultural product prices in Chile have been depressed deliberately by public policies aimed at controlling money prices and providing cheap food." Simon Rottenberg directed research on the Chilean social security system, the economics of Chilean education, and entrepreneurial behavior.[60] Aside from their pedagogical objective, the projects permitted these academics to show the general pattern of resource misallocation and the inefficiency of the system.

These were also the main emphases of the only general description available of the Chilean economy prepared by Chicago staff members at the outset of the project – "Memorandum on Chile" by Arnold Harberger. Written in July and August of 1956 and distributed in mimeograph form by the Universidad Católica, the article was printed in *El Mercurio* in December of that year. It served as the subject for the discussions in the first workshops and as the introduction for a "critical discussion of some of the leading works on economic development in Latin America."[61] In it, Harberger emphasized the consequences of resource misallocation in trade controls in Chile. "Tariffs and restrictions on imports," he argued, "operate in such a way so as to drive buyers away from the market. As a result, the exchange rate, which is supposedly free, is much lower than it should be if these tariffs and restrictions were not applied. With the exchange rate artificially low, many industries are prevented from competing in the world market when in fact their competitive position is very strong."[62]

Harberger's views on the Chilean economy, as well as others expressed by Chicago professors in a similar perspective, had a very important effect on the definition of the professional role to be adopted by the Chilean trainees. In fact, their fundamental hypothesis and their final conclusion was that Chilean economic problems were due basically to erroneous economic (technical) decisions and that well-trained economists, guided by the essential theoretical laws and methodological practices of the economics profession, would produce a substantial turnabout in the situation and lead to economic growth.

The reports leave no room for doubt about this assumption. The seventh report indicates that the "University of Chicago staff from the beginning of the project have held the view that the relatively low income per head and the slow economic growth of Chile stem, in a significant part, from inadvisable economic policy measures."[63] And what was the reason for this long series of ill-advised and mistaken decisions?

The answer appears briefly, diplomatically, while in a straightforward manner, stated in the fourth report:

The University of Chicago staff has found among Chilean economists and other professionals a certain distrust of free market processes and a conviction that free markets and the structure of free prices do not dispose of resources efficiently. The economists seem to be convinced that the traditional marginal analysis of economics is not useful for the Chilean (and other Latin American) case. The Chicago staff has sensed a certain reluctance among them to submit their points of view on policy to close critical examination.[64]

While the first part of this comment clearly suggests the idea of prejudices or confused beliefs devoid of any theoretical base or construction, which was obviously not true of developmentalist economists, the second constituted a derogatory remark with regard to their professional attitudes, a curious observation if one considers the eagerness with which some Chilean economists refuted the articles and papers by the Chicago professors that were circulated in Santiago at the beginning of the project. The report continues to affirm that,

partly because of this lack of confidence in market processes, pyramids of controls upon economic behavior have been introduced and the Chicago staff believes that these controls have often diminished income and output in the economy. The avowed objective of these policies has been, of course, to achieve an increase of income and output. That they should have had opposite effects reflects, in part, the failure to use aptly the tools of economics that permit prediction of the consequences of policies. It is expected that, over the long run, the research writings of the returning Chileans will find this gap.[65]

The mission

The main force orienting the project and its future was, as this last quote shows, the unshakeable confidence the Chicago professors felt towards these students as individuals who were technically capable of transforming a situation which had been basically created through ineptitude. The belief was obviously fostered by the noteworthy academic performance of the trainees, as well as by the cultural fitness and ideological permeability they possessed which led some of them to behave in exactly the manner they were expected to behave as soon as they occupied their full-time posts at the Faculty in Santiago. As the project developed, the students are described in the reports with increasing praise: "fully selected group," "highly trained," "well qualified," "outstanding," "young men of talent," whose "original and significant investigations" will have to be "appreciated in its full potential value" by the Chilean community and will make of them, "we hope, the leaders in Chile's economic profession."[66]

 More than hope, what was present was the belief in a mission. The Chilean group was seen and addressed as a secular team of scientific missionaries who would return to their country to spread science and rational behavior in teaching and research methods, in economic advice, in business practices, and in governmental decision-making processes. In the Chicago tradition, this missionary vocation was linked, as we have seen, with the psychology of a beleaguered minority, confronting the expansion of heterodoxy and error, and developing, as a result, an "adversary mentality" and a conception of economics – not wholly, but partially – as propaganda. This mentality appeared to be a necessity in this mission, which would have to be conducted in infidel and ignorant territories. But propaganda in the Chicago professional conception is not synonymous with superficiality. Rather, it is the social expression of a moral obligation, the obligation of the bearer of truth, who, from the objective position he has cultivated as a scientist, communicates his knowledge, and offers rational options.

The fourth report contains a reference to the question of scientific objectivity, which deserves to be quoted in full.

It is important that Chicago staff members be in Chile for some time while the staff of full-time Chilean professors is being formed in order to entrench these principles [of objective scholarship]. *It is very common for university teaching and research personnel to be actively and openly attached to some political party and to participate in its campaign and other activity. Since political parties in Chile are distinguished one from the other, by their respective doctrinal positions, associations with parties inevitably give the professor an ideological coloring. The Chicago staff believes that it would be wise that the full-time professors be induced to pursue careers of scholarship and that they eschew participation in politics that has been conventional.*[67]

This reinforcement of the technocratic definition of the role of an economist runs, of course, counter to a basic characteristic of Chilean political culture, in which parties and ideological options permeated, for reasons which were not superficial, as we shall see, most of the "socio-economic" alternatives. But, it also contradicted what had been the traditional behavior of the generation of

Chilean economists that had been instrumental in the organization of the Chilean post-crisis economy and the strong development of the state.

The claim for independence and autonomy was not limited, however, to the political sphere. The new economist had to be independent of any other organized interest in society. The fourth report continues:

It seems also to be conventional to hold the professor and his university faculty jointly responsible for the professor's writings. It is of some interest that, on two occasions, when the conclusions reached by a Chicago staff member in a published research report were found by persons in the industrial and banking communities to be distasteful, representations were made to the Dean of the Faculty. On both of these occasions, it was necessary to point out that the author was exclusively responsible for his writings, that he had freedom to publish, that neither the University of Chicago nor the Catholic University, as institutions approved nor disapproved his writing, and that every author simply stood in the judgment of the professional community for what he wrote. *It will be important to maintain these principles and to protect the returning Chileans from the pressures of special interests in the community that may wish to check their freedom to publish their research results.*[68]

The idea that the Chilean students had to be protected by their professors from the pressures of interest groups in their own country is in itself an unusual idea, not only because of its naiveté, but also because it gives an indication of the type of relationship established between professors and students in the Chile Project. This protective attitude, about which we will have more to say in later pages, led in the end to the involvement of Arnold Harberger and Milton Friedman in the economic policy decisions of the Pinochet regime in 1975. However, this is not the only point that stands out in this observation. For what the quotation reflects, in the first place, is the conception of the economist as a technician or, better yet, as a scientist placed above social conflict and the social process itself, adopting an attitude of social, political, and ideological autonomy from the concrete characteristics of his own society. It is true that the remark stems from a valid principle: the need for freedom of expression in academic activity. Yet, as we shall explore more extensively in the next section, what is of importance here is that the affirmation of this principle was made in the context of a belief that what was being protected was true science, the only true scientific standpoint, in fact, from which a rationalization of society could be promoted.

More than freedom of academic research and publication, what was at issue then was the credibility of that science *vis-à-vis* other groups in that society, which depended basically on the recognition of the superiority of its practitioners and the priority of the application of its principles. This application had to be made independently of any other consideration not stemming directly from the normative and methodological elements at its base.

A second observation is, of course, that these remarks had their origin not only in a simple lack of awareness of the peculiarities of the society into which the principles were being transplanted, but also in the belief that the ideas and the practices to be avoided were unimportant or inconvenient for the tasks the economist would have to accomplish. As a consequence, even when they were intended to indicate simply those practices and ideas falling outside of professional competence, they were received by most of the students – given their nature as individuals and the type of society in which they had to function – not just as pitfalls to be avoided, but as remnants of an irrational world to be left behind.

Before discussing these points more thoroughly, however, we need to address the recipient side: the students, their traits, and their world at Chicago.

The students: the objective and subjective environment

It seems evident that the careful and systematic program of instruction and professionalization we have described could not have succeeded in the way it did, or at least would have had a different development, if the students selected had possessed distinct personal traits. In fact, their common characteristics were not limited to knowledge of the English language, a deficient education in economics, good intellectual capacity, and excellent working disposition. They held in common certain social and ideological lineaments which helped to generate a very high degree of ideological receptivity to the notions being transmitted. Indeed, it was through these features that the Chicago School doctrine developed into a fully fledged ideology, becoming, one decade later, a program that would lead to the transformation of Chile.

What were the main traits of the students selected during the primary phase of the project? In the first place, most of them were conservatives or apolitical; secondly, they had a middle-class background and, thirdly, in most cases, their families had recently or relatively recently immigrated to Chile. Let us discuss these three elements separately.

The ideological characteristic seems to be, by far, the most important in shaping the favorable disposition toward the study program and the notions of professionalization transmitted in Chicago. The students selected in the first three groups were, with two recognizable exceptions, either conservative or apolitical before they left to be trained in the United States.[69] Their conservatism, however, did not imply an active adherence to a political party, although most of them would vote for the candidate representing the traditional Conservative and Liberal Parties in the internal elections for the student federation at the Universidad Católica. At the Economics Faculty, however, during the period preceding the first selection for the Chile Project, ideological differences were hardly noticeable within the student body. It was only before the 1958 Chilean presidential election when rightwing (or the Alessandrista position) and Freísta (or the Christian Democratic option) took on the appearance of being opposing views or at least clearly distinct political alternatives being offered to the students.[70]

In these students' view, conservatism appeared to be combined with a strong professionalist, secular, and individualist bent. These ideological features would distinguish the student at the Economics Faculty of the Universidad Católica from other types of conservatives at the university, who were of a different social origin, came typically from Catholic schools, studied law or agronomy, and adhered to "corporatist" and "integrist" (meaning more politicized and traditional) ideologies of Chilean conservatism. In contrast to these forms of conservatism, which were inherited from "hispanism" and authoritarian values, the economics students were prone to be attracted by American values and culture and less oriented towards European intellectual subjects and ideologies. For those who were not of a strong Catholic tradition, nor from an upper-class origin, the Conservative Party hardly served as an alternative with which they could identify. It was only natural, therefore, that the prevalent emphasis in their outlook was "professionalism," a type of professionalism which was, moreover, open to a technocratic vision of society.[71]

The first group of trainees included three students, who added one more commonality to those just mentioned, which seems to have been an important consolidating element in the constitution of the group, at least at the beginning. Ernesto Fontaine, Sergio de Castro, and Pedro Jeftanovic, three of the four students who went to Chicago, had received their secondary education at the Grange School, a British non-religious institution in Santiago for middle- and upper-class students. The Grange had certain qualities which may have been important in the process of forming the ideological tendencies described above, as well as in the receptivity that de Castro and Fontaine – probably the most important members of the group – manifested with regard to the Chicago doctrines.[72]

Professionalism was a typical attribute of the middle class in Chile during the 1950s and 1960s and, most particularly, of those sectors comprised of recent immigrants. The observation made by Silvert and Jutkowitz in the sense that "socially climbing professors tend to have foreign born fathers at the Catholic University" seems to synthesize this point quite adequately.[73] In fact, both professionalism and training abroad constituted strong elements favoring upward mobility in a society characterized by a relatively rigid class structure.

Conservatism, however, was neither a common trait of middle sectors, nor of immigrant groups. In our case, therefore, this conviction cannot be viewed as being a result of the students' social background. Conservatism here stemmed more probably from a factor which was salient in most of the interviews conducted with members of the Faculty of Economics, which is that the students following a career in economics were either members of families in which business activities were important or were interested in business themselves. This peculiarity leads to a very relevant point; the combination of a middle-class "professional" outlook with a conservative ideology was, in fact, a very fertile ground for the implantation of a technocratic mentality of autonomy and independence from interest groups. The students were conservatives in a society where the sectors in which they wanted to become influential were experiencing a state of defensiveness and confusion, and where reformist and revolutionary propositions were making headway. The adoption of the principles of professionalization offered by the Chile Project meant not merely having access to the power centers controlled by the dominant class, but also the possibility of transforming that class, of radically modifying its ideology and even its composition, something for which they were psychologically and intellectually prepared, for – in general – they had no kinship or property relations to defend and preserve, and their scientific practice would command sufficient respect and influence to erode the resistance they would encounter among these traditional interest groups.

These elements of homogeneity among the students would be reinforced even further during the 1960s, when the traditional rightwing parties were reduced to a minimal electoral expression and the country was swept by the multiple social and economic reforms adopted by the Christian Democratic regime of Eduardo Frei. It was then that the weakness of the traditional interest groups in the business and banking sectors offered a concrete opportunity to put this vocation into practice.

There were other elements in the initial constitution of the group that need to be explored here. This would refer to the material, and particularly to the psychological, living conditions in Chicago. It should be noted as a first point that, for Chileans at that time, studying abroad was not a common alternative for graduate students and that studying in the United States was even more unusual. The students selected to be the first participants in the "Chile Project" understandably considered themselves pioneers, and this occurrence alone created an *esprit de corps*.[74] Most of these Chicago students recall their period of training there as a very beautiful, challenging, and decisive period in their lives. In their recollections, three topics usually stood out: the difficulties they had to endure in order to keep up with the demanding level of studies,[75] the economic hardships generated by insufficient scholarships, and the warmth and affection with which they were regarded by the Chicago professors.

Friends and fathers: the Harberger factor

While the first two topics do not need further elaboration, the third seems to have been of importance for the future of the group and the development of the Chicago doctrine in Chile. The Chicago professors on the staff of the project did their best to provide the students with a friendly and agreeable atmosphere. They were warm, generous, and hospitable. While some students remember T. W. Schultz bringing them an armchair as a present one Saturday afternoon and most of them recall the ongoing interest of Professor Lewis in their material and personal well-being, all name Arnold Harberger as the "father" figure of the group. A man of strong emotions and a charismatic personality, Harberger and his wife, Anita, a Chilean, opened their home to the Chilean students and bestowed on them affectionate attention. Nobody has better described these efforts than Harberger himself.

In a letter to Dr. William D. Carmichael from the Ford Foundation, he wrote:

There are mundane "little things" like finding apartments for new arrivals when none seem to exist, helping them get settled and oriented in the university community and in Chicago as a city, getting to know them on a more personal and informal basis . . . Then there are consultations with them through the period of course work and prelims, which are both more frequent and more lengthy than is common with other students, perhaps in part due to the easier and more informal relationships that we try to establish with them. Finally, there are the special efforts that we make to help them find dissertation topics . . . and to advise them, again at frequent intervals, and in sessions that on the average are more lengthy than most, during the period in which their dissertations are being compared. Finally, it would be remiss not to mention our wives, who apart from extending their hospitality to the participants on any number of occasions during the year, spend substantial amounts of time helping the participants' own wives to become acclimated to Chicago life, coming to the rescue in times of illness or emergency, helping resolve difficulties that their children may have, etc.[76]

It was this type of relationship, along with Harberger's interest in development problems and Chilean economic affairs, in particular, which caused a long-lasting friendship to develop between the professor and his students. This friendship has been mentioned as one of the principal factors in the formation of their attitudes and ideas.[77] In fact, his intellectual influence seems to have developed more as the result of informal interchanges than as the product of his lectures or writings. Although the latter were attractive to the Chilean students due to his knowledge of underdeveloped economies and his use of an economic language which was more accessible than others at the Economics Department of Chicago, the main element of his message was more effectively transmitted through a more personalized intellectual relationship. It was the rigorous and exclusive technocratic approach, the concept of the economist as an engineer who finds efficient solutions for different governments without asking questions about values or ideological orientations.[78]

Harberger himself values enormously his relationship with Chilean and Latin American students and describes it with words expressing both affection and possessiveness. "A great piece of my life is involved with these *latinoamericanos*," and "I feel prouder about my students than of anything I have written, in fact, the *latino* group is much more mine than the contribution to the literature." Indeed, "a third of these students belong to me." He very often uses the analogy of a father when referring to his relationship with his students, and that of a medical doctor or an engineer when discussing their professional rearing. He also adheres, obviously, to what we have called the "theory of the pluralistic result," and observes the ideological differences between Ffrench-Davis and Massad and the rest of the students. The students, he says, "were never taught ideology by me, they were taught to be good professionals and I have always respected their differences because when you have children, you know that they are different." "They are like my children and I have a lot of them all over Latin America."

He is adamant in his distinction between the uses of science and the existence of political or ideological opinions which he considers to be of no relevance to the former: "I happen to own a science of cost benefit analysis which happens to tell you if it is better to have a cigar factory or a mill, and it is not Harberger who is telling it, its a science." There is simply no problem, therefore, with political or ideological considerations, for "when you ask an engineer to build a bridge, you are not supposed to ask him where the bridge leads."[79] In fact, he says, "good economics can be helpful to any society which is willing and ready to accept it." What does not work is "the attempt to combine good economics and demagogy." The ideal is to make political and economic objectives coincide, but "if they collide, you have to sacrifice something." Politics and economics are often, he thinks, in a situation similar to that between the irrigation man who wants to release the water from a dam and the water power man who wants to keep the gates shut: "when will they coincide?" he asks.[80]

Harberger's influence over the Chilean students, great as it was, has to be qualified, however, in the light of his work and his definitions of himself. For he has shown in his intellectual productivity and his professional work a degree of flexibility, which would not become a characteristic of his disciples. As Strassman argues, Harberger stands out at Chicago, "as both a genuine member of the School and yet beyond its usual somewhat petulant wishful thinking about the latent power of the markets." A review of his work shows that he cannot be described as falling into some of the misdeeds commonly charged to Chicago work on development: "that it fails to adapt neo-classical theory to the special characteristics of developing countries, that it makes a selective use of evidence in corroboration of his views and that it holds a 'reactionary belief' in the power of the market to produce 'desirable' solutions in all situations."[81] Taking his positions on public enterprises and state intervention, for example, topics which would become central targets for vilification during the Chicago Boys' period in power, his flexibility stands out rather clearly. He has written: "I am proud to say that I have never taken a dogmatic position on the issue of public enterprises. Probably this stems from the fact that I became involved in the operations of several of them . . . " He worked directly with electric companies in Mexico, Honduras, Costa Rica, Brazil, and Chile, and, through these contracts, he says he "gained great respect for their overall operations . . . Thus there is no question that public enterprises can be efficient and successful if given the right motivation . . . "[82] And, on the subject of government intervention, Harberger has called for "professionalization of the personnel involved" in the process of project evaluation at all levels. "He visualizes an evaluation corps, independent of particular operating agencies and, therefore, able to resist short-sighted pressures to overstate the case for one's own branch."[83]

It is also true that these heterodoxies do not separate him from the mainstream of his school. The role as "representative of the neo-classical tradition of economic science," he has written, "fits well with my own conception of what my life and career in economics has been all about."[84] Economics, he says, is a true science, useful in a great many different kinds of political environments and, while economic goals are not the only goals and non-economic considerations are certainly important in many instances, "they are not, in principle, part of the discipline of economics . . . The natural role for economists is to present in an adequate fashion what the economic considerations are, what are the economic costs and benefits."[85] Looking back at the characteristics of the School we described earlier, Harberger seems to side comfortably with the tradition of a normative science and constitutes one of the most formidable promoters of the missionary spirit idiosyncratic of Chicago. Yet, due to his interest in development problems and to his knowledge of some Latin American countries, he was much more drawn by "macro-economic" considerations than the rest of his colleagues. Perhaps the most perceptive comment about Harberger's professional orientation was made by Kalman Silvert, who observed once: "I have known for many years that Al Harberger is a macro man who wants the advantages of the total society view, as well as the rigor of the micro techniques." That was indeed the essence of a Chicago developmentalist.[86]

What we have indicated tends to confirm the point that Harberger's influence – which continued to develop with successive generations of Chilean students – was more related to the role that he assumed as protector and promoter of the expansion of professionalism in Latin America than to his views on development policies, and that what became the essential part of his influence was the technocratic model of the economist. After 1964, Harberger organized at Chicago a "Program of Latin American Economic Research and Training," supported by the Ford Foundation, which continued the Chile Project in an almost identical form, but aimed this time at a Latin American audience. Chileans from the Universidad Católica and from the Universidad de Chile were conspicuously a part of it and Harberger went to great lengths to try to secure the best of them for his program.[87] After 1964, Harberger also became an economic adviser to the Chilean Banco Central, and continued to visit the Research Center and the Faculty of Economics of the Universidad Católica more assiduously than any other Chicago professor. In 1964 he reviewed and endorsed the Latin American Teaching Program in Economics of the Universidad Católica, through which his former students extended their perception of economics to Latin American undergraduates.[88] During all this time, he maintained his paternal role over the Chilean students and their faculty. As Fontaine says, "he came to help and intervene whenever he thought the investment was being threatened."[89]

Harberger's influence seems to have been unmatched by other Chicago professors. The only other figure even approaching Harberger's role, although far behind, was Larry Sjaastad. Professor Sjaastad had a central role in the development of the Cuyo Project also using ICA funds, wherein a group of the Chilean Chicago Boys served as professors. His influence on Chileans developed after Harberger's. From 1964 Sjaastad, the quintessential monetarist, taught the Chilean students at a time when the new Chicago Latin American program was put into effect. Most of them would go on to form the technical cadres who occupied the middle levels of the economic sector of the Pinochet regime, under the leadership of de Castro, Baraona, Luders, and Kast. From 1976 on, Sjaastad had a crucial role as their adviser in the monetary policy of the government.

Some preliminary conclusions

We have just covered the main elements of the training and socialization process of Chicago. At this point, we should determine their applicability to the question we defined at the beginning of this chapter, namely, if training at Chicago was a factor influencing the development of the group and its ideas for the future.

It seems safe to affirm at this juncture that the efforts developed by the Chicago professors had an immediate effect on at least four very important aspects of the group of Chilean economists and its activities from the moment they returned to Santiago. The first was the creation of a team and not merely a group of economists, endowed with a mission to accomplish in Chile and Latin America. The second was the intellectual recreation of the Chicago tradition in Chile through the courses the Chicago Boys imparted at the Universidad Católica. The third and fourth are closely related: one refers to the constitution of a self-contained world of economic science with no reference to values and information outside of the closed system of scientific norms and principles; the other centers on the constitution of the University of Chicago Department of Economics as the "external authority referent" for the team of students and, consequently, for the institution that they and their professors would build in Chile. Clearly, these were not the only, nor even the most important, expressions of the ideological product that was transmitted. Rather, they represented the tip of an iceberg constituted by the doctrine. It was through these forms that the content would begin to unfold in a socially relevant way. And this would happen – as we argued at the beginning of this work – only when the political power structures of the Chilean political system permitted them to appear, not as mere symbolic expressions of a desirable social order, but as a meaningful collection of ideas capable of being put into operation.

Let us turn for the moment to an examination of these aspects, as we have been able to ascertain them, at the time of the return of the Chileans to Santiago. According to Ernesto Fontaine, their commitment to the mission with regard to the expansion of economic knowledge in Chile and Latin America was born in Chicago. The students came back to Chile having decided, in the first place, "to transform the Catholic University Faculty of Economics into the best of its kind, not just in Chile, but in Latin America." Secondly, they were eager to influence the way in which Chileans and, most particularly, the local business class thought about economics, introducing rationality into decision-making processes from "a strictly scientific point of view." Thirdly, they agreed on "the need to expand this knowledge throughout Latin America, confronting the ideological positions which prevented freedom and perpetuated poverty and backwardness." These points, Fontaine recalls, were explicitly discussed by the group in Chicago. Commitment to them oriented their development from then on, both in the academic or research fields – which was the activity to be followed by some members of the group, such as Fontaine, de Castro, Baraona, and Yver, for example – and in the business field, which others, most particularly Manuel Cruzat, would enter.[90]

The mission "to divert people from prejudices" had begun. The "adversary mentality," whose theoretical base stemmed from the courses and even the research methods learned at Chicago, would find a concrete field of action which was hostile and difficult, something the Chileans would realize after just a few weeks in Santiago. Difficulties would originate, as we shall see in more detail later, from the instruction of the basic elements of the doctrine: the courses on price theory.

Ernesto Fontaine was the first to teach the course. Like most other Chicago disciples after him, he closely followed the notions and the schema of the course he had been taught at Chicago, including, obviously, the literature. His instruction, therefore, as most of his students saw it, had the same "Marxist-like quality" discourse which Patinkin observed in the Chicago tradition: "simplicity together with apparent logical completeness," and, moreover, a degree of abstraction with respect to the Chilean economy, which shocked some students and seduced others. Through the price and monetary theory courses and their difficult and demanding nature, Fontaine, de Castro, and others who followed, reproduced the process of "acculturation" Reder has described. In sum, most students emerged with the unshakeable conviction that (a) these were scientific principles of a nature similar to those of the "hard sciences" which (b) gave them a scientific outlook of society unparalleled by any other social science (c) whose application to the social system would solve the perennial economic problems of their country, problems which (d) were due essentially to the ignorance of these principles or the inability to apply them.

Finally, Chicago, through its formal and informal processes of socialization, transmitted elements of social autonomy to the group that would have consequences of such importance that they cannot be sufficiently stressed. First, as we have repeatedly argued, the notions of professionalization along with the beliefs stemming from it, just summarized, tended to separate economic theories and techniques from any other consideration of a political, social, or moral type. *These were not necessary merely because they fell outside of professional competence, but also because they were – as norms – principles and beliefs already embedded in the notion of science proposed by Chicago. Norms and science, principles and methods constituted a closed system which knew no historical or culturally related boundaries.* The results of this earlier assumption would become painfully evident when the decomposition of the political system, within which these economists worked, gave way to an authoritarian application of science. Indeed, it was precisely when the opportunity, granted by authoritarianism, allowed the experimentation of the normative side of the equation represented by Chicago, that the ideology of science acquired its fullest expression. But this was not the only expression of the social autonomy embedded in the concept of professionalism. *In fact, the team, that would later be baptized "the Chicago Boys," was born with an authority referent which was external to the social conditions and processes in which their life as professionals would develop.* As a result, the Chicago tradition of strong affective bonds between professors and students was reproduced here in a stronger fashion. And this was so exactly because the ideological product the Chilean students represented was not in any way an outgrowth of an endogenous development – economic or political – of Chilean society, but was, in a very real sense of the word, "imported."

Throughout a relevant period of time, this "imported" quality was a painful reality induced by the isolation of the group and by the tendency, on the part of other groups or persons in these academic or political surroundings, to ignore, control, or be hostile toward it. During that period, which will be discussed in the next chapter, the protection that the University of Chicago gave to the students was essential for the survival of the group at the Universidad Católica. But, what is more important, this protection and this type of relationship in general strengthened the conception of *an external authority referent* in the most important figures of the group, as well as in the institution they finally came to control – the faculty – and this idea would constitute an essential element of the elite's self perception from then on.

Part of this conception was shown in the need for autonomy from internal interest groups. *As we have suggested earlier, autonomy did not mean just freedom of research and publication. It meant social unaccountability, which was different. For accountability was only possible, from the point of view they had been taught to believe, with respect to scientific entities. And for a long time Chicago would be the bearer of scientific validation, the main institution with that authority.*

It was, we believe, from this basic precept, that the reasoning governing their period in power emanated. When in power during the Pinochet regime, just as before, during their term as faculty members at the Universidad Católica, the group of economists known as the Chicago Boys did not recognize any local or national authority referent with respect to their options and decisions. Both their rationality and their affections as a group were oriented by an external authority referent which, incarnated first in the University of Chicago, came to be embodied later in different institutions and power centers of the international financial system: the private banks, the International Monetary Fund, and the multilateral lending institutions. They were, in fact, the main sources of their influence and constituted their best protection.

CHAPTER 7

The implantation of the Chicago School in Chile

An ideology out of place

Processes of transference of intellectual technology often seem very difficult to disentangle from what one might call the "implantation" of that cultural product within a group or society. Transference obviously implies the idea of an object in motion from one place to another, while transplant refers to the roots this object develops in a different soil. Yet the rhythm and velocity these processes adopt admit a wide range of possibilities and combinations: the former can develop simultaneously with the latter, it can precede it, or it can evolve as a merely mechanical process without ever being implanted. For by "ideological implantation" we understand the adoption and appropriation by "local elites" of that particular set of ideas – more or less systematized – which are the objects of the transference. But this appropriation may or may not occur. In this latter case, the "modernizers" – those to whom the set of ideas being transferred belonged in the first place – will continue to administer and reproduce them in the recipient society for an indeterminate period of time. Or the specific local elite, having adopted them, will operate as a group alien to what constitutes the mainstream of that particular area of ideas or of knowledge in their own intellectual milieu. Then the transferred ideas will be seen by a majority in that society as "foreign or eccentric ideas."

The first part of this chapter deals with the difficult process of implantation of the Chicago group and their ideas in their social space: the Catholic University. The changes introduced by the Chile Project in the curriculum, the composition of the staff of the Faculty of Economics of the Catholic University, and the growing internal power of the group of full-time professors arriving from Chicago, sets the stage for the first point we want to discuss: the obstacles raised against the expansion of the Chicago mission, both at the Catholic University, in the economic profession, and in society in general. The result was the group's isolation. The new economists coming from Chicago were secluded within their own faculty or had to leave, taking refuge in the network of Latin American activities promoted from the University of

Chicago by Arnold Harberger. The Chile Project seemed in fact to be in serious danger, supported only by the American professors and by a growing group of students who became in the end the main force backing the *coup de force* which in 1964 turned things around at the Faculty of Economics and left the Chicago Boys in control of the School.

During this difficult initiation as professional economists, the Chicago Boys saw their intellectual merits praised – sometimes lavishly – in internal memoranda of American private foundations or in private reports from the University of Chicago to these foundations – reports which described them as "the best economists in Chile." Yet in Chile they were scarcely known: their work was discussed only within the walls of the faculty.

In fact, the expansion of the "mission" among the groups which were culturally prone to be attracted by it was restricted during the 1950s and 1960s to a group of students at the Catholic University. Other "potential clients," like businessmen or rightwing politicians, accepted and needed the centrality of the state, and therefore of politics, in Chilean society. They saw the new "science of economics" as merely an academic discipline with little practical relevance. For the crux of the Chicago approach, namely, the freedom of *homo economicus* from any form of coercion or authority not stemming from the need to liberate his capacity to maximize utilities, confronted here a social system where the highest values were social integration and political equilibrium or the need to prevent social revolution by confronting "backwardness" without having to resort to violence and dictatorship and where – as a result – economic decisions were adopted, not in the light of efficiency reasons dictated by theoretical wisdom, but by very practical considerations – the degree to which they could combine growth with equilibrium between conflicting social and political groups in a system of political freedom. In a society characterized by increasing social and political participation and insufficient economic growth, economic thought would not necessarily develop as an exclusively economic product. It would incorporate what were called "social and political realities." This was the essence of the "structuralist" school of thought and of the developmentalist paradigm to which an overwhelming majority of Chilean economists adhered. And the Chicago approach was, of course, irreconcilably opposed to such a perspective.

In the second part of this chapter we want to address the question of the mechanisms of social and material reproduction of the ideology. We will discuss the mechanisms through which the University of Chicago continued its mission to transform the discipline of economics in Latin America and to promote the essential truths of its own economic tradition. Before that we shall discuss the role of the American foundations.

The social structure allowing the ideology's reproduction was formed by different generations of Chicago Boys who were able to transmit an ideological "ethos" based on the Chicago tradition. The overall architect of this regional effort was Arnold Harberger, and his main objective was to confront the ideas of the Economic Commission for Latin America of the United Nations.

The Chile Project was followed by the "Cuyo Project" in Mendoza, Argentina and then by different projects in different Latin American universities where Harberger's students came back to "modernize" their curricula with the ideas of Milton Friedman. In 1965, with the support of the Ford Foundation, Harberger organized his most ambitious endeavor: a program of graduate studies for Latin American students at Chicago. At the same time his former students in Chile organized at the Universidad Católica a program for Latin American undergraduates. This was the evolution of the Chicago mission up until the end of the 1960s.

Revolution in the faculty: the Catholic University at the beginning of the 1960s

With the hiring of three full-time professors trained at Chicago began the transformation of the School of Economics of the Catholic University. These professors were Sergio de Castro, Luis. A. Fuenzalida, and Pedro Jeftanovic.

The sweeping reforms initiated at the School in 1958 included a complete change in the curriculum of studies: a semestral system of courses was introduced and study programs were changed to emphasize statistics, econometrics, and monetary theory. As the final Chicago report asserted:

The system of relying on part-time professors has been replaced by a system in which the nucleus of the faculty consists of full-time professors devoting all of their time to the affairs of the School. This move has made possible the development of a solid curriculum giving emphasis to fundamental principles and tools and analysis in the first four years of the program and to research in the last year of the program. It has brought about changes in teaching methods and examinations designed to promote independent study and thinking on the part of the students.[1]

Transformations were also introduced in the requirements for students: from 1957, the degree of *Ingeniero Comercial* was separated from that of *Contador General*; from 1958 examinations were written, their frequency was increased, and reading courses were intensified. After 1960 failure in the first year of study implied the repetition of the admission process; and failure in three examinations during the following years of study meant repetition of the year. Students were also allowed to choose, in coordination with the members of the Research Center, the courses they preferred.[2]

These changes increased the number of applications to enroll in the School of Economics. The number of applicants was 70 in 1956 and 300 in 1959.

The number of students also increased gradually throughout these years: from 147 in 1957 to 289 in 1963.[3]

After 1958, more Chicago graduates came back to teach at the School on a full-time basis. In 1959 Ernesto Fontaine and Benito Vignolo were hired; in 1960, Rolf Luders, Mario Albornoz, Alberto Valdés, and Raúl Yver (who was shared part-time with the Faculty of Agronomy); in 1961, Juan Naveillán and Ricardo Ffrench-Davis; and in 1962, Mario Corbo, Gert Wagner, Pablo Baraona, Sergio Muñoz and Hans Picker.

On 1 January 1963, the following professors were employed on a full-time basis at the School of Economics of the Universidad Católica:

1. Mario Albornoz, *Ingeniero Comercial*, Universidad Católica; MA in economics, University of Chicago
2. Pablo Baraona, *Egresado de la Escuela de Economia*, Universidad Católica; MA in economics, University of Chicago
3. Mario Corbo, *Ingeniero Comercial*, Universidad Católica; MA in economics, University of Chicago
4. Ricardo Ffrench-Davis, *Ingeniero Comercial*, Universidad Católica; MA in economics, University of Chicago
5. Sergio Muñoz, *Egresado de la Escuela de Economia*, Universidad Católica; MBA, University of Chicago
6. Juan Naveillán, *Egresado de la Escuela de Economia*, Universidad Católica; MBA, University of Chicago
7. Hans Peter Picker, *Ingeniero Comercial*, Universidad Católica; graduate study in business administration, Northwestern University
8. Alberto Valdés, *Ingeniero Agronomo*, Universidad Católica; MA in economics, University of Chicago
9. Gert Wagner, *Egresado de la Escuela de Economia*, Universidad Católica; MA, University of Chicago.[4]

According to the Chicago report of that period, four Chicago graduates – Sergio de Castro, Rolf Luders, Raúl Yver, and Ernesto Fontaine – were on leave, the first two at Chicago under grants from the Rockefeller Foundation and the others at the University of Cuyo for the University of Chicago, Universidad Católica – Universidad Nacional de Cuyo Project.

The staff of the School was formed therefore by thirteen full-time professors – including those on leave – of which twelve were Chicago graduates. The School also included twenty-nine part-time professors, none of them from Chicago.[5]

This revolution in the School's curriculum and faculty could not fail to produce excitement in some and concern in others. The students and members of the old faculty received the new team of professors and their "new economics" with alarm: they saw the novelties as threats, either to the completion of their careers or to their positions in the faculty. The older and less specialized members of the faculty were soon alienated, incapable as they were of following the path opened by the newcomers. Dean Chaná was supposed to lead the transformation but was, in fact, as Sergio de Castro said, only "a sort of rubber stamp authority," a position that – as we shall see later – he began to resent after 1960.[6] When crisis came in 1962 and the dean turned against the group he had so enthusiastically helped to create, he echoed most of the reserves and criticisms that the old professors in the School, some of the students, and people inside and outside the university had privately or publicly expressed since the arrival of the Chicago Boys – indeed, since the first publications made by the American professors.

It is obvious that among these criticisms there were some which reflected simple incompetence or the impossibility of keeping pace with a more rigorous intellectual discipline. These are, of course, of little interest. Others, however, reflected deep differences in the approach to economics as a discipline and in the conception of the role it ought to play in society. As we shall see, in some cases these two dimensions became entangled.

Criticisms and misgivings

The Chile Project raised three sorts of initial critical reactions, within the circles – social or academic – in which it was supposed to develop.

The first oscillated between a certain private indifference towards the "abstract" and "inapplicable" character of their ideas and the public and often irritated rejection of the "esoteric" and "dogmatic" nature of this approach. The second, limited to circles within the Catholic University, focused on the contradiction between the normative elements present in this brand of economic thought and the Catholic social doctrine that was supposedly the main theoretical element orienting academic activities at the university. The third, which became the main argument used by critical students at the economics faculty in the Catholic University, was that the scientific pretension of this school of economics excluded or tended to exclude the teaching of other perspectives.

The first type of criticism was directed against the Chicago professors themselves. The Rottenberg team was not, at the beginning, particularly concerned with it: from its point of view the argument that their economics belonged elsewhere was not only expected but meaningless. As has been sufficiently discussed in chapter 2 of this work, the whole point of the Chile Project was to teach a science of economics for which the socio-historical development of the place of reception was seen as irrelevant in scientific terms. The medicine was good whatever the race and creed of the patient. But, quite soon, Tom Davis and James Bray – two of the Chicago professors –

became aware of the problems confronting their approach and of the importance of the socio-economic setting in which this type of economics was expected to be applied. Yet their criticisms and preoccupations, privately discussed with colleagues and friends, could not affect the development of the project. They were not influential enough in Chicago or with the students to modify the orientation of training and research.[7]

The initial confrontation of the Chicago professors with Chilean economists was mild enough and was centered, as could be expected, on the subject of inflation. Upon receiving the first paper written in the framework of the project by Martin Bailey, entitled "Aspects of the Theory of Inflation," Flavian Levine sent him a public letter in which he rebuked the idea he saw flowing from the paper that "there was only one theory of inflation" and that the phenomenon in Chile was only due to an excess of public expenditures. "Public expenditures do accelerate the inflationary process," Levine agreed, "but the process is in itself the result of other deeper causes." "You want to apply a specific model to explain the developments happening in this country. That is, you want to force facts in order to make them fit with a preconceived model," he wrote. Bailey answered with a long letter in which he accumulated data to show that the increase in unemployment due to restrictive anti-inflationary measures would only be transitory and could be followed by an equilibrium with more employment and higher salaries. He also noted that opposition to anti-inflationary measures came mainly from entrepreneurial sectors and not from the leftwing parties. He avoided, however, the structural discussion course proposed in Levine's letter.[8]

Some months later, a second and more widely publicized confrontation was provoked by the publication and circulation of a paper by Simon Rottenberg on industrialization and development.[9]

In this paper, Rottenberg criticized "the mystic [sic] of industrialization" which had possessed certain developing countries. His point of departure was as follows:

Let us assume that the resources of a country are being utilized in the production of different types and qualities of goods and services in a way that maximum production is ensured. It is proposed then that certain resources be destined to the production of other articles, different from those presently being produced, because these "other products" are a substitution of imports. The result is a decrease in total productivity which is detrimental to the well-being of the country.[10]

This line of reasoning was swiftly criticized by Aníbal Pinto. "How can anybody assume, even from such a high watchtower as Chicago," he asked, "that the total utilization of resources is a characteristic of underdeveloped economies? Can it be possibly affirmed that the margin of utilized factors is so ideally distributed as to reach maximum productivity?" Pinto went on by saying:

What Rottenberg supposes is that the world movement toward industrialization in the adolescent economies is fostered by a "mystic" without roots, by a pernicious "vogue" disturbing "natural" specialization and division of work at an international scale. What he suggests is that all those who have deviated through this inconvenient short cut should return to the traditional mold in which they were mere exporters of primary products while a minority of nations take charge of the most dense and refined phases of economic activity.[11]

The Chilean economist warned against these "esoteric 'economic formulations' proceeding from professors from the University of Chicago who, armed with excellent will, are disseminating among Chileans certain astroeconomic [sic] truths which paradoxically do not enjoy ready acceptance in their country of origin."[12]

The consequences of this sort of publicity for the project was that, as one of the Chicago reports shows, the visiting staff decided to avoid these sorts of general polemics. At the same time the attacks increased the degree of solidarity of some of the Chilean students with their Chicago professors.[13] Pinto's criticisms generated in the small group of local research assistants not just the "anti-leftist" reaction of students who were mainly of rightwing leanings, but stimulated the rivalry with the state university and the new and increasingly powerful sense of "professionalism" imbued by the American professors: as would be the case with most criticisms in the future, Pinto's criticisms were seen as "political."

In fact, these incidents reflected different conceptions of economics and of the role it should play as a discipline in an underdeveloped society. They went therefore beyond the sphere of "professional jealousies" or simple nationalistic reactions to "American intervention." They showed the clash between imported ideas and a social structure with deeply entrenched beliefs. For most of the Chicago professors and for the students who were trained by them, this clash was an inevitable expression of "modernization." Some others, however, began to read with certain alarm, not perhaps the reactions of the Chilean critics, but the characteristics of the place where implantation was being attempted, and they concluded that some revision of their programs and approaches had to be made. This was the position adopted by Tom Davis and also to a certain extent by James O. Bray.

In 1961, in a conversation with Clifford Hardin from the Rockefeller Foundation, Davis recalled that he had "come down from the States a Chicago-classical economist who believed that he could apply a few simple economic ideas and elucidate the problems for the Chileans."[14] Bray, in the same period, related to Hardin that "T. W. Schultz seems to have come down here with the idea that one could explain a few simple economic facts to the Chileans and change everything, thus exploding the Marxian dogma which had been accepted in an oversimplified form. The consequence is that the Chileans believe that the Chicagoans either were dishonest tools of Yankee policy or else they were very stupid." Rottenberg, he added, wrote "some popular papers that did more harm than good." Said Bray: "one has to learn in Chile to keep his trap shut until he knows something."[15]

What was there to be learned? Davis declared to Hardin that he had learned "that one has to apply economic analysis according to the institutional structure; that what is politically possible here and what is politically possible in the United States are two very different things." Hardin reported that Davis had written "a long manuscript [450 pages] on the evolution of the Chilean economy which is, he says, 40 percent political interpretation." Added Hardin: "He has emerged quite critical of the Chicago group identified with *Milton Friedman* and says that '*Arnold C. Harberger* has moved a little bit but not very much.' "[16]

Davis wanted to come back to Chicago to "see how much he can sell his shift in ideas," reported Hardin. He believed, the Rockefeller official wrote in his diary:

that Chicago is unquestionably the strongest place in theoretical economics in the United States, but that *this theoretical economics implies a certain social system, an institutional system, and that while it still remains authentic, it has to be adjusted considerably to apply to other institutional systems.* Davis feels prepared to challenge this because he also is trained in the same theoretical background, for example, as Martin Bailey. He knows exactly how Martin Bailey will approach problems and also why it is wrong in Chile. He will use the course in Monetary Policy which he will give in the United States (one Christ was giving in Chicago) to show that *you cannot get any place with monetary policy without considering the institutions of the country.*[17]

These criticisms, remarkable as they are, did not seem to include, however, an awareness of the impact that this approach to economic theory might have on the Chilean students. Bray recognized the existence of the problem but there is no indication in the Rockefeller papers that he seemed prepared to move from the initial teaching program: "Here," he said, commenting on the experience of the returning students, "*the boys have trouble adapting the Chicago classical theory of marginal utility without ever asking about the distribution of property, power and income in a country where, unfortunately, there was no social revolution a hundred years ago and where now revolution is just around the corner.*" "*Friedman's* influence," he added, "has been unfortunate and it has been expressed here by Harberger, although *Harberger* has modified somewhat."[18]

At the same time Bray thought that "the fact that the Chicago group of students has returned and are acting vigorously is extremely important" for the Chilean economic profession. He observes that, in his words: "Chicago has shaken up the pecking order in economics in Chile by throwing in a lot of roosters."[19] Like all the rest of the Chicago professors, Bray stuck to the idea that the learning ability shown by the Chilean students – the fact that "they were good" – made useless or irrelevant any other consideration on "the way in which they were good." It was, however, this particular conception of their profession and the models they wanted to apply in the Chilean context which led the Chicago Boys to a situation of complete isolation within their School, at the university, and more generally in Chilean society.

The Alessandri election

In a letter to the director of the Social Sciences Division of the Rockefeller Foundation written in December of 1958, Dean Julio Chaná expressed his confidence in the practical results of the Chile Project in the sphere of policy-making. He affirmed that Chile was "entering a favorable period of a liberal government in which all efforts towards furthering and improving the production and agricultural aspects of the Chilean economy are of invaluable help for the prosperity of the Nation."[20]

And in an attached document he added the faculty's point of view:

The fundamental belief of the group is that the levels of material welfare in Chile are disappointingly low in relation to the natural and human resources of the country. It is further believed that this state of affairs can be in part explained by the public economic policy choices which have been made historically . . . We view the economy as a conjunction of markets, the labor market, the capital market and the goods market. These markets are seen to operate within a set of cultural institutions.[21]

This expression of confidence in the future and of ideological coherence between the dean and his professors in the Research Center seemed justified: the election of Jorge Alessandri as president of Chile in 1958 had been welcomed by Chaná, who would become in 1961 Minister of Mining in that government,[22] and by all the incoming Chicago Boys, with only two exceptions: Ricardo Ffrench-Davis and Carlos Massad who were *freístas*.

Alessandri appeared during his first years in power as the modernizer who would impose technical decisions over political considerations. His economic experience was in fact – as Pinto has recently noted – a tentative and diluted attempt at the radical and traumatic economic transformation that would be put into effect by the Chicago Boys fifteen years later. The Alessandri government was certainly different: economic decisions were adopted within a democratic political framework; yet the affinities between certain basic characteristics of both models seem apparent.[23]

During the first period, emphasis was placed on the expansion of exports and the attraction of foreign investment. The experience was short-lived however: after a while the accent shifted to an increase in public and private investment in industrial development. The main purpose was to promote a policy of free external commerce with a stable rate of exchange in order to create favorable conditions for the import of new technologies that could allow national industry to compete in foreign markets. The basis for this program was, however, an abundance of external credit. In a relatively short period of time the external debt almost tripled and reached extraordinary levels by any measure. Under these conditions, the rate of exchange was kept stable from 1959 to 1961. This measure clearly showed that preoccupation with the expansion of exports had been removed from its initial predominant position.[24]

Since their return from Chicago, the new professors had the intention of influencing governmental decisions. They did not consider this a "political" activity. As Ernesto Fontaine says, they saw their role "as a group which gave information to the authorities which could help to diminish the state role; to make them [the authorities] understand economic problems and the effects that certain policies had on the economy."[25] Theoretical statements and research in economics could generate policy or at least could influence policy in a correct way. This was, in the end, what the whole Chile Project was about. Now the opportunity was open: a liberal administration like that headed by Alessandri seemed a promising field to test. The Chicago Boys were very critical of the lack of professional leadership in the different instances of economic decision-making in that government: the ministries of economics and finance were in the hands of entrepreneurs and industrial managers, without professional training in economics. This was one more reason to promote "sound economic analysis." It was therefore in this optimistic mood that they decided to enter the discussion which developed in 1962 on the value of the exchange rate.

Rolf Luders, as head of the Research Center, sent copies of an article entitled "Política Cambiaria, Estructura Productiva y Zona de Libre Comercio" to the magazine *Ercilla*. The article, written by Sergio de Castro, promoted an immediate increase in the value of the dollar and criticized the distortion produced by excessive protection and other incentives to local industry. This policy, the author argued, had given place to inefficient and anti-economic industries which formed pressure groups opposing any measure which demonstrated their inefficiency, with the argument that national industry had to be protected. The article proposed different ways of confronting the social and economic problems which the devaluation of the escudo would create, particularly within the most indebted groups and the poorer sectors in society.[26]

The article was evidently polemical. The government had been trying to resist pressures to devalue, and this sort of criticism, coming from a source which was not suspected of leftist or political opposition leanings came at a very bad moment. The paper was again commented on in a critical and derogatory manner in the socialist daily *Ultima Hora* and Dean Chaná's anger was understandably aroused: he had just left the Cabinet and continued to be a close adviser to President Alessandri.[27]

The Chicago report covering the activities of the Center between 20 June and 31 December 1962 said that "the issue of academic freedom in research and publication by the faculty of the Center arose in August 1962 and continues to cause considerable uneasiness on the part of the faculty. Prior to this time the Center faculty determined its own research and publication policy." The procedure had now been changed:

Certain political groups in Chile reacted adversely to recommendations that the escudo be devalued which were contained in a paper written by Sergio de Castro and published by the Center in July, 1962. The Dean then asked that papers be submitted to him prior to publication. A paper by Ricardo Ffrench-Davis, "Balanza Comercial, Tarifas y Terminos de Intercambio," further developing the case for liberation of trade and devaluation of the escudo was submitted in August, 1962. Its publication was disapproved on the grounds that the policy recommendations in the paper might be used by certain political elements to discredit the present government and might have adverse repercussions on the Catholic University . . . It was further indicated that the Dean's office might want to exercise some control over the choice of research topics. The faculty reaction to the change in policy was adverse. A very strong feeling was evidenced that faculty members must have academic freedom in research and publication as well as in teaching. There was talk of resignation.[28]

The Chicago staff rapidly mediated between the dean and the Research Center faculty. They proposed the creation of a "rotating review committee of competent Chileans" that would review prospective Center publications.[29] The stalemate continued however and conflict was aggravated and expanded in 1963. Eventually a provisional agreement was reached: individual staff members would be free to choose their own topics of research; they would have to submit their monographs for criticism and discussion by the entire staff of the Center which would decide on the basis of their technical merits whether or not they would be published. Approval by the dean's office was then required prior to publication. This solution was obviously unsatisfactory to the staff of the Center.[30]

Censorship was only the tip of the iceberg. The revolution in curriculums and certain personal characteristics of some of the new members of the faculty had gathered a strong opposition against the Chicago Boys. They had undeniably accumulated a lot of power in the School's decision-making and this factor, added to the systematic backing they received from the American professors, made their influence extremely irritating to the rest of the faculty and to some authorities at the university. Furthermore, the members of the group were considered arrogant. Their attitudes toward older colleagues were disdainful: while some were seen, and often described by them as "obsolete," some others were addressed as if they were definitely "gaga."

Most of the new professors were also seen as sectarian in an ideological sense. Increasingly irritated, Chaná soon began to consider the need to broaden the "theoretical spectrum" of the School and include a "variety of approaches." He made efforts to hire other professors with different academic backgrounds for the full-time staff. These intentions were resisted by the Chicago Boys who tended to see them as signs of "lack of confidence" in their own capabilities.[31]

Criticisms of the group began to expand outside the School boundaries: the Chicago Boys' characteristics created concern among those academics who were concerned with the religious or philosophical orientation of the university. One of them was particularly important: Father Roger Veckemans, director of the School of Sociology. An ambitious Belgian Jesuit with a strong intellect and a controversial personality, Veckemans was soon worried by the introduction of the Chicago conception of economics at the Catholic University. He had come to organize the School of Sociology and was celebrated at the university as the teacher of a "first generation" of professional sociologists well trained both theoretically and in research methods. Veckemans was, however, a Catholic modernizer. He believed that the Catholic University should not accept the predominance in any one faculty – most particularly in the social sciences faculty – of professors whose view of science excluded the moral values and social doctrines of the church. He considered, furthermore, that sociology and economics had to be interrelated and he came to perceive quite soon that this project would be impossible if the Chicago predominance was imposed on the economics School.

Initially, however, Veckemans made efforts to bring together the students and the young faculty members of both schools. In the Centro Belarmino, a Jesuit intellectual institution, he organized open discussion meetings to which he invited faculty members and students from both the Catholic University and the University of Chile. These meetings often ended in passionate discussions between two very definite factions: the Christian Democrats who defended the social doctrine of the church and the new liberals recently arrived from – or locally influenced by – the Chicago School, who defended their own view of science.[32] It was probably as a result of these meetings that Veckemans concluded that there must be intervention at the School of Economics. He therefore agreed with the dean on the need to hire other faculty members with different perspectives on to the full-time staff.[33]

During 1962 and 1963 the intellectual isolation of the Economic Research Center both within the university context and in society in general was remarkable. The group worked on different research projects, but their publications were internal. They were read only by themselves and the American professors.[34] Financial support came almost exclusively from foreign sources and there was no sign at the moment that "the local community" would respond to the Center's needs, as the Chicago professors had wished.[35]

The Center had, in fact, very little impact on Chilean society. One indication of this is the record of "visits to the Center" reported in the Chicago documents. Between July of 1962 and July of 1963, twenty-nine visits are reported – twenty-five from foreigners: eighteen from the United States, and thirteen from American universities of which seven were from Chicago. Only four of the "visitors" are Chilean: two of them were Chicago professors on leave at the University of Cuyo, Ernesto Fontaine and Raúl Yver.[36] The Chicago reports of that period describe a research center that existed apart from any institutional or social context. In fact the sole indication of a reality existing beyond the Center was the situation of conflict with the dean at the Catholic University and with some economists at the University of Chile.

Censorship and conflict were followed by an attitude of indifference from the dean's office. The report indicates that

The main problem here appears to have been that direct contact between the Dean's office and the members of the Faculty has been too limited to give the Dean's office a real "feel" of the research being carried on by the Center staff and the intellectual capacities of the individual staff members. This has resulted in misunderstandings and lack of accord with regard to various policies established by the Dean's office. It is exemplified by the fact that no joint meetings of the Center staff members and the Dean's office occurred between October of 1962 and March of 1963, despite the fact that the Center staff asked repeatedly for such meetings in order to discuss problems which were bothering them regarding publications.[37]

At the same time, the Center staff members were excluded from the university contacts with the outside. The same report states:

Some feeling existed on the part of the staff of the Center that insufficient support by the University and by the Dean's office was being provided in the matter of Center contacts with other activities of the university and organizations – both national and international – outside the University. This feeling was based on the fact that : 1) the Center personnel have not been invited to participate in various University activities – summer courses, seminars and conferences – in which specialists in economics and business administration could be expected to make contributions, and 2) the Center personnel have not been invited to participate in certain conferences with economic subject matter sponsored by both national and international organizations in Chile.[38]

The Chile project was in danger. And the impact of these developments upon the group of Chicago trainees was serious. Since 1962 the original

Chicago Boys' group had been weakened by the departure of some of its members for more graduate work at Chicago or for other University of Chicago projects in Latin America. In 1962 Ernesto Fontaine and Raúl Yver had left for Mendoza, under contract to the University of Cuyo. Sergio de Castro and Rolf Luders were on leave during that year at the University of Chicago.

At the beginning of 1964, in part as a result of the conflicts with the dean, de Castro decided to leave for Cali, Colombia, under contract to the Universidad del Valle, financed by the Rockefeller Foundation. These professors, along with Luis Arturo Fuenzalida, another of the original Chicago graduates, had been selected by Arnold Harberger who was the organizer of the first of these projects and had an important influence in the second.

The departure of these full-time staff members undoubtedly weakened the group and the new academic order established at the School. The ambience was tense and the group saw the future of the School as dismal, except for the relationship that was beginning to emerge with a group of the students, which would ultimately become the great area of success of the experience.

The Chicago Boys and the students: the hair cut incident

The creation of a group of Chicago disciples among the economics students at the Catholic University was not, however, an easy process. It began with some frustrating experiences. Sergio de Castro and Ernesto Fontaine's price and monetary theory courses initially produced an uproar among students. Going through their last year at school the students could not but perceive as a threat to their career completion courses which were exceedingly difficult, whose reading material was in English, and whose usefulness for Chilean economic problems they could not readily understand.

The first student reaction to these courses was, then, to meet and demand from the authorities of the faculty either the suspension of the courses or the removal of the professors. This was, at the time, almost a standard procedure. The bad quality of most of the professors had legitimated a student power which was difficult for university authorities to disregard. As a result, many incompetent professors had been literally dismissed by the students.

This time, however, the situation developed differently: the young professors took the matter into their own hands and after some weeks of tension decided to meet with some of the protesting students. Openness and informality worked so well that some of the leaders of the rebellion were soon convinced – as one of them put it – "that they knew nothing about economics; and that without these courses they would never become real economists."[39]

Criticism persisted however. Student discontent was centered on the difficulty and the pertinence of the courses being taught. The students used the new system of course rating introduced by the new professors to rate badly Ernesto Fontaine's monetary theory course. The extraordinary amount of failures in his exams and the rejection of the "abstract nature" of his approach, along with certain criticisms of Fontaine's arrogance and tough teaching methods, prompted the president of the student body, Cristián Ossa, to ask for his dismissal. It was, however, one of these small insurrectional incidents that helped the Chicago Boys to consolidate their position in the School and their influence on the students. The "hair cut incident" led to a strike, a conflict with Father Roger Veckemans, and a strengthening of the students' sense of belonging to the School of Economics, as well as to a closer relationship between the students and the new group of full staff faculty members.

In 1959 four fourth-year students took a mathematics examination which the course members had voted to postpone without consultation with the teacher. As punishment, their fellow students decided to cut their hair; something which they did in an episode not exempt from violent overtones. The reaction of the university authorities was swift and drastic: the student delegate from the course was expelled from the university. A strike in his defense followed, along with negotiations and discussions with the authorities. Friends and fellow students ran to other departments of the university trying to raise support for the strike.[40] But the expulsion was finally upheld and seven students, including the one expelled, left for the University of Chile, arguing, among other things, that they wanted to be taught economics that was relevant to the country's development.[41]

The departure of these students undoubtedly helped to establish an authority principle at the faculty, but this was not its most important result. The strike and the intervention of the university authorities, most particularly of Father Veckemans, appointed by them as "intervener" of the School, generated an *esprit de corps* among the students and an increasingly close relationship between them and the new professors. It was not simply that one of them had actually been favorable to the strike. What was more important was that these professors saw their teaching and life at the faculty as the most important thing in their profession; they were interested in the School more than in anything else. They had furthermore the "ethos" of the economics profession: professional pride and identity was their trademark. Their call to "defend the School" against outward interference was received by the students as the most articulate response to university authorities who appeared inconsiderate, archaic, and authoritarian. Criticisms against the "abstract character" of the "new economics," though subsisting, tended to dilute given the urgency to modernize felt by the students. In fact, the independence and the essential character of the School of Economics was probably the first and most basic element in the generation of the technocratic ideology that would link a group of students and their professors from then onwards.

Rolf Luders reports that, when he came back from Chicago in 1960, "the ambience among students was still very much against the Chicago group."[42] This situation changed however during the two following years; by 1962 a group of students tended to identify strongly with their professors. The prestige of the courses given by the Chicago Boys as well as of the students who mastered Price Theory 1 and 2 – considered to be the most difficult of all the courses – generated a group of *capos* (best students) who saw themselves as disciples of de Castro, Fontaine, Luders, and the others. This new relationship with students was an important factor in the resolution of the crisis that developed during 1962 and 1963.

The resignation of Dean Chaná

By 1963 a new element had been added to the School crisis – the insufficient salaries of the professors. The Chicago reports mention that there was "considerable dissatisfaction on the part of the professors with regard to salaries." In 1963 "average salary adjustments were not sufficient to maintain the real incomes of the professors at the same level that prevailed in 1962." The report warns that "the forces of the market will exert pressure: some of the professors are actively canvassing alternative employment opportunities. If the Catholic University is to hold its best young professors it will be forced to pay them competitive salaries."[43]

During the Chilean summer of 1964, H. Gregg Lewis and Arnold Harberger came to Santiago on one of their frequent trips. Both came to stay for a period of three months, lasting, in Harberger's case, until June of that year. The last Chicago report describes what Mr. Lewis saw on arrival.

Mr. Lewis discovered on his arrival in Santiago that the morale of the members of the Faculty generally was very low. Although employment contracts for the academic year beginning in March had not been offered by the University, the adjustment in their salaries that had been tentatively proposed by their Dean they felt were inadequate in the light of the inflation during the preceding year and alternative salaries outside of the University. Much more important, however, was their great uncertainty about their futures, individually and collectively, in the University. In part this uncertainty stemmed from lack of communication between the Dean and the faculty members. Such comments as the Dean has made to them in the preceding year, however, suggested to them that the future of the faculty team was threatened. Before the end of January the issue was brought to a climax by a letter to the Dean, signed by all of the full-time members of the economics faculty, presenting their grievances. Dean Chaná promptly resigned.[44]

According to Dean Chaná, the document included three main points. The first was that the decision to include professors coming from other universities in the full-time team of the School showed mistrust toward their professional capability. If this decision was maintained they could no longer remain at the university. The second point referred to salaries, and the third was that they (the Chicago group) had acquired sufficient experience to be in positions of command at the School.[45]

Sergio de Castro, visiting Santiago for a vacation from his Cali "exile," had met with Chaná and arrived at the conclusion that there was nothing else to be done but to confront the dean. After this meeting he talked to Pablo Baraona who, in de Castro's words, "had kept other fellow Chicago people who were out of the country informed." A series of hectic meetings followed in which Harberger and Lewis discreetly participated. Harberger decided to "risk everything" (*jugarse entero*) in order to "keep the investment going." The student group which was close to the young faculty members was informed of the development and it was agreed that they would see Chaná and give their support to the Chicago Boys. The resignation of the dean promptly ensued and was followed by that of Mario Albornoz, director of the Economics Research Center, and Alberto Neumann, director of the School of Economics.[46]

The Chicago report indicates that:

although the Rector, Monsignor Silva, was concerned about the manner in which the faculty had handled its differences with the Dean, he assured the faculty of his confidence in them and of his pride of their achievements and he asked them to continue at their posts, which they all agreed to do. In March Professor Hugo Hanisch was appointed acting Dean of the Faculty and Professor Pablo Baraona, Acting Director of the Economics Research Center. In the following month policy with respect to salaries was successfully worked out and employment contracts settled. In June Professor Baraona was appointed Director of the School of Economics and Professor Sergio de Castro, who had been on leave teaching at the University of the Valley in Cali, Columbia [sic], was induced to return to the Catholic University and to be the Director of the Economics Research Center. (Professor Rolf Luders, now on leave at the Brookings Institution in Washington DC, was also invited to return to the Catholic University.)[47]

The Chicago Boys were suddenly in control. The rector had supported them in rejecting Chaná's and Veckemans' objections over the type of economics they were teaching. This decision seems to have recognized the fact that the School of Economics had become identified with the "Chile Project" and that the Chicago Boys and their American professors had carried the conflict to a situation in which accommodation was no longer possible. From their point of view the School had to be in the hands of professionals and had to teach the only science of economics there was. This was in fact a compelling argument given the virtual absence of other economists at the School, and the type of conflicts that had developed in the previous years with the dean.

At the same time the rector's decision also responded to more practical considerations. The resignation of the young Chicago faculty would have meant the failure of a project that had attracted the attention and the interest of the American foundations. The university could not risk this sort of outcome to the crisis in the School without suffering financially. In fact, it would have been practically impossible to continue with the modernization of the School of Economics after a mass resignation from the young Chicago-trained professors. The Center was totally dependent on American sources of finance. During Harberger's stay in Santiago a one-year contract had been achieved with the AID Mission in Chile under which the Center would provide consulting services and undertake research studies for the mission. As the final report indicates, "preliminary discussions with the representative of the Ford Foundation in Chile indicated interest by the Foundation in the project and the Center has now requested the Foundation to support the project."[48] There was also, finally, the support from the Rockefeller Foundation. Furthermore, the AID mission in Santiago had instituted a five-year program of scholarships for advanced training in the US of Chileans in economics and economic development planning. None of these programs would have been likely to continue had the rector decided otherwise.

The last Chicago report ends with a note of optimism and satisfaction:

as we take our leave of the Chile Project, the prospects for the Faculty of Economics at the Catholic University look good. The Faculty, we believe, has won the confidence and support of the high officers of the University. The curriculum in economics has been thoroughly modernized and the exclusively part-time faculty replaced by a largely full-time faculty with advanced training in economics. An effective library in economics has been established. Research has been made an integral part of the scholarly activities of the faculty and steps have been taken to plan and obtain financial support for the research in the years immediately ahead. Efforts are being made to make the Faculty a center for training in economics in Latin America. *The members of the faculty have become keenly aware of the importance of providing their own replacement as they leave temporarily or permanently and they have worked diligently and with considerable success to obtain scholarships for advanced training abroad for their best students.* Their *esprit de corps* is excellent. [49]

The Chile Project had come to an end and the seeds had been successfully implanted. Yet, the University of Chicago professors had to defend their creation from the beginning. Their conservative reputation had been transmitted to their disciples eliciting concern not only in Chile but also at AID where some were now wondering about the wisdom of having concentrated all their support in a single university. In a paragraph entitled

"Should the training have been entirely at Chicago?" Gregg Lewis attempted in the last report to answer these concerns. He recognized that there was a danger that "when all of the newly trained faculty in the host country university have had their training at a single US university, there is a danger that this faculty will be criticized as being an 'image' of the US University and faculty." "This was," he said, "the case of the Chile Project, where, due to the mistaken but generalized idea of a 'Chicago School,' the faculty members of the Catholic University are regarded as having been 'brainwashed' at Chicago to adhere to a 'conservative' political position." "This erroneous criticism," he said, "has been a source of internal tension in the [Catholic] University that at least temporarily has interfered with the most effective functioning of the faculty." Lewis continues by saying:

As time passes the association of the University of Chicago with the Catholic University will be less obvious and more easily left unnoticed. Furthermore, time will tend to cure the mistaken notion that all of the Católica economists are conservatives politically. This process could be accelerated, of course, by discharging some of the Chicago-trained faculty, especially those regarded as most conservative, and replacing them with persons trained elsewhere who are not regarded as conservative. The *adoption of such a policy would be a tragic error.* It would greatly lower the quality of the faculty – and thereby the quality of instruction and research in economics immediately and for a long time to come, not only because the present supply of highly trained economists from which Católica can draw is almost entirely Chicago-trained, but also because as a long run matter the selection of faculty on other criteria than quality – such as political or religious affiliation – is a sure way to obtain a mediocre faculty. We hasten to add, however, that the recent actions of the Catholic University give us much confidence that they will not follow that policy.[50]

Lewis finally considers what was at the time a purely academic question: whether the problem could have been avoided by having some participants trained at other centers in the United States like Harvard, MIT, or Stanford "We think so," he says, "but such a diversification policy would not have been costless of course. Administrative control would have been a bit more difficult and some of the participants would not have benefited from the community of experience and from the special attention we were able to give them."[51]

In the Latin American programs developed later by Arnold Harberger, Gregg Lewis, and Larry Sjaastad there was never a mention about the readiness to explore such a diversification policy. It was clear, on the contrary, that "the community of experience" – as Lewis calls it – was anxious to incorporate more Latin Americans into its own training mission.

CHAPTER 8

The export of the Chicago tradition

In 1965 Sergio de Castro became chairman of the faculty and the control of the Chicago Boys over the School was completed. The year also marked the beginning of the plan to transform the School in Chile into an outpost of Chicago in the expansion of the original doctrinal mission in other Latin American countries. The plan, whose father and main organizer was Arnold Harberger, was principally financed by the Ford Foundation. Its objective – as seen from the Foundation – was to modernize the teaching of economics in certain countries of the region. The intention of the economists in charge went much further however. Their long-term purpose included the introduction of a scientific methodology, of rigorous analytic practices and of a professional ethos but was also motivated – as we plan to show in the following pages – by the idea of transforming the conception of economics prevailing in Latin America by specifically confronting the influence of the Economic Commission for Latin America and of Raúl Prebisch all over the area. The idea to reproduce the Chile Project in other Latin American countries had been present almost from the beginning in the minds of the American professors, most particularly in Harberger. In fact, a first effort was made in 1962, during the development of the Chile Project. This new project was formally known as "The Cuyo Project of the National University of Cuyo, Catholic University of Chile, University of Chicago and the US Agency for International Development in Mendoza, Argentina, under Contract No. AID/1a-1 (Argentina)." The origin of this project was very similar to the Chilean one. In early December 1960, Arnold Harberger visited Mendoza to consult with Albion Patterson, who was by then in charge of the AID in Argentina. On that visit Harberger negotiated with Dr. Corti Videla, then dean of the Faculty of Economic Sciences at the National University of Cuyo, a memorandum to serve as basis for an agreement between the Argentine University, the Catholic University of Chile, and the University of Chicago. In Santiago, Harberger negotiated with Chaná the participation of the Catholic University and corrected the draft aided by Rolf Luders and Luis Arturo Fuenzalida. By late 1961 the documents had been signed, but it was only in September of 1962 that the project got underway with the arrival at Cuyo of four Chicago staff members. These were Arnold Harberger, Larry Sjaastad, Ernesto Fontaine, and Raul Yver. The contract established that the two Chilean participants (Fontaine and Yver) would operate in Argentina as University of Chicago staff.[1]

The general purpose of the program, stated in the three-part agreement declared:

The objective of this agreement is the development in the National University of Cuyo of a center for high level training and research in economics. The University of Cuyo has already embarked on a program (hereinafter called the Cuyo Program) for modernization and improvement of its Faculty of Social Sciences. This agreement enlists in this effort the resources of the University of Chicago and the Catholic University of Chile. It is based on a recognition of the need for superior economic training and research in Argentina, and of the important role which the National University of Cuyo fulfills in its region and in the country. It also recognizes the high standing of the University of Chicago in economics, and the achievements which have been attained in the development of economic training and research at the Catholic University of Chile.[2]

As in the case of the Catholic University, the Chicago group drastically transformed the curriculum of the Cuyo school. As one of the Cuyo reports from Chicago to the AID established:

The Program was largely modeled after the program carried out by the University of Chicago and the Catholic University of Chile some years earlier, there being two major differences. Whereas in the Chile program, the University of Chicago professors devoted nearly all of their time to research and the Research Center established at the Catholic University was an institution dedicated to research, at Cuyo the professors were used primarily for instruction . . . The other difference was that in the case of Cuyo, we were able to draw directly upon the experience and resources of the Catholic University of Chile. The Catholic University of Chile agreed to loan two full-time professors to the Cuyo program. These were professors who had been trained under the earlier program with the Catholic University, and were ideally equipped to function in the role designated for them at Cuyo.[3]

In concrete terms, the Cuyo program included a "specified number of man–years of graduate training at Chicago for Argentine students; for the creation of several new full-time professorial posts with the Faculty of Economic Sciences at Cuyo, for curriculum revision of the Faculty, and for the creation of an Economic Research Center."[4]

Between 1962 and 1967, twenty-four Argentine students were trained at Chicago. At Cuyo, the Chilean and American professors taught the main courses of price theory, mathematical economics, and economic development. Eventually other Chileans like Alberto Valdés and Mario Albornoz came to teach there, and the relationship between the three institutions became quite fluid; yet – from the Chicago point of view – the program was not as successful as its Chilean predecessor. Among the reasons for this were the relative unimportance of the University of Cuyo in national terms, and the ideological and personal disputes between the Argentine faculty members. The final evaluation of the program made by Arnold Harberger was quite optimistic, however, and indicated considerable satisfaction with its results. It stated that the terms of the contracts had been fulfilled by all participants except by the Argentine government which had suspended – due to unnamed reasons – some scholarships for Argentine students. It praised the modernization of Cuyo's teaching of economics and commended – in more moderate terms than the Chile Project reports – the performance of Argentine students at Chicago. The evaluation concluded with certain remarks about the Argentine economy and the positive impact that well-trained economists could potentially have in decision-making in that area. As in the case of their comments on the Chilean situation, the Chicago professors described the economic evolution of Argentina as a series of bad economic policy decisions. Depressions, devaluations, and crisis were due to ignorance, misconceptions, and ideological beliefs. "It seems quite clear that a good part of Argentina's dismal performance with respect to economic growth can be directly attributed to bad economic policy. We are also convinced that these failures can be avoided in the future only via a sustained effort to accelerate economic research and to further increase the number of professional economists practising in Argentina." The report finally advised the AID to continue its programs of training of Argentine economists in the United States.[5]

One year after the initiation of the Cuyo project, Chicago influence extended to the University of del Valle in Cali, Colombia. The Department of Economics of that university had been receiving support from the Rockefeller Foundation and, in 1963, Clifford M. Hardin an executive of that Foundation suggested that Arnold Harberger should arrange the curriculums of study. Harberger visited Cali in March 1963. As Rockefeller was also supporting the Catholic University in Chile at the time, the proposition to deploy some of the Chilean Chicago Boys in the reorganization of the Cali institution was easily worked out. Hardin asked Harberger his opinion about an agreement between the Catholic University and Cali "to bring an economist like de Castro for a few years." Harberger thought that "it might be awfully good if Católica could get a little assistance out of it, for example a 50 percent overrun in order to meet its pressing expenses in Economics which come as a result of Chilean inflation." In a short time de Castro's and Luis Arturo Fuenzalida's appointment had been agreed. In 1965 Harberger was formally appointed by the Universidad del Valle as consultant for the project with funds provided by the Rockefeller Foundation.[6]

The development of the initiative – carefully recorded in the letters and internal documents of the Rockefeller Foundation – is a remarkable example of the way in which Harberger commanded a network of Latin American economists – his students at Chicago – by distributing them in different universities in the region. *It shows at the same time how the most important academic criteria in the selection of the students were their capacity to influence economic policies.*[7] His description of students includes adjectives like "solid" and "strong." He swiftly compares his disciples across countries describing them as "a notch better than" or "the equal to" so and so. In some cases his praise exudes the deep ambition sustaining the Chicago mission. Speaking of Rodrigo Nuñez, a Panamanian student, for example, Harberger writes: "I feel that, with the possible exception of Carlos Massad, Nuñez is the most likely of all Latin Americans we have trained at Chicago to leave his mark on the world in terms of his influence on policy."[8]

The experience of teaching in different countries undoubtedly enriched the academic experience of the young Chilean professors. This pedagogical training – added to their Chicago experience – contributed to the quality of their teaching performance in Chile and to the classroom attraction that some of them – Sergio de Castro in particular – exerted towards their Chilean students. It reaffirmed, at the same time – now in practical terms – the idea that national characteristics, institutional organizations, and social phenomena were of no relevance to economics. The teaching of economics was the same in Chicago and in Panama, or Cali, Colombia. The experience also deepened the distance that separated them from other economists in Chile. Their success with American foundations and American economists contrasted with the isolation they had to tolerate in Chile and with the absolute indifference toward their "science" implicit in the evolution of a society whose elite seemed ineluctably opposed to everything the Chicago Boys believed in. Their science as well as their friends seemed to belong elsewhere.

In a letter between two Rockefeller Foundation executives, great admiration is expressed "by the role which faculty members of the Universidad Católica de Santiago are playing in the development of the graduate program in industrial administration in Cali."[9]

Between 1962 and 1964, Arnold Harberger and his Latin American colleagues at the University of Chicago had successfully established a network of students and institutions in the region. Their contacts and projects went from Monterrey in Mexico to Cuyo in Argentina and the Catholic University in Chile. From the moment that the Chile Project began to look like a success, Harberger developed the idea of building a Chicago center for the study of economics in the area, a center to disseminate economic truth and prevent the advance of heterodoxy and nationalism promoted by ECLA. The Chile Project had been, in fact, just an experiment from which to launch such a project.

By the end of 1962, Harberger told Clifford M. Hardin of the Rockefeller Foundation about his plan. Hardin reported that:

Harberger believes that the University of Chicago might develop a Center for the study of economics in Latin America. *He notes that Raúl Prebisch et al. reject the tools of economics and talk about the vast and vague things like the relationship between the center and the periphery; but Harberger insists that the tools do not change, only the applications. What is needed is a revamping of price theory, monetary theory, international trade theory . . . also other branches of economic theory. Harberger believes that the University of Chicago has demonstrated its effectiveness and has developed links and programs which enable it to make a real contribution.*[10]

In his conversation with Hardin, Harberger indicated his intention to approach the Ford Foundation for this project. The initiative took some time to materialize however. Its postponement, and the changes in its conception were due in no small part to the difficulties experienced by the Chicago disciples in Chile. The "Chicago image" and everything that Chicago economics had come to imply in Chile and among economists in other Latin American countries, did not give much credibility in the Foundations to the argument that Chicago could organize a training center in the region itself. A failure of the project in Chile would have implied something even worse: that it was not a good policy to go on filling the departments of economics of universities in the region with Chicago graduates.

But in 1964 the control by the group of Chicago Boys of the faculty and the School of Economics at the Catholic University gave new strength to Harberger's mission and to his credibility in American foundations. The Chicago expansion was mainly organized around two projects, one conducted at the Catholic University in Santiago for Latin American undergraduates, and a second conducted by Arnold Harberger at Chicago for Latin American graduates.

The Latin American program at Santiago and Chicago and the Ford Foundation

In 1965 the Catholic University and the University of Chicago initiated Latin American programs financed by the Ford Foundation. These were formally independent programs and there is no indication from the Foundation's files that Ford staff saw them as related. Observed under the light of Harberger's vision, however, it seems evident that these two projects had a common design and responded to the same strategy. They were indeed very influential in the consolidation of the group of professors in charge of the Department of Economics in Santiago, in the continuing relationship between the University of Chicago and the Catholic University, and in the reproduction of the Chicago tradition in Chile and its expansion to other Latin American countries.

The examination of the grant records at Ford shows that the Foundation had no perception of Harberger's "anti-ECLA" crusade; or that if some of its staff did, they thought it was not a matter worthy of discussion. The Foundation had no intention of deliberately promoting the Chicago doctrine or any other particular ideological viewpoint. In contrast to USAID, Ford was not involved in a conscious attempt to "right the balance of economics in Chile," or to prevent the development of Marxist or socialist tendencies in economic thought. The Foundation's purposes in supporting economic studies in Chile were therefore in accordance with its stated policy of helping "to meet Latin America's need for an expanded supply of well trained professional economists in universities and government."[11]

This ideological neutrality is demonstrated by the fact that there is no indication of a Foundation preference for the Catholic University over the University of Chile in economics. On the contrary, between 1960 and 1973, for example, the Foundation gave $1,389,689.98 in different grants to the Institute of Economics of the University of Chile and its graduate program compared to $552,000 granted in 1965 ($300,000) and in 1972 ($252,000) to the School of Economics of the Catholic University.[12]

It is also a fact that the Foundation considered the programs promoted by Arnold Harberger at Chicago and most of the development of the School of Economics at the Catholic University to be a complete success. As we shall see, even when describing it, Ford officials in Santiago did not take seriously the Chicago ideology, preferring to depict it as an "image," something more the result of prejudice than of reality. The record shows a certain amount of naiveté in the evaluation of "pluralism" in the School of Economics at the Catholic University, and some indifference vis-à-vis the relationship of the type of economics being taught and Chilean society.

The Ford Foundation records provide an invaluable source of information on the development of these initiatives and the careers of the Chicago Boys. They exhibit, at the same time, the enormous influence of the Ford Foundation in the development of the discipline of economics in Chile. From 1961 the Foundation became the principal foreign contributor in that field, followed by USAID, the Rockefeller Foundation, and the Organization of American States. As Ronald Hellman's study on this subject shows, during the first ten years of the Foundation's involvement "the number of Chilean economists increased some six-fold, from approximately 121 at the beginning of the 1960s to an estimated 727 by 1970. At the same time the number of academic institutions in the field of economic studies in Santiago increased from four to ten."[13] In 1972 Hellman wrote that:

changes in the number and quality of teaching and research staff in these institutions vividly illustrate the remarkable evolution that the discipline has undergone in only a decade's time. For example in 1960 both Universities together employed a total of 32 economists as teachers and researchers. Many of these professors were largely part-time members of their respective staffs. Today, in large part because of Foundation assistance there are some 79 faculty members who are dedicated full-time at the ten schools and centers of economic studies at these two Chilean universities. Beyond their increased numerical strength, Chilean economists are today far better trained than ever before. In 1960, most of the 32 economists only held the Chilean undergraduate commercial engineering degree. By 1971, more than half of the full time economists (46 of 79) held foreign graduate degrees in the discipline; 16 have the Masters, 14 are ABDs and 16 held the PhD. The Foundation assistance has greatly contributed to these changes over the decade. For example, at least 17 of the 30 combined ABD and PhD holders have received some kind of Foundation assistance.[14]

In 1961 the Foundation made its first contribution of $500,000 to the University of Chile Escolatina program, which attempted to develop within four or five years graduate training to the PhD program.[15] In the following decade, the Ford Foundation contributed more than two million dollars to economic studies in Chile.[16] At the beginning its main recipient was the University of Chile. This was in fact an explicit decision, stemming from the fact that the Catholic University was supported by USAID and the Rockefeller Foundation. As Hellman remarks, it is a highly ironic fact that, in spite of this decision, the Foundation's impact was much greater at the Catholic University than at the University of Chile.[17] The initial step in the building of this influence was the support given in 1965 to the Institute of Economics' Latin American undergraduate economics program (PREL).

The program at the Catholic University

In June 1964, the interim dean of the Faculty of Economics and Social Sciences of the Catholic University requested the Ford Foundation for assistance in establishing within the faculty a two-year course to train students from other Latin American countries in economics. The grant would help the Catholic University to create "a special program leading to the approximate equivalent of a bachelor's degree in economics (*Ingeniero Comercial*) for students in economics from other universities in Latin America and, second, to help the economics and the sociology departments of the university to create a permanent new center for research in educational development."[18] The proposal provided for the acceptance of twelve selected foreign students each year as fourth-year students at the Catholic University, giving them a two-year period of intensive training designed to raise them to the same level of competence as the Chilean students. In January 1965 the Ford Foundation approved a grant of $300,000 divided into $213,000 for a five-year support of PREL and $86,800 for a three-year support for a program of social and economics research in education.[19]

There were three assumptions behind PREL. The first was that the quality of economic education at the Catholic University was not only better but greatly superior to that available in most Latin American countries. Secondly, it was assumed that training at the Catholic University was less costly and created fewer problems of adjustment for the Latin American students than sending them to the US or Europe. Third, and most important, as Ronald Hellman's notes indicate, "*because Católica's curriculum and faculty are patterned after US institutions, graduates will be able to do productive graduate work in the United States immediately (in contrast to the early years of the Chicago–Católica program when it was found necessary to utilize much of the first year at Chicago to fill in weak spots in the students' undergraduate training)*."[20]

This was in fact a very important objective of the program. Training at the Catholic University would help students to follow further training in the United States, which meant, in the Chicago Boys' perspective, almost exclusively the University of Chicago. The proposal written by Sergio de Castro, who was soon to be named dean of the faculty and director of the Project, included an indicative reflection on this matter:

Alumni from these [Latin American] institutions, going abroad for advanced training, frequently encounter difficulties in keeping up with the pace of studies in, for example, the better graduate schools in the United States. They tend to get relatively poor grades, at least initially. They require relatively long periods of study in the United States to become well-trained professional economists, and if they can only study for a relatively short time, they typically return to their countries still handicapped by rather serious deficiencies.[21]

There were also other reasons for the Catholic University's interest in this program. The School of Economics wanted to justify the employment of full-time economics professors for a faculty where the vast majority of the students were unwilling to take upper level economics courses, preferring business administration. Finally there was also the interest in competing with the University of Chile and with Escolatina strengthening a faculty which – as the Chicago Boys saw it – would "develop into the first genuine faculty of social sciences in Chile."[22] These objectives converged into the main driving force inspiring the group of Chileans trained at Chicago and their professors – the mission to disseminate truth in economics. This was what impelled the reproduction of the Chile Project and the maintenance of a flow of graduate students from the region to American universities, most of all to Chicago. With PREL the School of Economics at the Catholic University had the opportunity to become the selecting ground not only for Chilean but for other Latin American students following graduate studies at Chicago.

Admission to the program would be by examination and interviews to be conducted by the Catholic University professors. A Ford Foundation document indicates that: "In March 1965 Mario Corbo and Sergio de Castro traveled to different Latin American countries to interview students. Corbo went to Peru, Bolivia and Ecuador; de Castro to Colombia, Panama and Mexico."[23] The program designed was reviewed and endorsed by Arnold Harberger; it followed closely the experience of the Chile Project. Dr. William D. Carmichael, dean of the Graduate School of Business and Public Administration and professor of economics at Cornell, a consultant for the Ford Foundation, also gave his approval.[24]

The program at Chicago

While the Catholic University requested Ford Foundation support for an *undergraduate program*, the University of Chicago requested that same year Foundation support for *a graduate program* directed towards Latin American students. In April 1965, Arnold Harberger sent to the Ford Foundation *"a Proposal for the Establishment of a Center for Latin American Economic Instruction and Research at the University of Chicago."*

Harberger's proposal had the following general objectives:

(a) To help meet Latin America's vital need for a greatly expanded supply of well-trained professional economists, both in their universities and in government.
(b) To provide for Latin American graduate students of economics a curriculum which includes, both in the principal courses and in specialized courses, materials that are directly relevant to the types of problems Latin American economists are likely to encounter.
(c) To provide a continuing flow of high quality research on Latin American economic problems by American and Latin American economists.[25]

The program was the continuation of the "Chile Project." In his proposal, Harberger describes the "deficiencies" in the patterns of training of the major centers of graduate studies in the US and insists on the need to expose students to theory and to its application to the Latin American cases. For this purpose he proposed the introduction of at least one course and one seminar meeting throughout the year devoted to Latin American topics.[26] The proposal describes the enthusiastic evaluations made of his program in Chile by AID, ICA and "external observers." The US Advisory Commission on International Educational and Cultural Affairs, for instance, had this to say about the contract: "the relationship of the University of Chicago with the Catholic University in Santiago . . . has resulted in an impressive revitalization in the study of economics in Chile, spreading even to other Latin American countries." Harberger does not include evaluations made by Chileans.[27] He concludes by saying: "we feel that the results of this program have demonstrated the capacity of the University of Chicago to produce economists who can become leaders of their profession in Latin American countries."

In May 1965 an initial grant of $400,000 was authorized after what a Foundation document described as "lengthy negotiations." This grant extended to 1972, when the Foundation staff concluded that "Chicago had achieved considerable success" and a $125,000 terminal grant was approved for three years. Grant funds were provided for reduced levels of faculty salaries and graduate fellowships and for seminars, travel, and secretarial support.[28]

The two programs financed by the Ford Foundation developed during different periods and had different impacts. We shall first describe their formal results beginning with the undergraduate program conducted at the Catholic University.

Between 1965 and 1970, the Catholic University professors enrolled in PREL sixty students coming from ten Latin American countries.[29] "Through 1969, twenty-nine completed all course requirements, and ten also met thesis requirements and obtained the degree of Commercial Engineer (economist)."[30] The results were mixed. As the Ford Foundation report indicates:

in strict terms of the main stated objective, the record is mixed. About two thirds of the grant-financed students completed all courses, some with grade average among the best and fully equal to Chilean classmates. Yet from the reports and our files, only three of the participants are known to have gone to graduate work and they only after some delay. It does appear that most returned to their own countries, and often to teaching posts.[31]

The report adds elsewhere that six of the eight participants who began in 1965 and completed course work in 1966 or 1967 were later teaching at universities in Colombia (del Valle), Ecuador (Guayaquil), Mexico (Monterrey), and Peru (Católica de Lima). But the limited number of students following postgraduate studies was obviously a setback for the program.

The problems were of three different kinds. The first was related to the students selected. Most of the candidates for the program came from provincial universities in Ecuador, Bolivia, Peru, and Paraguay and, as the Ford evaluation says, "couldn't cope with intensive, full-time study, nor with English bibliographies and rigorous classroom discussion led by energetic teachers." A second area of difficulties stemmed "from the University revolution of 1967" (at the Catholic University of Chile). The student-led reform of that year – the report says – "affected PREL's recruiting and derailed efforts to get fellowships funded by international agencies. In 1967, eleven students had such financing; there have never again been such resources available, though in part this reflects a general cut in budget of USAID in Latin America."[32] The third type of problems appears to be related to unrealistic expectations of the Chilean recipients with respect to other funding for the program and to certain misunderstandings between the faculty of the Catholic University and the Foundation.

The Foundation decided to stop the financing of the program in 1968. The denial of the supplementary grant requested by Dean Rolf Luders seems to have come more from internal contradictions in the Ford Foundation than from outright criticisms against the program.[33] It is interesting to note, however, that Luders and the other Chicago Boys thought that this decision stemmed either "from a bias against supporting undergraduate studies, or a bias against them for the 'Chicago image' and for not being the National University."[34] That this was not the reason is shown by the fact that – as we shall discuss in the next chapter – the Foundation generously supported in 1972 the Masters program at the Católica. At the same time, the records show an almost repetitive description of the Catholic University School of Economics as "the most competent economic group in Latin America, with a solid record in publications and generally high standards in research and teaching."[35]

Before discussing the image of the Catholic University at the Ford Foundation, let us turn to the Chicago program.

The final report submitted by Arnold Harberger to the Ford Foundation is a short document indicating in a concise and straightforward manner the enormous productivity of his program. During the period between October 1965 and September 1973 – he says – the enrollment of Latin American graduate students in the Department of Economics ranged upward from about twenty-five at the beginning to over forty at the end. By 1975, over a hundred students had been involved, and twenty-six Chicago PhDs and seventy-four MAs had returned to Latin America.[36] Those who failed to do so "are overwhelmingly concentrated in Washington in the international organizations, where their work deals with and impinges directly upon the economic situation of Latin America."[37]

As always, Harberger emphasized theory over everything else. In his reports to the Foundation he states that "on the training side, the emphasis was always on putting out first class economists," with a command "over the tools of the discipline which would enable them to function well anywhere." In this framework, a first prerequisite was the "de-Latinamericanization" of the students. At Chicago – he wrote – unlike other places in the United States, "*it was not the area interest which predominated over the disciplinary orientation, but the disciplinary interest that predominated over the area orientation*":

As has been repeatedly noted in prior reports, conversations and correspondence, *our* Latin American orientation did not at all have the purpose of "keeping up to date" with everything going on on the economic scene in Latin America. Instead its aims were a) *to keep our Latin American students from being "culturally alienated," by continually showing them that the economics that they were learning could really be applied in useful and productive ways to problems emanating from the Latin American environment,* b) to see to it that our general course program for all students incorporated in the numerous special insights that could be distilled from study of the Latin American economic scene (viewed in the sense as a laboratory in which, for historical reasons, certain general economic phenomena could be studied more deeply . . .) and c) of providing special attention to our Latin American students so that they would actually achieve their full potential growth as professional economists during their stay at Chicago.[38]

The Chicago professor adds elsewhere: "The same spirit pervades the faculty research efforts . . . Though many of the works . . . have to do with specific countries, the spirit underlying them was not country- but problem-oriented. Our studies of inflation in Chile, of planning in Argentina or of fiscal policy in Panama were obviously strongly influenced by the country setting, but mainly they represent the application of good economic analysis to a specific environment."[39]

In a review of the Chicago grant made in 1970, Eduardo Venezian, a Chilean Chicago graduate who was a consultant for the Foundation, made a very precise description of the program and of the attitudes of the Latin American students toward it. "Through my contacts with students," he says, "I could detect a high regard for the Chicago Economics Department (staff, teaching, system, etc.) generally, but less enthusiasm with the 'development' side of it. Probably the main reason for this is that students coming to Chicago typically get concerned with becoming good *economists* and take a theoretical bent (a result of the 'Chicago approach'); hence they discount the more applied fields and especially those that are associated with 'weak' professorial people (such as development)."[40]

Though the situation changed with different generations of Latin Americans and of Chileans, Venezian's observation seems correct. In our case Chileans were directly influenced by Martin Bailey and Harry Johnson (the first group), by Larry Sjaastad and his monetary approach (the second), and by Milton Friedman (all of them). While some students did not follow the price theory and monetary theory courses with Friedman, all of them were strongly influenced by his books. But the development courses were also in a way "theory courses." Venezian describes the "Chicago approach to development" saying that "it differs from the typical economic development programs at other universities and one often encounters rather sanguine reactions about Chicago economics around Latin America":

I believe the essential points are: a) there is a heavy emphasis on economic theory, particularly micro or price theory; b) there is less emphasis on the macro side and almost complete neglect of "organic" approach theories; economic development is not treated as a field, but rather as a collection of problems cutting across many subjects . . . That is, the approach is to apply what economic theory is known to specific problems of countries in different stages of development, rather than taking the total problem of development all at once. For the same reason, little use is made of country case studies; instead, examples are used to illustrate specific micro-problems.[41]

Venezian added: "whether this approach is better or worse than others is largely a matter of judgment and is not to be settled here. The important fact is that Chicago is producing good economists, who are working on applied problems in Latin America. Time will show which brand of training turns out to be the best."[42] This statement summarizes perfectly the attitude that the Foundation had to the Chicago tradition and its export to Latin America.

Let us now discuss in a more detailed form the Foundation perception of the characteristics which gave to Chicago – as Kalman Silvert wrote in a memo – "an excellent reputation plus a controversial ideological aroma in Latin America." We should begin by saying that it would be unreasonable to expect a "joint evaluation" of the Chicago and the Católica programs. From the Ford Foundation perspective these were two separate projects and two separate grants, managed by two different offices in the Foundation. Even when – after the military coup of 1973 – a drastic decision was taken to cut all support to Chilean universities, the Foundation continued to perceive the Chicago project and the training of Chileans at Chicago as a success story.[43]

At the same time, the documents in the Foundation archives give sufficient information on the impact that the Chicago program was having at the Catholic University and of the mimetic relationship between the Católica faculty and some professors at Chicago. There was also considerable discussion and concern about "ideology" in the program as well as in the methods of recruitment of Chilean students by Harberger. In the evaluations of the Chicago program made by the Foundation, one finds sufficient comments on the "closed" character of the group, as well as on the lack of interaction with other economists and other approaches, to elicit concern. But none of these questions led the Foundation to seriously question its support for these programs or – as far as we could ascertain – to discuss in writing its concerns with Arnold Harberger. Moreover, none of these concerns changed the characterization of the program as a "success," which was in fact the most common concept in the Ford Foundation staff description of the Chicago program: "I am impressed by the formidable array of students and faculty research, the cross fertilization, and Chicago's tested ability to identify talent in Latin American economics," said one of the Foundation members.[44] "This is one of our most successful grants. Chicago has recruited, trained and returned an impressive number of economists to Chile, who have already made significant contributions," said another.[45]

Why was this image of success unmarred by the criticisms and doubts that the Foundation seemed to have?

The answer to this question lies, probably, in the perception that the Foundation had about the situation in Chile and Latin America at that time, and of the type of ideological and political challenges confronting the social sciences in these countries. Reformism and revolutionary perspectives were the sole competing approaches in sociology and economics. A tendency to political partisanship was observable at the universities which – from the mid-1960s onward – began to experience a revolutionary process of transformation led by the students. At the same time the experience at the University of Chile, which had been heavily supported by the Foundation but had lost – after 1964 – the best of its professors to the Frei government, initiating a process of academic decay, left the impression that "institution building" was a first priority.

Contrary to that experience, the Catholic University had managed, through its agreement with AID and Chicago, to establish a permanent full-time faculty, and had apparently been able to weather all political crises. Its conservatism was harmless in a political sense; it simply could not be effective in a country going leftwards. It forced the Chicago Boys to remain at the university and to be academics. It kept politics out of the faculty. Ideology, more than a hindrance, appeared in this case as an asset.

Furthermore, as we have already mentioned, the Foundation continued to give support to the University of Chile and – as Hellman has argued – increasingly developed a favorable bent toward Christian Democrats and their efforts to promote a social science linked to the solution of the main problems of the country's development.[46] The School of Economics at the Catholic University and the Chicago University programs were never assumed, therefore, by the Foundation to be their only horse in Chilean economic studies. As Hellman points out:

the Foundation staff during the last decade had been overly concerned with academic criteria narrowly construed. In its desire to achieve institutional stability, the Foundation's staff overlooked or failed to weigh significantly such factors as the ideologies of the participants it was supporting and the political process of Chile at the time.[47]

The Foundation did not perceive therefore the impact that this ideological implantation was having among students both in Santiago and in Chicago up until the end. In its final formal comment to the program, James Trowbridge writes that: "*Through careful negotiation at the outset and diligent administration and maintenance of quality thereafter, Professor Harberger made the Foundation's investment in the University of Chicago's Department of Economics a highly fruitful one for the economics profession in Latin America.*" His conclusion received the following hand written comment by Jeffrey Puryear: "*Although the quality and impact of this endeavor cannot be denied, its ideological narrowness constituted a serious deficiency. The interests of developing countries are not well-served by exposure to a single point of view. Thus programs like this one should be balanced by others that are equal in quality but different in values and intellectual perspective." To which William Carmichael added: "I concur with this very important observation."*[48]

Let us now review some of the remarks in the Ford Foundation records on the Chicago and the Catholic University grants.

The most remarkable expressions of concern came, of course, from Kalman Silvert. In a memo to William D. Carmichael dated 7 January 1972, he comments on the Harberger reports on the dissertations written by Latin American students at Chicago in the following terms:

I have known for many years that Al Harberger is a macro man who wants the advantages of the total-society view as well as the rigor of the micro techniques. If he is managing to get the two together, however, we should know about it. Harberger several times states of these dissertations that they break new paths. I am not competent to judge whether they do or not, but I suggest that we should find out in connection with a more sustained effort to rethink our position in regard to economics. I have made the point before, and repeat it merely to summarize: institutional economics and political economy need immediate revival. To what extent are these Chicago students contributing to that revival?[49]

From the particular viewpoint of Chicago, the answer to this question could have been positive. In fact it became explicit in Chile some years later. The Chicago Boys were reviving classical economics, which in their view was the only true science. As most of them adhered to the radical vision of the market as a substitute for the state, and of science as a substitute for politics, they were indeed producing a particular vision of political economy. But this answer, which would have seemed abhorrent to a man so aware of cultural and historical phenomena as Silvert was, did not emerge at the time. Then, in fact, the answer lay probably where Silvert proposed to look – in the dissertations – but it was hidden by a conceptual and methodological framework, a scientific paradigm, which insulated the normative considerations implicit in the economic approach. It was not evident at the time that this scientific paradigm constituted by itself a normative proposition. Silvert, then, could only put his finger where ideology was apparent: in the image that the University of Chicago had in the eyes of the Chilean and Latin American students. As he said, "the Latin Americans themselves are generally aware of the differences between LSE and Chicago, say, and have successfully sought training in very different kinds of departments as well as in many different countries; and, lastly, the discipline of economics in Latin America has matured sufficiently to incorporate differing sets of attitudes toward the discipline and its practice. Nevertheless, this Chicago grant raises the problem of a tie-in between fellowships and at least an alleged ideological bias toward the discipline."[50]

In Santiago, John Strasma, the economic consultant for the Foundation, also gave his opinion on the ideology question. His comments make extraordinary reading more than two decades later:

Yes, a definite ideology permeates this program, but it is a far cry from the ideological view commonly attributed to Chicago in Chile. Contrary to the impression left in Chile by visiting professors sent by Chicago between 1955 and 1963, this program does not advocate unilateral free trade in a world full of trade barriers, nor monetary restrictions as the single important tool of stabilization policy, nor higher food prices as the sole policy change needed to resolve all problems of production and employment in Latin American agriculture. These views were advanced in Chile by two professors not good enough for Chicago's own faculty, but hired to fulfill Chicago's obligations under an AID contract . . .

From the reports, my visits, and conversations with professors and graduates in the program over recent years, I would describe the essential ideology of this program as a cult of rational decision-making at project levels and in the aggregate.[51]

This is a remarkable definition: in fact Chicago ideology appeared a decade later in Chile as precisely the combination of the first diverse elements that Strasma does not consider as part of the tradition, and that "cult of rational decision-making" which was nothing but the simple adjudication of an overall rationality to the market. But, as we have observed before, a cult for rational decision-making was not in itself a particularly controversial characteristic at a time in which political partisanship and Marxism seemed to invade the campuses, threatening "objective" academic practices. Furthermore, as Strasma said, it was a characteristic of the whole economic profession. The extra emphasis that Chicago gave to the matter was what originated the "Chicago image."

Another problem addressed in the Ford Foundation documents refers to the closed character of the group and its inability and unwillingness to open its academic discussion to representatives of other currents in economics or the social sciences in general. In 1972, Reynold E. Carlson from the Ford Foundation office in Lima wrote to New York saying: "the distinguished list of speakers at the Chicago seminars . . . seem to be limited to ad hoc case studies. Then too, the list is already weighted with PhDs already trained in the 'Chicago School.' I do not see the equivalent of a Jaguaribe [political science] at Stanford or a Furtado [economics] at Yale as visiting scholars."[52] Carlson was right; in fact, between July 1970 and September 1971 the outside speakers from Chile invited to address the Latin American Seminar were Ernesto Fontaine, Rolf Luders, Marcelo Selowsky, and Vittorio Corbo, all of them Chicago graduates.[53]

In Santiago, however, the Foundation office seems not to have taken too seriously the criticisms of "lack of alternatives" that the program at the Católica offered to those students looking for a different perspective from that of the Chicago tradition. These criticisms were – as we shall see in the next chapter – one of the main points of the internal discussion at the School. From the Foundation point of view, however, students taking Marxist economics at CEREN (Centro de Estudios de la Realidad Nacional, a leftist academic institution) or the Ricardo Ffrench-Davis course on "international commerce" at Escolatina were seen as simply "taking advantage of the other institutes and centers"[54] without any questioning of the reason why such a numerous staff of professors could not develop these alternatives within the School. At the same time, the Foundation took at face value the explicit promises made by Sergio de Castro of cooperation with the Escolatina program at the University of Chile without seeing that – as Hellman wrote later – the Chicago Boys considered the Escolatina graduate program as inferior to their own undergraduate program.[55] The fact that there was no institutional cooperation with Escolatina or with the Institute of Economics of the University of Chile tended, however, paradoxically, to strengthen the Foundation conception of a mythical institutional "pluralism" in economic science in Chile. In fact, the existence of multiple institutions with different perspectives did not imply pluralism. It did not lead to an open academic debate or to a minimum exchange of ideas. What should have been observed, on the contrary, remained ignored: the fact that from the Chicago Boys' viewpoint the other economic orientations present in Chile had no academic stature; in some cases they did not even belong to the profession. The peaceful academy of economists described in some Foundation documents was in fact quite distant from reality:

The Catholic University Institute group studies policy formation with a relatively "orthodox" set of models, adapting them to the Chilean situation, while the staff of the University of Chile's Institute is seeking to study the same sort of question from the starting point of Marxist economic theory, also considerably modified and adapted for Chilean applications. As the rancor of the 1970 election fades [sic], there is growing interest in communication but it is already clear that the Institutes are seldom duplicating each other's work.[56]

The Chicago Boys were not characterized by a big publication output. On the contrary, their academic publications were very scarce and limited to very specific topics. The Foundation staff seem to have been aware of this factor which did not, however, change their description of the Institute as "one of the best." In his evaluation of the Chicago program Eduardo Venezian wrote: "I think that the output of published research by Latin American–Chicago students is quite small (although some of top quality) relative to the number of such students turned out over the last ten years. I suggest that one reason may be the limited (or lack of) training in research received in the course of their studies."[57] The observation is surprising when compared to the "great emphasis on research training" invariably indicated in the Chicago reports.

In Santiago John Strasma shared this concern. In a detailed report including a portrait of each of the professors teaching at the Católica, Strasma mentions the lack of publications of some of the professors who most fitted the "Chicago image." Of Sergio de Castro he says: "his administrative load may explain the fact that his published articles are mainly descriptive or theoretical essays at the level of a professor's lecture notes." Of his research work he adds: "he set out to replicate in Chile the work on the economics of education à la Theodore Schultz, his old mentor." Sergio de la Cuadra – Strasma says – "has written several essays all circulated in a mimeographed form." Gert Wagner has "no publications other than a pedantic note on the reverse ratio in Chilean banking legislation."[58] While some of the other members of the faculty like Alberto Valdés and Dominique Hachette had a good publication record, the fact is that the Chicago Boys in general were not known for their academic productivity. Besides the reason argued by Venezian, this might well be another indication of the isolation of the Chicago graduates and of their tendency to develop their work and discussion within the closed circuit of the Chicago School initiates.

The Chicago subsidiary: some final notes and comments

From 1965 onwards the Catholic University School of Economics incorporated into its faculty new professors trained at Chicago. As Gregg Lewis had written in his last report to USAID: "the members of the faculty had been keenly aware of the importance of providing their own replacement as they left temporarily and permanently and . . . worked diligently and with considerable success to obtain scholarships for advanced training abroad for their best students." The "social reproduction" of the first group of Chicago Boys was remarkably successful. In 1967 the Economic Research Center of the School had sixteen full-time members of which ten including the dean of the faculty (de Castro), the director of the School (Baraona) and the director of the Research Center (Luders) were Chicago graduates. But the important fact was that new Chicago-trained professors were coming in and a new generation was being formed.

The words of concern expressed by some of the authorities of the faculty about the "Chicago image" was at best a screen to dissipate the Foundation's concern. Robert L. West from the Rockefeller Foundation reported in 1964 that:

Baraona, at least, is somewhat disturbed by the heavy emphasis on training at the University of Chicago, but he insists that it has not resulted in a single emphasized viewpoint, but rather has resulted in a wide array of viewpoints being brought back from Chicago to Chile. He states that the structuralist emphasis is represented within the Faculty, but not as strongly as at the National University. Perhaps the most disturbing feature of the influence of the University of Chicago is that the better graduates of the Catholic University, on which the faculty will rely for its future recruitment of professors, continue to go to the University of Chicago for their doctoral training. Baraona is aware of the dangers of this sort of inbreeding but has found it difficult to influence the graduates who are familiar with personnel from the University of Chicago and know little of the opportunities provided for graduate education in economics in other centers of the US or abroad.[59]

What Baraona called the "familiarity" with the Chicago professors was a characteristic actively promoted among the students of the Catholic University School by the first generation of Chicago trainees of which Baraona was a member. In fact, some of the best students at the Catholic University – those of a rightwing persuasion – were incorporated into an "intimacy group" with the old boys and their highest ambition was to go to the University of Chicago. "Going to Chicago" was the uppermost distinction a rightwing Catholic University economics student could receive. More than ever before, Chicago played, at the end of the 1960s, a role of "external referent" to the old boys and their new recruits. It became an ideological and a professional referent. Tom Davis saw this process from the beginning.

Davis said that going to Chicago has taken on a special meaning, so many having gone and returned, having taken the same courses that the comparison of grades has made a curious situation. Those that have nothing to lose are glad to go to Chicago, but anybody who has something to risk is afraid to go because he is already set up here and goes there and gets a poor grade in an important course and is badly hurt here; whereas, if his reputation here is not established, he can go there and if he does well he comes back and his fortune is made.[60]

While some changes were introduced after the university reform of 1967 and new professors representing different points of view were recruited, these changes did not alter the basic fact of Chicago hegemony. This control was not only based on the right of the Chicago Boys to determine their own replacement and on their rule that new faculty members had to be approved by a unanimous decision, but also in the identification of rightwing students with Sergio de Castro, Ernesto Fontaine, Rolf Luders, Sergio de la Cuadra, and Pablo Baraona. This identification expressed itself most of all in the decision to prefer Chicago over any other foreign alternative, a preference which Arnold Harberger was ready to accept.

In a memorandum to Peter Bell, John Strasma denounced Harberger's tactics to recruit students from the Católica. The story is worth reproducing, for it involves the student who would be the leader of the second generation of Chicago Boys, Miguel Kast. Strasma wrote to Bell:

In at least one case [Kast] a brilliant student failed even to complete applications to Harvard, MIT and Oxford because Harberger passed through Chile, met him and assured him on the spot of admission and a tuition fellowship. Kast is doing well, but told me in February that he is aware of the Chicago image in Chile. He now realizes he should have gone to Harvard or MIT for his own professional prestige and for the image of the Catholic University here. I just reviewed our files, finding that none of the students receiving funds from us to study at Chicago in the last three years even applied to another graduate school, despite our advice. Chicago thus actually worked against this office's program goal of diversification . . .

This office made 17 individual fellowship awards in economics and agricultural economics in 1969, 1970 and 1971, six of them for study at Chicago. Five of these received tuition waivers from Chicago, presumably with grant funds, before applying to us . . . For new students then, Chicago has behaved more like a football recruiter than a last-resort source of funding for good men overlooked by this office.[61]

In search of politics

The Chicago Boys' essentially academic project met obstacles that were
unforeseen by, and frustrating for, those behind the introduction of economic
science into Chile in the mid-1950s. The professional and pedagogic success
of the Chicago disciples gave them great influence over their pupils, but this
did not extend itself to the rest of society much less to government decision-
making.

In 1967, the bulk of Chile's conservative forces began to contemplate an
authoritarian solution to what they saw as a crisis in the basic tenets of the
social order that hitherto had ruled society. The Chicago Boys shared this
sense of rebellion against state-induced change. In this and subsequent
chapters, reference is made to two processes that converge and decisively
mark this collective biography: on the one hand, the economists' conviction
that they needed to take more decided steps towards becoming involved in
politics and, on the other, the increasing receptiveness of the business world to
the free market discourse propounded by the Chicago Boys.

Nineteen sixty-seven was the year of the student revolution in Chilean
universities. The student organizations led by members of the Christian
Democratic Party first occupied the buildings of the Catholic University in
Valparaiso, then the Catholic University in Santiago and finally the University
of Chile, the state institution. The occupation of the Catholic University, on
11 August 1967 was, however, the most resounding event in this series of
student revolts. The Catholic University was still seen by the Chilean
conservative sectors as a stronghold of tradition – the last expression of
conservative Catholic thought resisting the reformist and progressive tendencies predominant in the Chilean Catholic church.

The revolt, however, was the last step in a long process of organization and
discussion among students on the character of the university, in a society
undergoing rapid social change. Prior to the measure of force, the students
had attempted to negotiate, without result, with the conservative *Consejo
Superior* of the university and had finally carried out a plebiscite asking the
students to vote in favor or against the resignation of the rector, Bishop Silva

Santiago, which obtained an overwhelmingly favorable response. Their two main demands were for a university linked to and in the service of Chilean society, implying by that a change in the oligarchical or upper-class character of the institution, and for the democratic election of the university authorities. This meant the election of the rector and all other authorities by *claustros*, or conventions where the university community, represented proportionately by faculty members, students, and administrative employees, would vote and elect the authorities.

The students led by FEUC, their organization, occupied all the university buildings except one: the School of Economics. A majority of the students in that school were conservative and opposed the occupation; moreover, the bucolic place chosen by the Chicago Boys to establish their own independent campus was located in the upper side of Santiago, too far away from where the majority of students were concentrated and the battles were being waged.

After twenty days of occupation of the central building of the university, FEUC won a complete victory. During that time it had received overwhelming support from the students and the backing of a majority of the faculty members of the university. Even those who rejected "the use of force" thought that the archaic university structures were doomed and students were instinctively promoting modernization. Rector Silva Santiago and the old Superior Council resigned. Authority was given by Rome to the Cardinal Archbishop of Santiago, Raúl Silva Henríquez, who appointed as "prorector," with authority to organize the *claustro*, a young professor of the School of Architecture who had been chosen by the students from a list of names provided by the cardinal, Fernando Castillo Velasco.[1] The "New University" had begun: within one year sweeping reforms had been introduced in all universities in Chile.

The process of reform at Chilean universities cannot be understood in isolation from the general situation in the country since the election of the Christian Democratic government of President Frei in 1964. Yet we have chosen to address first the situation inside the Catholic University, more precisely in the School of Economics. We will turn later to the general characteristics of the political and ideological process in Chile during the 1960s. This is in fact the order in which the Chicago Boys observed the development of events: it was not until the ideological battles sweeping the country penetrated their own ideological stronghold, threatening their views and their influence over students, that they decided to move at least part of their activities out of the university, into the power centers of the political right. For the student revolution highlighted and gave new impetus to the old criticisms raised against the Chicago Boys by a group of students and professors at the School of Economics and, this time, it was impossible for the group of economists to discard them as simple expressions of ignorance or prejudice. Neither the situation in the country nor that in the university allowed a careless reading of the strength behind the demands for a drastic change in the orientation of the teaching of economics.

The Chicago Boys were slow, however, in understanding the dimensions of the reform movement at the university. In fact, the first reaction to the university occupation, coming from Dean Sergio de Castro and the permanent faculty members at the Economics School, was unusually angry and tough-worded. In a first draft prepared by de Castro, the Faculty of Economic and Social Sciences agreed to condemn most emphatically the attitude of what it described improperly as a "group of students and persons from outside the university" who had committed "an act of thuggery" (*un acto de matonaje*) which prevented academic freedom. Dean de Castro's statement drastically repudiated the idea of a 25 percent student participation in the *claustro pleno* (the university convention), it declared the *a priori* illegitimacy of any such convention, and demanded the immediate cancellation of membership of the university for all the students involved, which meant in fact their expulsion. It ended threatening the Superior Council that the faculty would not tolerate any solution to the crisis which did not consider these previous points.[2] Some days later, Sergio de Castro resigned as dean of the faculty in solidarity with the rector.

During the frantic days following the university occupation, the Chicago Boys held tight against the reform, joining the most conservative groups at the university. Their view at the time was that "violence" could not generate any legitimate order and their reaction was an apparent moral revulsion to the students' attitude. It was then that their relationship with the groups calling themselves *gremialistas* – the ultra-conservative Catholic youth headed by Jaime Guzmán – was established.[3] The occupation of the university had the effect of uniting them with other faculty members from departments with which they had no previous relationship. The impact of their discourse and analytical abilities in meetings with other more traditional conservative groups was immediate. Sergio de Castro became one of the leaders of the anti-reform movement.

The rebellion also attracted the attention of the conservative newspaper *El Mercurio*, with which by now some of the Chicago Boys were associated. In angry editorials the paper denounced the occupation as a result of a communist infiltration in the student organizations. In response, the FEUC leaders placed a gigantic sign on the front of the central university building announcing: "*Chileno: el Mercurio miente.*"[4] The victory of the rebels generated an intolerable situation for the Chilean right, for conservatives in the Catholic church, and also for the Chicago Boys.

A Rockefeller Foundation staff member reported:

I attended an economics faculty meeting last week in which the topic of discussion was whether to resign now or wait and see who wins the Rector's election in November. Some cooler heads prevailed [e.g. Luders and de Castro] and a wait and see attitude was adopted. Nevertheless Pablo Baraona's resignation which had been previously tendered was not withdrawn. It was a bit unpleasant to be sitting in on a session which at times seemed to herald the dissolution of that group of professors.[5]

Pablo Baraona indeed resigned as director of the School, but he became at the same time the most active polemicist against the critics within the faculty. He felt the obligation to defend the School and its history against what he saw as prejudices and political attacks.

Criticisms had increased in fact since the School's change to the new building in Los Domínicos almost two years earlier. The new School, located far away from the main university campus, was the concrete expression of the "autonomy" of economic science from other disciplines.[6] As might be expected, the independent campus had the intended result of increasing the *esprit de corps* of the faculty and the students. But a minority of students and faculty members realized that this independence also meant a tighter control by the Chicago Boys over what was taught and what should be excluded from the teaching of the discipline. They were worried, for example, by the lack of courses on the role of the public sector, or of courses in economic development.[7] More than that, their criticism was directed against the values orienting the teaching of the discipline and the implications this had for the development of Chile. This was the discussion which would emerge after the events of August 1967.

In a leaflet published immediately after the resolution of the conflict entitled "Our Vision of the Catholic University of Chile" and under the heading of "The Unexpected Dividends of Violence" the majority of the faculty of the School declared:

After a solution to the students' conflict was imposed, our School has received the visit of numerous persons who suggest changes in its "orientation." We are not against changes and we like constructive criticism . . . We find strange however that these suggestions, which did not appear during the many years in which these "advisers" have been related to the School, emerge precisely at this moment. We are even more stupefied when, attempting to define precisely the content of some of these suggestions, we verify that what is attempted is not the intensification of the study or the research in some of the fields of economic science, but of the introduction, under the guise of formative courses, of topics which fall more properly in the field of ideological indoctrination. While we respect all ideologies, we oppose – and we shall oppose – what seems to be the intention to present ideological judgments as positive conclusions of economic science.[8]

The document was answered some days later by Mario Zañartu SJ, a Jesuit priest who held a PhD in economics and was a part-time professor at the

School. Zañartu, a close friend of Roger Veckemans, the old adversary of the
Chicago Boys, and one of the "advisers" alluded to in the document, bluntly
responded that "the intention to present ideological judgments as positive
conclusions of economics science" was precisely the characteristic of the
School of Economics of the Catholic University and not the suggestion of the
reformist "advisers" or the "dividend of violence." "The present group of
professors," he wrote, "does not acknowledge that their teaching implicitly
contains a series of ideological judgments which coincide with the positions of
certain economic power groups in Chilean society." "What the new School
demands," he continued, "is that these ideological judgments be acknowledged, that their convenience be judged and that certain corrections be
applied, corrections which could consist, maybe, in the introduction of a
plurality of ideological backgrounds or in the selection of ideological
backgrounds more in accordance with the reality in which the national
community or the Catholic University lives."[9] Quoting some underlined
sentences of the Chicago Boys' document Zañartu added, among others, the
following criticisms:

the present faculty body of the School of Economics tend to disqualify as "ideological
indoctrination" any subject which is not reduced to the empirical verification of some
variables . . . Even courses which are as proper for an economics school as Economic
Development or as proper for a Catholic University as Socio-economic Doctrine of the
Church tend to be qualified as instruments of "ideological indoctrination."

"Logical rigorousness and empirical content." These two basic requisites that the
faculty body repeats as fundamental for the orientation of the school of economics can
be utilized in such a way as to cancel each other out . . . logical rigorousness and
empirical content can be alternatively used to disqualify conclusions of logical
rigorousness and empirical content disliked by the ideological background of the
present faculty body of the School.

"The actions of the authorities [of the School] result from a general consensus and
important decisions are always taken as a body." Yes, but only belong to the body of
professors who are in agreement beforehand with the ideological orientation of the
present constituents of that body.

"The untouchable role of positive science in the scientific and professional education of
the students." Should not be confused with the role of the ideology underlying the
positive science transmitted by the present faculty body; this ideology is not
untouchable, and to touch it does not imply questioning the role of positive science in
the scientific and professional education of students.

"[Economics should be taught] with arguments derived from reality and logic in the
framework of terrenal life." Of course, but with the condition that reality not be
reduced just to what interests the present faculty body to verify empirically, and that
logic not be reduced to what agrees with presuppositions dictated by a specific

ideological background. Besides, the reference to the type of life under discussion does not seem necessary: the suggestions made at the demand of some of the School professors do not refer to the organization of celestial life.[10]

Zañartu's attack was the first "illustrated" criticism the Chicago Boys had received at the university. The Jesuit economist could not be accused – as Chaná had been – of academic archaism or ignorance of economics. He had come back with a PhD in economics from Columbia University in 1962 and had found – in his words – that the Catholic University School was "almost 100 percent Friedman oriented" and that "the importance of price theory permeated everything intruding into just about all courses: *finanzas públicas*; *economía internacional*; *economía política*, not to mention of course the more micro fields." Zañartu saw "the Chileans who returned from Chicago after 1960" as "even more Friedmanite than Friedman himself."[11]

Observations such as these were muted criticisms, however, at least until Frei's election in 1964. For Frei's "Revolution in Liberty" – as we shall see – had affected the debate about the need for more planning and government intervention in the economic process, reinforcing the position of "the anti-Friedman forces" inside the School and unveiling the polarity of social and political views which certain "academic" positions implied. Even after that election, however, the uncontested hegemonic position the Friedmanites enjoyed at the School allowed them to effectively suppress every criticism and dismiss each argument they disliked as ideological. Only the drastic change introduced into the School's immediate environment by the 1967 reform could also produce a change in the group's attitude towards criticism. Zañartu's observations were not now treated with indifference but infuriated and threatened the group. Outraged letters were sent to Sergio de Castro demanding a meeting of the faculty in which Zañartu be compelled to "personally substantiate" his charges.[12]

Some of these letters show the difficulty that the group had in understanding the nature of the criticism being raised. Ernesto Fontaine, for example, tells Zañartu that he cannot understand "what impels you along this road which . . . should be forbidden to persons with sound principles and even more to a priest of the Catholic Church." These "slogans," Fontaine wrote, "transgress the most elemental rules of Christian charity" [*sic*]. As acting director of the School, Fontaine "demanded" Zañartu to "present proofs of your accusation of dishonesty to the group, and to publicly specify . . . the ideological background of [the courses dictated by] each one of the nineteen full- and part-time professors that you include in the present faculty body of the School." And he named them.[13]

Not all the group members, however, reduced Zañartu's criticisms to an accusation of "dishonesty." While reproaching Zañartu for not having made these accusations before and also demanding "proofs" for the existence of their ideological background, Pablo Baraona agreed to debate Zañartu's point at an intellectual level:

Let us suppose that an "ideological contraband" does exist in our teaching. I am convinced that this is not true but nonetheless let us suppose it. It would be in any case an involuntary or inevitable phenomenon and very difficult to detect, even for the most independent, good willed and intelligent person. If this person could find it however he would not think of a solution like the one you propose. Our position is that if this problem exists the solution is to extirpate all ideology from the scientific courses . . . Your position is that, on the contrary, if the problem exists it could be solved choosing another ideology more in accordance with yours.[14]

Yet Baraona rejected the accusation of ideological homogeneity in the faculty body. This was, he said, "a very grave accusation of discrimination, not for academic excellence but for *political* ideology." By introducing the term "political," which Zañartu had not used, Baraona changed the character of the accusation, for the point was not that the Chicago Boys had the same political opinions, even if that was true for most of them. What Zañartu pointed out was the existence of a common set of normative orientations which existed as a background to economic science. Without mentioning it by name, he alluded to the Chicago tradition in economics, an ideological product which is not strictly "political."[15] At the end of his letter however, Baraona confronted this point, producing a remarkable even if inadvertent reflection on the Chicago tradition:

the ideology lying behind positive science is contradictory in its terms, as you should find obvious. A positive science with ideology ceases to be a positive science. An ideology which is only positive science does not have an element of ideology. The phrase should rather be something like: "A positive science limited or distorted by the eagerness to carry out ideological indoctrination." But a phrase like that does not correspond to the truth.[16]

The Chicago Boys could not accept, in fact, that "true economics" were value-based. Not even a period like the 1960s in Chile, in which explicit ideologies were proclaimed as inevitable and indispensable elements of identity, would induce them to concede that their adherence to A. J. Ayer's *Language, Truth and Logic*, which they had translated and distributed to the faculty, was also ideological. This conception of science was in fact the only knowledge they had and they fully believed that as far as the social sciences were concerned, it was the only real knowledge there was. The fact of their unanimous opposition to the university reform was not seen by them as an ideological reaction; it was a "defense of science against ideology." There were not many at the university at that time who fully understood these ideological characteristics of the group. Zañartu was right in saying to Ernesto

Fontaine that he was "one of the few professors in agreement with the orientations of the New University who is able to fully apprehend in all its deepness, the reasons" for the Chicago group's opposition to the reform.[17]

A brief reflection on the Frei government and the spirit of the times can shed further light on these deep reasons.

The Frei government and the Revolution in Liberty

The Christian Democratic government, elected in 1964 with a landslide victory over the leftist coalition supporting Allende, had received the reluctant vote of the traditional right. The right had supported Frei reforms in an attempt to prevent Allende's revolution. Yet Frei's Revolution in Liberty was imbued with a moral will of transformation of social structures which would threaten the most deeply rooted value of the right: the sanctity of private property. Agrarian reform, state planning, "Chileanization" of the copper mines, or the "popular promotion" plans oriented to the shanty towns; in fact each one of the pillars of the Frei program was not only a task resulting from a modernization imperative, it was also seen as an ethical duty. Social structures were unjust and it was a duty of the state to render them more equitable. Christian Democratic ideals stemmed mainly from the teachings and practice of the Chilean Catholic church. After a lapse of three decades the remarkable development of Catholic social thought had turned the defender of the old oligarchical order into an advocate of the rights of the poor and oppressed. This was the main element giving Christian Democracy its ideological strength and legitimacy as "peaceful revolutionaries."

The idea of justice was linked in the Christian Democratic government with the concepts of "marginality" and of "national community." Chile was above all else a "national community," not only in the sense of a nation but of a community of people bound by common ethical principles. "Marginals," like peasants and shanty town dwellers, for example, had to be "incorporated" into that national community. Their marginality was the main concern of the national community not only because it certainly contradicted the Christian culture to which the majority of Chileans adhered but also because the injustice committed against them – the violence implicit in their marginality – was the main source of communism, revolutionary violence, and extremism.

At the same time, their marginality conspired against national development. Injustice and development were antithetical terms. A national development program assumed the need for efficiency and technical modernization *and* the struggle against social injustice. The incorporation of marginal sectors into the "national community" would increase the size of the national market, while the state impulse to industrialization, added to the participation of Chile in an Andean Pact with its neighboring countries, would result in a big step forward in terms of development. Besides, Christian Democracy carried with it the best intellectuals and social organizers in the country and could put economists and sociologists to the task. Moreover, its effort was fully supported by the United States, it was seen with enormous sympathy in Europe, and had a big impact all over Latin America. For once modernization and social justice had found a common ground; "international cooperation" and national development converged; ethics and economics coincided.

The right was overwhelmed by the historical optimism of the Frei reformist movement. Condemned by its incapacity to offer a program going beyond the mere defense of its corporatist interests, the traditional right was forced to support Frei in 1964 and saw its electoral support evaporate in the congressional elections of March 1965. In fact, Christian Democracy destroyed the two proud and traditional political parties of the Chilean oligarchy: the combined vote of Conservatives and Liberals went down from 30.7 percent of the electorate to 12 percent.[18] As a result the National Party was founded to gather the members of the two traditional ones. The search for a new right had begun.

The Chicago Boys did not view the Frei government with overt antipathy, at least at the beginning. Of course most of them – Pablo Baraona and Sergio de Castro in particular – abhorred agrarian reform and rejected the principle of state intervention in the economy. But at the same time – in contrast to the Alessandri government – Frei was appointing economists to the decision-making posts in the economic sector. Chicago-trained Christian Democratic economists like Carlos Massad and Ricardo Ffrench-Davis had been invited to join the government, the first as president of the Central Bank, the second as director of studies in the bank. From the group's point of view, therefore, this was a government which at least had some respect for technical capability and was making an initial effort to introduce rationality in decision-making. The impression however was short-lived.

Each Friday morning, the group would meet with Ffrench-Davis to discuss the economic decisions of the government. As Luders recalls, what became their main point of criticism was that "irrational decisions" were still forced by interest groups, mainly trade unions or industrialists.[19] This criticism, which would increase as time passed, reflected their opposition to the introduction of economic measures as a factor in the negotiating process between power groups in society. As Luders said, however, the discussion never included "politics." It was exclusively restricted to economics. This left out any consideration about the importance that this negotiation had for the existence of a democratic political system in Chile. Democracy or social development were political questions and therefore were not included within the scope of their interests. The main thing they knew was that economic policy was not negotiable, because science is not negotiable.

Even more unacceptable for them was the Revolution in Liberty pretension that economics was at the service of and thus should be adjusted to a program of political engineering organized by an ethical idea. The fact that this belief had – for obvious reasons – more adherents in the Catholic church than anywhere else had serious implications for the teaching of economics at the Catholic University. The notion implied the need to transform the "orientation" of the teaching of economics, adjusting it to the needs of the national community and to the imperatives derived from the social teachings of the church.

During the period of university reform some students wrote brief papers with personal reflections on their Schools and the change that was needed in university orientation. These documents constitute today interesting examples of the "spirit of the times." We quote them here to illustrate the ideological ambience surrounding and threatening the Chicago Project in the period from the end of the 1960s up to the Allende election in 1970.

In a document entitled "Reflections on the Orientation of the University and the School of Economics," José M. Piñera, a student of the School, affirmed that:

in order to fulfill its mission at the service of society the University has to be immersed in it, it has to detect where that society is evolving to, elaborating the scientific models and the cultural forms to channel that change. *This task has to be fulfilled creating formulas which respond to our own characteristics as a people, overcoming the implantation of models elaborated by cultures which are exogenous to ours . . .* [20]

Our country lives in a situation of underdevelopment . . . There is a certain structure of society which has brought with itself injustice putting obstacles in the way of the fulfillment of man. A great part of our people live in misery, marginalized from society in conditions that constitute an affront to human dignity . . .

A University which should be inspired by the values of Christian anthropology cannot remain indifferent to this situation. It has to be conscious of it and commit itself in the struggle to change the structures which oppress man . . .

Within this global conception [the School of Economics] has to respond to the demands coming from society and be conscious therefore of the situation of underdevelopment . . . and of the impossibility of certain economic structures to obtain the objective of liberating man, giving him the role he should have in the economic units and allowing him to live in conditions which are compatible with human dignity.

So, priorities should be established in the teaching programs and in research, expressing the role of a School of Economics which effectively serves the country and prepares professionals who effectively understand the processes of social change and are able to orient it in the best possible way.[21]

Piñera argued that the School should pay special attention to the transformation of private enterprise. He thought that the "present power relationship at the enterprise alienates man for he is considered just as a productive factor who receives a salary determined by the forces in the market." To "consider man simply as a productive factor . . . is to deny his human quality." The School of Economics has to contribute scientific elements and Christian values in order to remedy this situation.[22]

Other students led by Nicolás Flaño emphasized the "imported character" of the models being taught at the School. "Economic models imported from developed countries are producing an underdevelopment within under-development," they wrote. "Techniques imported from developed countries have been conceived for a type of reality totally different from ours . . . " – a reality "where there is a type of highly specialized Administration and economy . . . " At the Catholic University "economics and administration have not been integrated to an interdisciplinary perspective with the rest of the social sciences. On the contrary they have been kept apart from any social perspective." At the School, they thought, "the automatic application" of abstract theories "responds to the fact that there is no knowledge of our reality and of the problems it reflects."[23]

Most of these ideas were also present in documents prepared by dissident faculty members for discussion by the *claustros*. One of these texts entitled "Our Vision of the Catholic University of Chile" was prepared by Roger Veckemans, SJ, Ricardo Ffrench-Davis, Franz Hinkelammert, Roberto Maldonado, Cristián Ossa, and Mario Zañartu. The document included reflections on the structure of the university; a discussion on "statements of fact and value judgments in science"; general problems of the social sciences; and a program for the restructuring of the School of Economics and Administration. Some themes stood out as central: the role of economics and its relationship to other social sciences; the problem of ideology and the social sciences; the question of the Catholic character of the university and the topics that should be included in a new program for the study of economics at the Catholic University.

"In the developed world there is no tendency towards the sort of isolation of a faculty of economic sciences which is being attempted here in Chile," wrote Roger Veckemans. An interdisciplinary perspective, he argues, is needed not only in the teaching programs, but also in the research projects. "When one enters into the research of inflation one quickly realizes that along with economics comes sociology, psychology and technology, etc. Research does not allow epistemological classifications." In the research field an "institute of economics" is as inconceivable as an "institute of sociology." What was needed was an "institute for Latin America" reuniting people from different academic perspectives, Veckemans affirmed.[24]

The two Jesuits – Zañartu and Veckemans – addressed, then, the arguments in favor and against "logical positivism," concluding that "logical positivism sustains itself as long as the famous distinction between 'pure science' and 'applied science' is accepted without discussion . . . From the moment in which science claims to be applied and becomes operational, then values are necessarily filtered towards the diagnosis." What "these scientists" claim, they argued, pointing clearly to the Chicago group, is "to retreat to the pure, the basic, the gratuitous . . . Can they maintain this position?"[25]

Under the heading of "the Christian element in social sciences," the document addressed what was probably the most critical element in the polemics:

If the most fundamental element in a Catholic University is the elaboration and transmission of a Christian culture, this culture shall not consist in the simultaneous but separated elaboration and transmission of a social science which pretends to be pure and a social doctrine which is considered ideological and a-scientific. Only a doctrinal synthesis which comprehends both scientific rigor and Christian values shall constitute a Christian culture. It is not a matter of a "Christian economics" with laws and theories different from the laws and theories of "pure economics." It is a matter of the creation and verification of models in which institutions and values more in accordance with a Christian anthropology are inserted.[26]

These ideas needed a new type of economist and business administrator who was obviously very different from the dominant type in the current faculty. In the program sketched at the end of the document their characteristics were spelled out. The economist had to have the following traits: "analytic excellence"; to be an "economic planner"; a "macro-economist"; a "developmentalist"; he had to be well informed on the reality of underdevelopment, Latin America and Chile. The business administrator had to demonstrate equal "analytic excellence"; had to be knowledgeable in "sociology, reform of the enterprise" and "microeconomics"; he had to be a potential "leader of a working community," well informed on "business reality and macro-economics."[27] The new ideas needed at the same time a new orientation for the School. The new objectives were: the formation of professionals (economists and business administrators); the formulation of an "economic culture" for the present historical period (*la actual coyuntura*) and the diffusion of an economic culture to all levels and sectors. The program proposed the transformation of the curriculum and the establishment of new and different levels of study in the course. They included first a "basic humanistic level" oriented to the formation of a "university character" and a "basic social science level" in which the student had to "integrate" the basic knowledge in sociology, political science, anthropology, and social psychology. The "basic economic science" level coming afterwards distinguished between abstract economic theory and applied economic theory. The first included "history of economic theory"; "macro-economic theory, microeconomics and development theory"; "price theory (products and factors)"; and "planning theory." The second required (for economists) international commerce; monetary and fiscal policy; and (for administrators) bookkeeping, auditing, project evaluation, programming.

To this program, rather different from the one currently in practice, was added the "formulation of an economic" culture "for the present historical moment." This culture had to integrate, the document said, "the situational elements leading to an economic conception in: underdeveloped countries; countries going through a process of social revolution; countries with a determinate ideological framework."[28] The description of these propositions was identical to the text quoted above on the integration of a positive science and Christian doctrine written by Mario Zañartu. These ideas, the document concluded, had to "impregnate teaching and research."

A document like this, dated October 1967, was inconceivable six months before: such was the velocity of the discussion opened by the occupation of the university. The response of Pablo Baraona to the document was also surprising. Ideas that were anathema to the Chicago mentality were answered in a restrained and almost conciliatory tone. "Calm has returned," he said, "and we have at least the proper ambience to begin a dialogue."[29] He added elsewhere: "even bad actions have sometimes their merit; it seems to me that the student conflict will accelerate change in the structure of the Catholic University."[30]

Baraona began his comments declaring that "the present School of Economics and Administration (the majority of its students and almost all its faculty members) defend an accomplishment and stand behind it with just pride. This accomplishment responds to a set of ideas which, obviously, have not been understood or have not been clearly expounded. This explains how the group 'New University' infers from that reality an ideology of the School which does not correspond in fact to that of its members."[31]

Baraona cautiously addressed the argument favoring a different and wider social science formation for economics students, stating that he favored a system in which the student would be "informed about the alternative options to adopt *vis-à-vis* problems, but he would study and research within a discipline getting to the most advanced level of knowledge within it." He found "risky" the proposition of an "Institute of Latin American Studies" adding that "to take problems like inflation into an interdisciplinary program would be as inappropriate as to extract cancer from its own house: a Faculty of Medicine and Biological Sciences."

The main part of his paper, however, was dedicated to discussing the question of values and science. He proposed the position that even if total objectivity (*asepcia valórica*) was impossible it was the duty of the scientist to pursue it, in the same way that a human being pursues perfection.

We come to what I think is the center of our discrepancy. Is there in our teaching an intrinsic relationship between judgments of fact and value judgments? If that were the case it would constitute a serious situation. I hope that the writers of the document will tell us if this situation does exist and which is its expression.

Is there between the present faculty members of the School a homogeneity of values which, even if maintained outside the practice of the social science, expresses itself through the selection of the classroom or the research topics, through the examples given in lectures, etc.? If this is so, I would love to receive examples of this homogeneity and of the ways in which these values come about.[32]

With respect to the catholicity of the university, Baraona was very clear: "As far as I know," he said, "the Catholic University of Chile does not have any other value requirement than those of every University, besides being a privileged place for the cultivation of Theology."[33] The whole argument of the doctrinal integration between economics and the social doctrine of the church was thus rejected summarily. As the Catholic University had no particular "value requirements" the only reason to "put on trial," as he said, the School of Economics' professors was for their supposed lack of objectivity. They should be put on trial not because of being in disagreement with the Catholic University but for doing something improper for any university.[34]

The polemic went on for some time and it developed without the acrimony of the university occupation period. There was no possible agreement, however, and not everybody among the Chicago group was as well disposed as Baraona to maintain the discussion. Sergio de Castro was as always much more categorical, and plainly rejected the introduction of any course presenting a different approach to the question of development. In his view there was no other economics than that which was taught at the School. The rest was rhetoric.[35] The development of the university reform produced in de Castro a growing disinterest in the university and the School itself. While remaining in the faculty, he grew more and more involved in political activity and in the relationship with economic power groups especially with the Edwards group.

Following these events Rolf Luders was elected dean of the faculty.[36] While his election was seen by the Chicago group as a response to the "Catholic theme" (Luders was a Lutheran), it meant, in fact, a concession and a negotiating position towards the ideological pressures coming from the reform. Luders who, as we have seen, was not particularly close to the de Castro–Baraona team, adopted the pragmatic position of attracting to the faculty persons who clearly represented the "new economics" demanded by the reform. The three most important cases were those of Osvaldo Sunkel, considered a follower of Rául Prebisch and Cepal ideas and one of the most important exponents of the dependency theory; Eduardo García, an MIT PhD in economics linked to the left of the Christian Democrats; and Sergio Molina, a former Finance Minister of the Frei government who had later been in charge of ODEPLAN, the state planning agency. These new professors entered, however, the part-time group of the faculty which, as Luders told this author, "continued to be under the control of the original group." The new dean justified the hiring of the new professors as a requirement for the transition towards a more modern School. He stated that "the Chicago alumni's training had to be modernized."[37] Thus, the School of Economics underwent a certain transformation and topics such as Keynesian theory, economic development, comparison of different economic models, fiscal policies, Marxist economics, etc., were included in the curriculum. Accommodation would gradually transform itself into a serious threat to the hegemony of the Chicago School at the School. The democratization wave that characterized academic politics in those years led the group to electoral confrontations with an ever-increasing number of ideological foes, exposing the School to intervention by the new authorities who were in clear opposition to its neo-liberal orientation. In January 1971, the School's organization underwent changes that further reduced this group's influence. The post of dean was eliminated and the School of Economics and Business Administration merged with the Center for Economic Research into an "Institute for Economics." Eduardo García, a leftwing Christian Democrat economist who had been deputy director of planning during Frei's administration, was appointed acting director of the Institute.

García was an expert on economic planning and was decidedly set against the market doctrines that characterized the Chicago School. During his term as deputy director of ODEPLAN, the planning agency, he had experienced Arnold Harberger's rejection of a project to study development policies based on an agreement between ODEPLAN, the Ford Foundation, and MIT, under the direction of Paul Rosenstein-Rodin. According to García, Harberger – who had asked to evaluate the project together with Richard Mellon, from Harvard – issued an extremely negative confidential report to the Ford Foundation. The issue of this report, also signed by Jorge Cauas, left a permanent scar on the relationship between the new director and some of the professors at the Institute.[38] What needs to be stressed, however, is that García's arrival at the Universidad Católica, which coincided with the socialist candidate's victory at the presidential election of 1970, strengthened the apocalyptic perception of the times held by the Chicago Boys. In fact, the group of Chicago professors, reduced to de Castro, de la Cuadra, Gert

Wagner, and Dominique Hachette, vetoed García in the presence of all the professors. However, they had lost control and García was confirmed as director. Baraona and de Castro left the School. De Castro traveled to Chicago to finish his long overdue doctoral dissertation. Apparently the Chicago Boys had completely lost control of the institution that they had worked so hard to create. Some of the students, led by Miguel Kast, warned the new authorities that they were prepared to defend the Institute from the "Marxists lying in ambush" who controlled it at the time. However, the majority of the students were not concerned with who was in power at the School of Economics, but rather with the usefulness of their studies. Therefore, they did not have a negative attitude towards the changes to the curriculum introduced by the university reform: these pointed in a direction in which their careers were linked not only to the rest of the university, but also to the nation's situation in general. Among the Institute professors who favored the change, more than a few considered it was time to "be done with the Chicago Boys" and to sever the links between the Institute of Economics and the University of Chicago, and with the orientation it represented.

Yet power at the Institute would soon come back into the hands of the original founders. It was a paradox that the Chicago group was helped by the alliance between professors who represented the Marxist left at the university's Higher Council, and the conservative academics who gave a paradigmatic importance to the leadership of the Chicago Boys at the School of Economics. This "tactical convergence" responded to the need to defend certain parcels of ideological power from what was perceived as a wave of Christian Democratic control over the university. The right and the left pushed for a vision of *pluralism* within the university, defined not in terms of the existence of different lines of thought within each school or institute, but rather as the existence of schools and institutes that, between them, reflected differing lines of thought. A tacit agreement was thus brought about between the Institute of Sociology, controlled by the left, and other schools that wished to maintain an essentially leftist orientation, and rightwing professors who wished the School of Economics to return to a neo-liberal orientation. The agreement was expressed through various rules regulating the participation of professors in the election of authorities, rules that ultimately favored – both in the School of Sociology and in the School of Economics – the relative majorities of professors that existed *prior to the university reform*.[39] When the election of the non-acting director of the School of Economics was discussed, García was faced with a majority against him which led him to submit his resignation. In May 1971, the Chicago group and the Christian Democratic professors jointly agreed to elect Jorge Cauas as director. The latter, a civil engineer, had been chairman of the Chilean Central Bank between 1967 and 1970 and had done graduate studies in economics at Columbia University. At the time, Cauas was a Christian Democrat.

During Cauas's term as director, graduate courses in economics were established at the Institute, the courses on mathematical economics were strengthened, and the emphasis was placed on research and publications that favored the analysis of economic policies rather than the more theoretical approaches. The presence of professors with different economic approaches was maintained, but those with greater influence – Sergio Molina and Osvaldo Sunkel – remained as visiting professors, despite Cauas's efforts, who wished for, at least, Molina's incorporation as a full-time member of the Institute. Cauas tried to keep a distance between himself and the Chicago team, without breaking with a tradition that he viewed as a source of academic excellence. Despite the absence of de Castro, who was in Chicago at the time, and of Fontaine, Luders, and de la Cuadra who were with the OAS, the influence of the Chicago professors was gradually reestablished during Cauas's term and Harberger was able to patiently continue with his task of recruiting students for his university. In September 1971, Miguel Kast traveled to Chicago, marking the beginning of a real second generation of Chicago Boys, to which Juan Carlos Méndez, Juan Ignario Varas, Martín Costabal, Ernesto Silva, Alvaro Donoso, and others would belong. The group also included some Christian Democrats such as Juan Villarzú. When Jorge Cauas resigned in 1972 to take up a post with the World Bank, the directorship of the Institute came once more into the hands of a Chicago graduate: Dominique Hachette. The School of Economics of the Universidad Católica thus returned to its tradition.

CHAPTER 10

The elusive hegemony

The entrepreneurial movement

In 1968, Chilean private entrepreneurs organized a movement, through their business associations, in order to face both the threat posed by the reforms that the Frei administration was carrying out at the time and the social processes set in motion by these reforms. In the name of "solidarity between entrepreneurs" a "National Convention of Production and Trade" was organized in an effort to make the Confederation of Production and Commerce the visible head of the associations of entrepreneurs, representing the private sector as a whole. Its aim was to incorporate, if possible, 100 percent of "the 650,000 entrepreneurs and self-employed persons" in Chile to active business associations.[1] The National Convention, therefore, was not merely an annual meeting for representatives from different lines of business. The preparations made for the Convention and the dissemination of its conclusions indicated that it was a movement reflecting the concern felt by Chilean entrepreneurs in relation to a process of change viewed as a threat to private property and the principle of authority. The movement also expressed the opposition of a sector of "owners" to the government's attempts to make a distinction between backward agricultural sectors, that were being subjected to agrarian reform, and "modern" industrial sectors that the government wished to favor. In the years 1967, 1968, and 1969, when students, workers, and peasants increased their mobilization, private enterprise elites managed to reduce their internal conflicts and unify the entrepreneurial movement. Simultaneously, they launched a campaign intended to mobilize public opinion and to urge political actors to defend property rights and free enterprise; to this end they used methods that ranged from using their influence in governmental and parliamentary spheres to propaganda through the press, television, and radio. In addition to the reorganization of entrepreneurs, in practice the movement managed to halt the reform process attempted by the Frei administration, which from 1968 onwards shifted to the right in its economic policies, and also served to launch Jorge Alessandri's campaign for the 1970 presidential elections.

At the time, the Chicago group economists, with the support provided since the early 1960s by a group of powerful entrepreneurs headed by Agustín Edwards, managed to become involved in the business movement and to disseminate their model of economic organization. Once again, however, their intentions were opposed by most entrepreneurs who viewed these theories as inappropriate. Nevertheless, some economists in the group promoted their ideas from highly influential positions and established what has been viewed, since then, as the "liberal" pole in economic debates in Chilean rightwing sectors. In this chapter we will evaluate the accomplishments and failures of this endeavor. In order to understand the process, however, a brief review of the overall process is necessary. What was the actual situation of the right and private enterprise at the onset of the Frei administration?

Compelled to vote in 1964 for a program of changes in which they did not believe, and for a government that they did not trust, at the outset rightwing groups had to be satisfied with observing the economic success achieved by the new administration during its first two years in government, and to bear the worst political crisis suffered by the right since the 1938 election of the *Frente Popular* (Popular Front). As mentioned previously, in the 1965 congressional elections, Christian Democracy drained the traditional political parties (the Liberal and Conservative Parties) of a significant part of their electorate, reducing it from 30.7 percent to 12.5 percent.[2] The great party of the center thus appeared, at first, as a force capable of representing some of the traditionally center-right social sectors, by offering a program of changes that contemplated modernizing capitalism and preserving democracy. The participation of capable technicians in government and policies fostering industrialization initially helped to obtain the support of a considerable number of medium-sized and small entrepreneurs who shared the social and Christian principles that the government supposedly represented.

In the short run, however, the alliance between the reformist government and the most powerful entrepreneurial forces proved to be an impossible venture. Christian Democracy had set itself the task of carrying out, on its own, the pending modernization required by Chilean society. Their theories on agrarian reform, property tax, the reform of property rights, and the redistribution policies had, in political terms, a "centrifugal" effect on the political system.[3] They drove the left and the right to their respective extremes. For the left, reforms implemented by the Christian Democrats were a mere cosmetic palliative, a resource used by imperialism to halt the true revolution that Chile required: Christian Democracy was "the right's new face." For the right, however, Christian Democracy threatened to unleash a process of change that would endanger not only the interests of the more backward agricultural sectors but also those of the propertied classes as a whole.

The main political objective sought by the Frei administration in combining policies of agrarian reform with a policy aimed at increasing industrialization, was to destroy the traditional entente between landowners and the more modern industrial entrepreneurs. There was good reason to believe that this was a feasible objective. In fact, the government initially believed that the industrial sectors were indifferent to the fate of agricultural entrepreneurs. This indifference, which to a certain extent was real, was based on the fact that the groups affected by agrarian reform were a minority, even within the group of agricultural landowners, and that private enterprise would benefit from the domestic market's expansion resulting from the incorporation of peasants into the negotiation system. If, as Moulian and Torres have held, the plan actually failed, its failure was due to "the government's underestimation of the land owners' political influence in the rightwing ruling class and the weight of ownership for entrepreneurs as a whole."[4] But the association between these social sectors did not come about automatically as a mere process of reaction. In fact, it may be argued that "solidarity between entrepreneurs" would not have developed if the entrepreneurs had not organized a movement, and if the social radicalization complementing the political efforts made by business associations had not become more intense. The "fear" experienced by expropriated agriculturists was thus transmitted first to other rural landowners and then to small and big business, through a gradual and complex process steered by a new political force: the movement formed by associations of employers. In practice, this force replaced rightwing political parties and became the defender of the principles of order and property and promoted, from 1969 onwards, the return to the presidency of its greatest leader, Jorge Alessandri.

The Confederation of Production and Commerce (CPC)

Thus, agrarian reform not only set in motion a process of defensive organization against what the president of the National Agricultural Society (SNA) described as "the process of destruction of an entire economic system in our country"[5] but also a process of collective reflection by the entrepreneurs who began to discuss and criticize their own forms of organization, their beliefs, and future projects. The instrument used to organize this mobilization was the Confederation of Production and Commerce.[6]

At the beginning of the Frei administration, the CPC comprised the National Agricultural Society (SNA), the Industrial Development Association

(SFF), the Central Chamber of Commerce (CCC), and the National Mining Society (SONAMI). Once the movement began, and after a legal battle, the Cámara Chilena de la Construcción (Chilean Chamber of Construction) became a member of the CPC, thus signaling a change in the CPC's legitimacy and strengthening the incipient movement.[7] Up to then, the CPC had been the weak and unenterprising head of an entrepreneurial movement which was frequently disjointed, if not down-right divided. The conflicts of interest between the different business sectors in the movement were, at times, fundamental. They stimulated recurring debates between protectionist industrialists, free-trade merchants and export-oriented miners, between miners with restricted mining rights and agricultural interests with privileged surface rights, and also between modern merchants and entrepreneurs who needed the mass peasant market and anti-reform landowners. These groups also held different opinions regarding the Frei administration's policies and, ultimately, they represented differing ideological orientations.[8] As Cusack says, between 1942 and 1958, the CPC served as little more than a prestigious office and a basis for launching Jorge Alessandri on the road to the presidency.[9] A threat that apparently affected the interests of the Confederation's associates was necessary for these differences to recede into the background and for the CPC to start playing an active leading role. This function was fulfilled by agrarian reform and the changes to property rights passed by Congress, that acted on the Frei administration's suggestion. The SNA was charged with demanding that the CPC fulfill its obligation as defender of property owners and making all entrepreneurial sectors aware of the danger that, if unity was not achieved, all property owners in Chile would soon share the fate of landowners affected by agrarian reform.[10]

In 1986, Sergio Silva, former president of the Unión de Empresarios Católicos (USEC), was elected president of the CPC. As we shall see later on, he represented a moderate point of view that did not differ greatly from the ideological views held by Freism. His stated purpose, as president of the CPC, was to change "the atmosphere of distrust among entrepreneurs as a result of certain projects and initiatives promoted by Congress and the Executive."[11] Silva and his group of advisors set up a policy to strengthen the CPC in order to revitalize the initiatives and prestige of the entrepreneurial movement in Chile and to deter groups perceived as a threat to free enterprise. They intended to create an operational footing from which *entrepreneurial elites could go beyond their merely corporate interests and discuss issues of Chilean politics affecting their interests.* To this end, they were willing to avail themselves of all their political, economic, and financial resources, obtaining the necessary social backing for their cause.

The radicalization of the social and political process in 1968 added new impetus to the entrepreneurial movement. Farm "take-overs" and other incidents of occupation, including the destruction of factories, helped to cement the unity between agricultural entrepreneurs and other lines of business. In view of these facts, the CPC denounced the "Marxist activists" who had been joined by "government agency employees" who "use the taxpayers' money" to arouse hatred against those who have devoted their efforts to production.[12] These incidents hastened the launching of a "campaign of solidarity with entrepreneurs" which, in addition to uniting and organizing all property owners, intended to influence public opinion and seek support for private enterprise.

This was, in fact, one of the movement's most outstanding features: the awareness that business associations needed to achieve some overall influence and not merely seek influence with the government through political parties or a newspaper such as *El Mercurio*. The campaign had to address public opinion, but the difficulties involved were obvious. Hernán Errázuriz Talavera, a leader of the Sociedad de Fomento Fabril, in a letter addressed to Eugenio Heiremans, president of the SFF, said that "this is the essence of democracy" for "the administration has the obligation to capture the feeling of the masses and project its actions in order to satisfy them." He adds that if the entrepreneurs want to have influence on the future, they should begin by trying to educate the masses, since it is their views that the authorities project through official policies. But if matters are viewed in this way, he concludes, the situation of the entrepreneurs is particularly serious: "It is no mystery," he says, "that the majority of the Chilean electorate is essentially in favor of state control. This is a circumstance which, to further accentuate the problem, will shortly lead to the extinction of private enterprise and the failure of the association that we belong to as well."[13] Therefore, rather than having greater influence in government, it was necessary to launch a campaign aimed at contacting the most influential public opinion sectors, showing entrepreneurs as "modern and realistic" people, thus improving their image as "outdated, ambitious and harmful" that seemed to prevail in society in general.[14] *In addition to its inherent functions of organization and information, the movement should also fulfill a political function.* The dissemination of the Convention's conclusions was ideally suited to this purpose. Therefore, a dissemination plan was set up, through the radio and the press, which did not primarily intend to have polemical effects, but rather to inform the public of the advantages inherent in private enterprise. Different organizations, closely linked to business, such as ICARE (Instituto Chileno para la Administración Racional de la Empresa), CESEC (Centro de Estudios Socio-Económicos), and other *ad hoc* organizations and foundations, carried out various activities of dissemination and propaganda which included radio programs, training and technical courses, loans for cooperatives and small businesses, building public playgrounds for children, etc.

The second objective was to promote an "entrepreneurial mentality" and a "business association mentality," especially among craftsmen and small businessmen "emphasizing that to be an entrepreneur was a vocation, a realization of subjective aspirations."[15] These efforts led to the organization of hundreds of business associations, some of which, particularly those in agriculture, became so militant that they even went as far as resorting to violence. But this entrepreneurial mentality and the way in which it was manifested in Chilean society, could be interpreted in different ways. The issue of the relationship between entrepreneurs, the state, and Chile's development was subject to different, and occasionally contradictory, ideological perspectives. It is therefore necessary to analyze the ideological differences between CPC members.

The National Convention of Production and Trade expressed, for the first time, the conflict between two ideological perspectives: the "liberal" view and the more traditional "entrepreneurial" view. Furthermore, at the Convention, three groups became evident: first, the group formed by USEC (the Catholic entrepreneurs); second, entrepreneurs as such, that included many presidents of the different lines of business who shared the ideology of pro-Alessandri sectors; and, lastly, those of the Inter-American Committee on Trade and Production (CICYP) which assembled the most powerful and "international-ized" group of Chilean entrepreneurs.[16] While the first two groups clearly represented the more traditional ideological outlook of business, the third was the group where "neo-liberal" thought clearly concentrated.

The association of Catholic entrepreneurs sought to "disseminate, in entrepreneurial circles, the Christian conception of professional life and the pontifical teachings in socio-economic matters," to "turn enterprise into a service to the community," and "to strive to implant this Christian conception as the basis for reforming society as a whole."[17] The approximately 500 members who formed the association were obviously in good standing to influence the Christian Democratic government or, when relations deteriorated, to keep the possibilities for dialogue open. Sergio Silva, the president of the CPC, was a member of USEC, as were other outstanding entrepreneurs such as Eugenio Heiremans, president of the Sociedad de Fomento Fabril. Some members of Frei's Cabinet, such as Sergio Ossa and William Thayer, were also outstanding entrepreneurs.

As indicated in preceding chapters, most entrepreneurs shared an outlook commonly identified as pro-Alessandri. They accepted the existence of a state that was active in protecting private enterprise and they shared the belief that it was necessary for Chile to achieve industrial development. As they frequently stated, "they did not understand politics and did not care for politicians" but they understood the social functions that development needs imposed on the government. In any event, *they had no specific ideas about politics*

and they lacked, and did not intend to have, an overall and comprehensive project.
However, they held a series of opinions that referred mainly to the type of
economic policy that they wished to have, and political relationships were
established on this basis: their support for the *Partido Nacional* was based, firstly,
on the class background of its leaders and, secondly, on a political program
that coincided with their ambitions.[18] The great majority of entrepreneurs
lacked, however, a specific plan for the Chilean economy, society, and politics.
Alessandri inspired them fully, primarily because he did not represent, in that
sense, an ideological program. "Alessandri did have, nevertheless, an
economic standing, a respect for certain values of free enterprise and an
intelligent way of handling politicians which prevented social disruption and
helped to preserve social order."[19]

The third group of entrepreneurs at the Convention was identified with
CICYP, whose Chilean branch was presided over by Jorge Ross, a powerful
entrepreneur, and in which other influential businessmen such as Agustín
Edwards and Carlos Urenda also participated. The CICYP was established in
Montevideo in 1941 to "provide Latin American entrepreneurs with a system
of international contacts [mainly with the United States] similar to those
already established by government and labor."[20] CICYP's main objective was
to "promote the principles of private enterprise and individual initiative" and
had been established in Chile, according to Cusack, as a "club to promote
international connections and prestige, assembling the largest independent
businesses in Chile and 'advised' by influential intellectuals and politicians
interested in promoting free enterprise."[21] In 1968, CICYP included
approximately forty members who directed Chile's most important corporations, mainly in mining and industry, but also in banking, oil, agriculture,
trade, construction, and the press. Many were multinational businesses,
largely US based (First National City Bank, Bethlehem Chile, Standard Oil,
etc.) and some represented the more prominent Chilean monopolies (United
Breweries, Chilean Tobacco Company, South American Explosives, etc.).
Minera El Teniente also belonged to this organization, but it was not affiliated
to any other national organization; this mining company was owned by a US
firm that had two representatives on CICYP's board of directors.[22]

However, CICYP operated primarily through a team of "advisors" formed
by economists, attorneys and politicians. Pedro Ibáñez, an entrepreneur and
senator for the *Partido Nacional*, presided over the organization in 1963.
CICYP's public activities were non-existent: it had no publications and did
not sponsor congresses or conferences. This approach was functional to its two
main tasks. The first was to finance causes considered important by the
entrepreneurs for their common interests, such as the National Convention of
Production and Trade. Even firms compelled by law to stay out of politics,
such as El Teniente, made large contributions to causes that bordered on the

political such as the "campaign of solidarity with entrepreneurs." The second was to represent and promote the interests of Chilean entrepreneurs in the United States, which was done through the contacts that Agustín Edwards and Jorge Ross had in the private sector and in many government organizations in the United States.

This was the business group that protected the group of Chicago economists, provided them with the infrastructure and a network of connections to enable them to efficiently fulfill their role as "organic intellectuals in the project for creating new foundations for capitalism in Chilean society." Let us return now to our specific area of concern.

The Chicago Boys and the Edwards group

The group of entrepreneurs headed by Agustín Edwards, Jorge Ross, and Carlos Urenda, immediately showed great interest in the transformation that the University of Chicago's Chile Project entailed and the training of new generations of economists at the Universidad Católica. After the return of US professors to Chicago and the appointment of Sergio de Castro as dean of the School of Economics, these entrepreneurs began to support the economists' main activities. Some activities were directly linked to work carried out at the School of Economics. The Edwards group gradually began to employ some professors and students as research directors at the Banco de A. Edwards and as executives in their firms, and subsequently, through the Fundación de la Escuela de Economía and the network of CICYP members promoted by Carlos Urenda, they managed to collect the capital needed for a new campus for the School.[23]

Other initiatives promoted by the association between entrepreneurs and economists aimed to disseminate the "economic science" of the Chicago School among the business class and to achieve a greater degree of social influence for business associations. The most important initiative was probably the creation of the Center for Social and Economic Studies (CESEC), which played an important role in the period prior to Allende's election in 1970 and the military coup in 1973. Another significant decision was the creation of an economic section in *El Mercurio*, in 1968. Its purpose was to disseminate research done by professors at the Universidad Católica, but it actually consisted of brief courses in economics that helped to train them for the editorial work that they would carry out after the military coup. These activities enabled some of the Chicago graduates to form part of the advisory team of the group affiliated to CICYP, which thus served to orient many of the group's opinions and activities. These activities also determined the economists' participation in the development of the business movement in the 1960s.

The relationship between this specific business group and the Chicago Boys was based on ideological factors although, as we shall see later on, they include some practical motives. The first one, the intention of these economists to exert an ideological influence on Chilean entrepreneurs and convert them to a free market doctrine, was shared by these entrepreneurs.

Another important factor that should be taken into consideration is the "lobby" organized by United States professors, in particular by Arnold Harberger, among some Chilean businessmen; in addition, the strong attraction that Jorge Ross and Agustín Edwards had for any conservative initiative coming from the United States, was equally significant in this respect. Ross was very well connected in the United States, and was considered to have great political abilities and contacts, both in the United States and among Chilean entrepreneurs.[24] However, it was Agustín Edwards who, from the beginning, showed the greatest interest in the dissemination of this doctrine expressed by United States professors and continued by their Chilean followers. According to Orlando Sáenz, a former SOFOFA chairman, Edwards' connections in the United States "were far greater than those arising from mere affinity, friendship or commercial interests."[25] A strong US cultural influence,[26] plus business and social activities linked to the United States, enabled Edwards to keep a great ideological distance regarding Chilean society, which brought him closer to the characteristics of the Chicago economists. Edwards and Ross were, therefore, the first of a "group of business *caciques* [clan chiefs] who were always on the alert, were helpful, and offered jobs and money in order to improve the level of economic debate."[27] Carlos Urenda explains the group's feelings towards the School:

for us, the Chicago School guaranteed an orientation in favor of free enterprise, and it was our duty to support it, particularly in view of the fact that, apart from the Adolfo Ibáñez Business School [in Valparaiso], a minor school, all economists graduating from national universities were either socialists or statists. We thus supported a school that favored free enterprise. Chicago sent professors and scholarships, but no money. At the same time, they [the Chicago teachers] demanded modernization. We backed them because they demanded support, local investment.[28]

However, the doctrine advocated by the economists appealed to this group of entrepreneurs for a more basic reason. Since these businessmen were linked mainly to financial and international sectors of the economy, they fully adhered to the efficiency criteria characterizing the orthodox discourse and its principles regarding the use of comparative advantages as an essential element to enter the international market. Therefore, they agreed, to a greater extent than other businessmen, with the criticism made of Chilean industrial development and the incentives it received from the state.

Let us now examine each initiative taken by this group of entrepreneurs and economists, and their impact on the Chilean rightwing sector during the 1960s.

CESEC

The first expression of this local investment was the organization, in 1963, of the Center for Social and Economic Studies (CESEC). The Center was created by Agustín Edwards. The initiative responded to a concern shared by Edwards and the group of economists regarding what they called "the lack of economic ideas in the rightwing sectors." Pablo Baraona and Sergio Undurraga, among others, had persistently expressed the need to address the problem by searching for mechanisms to disseminate economic science and create a coherent ideology among entrepreneurs. The adherence or acquiescence that most entrepreneurs had shown until then to the idea of a "mixed economy," in which the state plays the role of entrepreneur and also promotes economic activity, was not viewed by these economists as a genuine ideology, nor did it respond to the specific development of the Chilean business sector, but was rather a feature indicating submission and ignorance. Even the Alessandri administration was to be censored for the way in which it handled certain economic decisions and for its inability to withstand social and political pressures.[29] These reflections, together with Agustín Edwards' perception of the statist and socialist nature of the options envisaged in the electoral scenario of the forthcoming presidential elections, drove Edwards to create an "instrument to defend the principles of free market and economic efficiency."[30]

Initially under the direction of Guillermo Chadwick, CESEC's most prominent members in different periods were Pablo Baraona, Sergio Undurraga, Pedro Jeftanovic, Sergio de la Cuadra, Adelio Pipino, and Emilio Sanfuentes. Baraona and de Castro worked only in an advisory capacity *ad honorem*, but given their personal influence over the other members of the group, their presence was constantly felt in the Center's development.[31] Initially, the Center carried out a series of economic studies, such as "The Demand for Non-perishable Goods in Chile" and others on national agriculture, that indicated that the group's academic orientation was too strong a feature not to influence, at least in the beginning, any activity in which they were involved. However, CESEC's strategic purpose was quite evident. Frei's election, and the disastrous situation of the political rightwing sector after 1965, justified the Center's objectives and led it to a gradual involvement in the political and economic debate. CESEC started to include studies on public opinion and carried out surveys and sociological studies oriented to support the struggles that the entrepreneurs launched against the government in 1967. Its studies on the organization of the private sector, and those on the people's opinions and attitudes regarding private enterprise, played an important role in the preparation of the CPC Convention.

CESEC's creation seems to demonstrate the strategic talent of the most intellectually active parts of the rightwing economic sectors, and their ability to initate a very different type of organization and knowledge-producing system, typical of the United States, such as think-tanks. Agustín Edwards and the Chicago Boys perceived, much earlier than the leftwing intellectual world, the usefulness of private institutes as means to influence and achieve communication between technical and scientific production and the social and political powers. CESEC was the first step taken by the Chicago team outside the university. It was carried out with the same *esprit de corps* used to build their identity in Chicago and later at the Universidad Católica.[32] It therefore strengthened the group's identity in an area where they had severe ideological difficulties and in which they were regarded with great mistrust – the world of business and enterprise. As we shall see later, however, this mistrust was transferred to CESEC which, at least until 1970, was viewed by pro-Alessandri sectors as the "Edwards' group Center."

Business administration graduates

Significant evidence of the relationship between the Chicago group and the entrepreneurs committed to their development can also be seen in the way that companies absorbed graduates from the Department of Economics and Administration of the Universidad Católica, as advisors, consultants, and executives. In the mid-1960s, the Department of Economics primarily trained business administrators. In 1964, for instance, there were 332 students: 135 were first-year students, while third-year students dropped to 50 and fifth-year students only amounted to 31. The decrease in the number of students through the years was significant, but could be considered normal in relation to other Chilean university courses. There was a great disproportion, however, between the number of students in economics and those in business administration: between 1961 and 1964 only 19 of the 107 fifth-year students had chosen economics over business administration.[33] Administration courses were considered easier and, from an economic viewpoint, future professional prospects were thought to be safer in the business world than in academia.

The impact resulting from the incorporation of these administrators into business was not restricted to modernizing management practices. Chicago School administrators radically modified the rationale that had traditionally guided production enterprises and banking services in Chile. Their monetarist training led them to favor financial aspects over production in the enterprises, thus introducing a rationale of accumulation that, after 1973, characterized the behavior of economic groups created under the protection of the military regime.[34]

Some administrators from the first generation of Chicago students viewed the task of reforming private enterprise as a "redeeming mission." The most outstanding case is that of Manuel Cruzat. In 1966, Cruzat, who had been a brilliant candidate for a PhD in economics at Chicago, and later for a PhD in administration at Harvard, told his friends in the Economics Department at the Universidad Católica that he wished to leave his academic career and devote himself to business. His decision aroused a long debate in the group of professors.[35] Some of them thought that Cruzat should not leave the university, since he played a vital role in training business administrators. However, Cruzat believed that the task of training businessmen should be done "from within." He also believed that the elite of economists bequeathed to Chile by Chicago should participate in the business world. Cruzat told his friends that he felt that leaving the university to reform the business sector was an imperative mission. According to Ernesto Fontaine, Cruzat said that "it could not be postponed any longer; private enterprise in Chile was on the verge of blowing up." As Fontaine puts it: "Manuel Cruzat left, took over the Banco Hipotecario de Fomento and dismissed all the old men who worked there."[36] Subsequently, as research director at the bank, and in association with his brother-in-law, Fernando Larraín, and Javier Vial, he conducted the sale of the bank's real estate properties and bought shares in the main Chilean enterprises. The group's financial voracity soon led the press to give them the nickname of "the piranhas": in 1970, four years after the group was created, it had become the third or fourth most important economic group in Chile. After the 1973 military coup, Manuel Cruzat's group became one of the two most powerful groups in Chile. Their control over hundreds of companies soared, thanks to bids for public companies that their former Chicago classmates implemented from their government posts.[37]

However, Cruzat represented an exceptional case of personal initiative and autonomy. The usual case was, rather, for administrators and economists to be employed as research directors and executives in companies linked to Ross or Edwards. Emilio Sanfuentes was a leading figure in this area. After returning from Chicago in September/October 1961, Sanfuentes took over as executive secretary to the Center for Economic and Social Studies (CESEC). He also worked at OPLA, one of the planning offices for the Edwards group of companies, which was directed by Hernán Cubillos and in which Sergio Undurraga and Javier Fuenzalida also participated.

A new campus for the School of Economics

With the appointment of Sergio de Castro as faculty dean, an idea that the group had been contemplating since their return from Chicago, began to take shape, i.e. that the School of Economics of the Universidad Católica should have its own campus. They had good reasons to support this argument. The facilities that the School of Economics had in the old central university campus were inadequate and uncomfortable. The "flexible curriculum," adopted in December 1966, that replaced the annual system for a system of credits, implied an increased daily attendance of students and therefore the need for more space for libraries and study areas. This need conveniently served to justify separating the School from the rest of the university. From the teachers' viewpoint, the ideological contamination of their students resulting from contact with sociology and law students, both highly politicized schools, and with the rest of the university, was detrimental to the *esprit de corps* that they wished to create.[38] Furthermore, some deans of other schools were considering the possibility of transferring the whole university to a general campus, based on newly adopted ideas on the university's mission in society, which also included plans for curricular integration, which was unacceptable to the economists.[39]

At this point the complaints expressed by United States professors on the need to modernize the School began to have an effect on the group of Chilean businessmen linked to Agustín Edwards. "External suggestions in favor of the School of Economics" led Carlos Urenda to obtain "logistic support for the Chicago agreement."[40] For several months, Urenda organized luncheon meetings with businessmen, in which Sergio de Castro explained the School's role as promoter and defender of the concepts of free market and economic science. The idea was to emphasize the School's importance for the Chilean entrepreneurial movement and its future development. Thus, in a short time, Edwards and Urenda – supported by Jorge Ross, Sergio Vergara, CICYP partners, and the board members of the Foundation "Escuela de Economía de la Universidad Católica," formed by alumni – managed to collect nearly 50 percent of the funds needed to purchase a new building for the School. They bought a property owned by the United States Congregation of the Holy Cross, located in a remote and beautiful suburb in Santiago. Funds were mainly provided by national companies such as Banco de A. Edwards, *El Mercurio,* Papelera de Puente Alto, and Banco de Chile, but there were also contributions from foreign companies with investments in Chile.

Transfer to the new campus took place in March 1967, and classes started in April. Four months later, the independent and bucolic life at the "Los Domínicos" campus was interrupted by the student "takeover" of the university's central campus and other university facilities. Apart from the problems previously mentioned, this caused an additional complication: many companies and alumni who were committed to pay installments for purchasing the new campus, suspended their contributions in view of the situation at the university. This forced the School to request funds from the university administration in order to cover the cost of the property. For this reason, the land was purchased by the university and not by the Foundation, as the donors had initially intended.

El Mercurio

The relationship between Edwards and the Chicago Boys was crucial to the change of *El Mercurio*'s character in the late 1960s and early 1970s, which altered its style and role in the media.

Up to then, *El Mercurio* was noted for being a liberal newspaper adhering to the model of "objective journalism." Simultaneously, although *El Mercurio* was invariably linked to the interests of large economic groups, in its internal operation it was careful to keep separate the business activities conducted by Agustín Edwards and the organization of the newspaper itself. Similarly, it was independent of the various rightwing political factions. On the one hand, this relative independence provided *El Mercurio* with the necessary authority to act as arbiter in rightwing sector conflicts and, on the other, it enabled it to appear as a newspaper that was "open" to different political and ideological trends in the ruling class. However, the crisis in the right after Frei's second year in power introduced an important change in this traditional perspective. *El Mercurio* began to appear as the promoter of new and highly controversial ideological positions in the rightwing sectors. These positions were a coherent anticipation of *El Mercurio*'s central ideological line during Pinochet's dictatorship – the neo-liberal project for restructuring capitalism.[41]

This change is closely connected to the relationship between Edwards and the Chicago economists, but even more so to the fact that Adelio Pipino joined *El Mercurio* as editor for the new section on economics. As indicated in previous chapters, the newspaper had traditionally included articles and editorials dealing with economic issues but they were merely informative and frequently polemical. The idea of *educating the readers on economics*, and specifically businessmen, through the newspaper, stemmed mainly from the influence exerted by the group of economists on their mentors in the Edwards group. However, this does not mean that the newspaper had not previously intended to improve information on economic matters. In fact, this idea had first come up in 1963, when the heads of *El Mercurio* participated in an international conference on economic journalism in Rio de Janeiro. They became aware, at that time, that the economic information published by the newspaper was insufficient.

However, it took several years to put the idea into practice. An important obstacle was the skeptical attitude of the newspaper's director, René Silva Espejo; his skepticism increased in 1966 with the publication of a series of analytical articles on economics. Silva – a prestigious journalist of the old school, whose ideas tended towards liberalism with ECLA overtones – viewed the economists' articles as unintelligible and remarked that they "seemed to be translations from English."[42]

In May 1966, Pablo Baraona asked Adelio Pipino to furnish *El Mercurio* with articles of economic analyses. Initially, these articles appeared irregularly and their contents were not too significant, but they gradually became more sophisticated. Towards mid-1967, Silva Espejo asked Pipino to publish all the articles on one page of the Saturday issue. The page was published with no by-line and was first checked by Arturo Fontaine and then by Hermógenes Pérez de Arce. Pipino wrote all the economic sections published by *El Mercurio* between June 1967 and October 1969, when he left Chile to work for the International Monetary Fund. Prior to this, whenever Pipino was absent from the paper, one of his Chicago colleagues took charge of the economic section.[43]

As was to be expected, the articles clearly opposed both the main premises of Chile's economic organization and the orientation of the Christian Democrat government. Unlike articles by other members of the team,[44] they tried to avoid ideological considerations and non-economic debates, which were left to the paper's editorial columns. However, quoting the subtle words of the editor, the articles had "tinges of opposition to the Frei administration."[45]

What can be learned from these articles? A selection of topics and statements published in 1968 shows the enumeration of the main principles: they state that efficiency lies in the market; that inflation is invariably caused by state expenditure; that the state's economic and social activities are inefficient and disrupt the economy; that businessmen are the main injured parties when the state intervenes in the economy and, indirectly, that Chile did not need social changes for its development, but rather that it simply needed to face the main problems, i.e. inflation and the need to liberalize the economy. However, it is interesting to note the tone and style used by the newspaper to educate its readers in the Chicago economic science. An article on "Loan trends between 1940 and 1967" says:

In capital markets free from state intervention, the interest rate will equate the supply of funds with demand. If there is a shortage of loans, the former will tend to increase. A higher return on savings will increase the money supply offered by financial institutions (banks or others). It would thus be possible to partially satisfy the increased demand for loans. Unfortunately, in our country, due to a misunderstanding of the concept of usury, the cost of credit has been fixed and regulated by law since 1929. Therefore, the instrument that regulates savings and loans has not been allowed to balance the financial market.[46]

In their usual style, the analyses "demonstrate" not only the inefficiency of the state's social action, but also that it is an unjustified effort. A study on agrarian reform, one of several written under Pablo Baraona's direct guidance, used a style very different to the ardent one characterizing many of the newspaper's articles or statements made by associations of agricultural entrepreneurs on the subject. A report by FAO and ICIRA on peasant settlements that had been functioning for a year is used to show that peasants would have earned more if they had continued working on the old farms, instead of working as settlers awarded land through agrarian reform. It further states that, during the period under study, capital invested in settlements by the Agrarian Reform Corporation yielded lower profits than private farms. The report acknowledges that "the study [by FAO and ICIRA] was based on data for settlements that had only functioned for a year and that their productivity may have improved later on"; nevertheless, it concludes that "far from showing favorable results under the new system for working the land, as intended, it provides irrefutable evidence that the expensive Chilean Agrarian Reform only led to a reduction in the country's capacity to feed its own population."[47] It must be pointed out, however, that the scope of the articles did not include social processes and that they dealt with phenomena such as agrarian reform only as an "economic measure" which was assessed according to the same criteria used by commercial enterprises. Furthermore, the articles did not take into account the "values" involved, at least those differing from the ones contemplated in their own concept of economic science. Finally, in their opinion, the criteria regarding social and economic efficiency that motivated the Christian Democrat government's efforts to redistribute income were also completely unwarranted. In their comments regarding the report by the Treasury Minister on the state of the public treasury, the authors stated, in their usual style:

The third objective in the Government's program was to improve the distribution of income and wealth. Without making value judgments about this goal, we would like to emphasize that in a previous issue of the Economic Section ... we pointed out that income distribution in Chile is relatively similar to that of Western European countries which are usually taken as the model: Sweden, Denmark, Norway, England and West Germany. Moreover, according to the same study, income distribution is more egalitarian in Chile than in France, Italy and the other Latin American countries. In view of these facts [sic] the question that arises is, whether it is really worthwhile to insist on adopting drastic measures in this respect, in detriment of economic development and anti-inflationary plans.[48]

Evidently, some of these articles gave rise to conflicts with economic authorities in the Frei administration. What is even more interesting is that, in some cases, the articles also met with opposition from the editors of *El*

Mercurio. Two examples are worth noting. The first one was an article by Pipino on foreign competition and tariff policies. The theory favoring tariff latitude and promoting foreign competition as the way to improve efficiency in resource allocation was objected to by Arturo Fontaine and René Silva Espejo, who adhered to the traditional theory that this policy would destroy Chilean enterprise. The article was thus rejected by Fontaine, who demanded that articles should be delivered sooner and only agreed to publish the text as the personal opinion of an economist, intended to open the debate on an interesting issue.[49] An even more contentious case came up when Adelio Pipino and Sergio de la Cuadra wrote an article on the "Chileanization of copper," a policy announced by President Frei consisting of a form of nationalization agreed to with the large copper mining companies, which until then had been fully owned by US enterprises. The article, carefully reviewed previously by other members of the group such as Sergio de Castro, Sergio Undurraga, and Javier Fuenzalida, was violently rejected by Arturo Fontaine, who demanded its substitution by another article on a relatively harmless subject.[50]

Even though the relationship with *El Mercurio* was highly harmonious, these incidents show the difficulties encountered by the Chicago group in breaking away from the outlook held by the entrepreneurs on Chilean development. Therefore, the relevance of *El Mercurio*'s economic page does not lie in a "subversion" of the ideological relationship between the entrepreneurs and the state. Its importance resides in the fact that it was an attempt to educate the Chilean ruling class regarding the social prevalence of so-called economic science, which should not only regulate entrepreneurial activity, but should also subordinate political principles regarding the state's organization and the country's social structure. This therefore gave rise to the development of the belief that there is a technical explanation for every socially relevant issue. Conversely, everything outside the market scheme, and the science that regulates it, is viewed as socially irrelevant. What is not related to the market is of a political nature, and political issues should be viewed as a social obstacle stemming from prejudice and ignorance, which is undoubtedly responsible for some of the inefficient features of the system. *El Mercurio*'s economic section thus helped to train the group and its readers in a style used to disseminate Chicago "economic science" through the press, paving the way for the overall campaign launched by mass media to spread "Chicago ideas" after 1974. Ten years after the arrival of professors from Chicago, Simon Rottenberg's idea of producing leaflets addressed to "the business community and public opinion" on topics such as inflation and public expenditure, the credit system, social policies, etc., an initially unsuccessful campaign, became a reality through none other than Chile's most important newspaper, i.e. *El Mercurio.*

PEC magazine

The articles published in *El Mercurio,* adhering strictly to economic science, avoided dealing with the political obstacles that hindered the implementation of the kind of world envisaged by the Chicago doctrine for a society such as the Chilean one. However, a different style was used in articles published by *PEC* ("politics, economics, and culture"), a magazine of the extreme right which served to spread, in a less academic and restrained manner, the radical standpoint that characterized the Chicago group. The style used in articles against the Christian Democrat government and its doctrines can easily be seen in the following title – "From Rosenberg to Veckemans" – in which an anonymous writer compares the priest Roger Veckemans and his theories on marginality with Adolf Hitler's ideologue and his ideas.[51]

The social doctrine of the Catholic church and Christian socialism was an important topic of concern for the magazine and reflected the permanent and irreconcilable struggle between the ideas promoted by Chicago and the Catholic point of view. Two articles by Dr. Wilhelm Roepke, translated from German, discuss Catholicism's rejection of neo-liberalism and the socializing trends of Catholic doctrines. Re-reading these at present, one recalls all too vividly the arguments used by the Chicago Boys to confront criticism by the higher echelons of the Catholic church under Pinochet's regime.

It is obviously irresponsible, and therefore improper, for any Christian to ignore the simple fact that the economy's full scope and complex patterns give rise to annoying problems that science has been trying to elucidate for the past two centuries in order to provide an adequate interpretation. Whoever demands attention and adherence to their own viewpoints must, in the first place, possess the necessary knowledge and look into the respective sciences . . . even though the economists providing the necessary knowledge and answers to their problems appear to be bad Christians.[52]

In the Chicago group, the most conspicuous article writer for *PEC* was Javier Fuenzalida A., who wrote under the pen name of Coriolano. His essays, which were skillfully polemical, dealt with the usual issues: "state inefficiency," "re-privatization," and the advantages of private enterprise. He also denounced, offhandedly, the Chilean state's "dossier," "the love affair" of a generation imbued with state intervention, and dogmas establishing, for example, that the postal service should be state owned. Nevertheless, these essays also got involved in clearly political debates, usually against Christian Democrats.[53] The articles show two features that characterized the Chicago School's style in dissemination activities: thoughts on the operation of the economy and private enterprise based on a non-existent ideal and theoretical model; and inadequate – if not absurd – national comparisons and examples. "When a private company cannot face competition it disappears and neither public opinion nor the government comes to its rescue. At most, there might be some nostalgia, but everyone agrees that the company is to blame for not having been able to survive," wrote Coriolano in reference to the world of free enterprise and its advantages over the Chilean world of statism. And in recommending *re-privatizacion* ("an idea that does not exist in the Spanish language ... which refers to *making private once more*") he states that "to a certain extent" this "re-privatization of social activities and tasks" has been "underway in Yugoslavia and Czechoslovakia, and in the Russian association with Fiat."[54] His articles touch on – without discussing it directly – the political feasibility of implementing the Chicago model in Chile. Perhaps the article that approaches this issue more directly is one by Ludwig Erhardt on the "German miracle." After praising the German model (in which "there was freedom to succeed in business, as well as freedom to go bankrupt when consumers no longer wanted the company's product") Coriolano asks if it is possible to transfer the experience to Chile. His thoughts are extraordinarily premonitory:

Transferring the German scheme to a country like Chile might raise the need for variants, but the principles remain the same . . . it would imply re-orienting our whole system of production that developed according to the theories of forced industrialization and extreme protectionism . . . which would cause some suffering, although not as much as that endured by the Germans, so that it would not be more difficult for a government in this country to carry out the *neo-capitalist revolution* which in the initial period of adjustment, implies some sacrifices. The Erhardt model requires formal changes, but the essence would remain unaltered, although it is necessary to acknowledge that some of the formal changes would be difficult to attain. One example is the need to amend our Constitution in order to re-establish private property.[55]

The reference to "formal changes" seems to point to the great political difficulties that would have to be overcome in order to carry out in Chile what Coriolano called – with great foresight – "the neo-liberal revolution." These were precisely the difficulties that posed an obstacle to the Chicago Boys' influence in entrepreneurial and intellectual circles that were actively preparing for a forthcoming rightwing government.

The Convention and the political program of Jorge Alessandri

Carlos Urenda, president of the National Convention of Production and Trade, enabled the Chicago Boys to participate in committees that prepared the background documents for this event. Except for Pablo Baraona, appointed to the Agriculture Committee, the other CESEC members only participated through unsigned documents presented by the president of the

Convention. Quoting Urenda: "the CESEC background documents were expounded in detail at the Convention."[56] This was probably one of the reasons why the committees became an area for agreement, but also for confrontation and debate between entrepreneurs and their technical advisers. The studies, conceived as a preliminary government program, dealt with a wide variety of issues regarding economic development. It is beyond the scope of this book to analyze these documents. However, it is interesting to note that it was possible to identify – in a single document – the differing views of the Chicago Boys and those of technical advisers and entrepreneurs who perceived reality in a more segmented, varied, and less radical manner.

The main difference between these groups, which at times was evident only in nuances, was their *assessment* of Chile's development. Evidently, the magnitude of the proposed changes for the Chilean economy depended on the moderation or radicalism of the assessment. This point is highly significant because these differences effectively prevented the Chicago Boys from participating in the team responsible for preparing the economic aspects of Jorge Alessandri's government program. The elements used to assess the situation, however, were probably much more important since, after 1973, they provided the *justification for drastically modifying the development plan applied in Chile since the 1930s*. The documents presented at the 1968 Convention, written prior to the *Unidad Popular* government and the crisis of 1972–3, show that although, at the time, entrepreneurs adhered to a concerned but "reformist" perspective regarding Chile's economic development, the group of economists had already prepared their assessment leading to a "revolutionary" and neo-liberal perspective.

One of the most significant articles presented at the Convention was a document on "Private Enterprise and its Participation in Economic Development." Chapter I of this document, entitled "Assessment and Strategies for Economic Development in Chile," included a series of subsections analyzing the economy's general performance: investment and savings, employment and the efficient use of human resources, etc. Several sections of the assessment presented a complex outlook on the issues under study and the various authors found reasons to express both their concern and a relative optimism based on their positive evaluation of some economic achievements accomplished in the period 1960–66. There were also some documents that proposed policies or policy outlines reflecting many of the classical principles of neo-liberal economic thought, such as public expenditure reduction, fiscal reform and the elimination of wealth taxes, liberalization of foreign trade, development of private capital markets, etc. One of these sections, dealing with "the decentralization of economic decision-making and improved efficiency," stands out for its typical Chicago-style language and approach to the subject of economic organization. It is not a specific but an overall assessment, in which problems are not viewed as isolated issues but rather as a corrosive evil that not only threatens individual economic efficiency but also individual freedom.

In general terms, the assessment combined the good with the bad: "in the course of the current decade, up to 1966, the Chilean economy has grown at the fastest rate ever."[57] It added, however, that it was not possible to be satisfied with this rate of growth because, in the first place, "social pressures demanding improved living conditions are as strong as those in 1960, or even stronger," because Chile's rate of growth was much lower than in developed countries and, finally, because in 1967 there were indications of stagnation. The introduction pointed out that "despite the unique growth experienced by the Chilean economy's rate of development in 1960–66, it is necessary to adopt measures to ensure that the standstill observed in 1967 will be corrected in 1968, and also to achieve a higher growth rate, similar to that observed in more dynamic countries. This is the best way to relax social tensions arising from demands for better living standards, which create so many problems for the country. This requires an in-depth analysis of the economic practices followed in the past few years."[58] Nevertheless, the section on "improved efficiency,"[59] included in the same report, defines a more global and disastrous image, stating that: "the basic economic mechanisms to achieve efficiency do not work in Chile."

Market mechanisms . . . have virtually been eliminated. Prices are fixed by the state, based on criteria modified in accordance with the ideas of officials in power . . . Domestic prices are not consistent with international prices and, therefore, the Chilean economy is isolated from the external market. The capital market is subject to strict state-controlled rationing, in addition to a permanent and soaring inflationary process, which adds another element of uncertainty to decision-making. The final result is a waste of resources and efforts under a regime . . . that does not reward efficiency and creativity but rather the ability and patience to overcome the obstacles imposed by the system and the acumen to take advantage of a complex set of rules. Rather than competing with each other, entrepreneurs . . . have to compete against government officials who are enmeshed in a web of totally incomprehensible rules and regulations. This has been the result of a long-standing and gradually increasing process of bureaucratization in the economic system, which can no longer be controlled by officials in charge of formulating economic policies.[60]

Obviously, this viewpoint required drastic changes in the economic system and, above all, in state organization. It also demonstrates that it was not Allende's administration and the *Unidad Popular* that created the need for the Chicago economists to prepare an assessment that warranted a "neo-liberal revolution" after they took over the state in 1974. However, their assessment, and the solutions offered, were far too drastic for pro-Alessandri entrepreneurs prior to 1970.

The Chicago Boys during Alessandri's campaign

These problems became evident when the team of economists began preparing Jorge Alessandri's government program. The first meeting convened to deal with economic matters was attended by a group of entrepreneurs, economists, and leading rightwing figures that started out by naming a Committee for Economics and Treasury Affairs (Comité de Economía y Hacienda).[61] Pierre Lehman, an entrepreneur, was appointed as president of the committee and Carlos Hurtado as technical coordinator. José Luis Cerda and Manuel Figueroa, two entrepreneurs connected to the construction sector, also formed part of the committee. With the exception of Carlos Hurtado, the group was originally formed by entrepreneurs and not by professional economists. Their first meetings focused on evaluating the experience of economists under Frei's administration and the difficulties they had encountered in carrying out their plans. These discussions led Carlos Hurtado to invite Pablo Baraona, Manuel Cruzat, Sergio de Castro, and Javier Fuenzalida to advise the group on technical matters. According to Carlos Hurtado, conflicts emerged when they started to draw up a brief document stating objectives. The Chicago group proposed swiftly opening up the country to foreign trade, the immediate and total elimination of price controls, and establishing market mechanisms for all sectors.

In view of the lack of agreement, the committee decided to discuss each issue separately and to invite a broader range of entrepreneurs and other leading figures. These included Enrique Ortúzar (a jurist), Víctor Graniffo (an executive at the Papelera paper manufacturing company), and Elios Picquer (an entrepreneur). The atmosphere got increasingly harsher and more aggressive at each meeting. The Chicago group did not change their standpoints in the least. However, decisions eventually had to be made. Pierre Lehman and Carlos Hurtado prepared a "white book" containing the report submitted by the majority; another was prepared by de Castro, Baraona, and Fuenzalida containing the ideas of the "minority." The latter harshly criticized the ideas of the majority. According to Hurtado "the exchange of opinions became increasingly heated and things went from bad to worse."[62] A conciliation was then attempted. The Chicago group proposed that committee meetings and work sessions be held at CESEC headquarters. Hurtado met with Alessandri and expressed his objections to this idea: CESEC belonged to Agustín Edwards and a poor image would be projected if the program was prepared at an institute belonging to the country's main economic group. Alessandri agreed with Hurtado and decided that the only solution was to separate the groups. Thus, INECON (Consulting Engineers and Economists Ltd.) was established. It was directed by Hurtado and Arturo Mackenna (an entrepreneur), and was dedicated to the study of economic development, prices and economic stability, and labor policies. CESEC was devoted to the study of agriculture, foreign trade, and capital markets. However, the groups were forced to meet again. Meetings held at the home of Carlos Urenda in Reñaca, and subsequently with Jorge Alessandri, showed the basic differences between them and ratified the rift between the Chicago group and the pro-Alessandri entrepreneurs. However, the situation between both groups would remain ambiguous until the end. Although Alessandri shared the doubts about the economists, he did not make a clean break with them and allowed them to continue working until the campaign was over.

CESEC did not confine its involvement in the campaign to the economic aspects of the program. It became the center of the so-called "terror campaign" against Allende. There they prepared the books *Triunfó Allende*, describing Chile's future takeover by the Soviet Union and *La Canalla Dorada*, addressed to officials working for international organizations, particularly at ECLA, who were getting ready to work for the program's economic area and subsequently for the Allende administration.[63] CESEC served to channel funds from CICYP members, especially foreign ones, to the Alessandri campaign or rather to the anti-Allende campaign. Unfortunately, it is impossible at present to prove that these activities actually took place. CESEC files and documentation were either destroyed or secretly dispersed when Allende won. According to CESEC members, this was necessary because they contained "lists of people who belonged to political parties, etc." As Urenda stated: "CESEC was always fairly underground."[64]

CHAPTER 11

Under the *Unidad Popular*

Three days after Salvador Allende's victory in the September 1970 elections, Arnold Harberger, who was in Santiago on election day, wrote a long letter to his Chicago colleagues reporting on the Chilean situation. The letter, which was nicknamed – probably by someone other than Harberger – "The Last Dope from Chile,"[1] is a lucid and well-informed document reflecting, with concern but also with political objectivity, the emotional state of mind of part of the center and the right in view of the victory of the socialist candidate with an electoral majority of 36 percent.

The first paragraph of the letter states: "Since Friday night, people here have talked about nothing but the election. God knows how many of the 800,000 or so who voted for Tomic, the Christian Democratic candidate who came in third, would love to be able to go back to the polling booth and switch their votes to Alessandri – but it's too late for that." He then goes on to explain the difficulties which Congress would encounter – since it was responsible, under the constitution, for proclaiming the winning candidate – in voting in favor of Alessandri, the runner-up, and thus breaking with the tradition of proclaiming as winner the candidate with the largest number of votes. The letter then adds that "perhaps the most interesting possibility that has been discussed during the past few days is a deal between Alessandri and Frei whereby the Christian Democrats would vote to confirm Alessandri as president while Alessandri in turn would commit himself to resign the presidency within a short time, say, one or two months, after assuming power. This would give rise to new elections, in which the Christian Democrats could present Frei to run against Allende." According to Harberger, Frei would win this new election easily, but an agreement between Christian Democrats and Alessandri supporters would undoubtedly foster civil violence. It might seem surprising that on 7 September, only two days after the election, Harberger knew about a plan that, at the time, was discussed in absolute secrecy. Harberger's information shows to what extent many of his students and friends were at the core of this secret political operation. The professor from Chicago further stated that another idea was being considered in those circles:

"In rightist circles," he writes, "*the idea of a military takeover is also sometimes broached*. Whereas in many Latin American countries such talk is common-place, as is indeed the experience of having a military government, the mere idea of a military coup is about as foreign to Chilean political traditions as it would be in the US. *That anybody should seriously contemplate this possibility is itself a measure of the level of stress to which the Chilean body politic is currently subject*." Harberger concludes this comment affirming rightly that: "in point of fact, military intervention is most unlikely."[2] He explains that military leaders have publicly stated their respect for the constitution, while "all the organizational force and discipline that the Marxists can now muster is presently on the side of 'keeping it cool.'"

The professor from Chicago continued his letter on 8 September, reporting that the meetings between Frei and Allende, plus Tomic's acknowledgment of the left's victory, made it possible to foresee that the Christian Democrats would vote for Allende in Congress. "The question in the minds of many at this point is whether the new course is reversible and whether one can travel in both directions along this road ... The people who believe in the irreversibility of the process are by and large also the ones who seriously contemplate the prospect of a possible military intervention. Those who do not feel that the process is irreversible place their faith in the strength of Chile's democratic traditions and institutions." Harberger believes that the Christian Democrats have clearly chosen this last position, on the assumption that Allende would lack a majority in Congress and that, should the institutions withstand this, the electorate would favor Frei in the 1976 elections. He then analyzes the reasons why the economic program of Allende's government seems doomed to failure:

The first and perhaps the most important source of such a failure is the high level of expectations that were aroused by Allende's campaign. Chile simply does not at this time possess the resources to accomplish all that Allende promised ... The second source of failure is the reaction of Chile's technical and managerial elite to Allende's victory. Perhaps the panic will subside, but panic is the only way to describe the current state of mind of a fair fraction of this elite group. Many have already left the country, and many others are planning to go. The black-market dollar, which had fluctuated around the price of a little over 20 escudos in the months prior to the election, was reported yesterday to have reached prices of over 60 escudos. The people planning to leave are ready in effect to sell all they can't take with them, to abandon their jobs and/or professional practices, and to leave their houses, businesses, factories, etc., to an uncertain fate. How large the exodus will be is entirely unknown.[3]

He states that the fear felt by these "technical elites" is greater than that of the political sectors since, although it would apparently seem feasible to reverse the situation on a political level, it is inconceivable at the economic level. "One young Chilean put it that 'we no longer have a real choice in regard to capitalism, but we can choose between being another Yugoslavia or another Rumania.'" Harberger adds: "I consider this to exaggerate the situation substantially, but nonetheless I must concede that if a third or a half of Chile's industry is nationalized, no more than a quarter or a third of the nationalized activities are likely ever to be returned to the private sector."

Professor Harberger then devotes himself to analyzing who is responsible for this "tragedy". He blames those who would like to change their vote from Tomic to Alessandri, as well as those who maintained a complacent attitude towards Alessandri's victory up to the last moment. "This is especially so since the Alessandri camp was so overwhelmingly status-quo oriented: elements favoring reform were present, but their voices were weak amidst the general clamor for Alessandri as the best man to keep things more-or-less the way they are."[4]

Although he did not expressly mention the situation of his disciples at the Universidad Católica, Harberger's letter is a remarkably faithful portrayal of the atmosphere in society in Chile which undoubtedly included those surrounding the Catholic University and most of its faculty, particularly of course the conservative professors at the School of Economics. Among Harberger's students, Allende's victory initially generated a feeling of panic that resulted in at least one emigration: Ernesto Fontaine left for Washington, preceded by a dramatic farewell from his students. Subsequently, Rolf Luders also emigrated to the same place. Fontaine, Luders, de la Cuadra, and Marcelo Selowski worked on a "Project on Capital Markets" at the Organization of American States (OAS) under the protection of Ardito Barletta, a Chicago economist from Panama.

Between politics and war

There were in fact reasons for serious concern. The three years of Salvador Allende's administration were a period in which all the political and ideological contradictions which had characterized Chilean society in the previous period reached their peak. The conflicts that had accumulated since the beginning of Frei's attempts at reform became irreconcilable primarily as a consequence of the fact that the political extremes had turned them into a radical synthesis. Political life gradually became an alternative defined by opponents as a choice between "communism or fascism." The radicalization of the political process took place amid a significant rise in social and political activity. The number of registered voters increased from 1.5 million in 1958 to over 3.5 million in 1970; the percentage of voters as a proportion of the total population, which stood at around 15 percent prior to 1960, had risen to almost 30 percent by 1970. Moreover, the number of trade unionists doubled during the Frei administration: in the space of six years, the unionization of workers increased by 38 percent and that of white-collar staff 90 percent. Peasant organizations expanded from some 2,000 members in 1964 to over 114,000 in 1970.[5] This level of participation contributed to a climate of social revolution. Violence was present from the very beginning, and did not stem simply from the activities of the left.

Immediately after Allende's election, the attempt to abduct the army commander-in-chief, General René Schneider, carried out by extreme rightwing militants who pretended to be a leftist revolutionary group – an attempt that resulted in the commander-in-chief's death – caused the failure of the military coup that the extreme right desperately wished to bring about. This murder marked, from then on, the atmosphere of hate and mistrust that characterized the confrontation between the right and the left. At the same time, the more radical groups in the *Unidad Popular* launched a systematic attack against the political center, i.e. Christian Democracy, in order to, as they said, "unmask its true reactionary nature." The Christian Democrats respected the tradition of voting in the National Congress for the candidate with the majority of the vote. In doing so, they allowed Salvador Allende into office. Initially, there was still hope for an understanding between the left and the center. However, this prospect proved ephemeral. Attacks on the Christian Democrats from left of the *Unidad Popular* gradually gave a more pivotal role in the PDC to those leaders who had always sought the failure of a left-oriented government. They found ample justification for their bitter criticism of the *Unidad Popular* in the oral violence and uncouth discrediting that they were subjected to by the leftist press which, in turn, confronted the patient sedition, promoted by *El Mercurio* and other rightwing media, by replying with insults and threats.

Such was the atmosphere prevailing at the time when the organized workers and large marginal urban sectors began increasingly to participate in politics. The organization and ideological indoctrination of these groups by leftwing political parties, through measures such as the nationalization of private companies and the increased scope of agrarian reform, began to give shape to a real process of social revolution. The secular fear of the poor felt by the wealthier classes promoted the radicalization of trade associations and associations of employers. Having already mobilized during the previous period, these associations now resorted to hoarding and even to terrorism, in order to foster confrontation and chaos and thus bring about the military intervention desired from the outset by some of their leaders.

From the standpoint of our study, the real interest lies in tracing the course of the events that heightened the appeal of neo-liberal ideas among business sectors and, more generally, the taking up of such notions in the discourse of the opposition to the leftwing government. From this angle, our argument could be summarized as follows: sectors of the center and the right, who previously had opposed one another, now worked together under a common banner based on "principles"; this alliance was prompted by the political and ideological radicalization provoked by the Allende government and, particularly, by its expropriation policy and the gradual disappearance of market mechanisms in the Chilean economy. Given these developments, the right, and especially the business community, began gradually to accept that the remedy for the political and economic situation had to be radical.

We therefore need to examine the new and slippery political context in order to discover why these ideas – previously rejected by the team of presidential candidate Alessandri – came to form part of an ideology which bound them together after the election of Allende. First, Allende's election and the characteristics taken on by political debate determined the radical *politicization* of the whole debate, including that related to economics. This meant that many of the conflicts regarding *specific economic policies*, that used to be highly important during the previous period, gradually tended to disappear. The acuteness of social and political conflict widened the scope of ideological disputes, which adopted the language of "principles" and became thus irreconcilable. It is easy to understand that this led to the disappearance of all possible spaces for negotiation, thus providing the more extreme sectors with an advantage in leading their more moderate allies. Gradually, the fundamental deterioration in society's economic, social, and political situation made extreme solutions appear to be more "realistic." The same radical force that sapped the prestige of moderate politicians and intermediate political solutions also assisted the rise of radical economists, who advocated the reduction of the role of government as part of the confrontation between the state and the market.

In practice, the most powerful groups of entrepreneurs – assembled under CYSIP – led the entrepreneurial movement in a campaign that achieved the flexibility needed to homogenize an entrepreneurial entity that assembled a wide variety of members ranging from big to small business. As we shall see later on, this eased the way for a close collaboration between Chicago economists and *the core* of the organizations of entrepreneurs. At the same time, the situation rapidly eroded the conflict between neo-liberal economists and Christian Democrat economists, which made it possible for the Chicago group, who had scattered following the university reform and Allende's victory, to participate in a more "pluralistic" organization, open to economists holding other theoretical orientations. Finally, and despite the fact that it never disappeared entirely, the conflict between Christian Democracy and the right was considerably diluted. The most radical sectors on the right were thus able to fix the parameters within which the contest with the Allende government would take place. Acting under the assumption that the left sought to destroy democratic institutions, opposition forces proceeded to manipulate and use these institutions in a spurious fashion, with the intention of utilizing them in the battle for power.

Within this general context, and in the space of barely two years, neo-liberal ideas and their standard bearers in Chilean society were to see a paradoxical shift in their fortunes. Immersed into academia, and apparently situated entirely outside reality at the beginning of the leftist government, neo-liberal ideas and their exponents gained rightful admittance into an intellectual gathering of "democrats" that gradually reunited all the economists opposed to Allende's socialist experience. Thus, and for the first time since their transfer to Chile, the Chicago ideas and their bearers did not adopt a position that was *antagonistic* to all other viewpoints and to the technicians existing in the field of non-Marxist economics in Chile. Furthermore, the intensely radical nature of the political and economic situation gradually provided these ideas, *vis-à-vis conservative groups*, with a degree of realism that in their previous perception of events they obviously lacked. The conflict was fundamental to such an extent that the issue was no longer the "economic policies" themselves but rather *the economic principles* underlying society's organization. The overall virtues of the market and free competition, the rejection of the state and its protection of industrial development that characterized neo-liberal ideas seemed then to combine without conflict with Christian Democratic concepts of a free market with state participation in promoting "social justice," worker participation, and income redistribution. The contradictions between these issues were considered to be less important than that of forming a defensive front against the uncontrollable "collectiviza-tion" of the economy. The radical nature of the situation led the business sectors to appreciate as virtues what they had previously seen as theoretical dogmatism in the neo-liberal group. In fact, the more foreign and "out of place" that these neo-liberal ideas seemed to be, the more they appeared to possess the virtues of realism and pragmatism. Faced with a rapid deterioration in the economy and by a revolutionary situation, business groups and their political allies soon deduced that corrective measures would require not just the use of force in overthrowing the government, but also the eradication of socialist ideas from Chilean society.

The center of the economics debate was no longer the university. The serious political and social conflicts that characterized the last three years of Chilean democracy fostered strong economic discussions in Congress, in the press, in political parties, and in social organizations. Economists in the opposition, i.e. Christian Democrats and rightwing economists, were under pressure from members of parliament and the press who demanded ammunition to wage the emerging war against the government presided over by Salvador Allende. Simultaneously, business organizations and some political parties began to explore more conspiratorial and clandestine ways to carry out their activities. The Chicago Boys were to play an important role in this respect.

The conspiracy

"Conspiracy"
no secret

Following Allende's election, the sense of crisis and personal insecurity that gripped rightwing political and social leaders had an immediate impact on CESEC. Any illusions of a political solution that would lead to fresh presidential elections, such as that described by Professor Harberger in his letter to Chicago, quickly evaporated. Moreover, the possibility of military intervention, always rather improbable, dissipated completely after the assassination of General Schneider, whose death anyway reduced the probability of a successful US intervention to prevent Allende's assumption of power. After visiting Richard Nixon and Henry Kissinger to request an intervention by the United States against the new Chilean government, Agustín Edwards took up a post as vice-president at the Pepsi Cola Company and settled in Connecticut. Carlos Urenda went to live temporarily in Buenos Aires. CESEC was formally closed. However, as Urenda stated, some of its members continued carrying out their activities in the "underground."[6] These activities led to two initiatives that subsequently shaped a significant aspect of the preparation for the military coup: the organization of a team of economists that acted as advisors to the Sociedad de Fomento Fabril and the preparation of an economic program for an eventual new government. Let us now examine each of these initiatives.[7]

In mid-1971, Orlando Sáenz, the new president of SOFOFA,[8] met Hernán Cubillos, who had replaced Agustín Edwards as chairman of *El Mercurio*. Cubillos organized a luncheon for the president of SOFOFA with the CYSIP group. Jorge Ross, Javier Vial, Manuel Cruzat, Arturo Fontaine, Fernando Bravo, and Emilio Sanfuentes attended this meeting. According to Sáenz, the discussion was so successful that the group decided to continue working together as a strategic and financial support to SOFOFA. The group, that later came to be called "the Monday Club," met each week at the office of the chairman of Editorial Lord Cochrane – the publishing house for *El Mercurio* – and, according to Orlando Sáenz, gradually became a "place for discussion and decision-making of even greater importance than SOFOFA's governing body." According to Sáenz, this was the source of all "the powerful foreign contacts," both in the United States and with the large organizations of entrepreneurs and big businessmen in Latin America.[9] At one of these meetings, Sáenz agreed to the group's proposal that he should reorganize SOFOFA's department of studies and enlist a group of economists whose names were suggested by the "Monday Club." The first person to be summoned was Sergio Undurraga, professor of the Institute of Economics at the Universidad Católica. Undurraga was not trained in economics under the agreements with the University of Chicago. He was, however, considered by his colleagues to be an "honorary Chicago Boy." Thus, he faced no problems in recruiting the principal members of the group to join in the work that would result in the preparation of an alternative program.

After assessing SOFOFA's requirements with regard to information and economic analysis, Undurraga presented Sáenz with a proposal for a project that included the elaboration of an overall view of the Chilean economy. He also convinced Sáenz that this work could not be done at SOFOFA, but should be done by an independent entity. A consulting firm was then established. They rented office space located very near to "La Moneda," the presidential palace. The firm was manned by three people: Undurraga, Emilio Sanfuentes, and Alvaro Bardón. While the first two were persons with direct links to Agustín Edwards and his group, Bardón was linked to the Christian Democratic economists. The group's objectives were to carry out a daily analysis, a monthly report, and an analysis of the projections they envisaged for the Chilean economy.[10]

The first report submitted by Undurraga and his team to SOFOFA was highly disappointing to the entrepreneurs. Instead of the economic chaos expected for 1971, the results of the government's actions appeared to be quite satisfactory. In effect, the Chilean economy experienced unprecedented growth that year, mainly as a result of highly expansionist economic policies. The growth rate was 8 percent, vastly superior to the 3.6 percent achieved the previous year and the highest recorded since 1950. Inflation fell significantly (from 36.1 percent to 22.1 percent) as did unemployment, which dropped to only 3.8 percent – the lowest figure ever recorded in Chile. There was also an improvement in wages and income distribution, thus translating economic growth into generally higher living standards and a sense of unfettered success among those on the left of the government.[11]

Success was, however, deceptive. The economic team was already able to detect, and report, a series of disequilibria deriving from the expansionist policies: a rise in the fiscal deficit, a fall in international reserves, a drop in investment, and a trade deficit. All these indicators pointed to serious problems in the following year. Indeed, by the end of 1971, there were signs of an impending, rapid acceleration in inflation. The technical team's ability to foresee events raised its prestige considerably in business circles and among opposition politicians: the importance of the team of economists and their science was recognized. From that point onwards, the group of economists felt free to develop and to take on new and different activities. Undurraga and Bardón established links with members of Congress from the National Party (*Partido Nacional*) and from the Christian Democratic Party, providing them with the economic information needed for their attacks in Congress against the regime's policies. In the meantime, Emilio Sanfuentes devoted his efforts to disseminating these analyses through the press. His efforts materialized through *Portada* magazine, where rightwing intellectuals wrote, and also in the creation of *Qué Pasa* magazine, for which Sergio de Castro acted as economic editor.[12]

Between August 1971 and mid-1972, with funds provided by SOFOFA, Undurraga and his team began to prepare a new government program. The scale and political importance of this initiative did not go unnoticed by those who drafted it. Undurraga describes the situation saying that, even if nobody could specify how the change was to come about, they were certain that it was clearly a prime necessity. The size of the task required the assistance of all members of the Universidad Católica group in Chile, even those that had initially belonged to the business advisory circle: Sergio de Castro, Luis Frederici, Manuel Cruzat, Pablo Baraona, and Juan Braun. Thus, the main Chicago team was reunited once more. The objective pursued for so many years had finally been achieved. The Chicago Boys were now the premier advisers to Chilean business organizations.

The president of SOFOFA, however, had his doubts about the representativeness of the group. Sáenz claims that he clearly perceived that the studies carried out by the consulting firm represented *only one* outlook of economic theory whereas SOFOFA's institutional objectives required the participation of all the economic ideas representing the opposition to Allende's administration, including Christian Democracy. The work done by the Chicago team was, in his words, "a very well-established munitions factory, so that when I spoke I would have the technical support required to destroy the state ministers in the Senate."[13] But the preparation of a government program required the setting of wider criteria.

By that time, the deterioration of the economic situation was clearly evident: in February 1972, Undurraga and Bardón had completed a study in which they predicted that inflation would rise to over 180 percent by the end of the year.[14] Despite signs of economic deterioration, the UP government did not hesitate to sacrifice economic equilibrium in order to enjoy continued political popularity, particularly among the poorest sectors of society. In this manner, wages continued to grow faster even than government plans envisaged. Subsidies to state firms also expanded, while tax revenue declined. The net result was that the fiscal deficit swelled to unheard-of levels: 24.5 percent of GNP in 1972 and 30.5 percent in 1973. The economy went into recession. Inflation shot up to 260.5 percent in 1972, and 605.1 percent in 1973. During these two years, Chile went into a period of economic collapse.

Sensing the precariousness of the situation, those preparing the new government program accelerated their plans. The group of economists contracted by SOFOFA heeded the recommendation of their president and decided to expand membership, bringing in economists linked to the PDC. Contacts with Alvaro Bardón led the Chicago group to put itself in touch with the *technical staff* of José Musalem, a senator from the Christian Democratic Party. Some University of Chicago graduates also formed part of this group: Andrés Sanfuentes (Emilio's brother), Juan Villarzú, and José Luis Zavala. In August 1972, the fully established group discussed the outline for the economic strategy to be implemented by a new administration. Ten economists participated in this discussion: José de Castro, Pablo Baraona, Manuel Cruzat, Sergio Undurraga, Emilio Sanfuentes, Andrés Sanfuentes, Juan Braun, Juan Villarzú, José Luis Zavala, and Alvaro Bardón.[15] According to Fontaine, "once the general plan was approved, the various topics were distributed among the economists. Thus, for example, agricultural matters were assigned to Pablo Baraona, capital markets to Sergio Undurraga, policies regarding income redistribution were left to Andrés Sanfuentes, state-owned companies were entrusted to Juan Villarzú, and so on."[16]

The work was clandestine, given that the idea of a program for "the next government that would succeed the current one" would only make sense in 1972 or 1973, under the expectation of a solution provided by resorting to force: Allende's administration was supposed to end in 1976.

The opposing sides both continued to allude to the unsustainable nature of events, yet neither wanted to risk being openly accused of preparing for the use of force. From mid-1972 until the parliamentary elections in 1973, opposition hopes centered on winning a sufficient majority to be able to constitutionally impeach President Allende and provoke new elections. The election results showed, however, that even though government support had weakened it remained strong enough to avoid a "legal overthrow." The UP won a surprising 45.3 percent of the votes in these elections, scarcely 8 percent less than in the 1971 municipal elections. Given the catastrophic situation preceding the elections, this result was viewed by parties in the leftwing coalition as little less than a triumph. Thus, the last constitutional attempt to depose Allende took place in March 1973. The only options now open to the opposition were either to pursue the difficult path of political agreements with the government, or to incite a military coup. The PDC systematically refused to reject the former, entering into a series of discussions with the government. These came to involve the president of the republic himself and persisted, even though continually frustrated, practically until the eve of the coup.

In this political context, the PDC had to keep secret the participation of its economists in the new program. Even though the party's leaders were perfectly aware of what was going on, the PDC economists always stated that their participation was purely personal. Former President Eduardo Frei was, in fact, duly informed by Orlando Sáenz about the technical team's existence and about SOFOFA's efforts to include in the initiative contributions that represented the viewpoint of the Christian Democrats.[17] The party was nonetheless kept out of the discussion and did not receive copies of documents originated by the working group.

A second, and more important reason accounted for the atmosphere of privacy in which this work was carried out. The program was part of a broader operation of the war against the Allende administration, organized by the movement of entrepreneurs as of late 1971. In September 1971, the nation's most important entrepreneurs met in Viña del Mar in order to plan their activities. According to Orlando Sáenz, they came to the conclusion that "Allende's government was incompatible with freedom in Chile and with the existence of private enterprise, and that the only way to avoid the end was to overthrow the government."[18] Years later, the entrepreneurial leader expressed the conclusions arrived at during that meeting as follows:

The first conclusion was the organization of a war structure; to systematically gather economic resources, search for funds, on the domestic and international levels, that could be used for activities in politics, propaganda and activism. We also decided to prepare specific alternative programs to government programs that would systematically be passed on to the Armed Forces. An intelligence service had to be organized, as well as technical departments. We decided on a form of organization that could guarantee that the information obtained, and our technical structure, were first rate, both of which involved funds. Furthermore, we needed the best possible means of dissemination and this also implied work and money.[19]

It has repeatedly been implied that this revolt by the middle classes was financed mainly by the United States and, specifically, the CIA. Those interviewed admit that the Agency did participate. It did so in conjunction with a network of business organizations from several Latin American countries, which officially channeled international funds to SOFOFA. "Money was coming in from everywhere," says Sergio Undurraga, "and nobody asked where it came from: one must keep in mind that with Allende, Chile had gone into a 'cold war' logic." Undurraga disagreed, however, that financing the work of the economists had required substantial resources. This is confirmed by others interviewed. This seems to rule out the statement contained in the report on "Covert Action in Chile" issued by the Select Committee of the US Senate which declared that the clandestine donations made by the United States government had been assigned to the economists and to the preparation of the program. The work carried out by the economists in preparing the various sections of the document did not require high financing: there were many previous studies that could have provided the basis for the program's recommendations. The issue remains unclear and is still in need of investigation. It is difficult, however, to discard the educated guess that the economists' program was used as a good academic excuse to justify the request for, and the granting of, funds actually used to organize the unemployed, student demonstrations, propaganda, and other activities in an attempt to create the necessary chaos that would finally persuade the military to intervene.[20]

In late 1972, two of Agustín Edwards' employees, former naval officers Roberto Kelly and José Radic, were asked by naval sources to obtain an economic program that would ease the way for the military coup.[21] "It is very easy to overthrow Allende. The important thing is what to do with the government; how to solve the economic problems" stated the naval sources.[22] Roberto Kelly tells that he approached Emilio Sanfuentes to request the preparation of the plan and that he promised to have it ready in thirty days. The mediator then returned to the naval sources and promised them that the program would be ready in ninety days.

The various studies included in the program were ready by May 1973. Kelly and the team met in Viña del Mar where, at a seminar, the studies contributed by the ten economists were compared. This was no easy task, since different criteria existed regarding significant measures of the economic policy to be followed. Compromise solutions prevailed, however, due to the urgency of the navy's request and also because of the way the economists perceived the situation in Chile. Arturo Fontaine vividly describes the culmination of this operation as follows:

Emilio Sanfuentes summarized the study in five pages and handed it to Kelly. He, in turn, passed it on to Admiral Troncoso. From then on, the Navy started to receive the program almost page by page as de Castro and Undurraga gave it the finishing touches. On September 11, 1973, the photocopying machines at Editorial Lord Cochrane, chaired by Hernán Cubillos, Agustín Edwards' highest representative and closely connected to several of the plan's economists, worked non-stop to duplicate copies of this long document – known under the pet name of "El ladrillo" [the brick]. Before midday on Wednesday, September 12, 1973, the General Officers of the Armed Forces who performed governmental duties had the Plan on their desks.[23]

The timing of the Chicago Boys' first program with the bombing of "La Moneda" and the death of the last constitutional president of Chile had thus been perfect.

Twenty years on: a postscript

The new Chile

A history of the Chicago School in Chile could formally end here. In previous pages, this book has described the academic success of the transfer of ideas and how, due to an authoritarian regime, these ideas had an enormous ideological impact on the workings of Chile's economy and society. The book has chronicled, from various angles and to varying degrees of detail, the events that seem most relevant: namely, the way in which an economic doctrine was transferred to a group of Chilean students, and the ultimate effect that this was to have on life in Chile. First, attention has been given to the manner in which certain ideas on the economy and on the role of economists spawned a cohesive elite and a sense of mission. Second, the book has analyzed the frustration of the economists in Chile and their proclivity to verge towards authoritarianism and become indifferent to democracy, as well as their rejection of politics, which they saw as an obstacle to a free market, an activity dedicated to conciliate, somewhat illegitimately, the interests of organized groups through the intervention of the state. Finally we have discussed the manner in which this set of ideas played a determining role in defining the economists' attitude to the break in constitutional order and the military coup of 1973: they understood it as an opportunity to carry out a revolution that would transform not just the economic structure, but also the way in which decisions were made and values created in Chilean society.

Almost twenty years after the experiment began, the most enduring consequences of such events for today's Chilean society still need to be reviewed. That is the purpose of this postscript. Although only a brief period of time has elapsed since the current democratic government took over from the military regime – something that should in itself caution against overly categorical assessments – Chilean society seems set on a surprisingly consensual course of development that promises to remain stable into the future. Stable liberalization policies and the rapid opening up of the economy to foreign competition have yielded enormously positive results, all made possible by the return to democracy. Renewed democracy has allowed a social pact between the government, business sectors, and workers, the tackling of the serious social effects arising from over a decade of neo-liberal policies and, above all, has given domestic and international legitimacy to a now clearly capitalist-oriented economy.

Neo-liberal ideas retain their importance within this framework, be this because they are antagonistic towards certain aspects of the government's economic and social policies, or because they form part of an ideological discourse that remains influential among business organizations and rightwing political elites. The main representatives of the neo-liberal approach – undoubtedly more diluted and less radical than in years past – continue to credit themselves with the economic success enjoyed by the Chilean transition, and to draw up principles and prescriptions for the construction of a "free society." Such ideas have a powerful resonance among elites on the Chilean and Latin American right and remain influential among certain economists and intellectuals at the center and on the center-left of the Chilean political spectrum.

The facts are known, but it is useful briefly to restate them. Since 1989, Chile has conducted a transition to democracy via negotiations and political accords. In the 1988 plebiscite, an array of center-left forces led by Christian Democrats and Socialists defeated General Pinochet and thus obliged him to call free elections the following year. Subsequently, Chile's political elites and armed forces have negotiated an admirably well-ordered political transition process. As part of this smooth transition, the civilian actors in the previous authoritarian regime remain organized – forming the political opposition to the new democratic government made up of center-left parties (the Coalition of Parties for Democracy, *Concertación de Partidos por la Democracia*). This is the coalition that has brought about macro-economic stabilization and the reform of economic policy, introducing such measures into a broader context of renewed public liberties, political participation, and electoral processes. The great electoral support enjoyed by the *Concertación* is shown by the fact that President Aylwin is retiring with a very high rate of support in the polls, while Mr. Eduardo Frei, the candidate of the coalition, was elected president in December 1993 by a substantial 58 percent majority.

What has happened to the main protagonists in this study? Some Chicago Boys have returned to academic life. Many are highly successful international consultants, others have joined Chile's main banks and companies, and most have a direct or indirect influence on the economic policy debate, be it through the rightwing parties, consultancy firms, or think-tanks. Their numerous disciples and intellectual descendants successfully populate academic economic institutes and the research departments of business groups. Nevertheless, from a political point of view, they have not been overly successful. Their incursions into political activity have left a sour taste, and the main party subscribing to their theses, the Independent Democratic Union (*Unión Demócrata Independiente,* UDI), remains the second party in a rightwing alliance that has failed either to achieve unity or to offer the public convincing proposals against the present governing coalition.

The other main actors in the Chilean drama, the armed forces – including General Pinochet whom the constitution authorizes to continue as army commander-in-chief until 1997 – are, for their part, returning gradually but not without difficulty to their traditional position of "influential subordination" to civil power. Inquiries into human rights abuses committed during the military dictatorship are being conducted by the courts. Progress is slow, punctuated by occasional friction with senior military officers. Yet such tensions apparently are not sufficiently serious to threaten overall political stability. Nevertheless, the stance adopted by the military high command, added to its close links to some rightwing politicians, have impeded constitutional reforms intended to facilitate a full return to civilian authority over the armed forces. Such factors have, moreover, denied political balance to a system whose main tensions stem from the impulse of the previous regime's authorities to "defend its achievements." All that said, the first government of transition, led by the Christian Democrat Patricio Aylwin, ended its term amid an aura of successful economic management and widespread recognition of its political ability to address the most difficult transitional issues. The question of the distribution of wealth is perhaps the only factor to have caused significant concern. Despite governmental efforts to raise spending on education and health and to augment investment in the poorest sectors, progress in this area has not been enough to reduce significantly the gulf in income distribution that arose during the years of authoritarian rule.

The economic success of the democratic government has clearly made a fundamental contribution to the high degree of political stability. Chile's economy has seen sustained growth, expanding by 10.4 percent in 1992 and by an annual average of 6.4 percent during the first three years of Patricio Aylwin's presidency. Falling inflation, rising investment, and a drop in unemployment have fueled domestic confidence in the government's handling of the economy, as well as optimism in Chile's real opportunities for development. Exports have grown by an average of 10 percent per year, export products have become diversified, and Chile is penetrating new markets across the globe, particularly in the Asia–Pacific area and Latin America. As a result, the opening up of the economy to foreign competition and export-orientation have become articles of faith for Chilean society in general, and have come to symbolize the type of country Chileans desire and to characterize the national interest.[1]

The return to democracy in Chile has thus not meant renewed state controls on economic activity, a return to a highly protected economy, or a relapse into populist management of the economy by the state, such as the Chicago Boys predicted during the campaign previous to the plebiscite of 1988. The return to democracy in Chile has been conducted with strict adherence to macro-economic equilibria, the promotion of economic growth, the attraction of foreign investment, and the stimulation of national savings. This continuity in the economic model, implicit in the definitive adoption by Chile of a free market economy, seems at first glance to suggest that, in economic terms, nothing has changed in Chile. The question is doubtless an important one, and leads to an array of other questions. Does this mean that, in terms of the underlying economic organization and criteria governing Chilean society, there is nothing to distinguish the dictatorship from democracy? Does it mean that neo-liberal criteria have been imposed on economic and social administration, and that both the decision-making process and the overall public debate still reflect the ideology of the authoritarian period? The answers to these questions are relevant to the underlying theme of this book, which is the usefulness of a particular type of economist and of economics in a situation of social and political reconstruction.

Debate on this issue has continued over the past few years, with very varied positions being adopted. It can be summarized, however, by two main lines of argument: one that emphasizes *continuity* between the economic policy and development prospects of the democratic government and the military regime; and a contrasting one that underlines the elements of *differentiation* between the economic and social orientation of both governments. Its main proponents are perfectly aware that neither position is exclusive; they agree that any reasonable discussion should identify elements of continuity in, and distinction between, the two regimes. That is, in fact, the primary characteristic of a "pacted transition" such as Chile's. Their discussion serves, however, to interpret the relationship between past and present ideas in Chile in terms of social organization and the concept of development.

Our objective in broaching this debate is to ascertain the degree of influence still exercised by neo-liberal thought *à la Chicago* over Chilean society. To do so, it is necessary to address the manner in which the neo-liberal discourse has been structured by its original proponents, and the way in which it has infiltrated other, very different discourses – some of which are, superficially at least, contradictory to the basic neo-liberal framework. To truly understand how an organized set of ideas evolves over time, one needs to track its ramifications and to observe how elements of what could be termed the "original doctrine" alter and decompose. Such elements can be employed in historically dissimilar situations, or can even be used to defend very different points of view. Equally, in the more specific areas of the economic structure of state and economic policy decisions, particularly when discussing the transition from an authoritarian to a democratic regime, it seems insufficient to simply assert that continuity is or is not present. Logically, there will always be a degree of continuity in some aspects and not in others. The question lies precisely in identifying those aspects where there is continuity and those where it is absent because the key elements have changed, decomposed, or been rejected. Those who assert the *continuity* between the two forms of government are, in reality, claiming that certain aspects of continuity are more relevant than other, *differential* elements in defining the conduct of the current government. This refers particularly to some key economic concepts adopted by the previous regime. One can imagine in fact a double-axis graph (representing continuity and differentiation) on which can be plotted the great variety of stances held in the debate regarding the economic nature of the Chilean transition. Let us attempt briefly to describe these in terms of the current course taken by each discourse.

The most paradigmatic of the *continuist* viewpoints claims that the current democratic government has made no substantive changes to the form of economic organization that characterized the military regime. This argument, present in some political debate, in press interviews, and in academic discussions, highlights the belief in a *continuity of success*. Briefly, it regards current economic success as being owed to previous achievements. According to this view, current success is due, fundamentally, to the maintenance of the economic structure forged under authoritarianism, to the rejection of previous attempts at *populism* and *socialism*, the preservation of a free market system and an open economy, strict adherence to macro-economic discipline, the allotting of a central role to the private sector and continued privatizations, etc. In other words, Chile has preserved the structural criteria established at the onset of the Chicago Boys' experiment. Hence, the notion of the continuity of success is closely linked to the maintenance of the economic structures and mechanisms established during the first years of the military regime.

Supporters of the *continuist* argument tend to be less unanimous or categoric when they move beyond considerations of the general structure of the economy and once they begin to ponder the degree of continuity in specific economic policies and, even more so, in the degree of faithfulness to the free market ideas that inspired the current economic order. Some will argue that socialist and Christian Democrat economists have learned the rules of economic science, and mended their old bad habits, especially their statist tendencies. Yet they will often claim that these economists remain suspicious of market mechanisms and that their hesitations delay and obstruct a more vigorous economic growth in Chile. In this sense, many supporters of the continuist view would claim that the democratic government's *ideas and attitudes regarding the economy* do not necessarily reflect the same economic principles held by the military regime, but that its practice confirms them. Others, however, continue to suspect deep ideological differences between the authoritarian and democratic regimes in terms of their view of the workings of the economic structure and call for permanent vigilance in defense of the free market.

The *continuist* position often perceives there to be a relationship of causality between authoritarianism, economic freedoms, and democratic politics. According to this perspective, the authoritarian regime resolved to return Chile to democracy; more specifically, the decision was taken by a technocratic nucleus within the regime which understood the relationship of cause and effect between economic and political liberty. In so doing the continuists concede, often implicitly, that authoritarianism was the necessary price to pay for economic reform and therefore for democracy, although they add that the two things are clearly independent of one another. Hence, the triumph of the "social market economy" is believed to reside in the fact that the Pinochet economy, having slipped its authoritarian moorings, became the economy of democracy. This "victory" seems to connote historic legitimacy not just for the Chicago Boys, but principally for Pinochet himself; the stability of the economic path that Chile is following today is precisely, in this view, the result of his leadership. The only possible threat lies in the current economic team's hesitation in continuing down the path of privatization as well as in politically induced distortions that were previously absent. In short, democratic rule has supposedly led to a clear expansion in the social role of the state as a result either of electoral obligations or of ideological backwardness. Accordingly, free market economists should be vigilant against such factors, since they could eventually threaten the entire economic edifice constructed during the military regime.

Naturally, the discourse that is closest to this *continuist* "ideal type" is that espoused by the supporters of the previous regime, as well as by those who today continue to identify themselves with neo-liberal ideology. We should, however, include an additional variant also present on our imaginary graph. This variant is just as close to the continuist axis as the sectors just mentioned, yet, at the same time, is radically different; it stresses the supposed continuity of model between the two governments, emphasizing that they are similar precisely because they retain the focus on "capitalist accumulation" that harms vast swathes of society and keeps people in poverty. The "model" remains in place precisely because current economic management resembles that of the previous regime in its refusal to conduct a true process of social development using the state. This has principally been a criticism of the radical left, close to the Communist Party, which has been up to now electorally insignificant. The communist view is similar to that of the neo-liberals in that it does not distinguish any appreciable difference between the economy under democracy and under dictatorship. Naturally, the critiques of both continuist views are not identical. One group attacks it for not going far enough along the road to a market economy, in particular for not making sufficient progress on privatization. Another group condemns the government for relinquishing social decision-making to market forces, abandoning the requisite leadership of the state, and upholding a situation of social injustice. One should add, however, that the criticism has been unimportant; the economic success of the first transition government has rendered marginal the attacks on economic policy.

Let us look now at the other axis, which we denominate that of *differentiation*. Those who stress the differences, rather than the similarities, between the economic policies of authoritarianism and democracy refer essentially to distinctions in the manner in which these governments conceived economic decision-making. In their view, the democratic government attempts to weigh up the links between economic and political decisions and their effects on society, aiming thereby to avoid negative consequences for the notions of justice that underlie social cohesion. On the contrary, the principal characteristic of the economy under the Pinochet dictatorship was the regime's indifference to the ethical, political, or social repercussions of its economic measures. Authoritarianism was not only a political phenomenon, it also extended to the economic arena; the regime took decisions without consultation or warning that led to increased inequality in society by making income distribution more regressive and bringing terrible hardships to the poorer sector of Chilean society. Democratic government, on the other hand, seeks to create consensus on the economy. Decisions are considered in conjunction with the various social actors, and attempts are made to correct their envisaged social effects.

A practical demonstration of this attitude towards the social costs of the economic measures – frequently cited in "differentialist" discourse – is the tax reform undertaken during the democratic government's first year in office. Given the high rate of inflation that it inherited, the new government felt forced to raise corporate taxes. Its specific goal was to spend the resources thus raised on the poorest segments of society. The measure was strongly resisted by some economists linked to the former regime, who opposed any policy they regarded as redistributive, yet it came to symbolize an economic strategy that President Aylwin himself described as *growth with equality*. From this viewpoint, then, the differences reside in the fact that the state has resumed responsibility for investing in people and has introduced as a fundamental issue for society the reduction of the enormous social deficit bequeathed by the neo-liberal experience. A strong social policy has been the complementary factor to a rigorously managed economy. This is the main differential factor.

Finally, those that share this *differential* perspective recognize the continuity inherent in the two governments' acceptance of the same economic structure, in rigorous fiscal discipline, and in the management of other macro-economic variables. However, they draw a strong contrast between the fostering of a "selfish and individualist" ideology, which they perceive as characteristic of the previous period, and the promotion of a social conscience in support of greater equity, which in their view symbolizes the efforts of the democratic government that followed. Therein lies, in short, the essential difference from the period dominated by the *Chicago model*. This view is shared among the elites and, to varying degrees, by members and supporters of the current government, trade unions, sectors of the Catholic church, and significant segments of the business community. There are also those who, having backed the military regime, now feel that it is time to take a fresh approach to poverty, not simply for ethical reasons but also because there is a social need. They see a difference in style and strategy between the two governments in this field.

We have already stressed that those who hold these positions in political or academic debate acknowledge the need for nuance and accept the value of some of the arguments sustained in the opposite discourse. In other words, some "continuists" do accept that – for better or worse – the current government has modified the previous scheme of things, though only in small ways. For their part, those that stress the differences inherent to the transition often accept that these do take place in the framework of a free market, and that the incoming democratic government found a relatively stable and modernized economy. In fact, only after the complexity of the legacy which the authoritarian regime left to Chilean democracy is accepted, does the debate become of real interest. For then the discussion centers on a synthesis between the elements which express continuity and those which reflect differentiation, a synthesis which focuses precisely on what is new about Chilean society, that is, on the distinct and different nature of current reality to the situation prevailing during both democratic rule prior to the coup and military dictatorship. This new analysis, which can be found among intellectuals on both left and right, acclaims the "modernizing" impact that the spread of market ideas has had on Chilean society, producing a belief in individual responsibility and initiative in civil society. It values the return to democratic institutions, which has brought this modernity a legitimacy of its own and removed the stigma of authoritarianism. It accepts that modernization has, meanwhile, been confirmed and consolidated by changes in the world economy, by internationalization, and by the generalization of free market ideas across the globe. With the restoration of democratic politics, the values of individual responsibility and competition in a free market have permitted the formation of a new generation of professionals, businessmen, and technicians who are efficient decision-makers, as well as audacious in the search for non-traditional exports and new markets. This view regards the rise of a "modern" group among the middle sectors of Chilean society as providing the main thrust behind Chile's leap to a new stage in its development. But, at the same time, this school of thought is critical of some elements of the "ideological contagion" transmitted from the authoritarian to the democratic period. Such elements affect the conduct of politics and the consolidation of democracy, and could do so more in future. Neo-liberalism endures, particularly in its economic reductionism. Moreover, it has spread into culture, introducing market logic into political activity and social relations in general. This form of "economic imperialism" attempts to reduce all social action to (individual) cost-benefit analysis; neo-liberalism, overtaken in the economic arena and in government policy, appears to have triumphed in the fields of culture and social activity. The political class begins to look as if its sense of public service has vanished. Hence, citizens are becoming increasingly distanced from politics and public affairs. As we shall see, this view outlines issues that may result in fresh controversies in a political system which lacks political debate and is currently conscientiously dedicated to the building of consensus on economic policy as well as on social development.

Before going on, however, we should revise the historical developments behind the arguments that make up the axes of continuity and differentiation. This will allow us to evaluate more thoroughly the impact on Chilean society of the ideas described in this book. It will also help us to review the distinct phases in the Pinochet regime's economic policy between the 1982 crisis – described in chapter 1 – and the inauguration of the first democratic government in 1990.

A brief historical review

In 1982 the calamitous results of the "automatic" adjustment policies, added to deep recession, forced the departure from the military government of the first and most famous team of Chicago Boys, led by Sergio de Castro. This marked an important point in the history of the group of economists, but did not end their influence on the Pinochet regime's economic policy. Members of the group continued at the helm during the confused and meandering period that followed the 1982 crisis, only to lose power for a brief period during which the military government appeared to return to more traditional economic reactivation policies – without notable success. Subsequently, a team of young neo-liberal economists, disciples of the first group, assumed the management of the economy. In this final period of the regime, from 1986 onwards, Chile enjoyed high growth rates and a generalized economic recovery. The "model" thus recovered its influence, and the profession of economist its prestige. However, the word "Chicago," unavoidably associated with perceived dogmatism, disappeared from the vocabulary of the political and social sectors who supported the regime until its defeat in the 1988 plebiscite. In 1989, former Treasury Minister, Hernán Buchi, was selected as the presidential candidate of the *Pinochetista* forces; it was the last political expression of the technocrats' endeavor to govern Chile purely from an economic perspective. Advisor to the original Chicago Boys' team directed by Sergio de Castro, Buchi was an engineer rather than an economist and had studied, not in Chicago, but at the University of Columbia. He was appointed head of the economic team in early 1985, and conducted the economic recovery process that began the following year. Buchi, a more pragmatic man with less ideological baggage, thus reaped the apparent success of the revolutionary process begun by his mentors at the start of the Pinochet regime. Let us now review events a little more closely.

As we saw in chapter 1, the 1982 crisis was extremely serious and threatened the structural reforms put in place since the coup. Chile had accumulated a huge foreign debt, fostered by the regime's triumphalist discourse and the open encouragement of consumption by the richest sectors. Moreover, during 1981, the terms of trade deteriorated and international interest rates rose. The terms of trade declined by 12.6 percent in 1981 and 13 percent in 1982.[2] Even prior to 1980, impelled by their desire to win the plebiscite in which General Pinochet sought approval for a new political constitution, the "Chicago Boys'" team adopted an expansive fiscal policy and simply hoped that external disequilibria would be overcome by "automatic adjustment." This adjustment never occurred. An outstanding member of the Chicago group, in a recently published and somewhat sympathetic catalogue of the series of errors that led to the crisis, mentioned "the perception that the terms of trade would improve, that there would always be abundant external financing and an excessive degree of optimism on the ability of an open economy to adjust automatically." He added that there was "a certain degree of political fatigue with the penuries of adjustment ... particularly as the crucial 1980 constitutional plebiscite approached."[3] From a different point of view, Meller has described well the effect that the crisis had on the behavior of the Chicago Boys: "Believing that the best alternative to economic policy is 'to do nothing' (since this is what believing in an automatic adjustment mechanism boils down to), when this mechanism fails and the economy enters deep recession, the 'Chicago Boys' face a serious conceptual and practical dilemma: what to do? In fact, the Chilean evidence shows that economists who are ideologically convinced of the existence of eternally valid economic rules and who believe that non-intervention is (always) the best alternative to economic policy, find themselves in great difficulty once they have to adopt active policies to deal with grave and urgent problems." "The 'Chicago Boys,'" continues Meller, "acquired this training on the job and this led them to experiment with a variety of monetary and exchange rate policies; Chile paid the price of this expensive apprenticeship."[4]

Thus began a period of very unstable economic decision-making. Between July 1982 and February 1984, following on from the resignation of Sergio de Castro in April 1982, there were a series of changes in economic policy. And the crisis deepened with the near rupture of the financial system. First, the government devalued the peso by 18 percent and implemented a policy of daily exchange rate adjustments. The change in policy quickly eroded overall credibility in the economic system and led to a run on the peso, with the Central Bank experiencing a sharp fall in reserves. The government adopted one measure after another in an attempt to control a situation that seemed to be deteriorating rapidly. The Central Bank implemented a program to purchase risky portfolios and set a preferential exchange rate for debts in dollars. This was set at less than the official rate and could be adjusted in line with domestic inflation. *Laissez faire* thus gave way to renewed state intervention. This peaked in January 1983 with government intervention in five banks, including Chile's two largest private banks; two other banks went into receivership, while two banks and a finance house remained under direct government supervision. Together, these ten institutions accounted for 45 percent of the capital and reserves of the entire Chilean financial system and 64 percent of the private banking sector.[5] The state "rescue" of the "privatized" economy advanced so rapidly that the period was jokingly referred to by Chileans as the "Chicago road to socialism."

Against this background of financial crisis, domestic recession, and frozen international credits, Chile began to negotiate agreements with the International Monetary Fund and, subsequently, the international commercial banks. These accords allowed Chile to obtain funds, conditional on the carrying out of an adjustment program. The Chilean authorities also assumed a number of obligations, the most important of which was to prioritize foreign debt payments. The multilateral organizations (IMF, World Bank and the IDB) supplied an annual average of $760 million during the 1983–7 period. For its part, the commercial banks allowed the re-scheduling of foreign debt repayments and opened new lines of credit to cover interest payments on the debt.

Two years later, the mechanisms thus established would allow Chile to pursue a strategy of foreign debt transfers (state subsidized repayments). This opened the way to debt reduction and would subsequently lead to new agreements with the commercial banks. Nevertheless, after 1983, IMF strategy defined and guided Chilean economic policy, something that continued to provoke opposition in the business sector. Indeed, business groups had been among the strongest critics of the regime's handling of the crisis and had laid much blame for their predicament on the "Chicago model." They regarded this option as designed exclusively for the benefit of the financial sector and speculators. Business sectors demanded more government action to encourage economic recovery and, given their preference for a political opening, enjoyed growing social backing. Such pressure paid off and, in April 1984, new Ministers of the Economy and the Treasury were appointed. On this occasion, the Cabinet appointments appeared to respond to disquiet in the productive sectors: the new ministers were, by reputation, relatively unorthodox and keen on dialogue. During the following months, measures were taken to deal with the predicament of domestic debtors. They rightly regarded themselves as the victims of an odious discrimination, given that they were often forced into bankruptcy while foreign banks and those with debts denominated in dollars were subsidized by the Central Bank. As a result, from 1983 to 1985, the Central Bank provided around US$6,000 million – then equivalent to 30 percent of GNP – in relatively generous subsidies to debtors in foreign currency, to the private banks, and to those owing Chilean pesos.

Some have observed that this prevented the bankruptcy and financial collapse of the bulk of Chile's private productive and financial system. But others have pointed out that, while the seriousness of the problems afflicting these sectors required action – which to some degree justified the transfers – there was no excuse for the policies that had led to the crisis. Neither can one avoid the fact that a substantial proportion of the Central Bank subsidies did not have a neutral impact on income distribution. Rather, they tended to worsen the already seriously skewed distribution pattern.[6]

Popular support for the domestic reactivation strategy was not enough, however, to bring about the desired result. The IMF applied pressure to restrain such policy because Chile had been unable to meet the agreed fiscal deficit targets. As a result, there were renewed changes among the economic authorities and fresh policies were introduced. Hernán Buchi took over the Treasury portfolio and a team consisting mainly of a younger generation of Chicago-trained economists assumed power. The priority in this period was to strengthen the external sector. Measures included policies to bring about a real devaluation and to stimulate exports, attempts to gain access to external credit via the multilateral organizations, and domestic austerity. Outside support for this program arrived immediately. Despite a deterioration on the current account in 1984, in 1985 Chile managed to attract almost the same amount of new money as the year before. Moreover, Chile signed an Extended Fund Facility program with the IMF and a Structural Adjustment

Loan program with the World Bank. The main characteristics of this phase in the military regime's economic policy were a cut in tariffs to 20 percent, and a second wave of privatizations. The latter focused particularly on the banks in which the state had intervened, as well as on firms it had hitherto regarded as "strategic." But more importantly for the future of the economy, the government introduced greater regulation of economic activity. New legislation was passed on the financial sector, allowing discrimination between banks according to the relative risk of their portfolios. The economic team headed by Hernán Buchi was much more protagonistic than its predecessors – whom Meller has described as embodying the "naive phase" of Chicago – showing greater concern for balance on the external and internal accounts. Benefit was derived from a recovery in the terms of trade, the decline in national and international interest rates, and the effect of the new legislation on a strengthened financial sector. From 1986 to 1989, the economy began to recover. GNP grew by an average of 7.7 percent per year. Beginning in 1987, the fiscal accounts moved into surplus, money supply grew moderately, and a trade surplus partially compensated for external debt service payments.[7]

At the end of the decade, however, the economy seemed to enter another of the destabilizing cycles that had characterized the previous few years. The economy grew by 10 percent, the result of increased spending by a government keen to bolster its position in the run-up to the 1988 plebiscite. However, such growth was not backed by real investment, which remained low throughout this period. Meanwhile, annual inflation reached 30 percent. This forced the democratic government, which took office in 1990, to adjust in order to decelerate growth in the money supply and rising inflation. Even so, Chile was now a "model" of economic order for the rest of Latin America. The multilateral bodies and commercial banks lauded Chile's positive economic performance, excluding the inflation rate; such an economic equilibrium was notable for a developing country and augured well for the desired transition to democracy. But above all, after great mishaps and at enormous social cost, the military regime had succeeded in implanting an open, market economy – something rendered necessary by economic globalization.

Instability and consolidation

What were the key features of the period that led from the Chicago revolution and 1982 crisis to the victory for democracy in 1988? And what is the net economic result of Chile's two periods of neo-liberalism under authoritarian rule?

A first response to these questions might seem paradoxical. The main characteristic of the period was the instability of economic policy. This engendered a series of extremely negative social and distributive costs, and put a significant limit on the rate of investment. Yet, at the same time, this series of ups and downs brought about a slow, albeit socially traumatic, establishment of a liberal economic structure, characterized by openness, deregulation, and privatization which derived directly from the reforms introduced by the Chicago Boys in the 1970s. In saying this, we refer to the enthronement of a free market system, characterized by the free functioning of economic agents. By 1987, however, the system was far from consolidated and lacked legitimacy. In fact, privatizations and market rules continued to be rejected by much of the population under the form of authoritarianism that characterized Chile until 1989. Indeed, all the polls carried out prior to the 1988 plebiscite and the 1989 elections showed that most Chileans favored state intervention and were suspicious of market mechanisms.[8] Hence, it was the democratic government and its policies of economic growth with equity that gave legitimacy and stability to the transformation of the Chilean economy.

In 1982 Chile suffered the worst fall in GNP of any Latin American nation, but went on to achieve, in 1989, the highest growth in the region. This is in itself a measure of the instability to which the economy was subject. It is worth recalling, however, as Ffrench-Davis has done, two aspects of this instability. First, both swings in the economy – decline and expansion – were associated with external events: a fall in the terms of trade and more onerous external debt servicing obligations (1982); and a surprising improvement in the terms of trade (1989). Second, the magnitude of the 1982 decline was the key to the strength of the ensuing recovery; moreover, economic growth rates of 7–10 percent between 1986 and 1989 failed to compensate fully for the plunge in GNP of 17 percent (1975) and 14 percent (1982). As Ffrench-Davis underlines:

apologist writings on the economic policy of the Pinochet regime highlight the evolution of the Chilean economy after the decline [of 1982] and pay particular attention to the 10 percent rise in GDP in 1989. This is a gross error for two reasons. First, the greater the fall in economic activity, the stronger the subsequent recovery can be. It is vital, therefore, to evaluate the results of economic policy, to consider the effects in their totality and not just one part ... The second reason is that the great growth of 1989 rested on temporary factors that were unsustainable for a prolonged period, and that left potentially damaging effects for future macro-economic equilibria.[9]

This tends to demonstrate that average economic growth during the two economic phases of the military regime was far from successful. During the two subperiods of the Pinochet regime, GDP grew by an annual average of 2.6 percent. This average included the falls of 17 percent in 1975 and

14 percent in 1982, as well as growth of 8 percent in 1977 and 1979 and of 10 percent in 1989.[10] Such trends in output demonstrate the instability of the economy, as do the low rates of investment. Over sixteen years, investment accounted for less that 16 percent of GDP. If one bears in mind annual population growth of 1.7 percent during the 1980s, per capita GDP growth was barely 0.9 percent yearly. Moreover, average wages in 1989 were still *less* than in 1970.

It is also important to remember that the economic growth from 1986 to 1989 – the last year of authoritarian rule – should be put in its proper context. The strong and sustained recovery in activity and GDP in 1986 and 1987 took place in a relatively stable macro-economic context. In 1988 and 1989, however, the situation changed: demand and economic activity expanded more rapidly, causing the economy to overheat and, consequently, a notable rise in inflation (to just over 30 percent). Hence, the democratic government elected in 1989 found a growing economy, no fiscal deficit, and moderate inflation as measured in relative Latin American terms. However, there were some important disequilibria that rendered necessary an initial adjustment process.[11]

In short, production expanded very gradually during the Pinochet years. Most output went to service the high foreign debt acquired between 1976 and 1982; finally, the Chilean economy became even more regressive in distributive terms. However, if these are the negative results, the positive ones included the expansion and diversification of exports. Sales abroad rose 8 percent annually in real terms from 1974 to 1989, with an even more notable 15 percent yearly rise in non-traditional exports; fiscal balance was maintained (although essential spending was greatly restricted) and new generations of highly dynamic businessmen came to the fore, applying modern management techniques to their firms.

However, the main observation concerning the Chilean economy of this period was its structural transformation. Alongside this rather unstable process, however, the Chilean economy took a liberal form – derived as much from the Chicago Boys' initial reforms as from the overall evolution of ideas and events in the international economy during the 1980s. If the economic results were, as we have seen, only modest, the great success of the Chicago Boys' experience was to transform Chile's economic structure into a free market economy albeit at any price. This endeavor received a strong push from the early 1980s onwards as a result of the spread of monetarism across Latin America and in the major industrialized societies. As Foxley has argued, the distinguishing feature of the new monetarist wave was its "strong long term component ... a form of structuralism using orthodox instruments."[12] The novelty of the new historical period was thus that the monetarists became structuralists and, in turn, that the monetarist wave swept the globe. The standard sermon of the "Washington Consensus" – the views of the governments of the industrialized countries, the commercial banking sector, and the multilateral lending bodies – included public sector reforms stressing fiscal discipline, the privatization of state enterprises, liberalization and deregulation of capital markets, trade liberalization, etc.

The "structuralist" aims of adjustment and the increasingly universal adoption of such policies after the late 1970s are important factors in understanding the evolution of the Chilean economy after the 1982 crisis. For one should not underestimate the importance of external factors in the way that the Chilean experience developed. Some members of the Chicago group, looking back on the reform model, now admit that the 1982 depression "was on the point of wrecking it."[13] However, they have also expressed as "surprising" the survival of the free trade model which, "having been declared dead during the turbulent years of 1982–1984, reemerged stronger and more healthy from 1985–1989."[14] They ascribe the continuation and success of these policies to their own "pragmatic orthodoxy," and to what they see as the "skillful combination of firmness in achieving basic objectives with flexibility and creativity in choosing the means."[15] The continuity of structural reform was not, however, so "surprising," nor was it due solely to the will and lucidity of a team of economists. Although political pragmatism played a relevant role in the successful consolidation of the reforms, it was the international context at the time – particularly the dominance of the "Washington Consensus" – that was the main reason for the maintenance of free market goals and making inviable a return to greater state control or trade protectionism. At the same time, the sheer size of the Chilean debt forced the economic authorities to follow the dictates of the IMF, as well as the priorities and forms of negotiation that the Fund and the commercial banks established for Chile. Moreover, the tremendous social cost of the reforms that had already taken place served to discourage even the most radical "statist" from seeking a new revolution in the basic structures of the economy. The continuity of structural reform was therefore not in the least surprising.

On the contrary, it is important to note that the 1982 crisis initiated the decomposition of a particular form of economic decision-making, and forced the at best surreptitious application of the ideological principles underlying the first phase of the Chicago model.[16] Much of the criticism of the economic policy towards the late 1970s had attacked both the simplistic nature of the model and the authoritarian manner in which it was applied. In the first phase of reform, the official concept of the economy and of economists, namely the ideological discourse of the Chicago Boys, so dominated the definition of social goals and was so meshed with the violent and authoritarian nature of the military regime, that one could not even imagine the functioning of a free market economy in conditions of social and political legitimacy.[17] Hence, the object of this criticism and the thing that effectively "sank" in the 1982 crisis was not the free market model. Given the international conditions of the time – and whatever the deficiencies in its administration by the Chicago Boys – the model had to be maintained. Rather, the crisis wrecked attempts at the automatic regulation of external crises, and the notion that euphoric market discourse was a complete panacea. The dogmatic approach to economic science was rejected, given its failure to deal with an economic reality that it found evasive and unmanageable. Then, following the crisis, there was censure of the fact that those who, having believed themselves to possess the perfect tools to understand the market, became perplexed when the market failed to behave as expected. What is under scrutiny was, thus, not "capitalism" but rather the dogmatism of an ideological scheme. The latter, unable to comprehend reality, lurches from propounding its totally market-oriented vision, to confused technical improvisation, only to return to a more disguised but equally dogmatic view, always under the shelter of the decision-making autonomy guaranteed it by the authoritarian regime.

If reforms were conducted more *discreetly* during the second phase of Chile's economic transformation, this was not because the regime's economic team had changed its view of the economy or the country. Rather, such discretion was due to a change in the political and social environment in which the reforms had to be implanted. The economic policy debacle gave rise to a new political scenario: one characterized by social mobilization and the regrouping of political organizations. Although the military regime used repression to put down the threat of being overthrown by "the protests" – the huge urban demonstrations that took place from 1983 to 1986 – the institutional machinery designed by Pinochet to keep himself in power indefinitely slowly took shape. Progressively, there developed the room for negotiation that precedes all routes to transition from authoritarianism to democracy. And this naturally conditioned the manner in which economic policy evolved.

Indeed, after Hernán Buchi's appointment to the Cabinet in 1985, economic policy still sought, in Fontaine's words, mainly the "dismantling of the interventionist regime created during three or four decades of redistributive policies."[18] But the group of neo-liberal economists now pursued their economic aims in a more discreet fashion, albeit with a sense of urgency to complete a task that they had always regarded as threatened by an eventual return to democracy. Buchi continued, first, to reform the role of the state. The fiscal deficit was controlled, accompanied by reduced spending and taxation, although the main emphasis was on selling off the bulk of public companies. As will be recalled, from 1974 to 1980 agricultural land, banks and industrial firms that had been nationalized by the Allende government were returned to private ownership. Despite this, in 1981, "state enterprises still accounted for a greater share of GDP than they had in 1965."[19] In 1982, the crisis forced the state to reacquire and control the bankrupt financial groups set up to take advantage of that privatization. Moreover, in many cases the state was obliged, until well into the period of democratic government that began in 1990, to administer what was called *el área rara* – an "unusual segment" of the economy made up of firms formerly belonging to these groups. But from 1985 onwards the privatization process resumed, this time directed at the state's most important holdings: mining, electricity, telecommunications, steel, airlines, etc. These privatizations would have the greatest impact on the economy after the onset of democracy, and would contribute most to the consolidation of a market economy in Chile.

As we have said, such changes were carried out in a manner very different from those of the first phase. Juan Andrés Fontaine recognizes that "political considerations ... greatly influenced the path taken by privatization. No program of privatization was announced containing a list of firms up for sale. On the contrary, preference was given to a case-by-case approach. A law was passed permitting the sale of up to 30 percent of the shares in each firm. Once the program had ended in satisfactory fashion, the subsequent steps to privatize the remaining shares were approved and applied."[20] At the same time, the government sought to avoid the mistake made during the first phase of privatization, which allowed two or three large economic groups to accumulate the bulk of privatized assets. During this second phase, the government decided to spread ownership as widely as possible. It used a variety of mechanisms, including subsidies, in order to encourage participation by small investors and employees of the privatized firms. These measures, added to the improvement in the international context – the support of international credit bodies and an improved terms of trade – allowed the Chilean economy to overcome the decline of 1982 and recover the growth rates now recorded.

The prestige of the neo-liberal economists and their view of the economy would prove more difficult to recover. The reasons for the loss of prestige derived not simply from the crisis, although this is where it originated, or at least how groups in Chilean society at the time gained sufficient liberty to criticize the economists. For the social groups backing the regime, the celebrated modernity provided by the new Chicago model had dramatically turned to uncertainty. Their admiration for the rapid creation of a powerful private sector which then assumed a central role in economic development, turned to criticism of the concentration of economic power in the hands of a few groups of speculators. Similarly, the opening up of the economy to foreign competition, previously seen as indispensable for Chile's ability to break into international markets, suddenly seemed to be at the root of the country's extreme vulnerability to fluctuations in the world economy. For the crisis highlighted a major feature of the economic model which had not been apparent during the period of expansion – its basically financial nature and its dominant tendency towards speculative activity. The fruits of the model seemed to boil down to the creation of a network of unbacked loans, granted between firms, using financial sources linked to the same economic group. The abundance of previous years now seemed to have been derived solely from external borrowing. The Chicago model lost prestige as fast as it had been gained.

However, there were other reasons why the prestige of the Chicago Boys diminished during these years. First and foremost, public opinion perceived a lack of ethical correctness in the behavior of many economists with responsibilities in the government. Many of these men moved between their ministries and a private sector composed of economic groups that arose precisely as a result of the privatization processes decreed by the government economists, that is to say, by these men themselves. This led to a debate on the boundaries between public responsibility and private business. The situation came to a head after the collapse of the financial system. The confusion of roles between the economists and executives of the main groups became all too apparent when the economist Rolf Luders was appointed Minister of the Treasury and the Economy. After criticizing the "volume of financial debt and the doubts about the solvency of institutions operating in the market," Luders decreed state intervention in the banking system and the liquidation of some financial groups – including the Banco Hipotecario y de Comercio de Chile (BHC), with which he had been associated only some months previously. This relationship soon caused him to leave the Cabinet – in April 1984 – and led him personally to face a judicial investigation into the financial management of this group. Few things contributed more than these investigations to knocking the Chicago economists from the pedestal of scientific neutrality on which they had managed to seat themselves.[21]

A further important factor in the group's loss of prestige was their evident indifference to the social results of their policies. Many Chileans saw the spread of poverty and unemployment, as well as the deterioration in public health and education, as tangible signs that the responsibility for their ills lay squarely with these economic policies. They blamed not just shock treatment and the sharp reduction in state spending on social services, but also the general instability of the economy. As Ffrench-Davis has said, "a society affected by instability tends to suffer enormous distributive impacts. In reality, instability is, definitively, extraordinarily regressive: instability in the level of prices, in the level of economic activity, in relative prices ... produces great concentrations of 'easy' profits, as well as enormous losses that are in fact absorbed by broad sectors."[22] The enormous transfers of resources that took place and the concentration of wealth and economic power among a few groups fed the popular perception that all norms of solidarity and social cohesion had broken down in Chile. This had grave political consequences for the military regime. The massive, multiclass phenomenon of social disobedience known as the "protests," and the brutal repression employed by the regime to keep itself in power from 1983 to 1986, scared the dominant social sector. It was forced to realize that social policies could not simply be discarded, and that an ideology which reduced political decisions to mere technical criteria was a dangerous illusion. The notion of the economists as the "police of a superior economic rationality"[23] began to crumble, even among those who had given and continued to give their full support to the liberal transformation of the Chilean economy. After General Pinochet's defeat in the 1988 plebiscite, groups on the Chilean right opted to give the regime's economic team an image of change and modernity. They proposed, as presidential candidate, Hernán Buchi, the last Minister of the Treasury under the authoritarian regime. The endeavor produced meager results: Buchi received the support of far fewer Chilean voters than General Pinochet had in the plebiscite the previous year.

Public opinion saw a great gap between the neo-liberal economists and democracy. This was the chief reason for popular rejection of the neo-liberal economists, and the factor that definitively turned the Buchi campaign into a pale imitation of the Sí campaign the year before. And quite rightly so, since the Chicago Boys, especially those belonging to the early phase, were the most implacable enemies of the forces that had coalesced to return democracy to Chilean society. Their principal discourse in this epoch concentrated on warning public opinion that victory for the Coalition of Parties for Democracy would fatally wound the market economy and destroy economic freedoms "won" by Chileans during the military regime. In this way, the Chicago Boys assumed the role of true Cassandras, prophesying that behind the calming discourse of the democratic economists lay the infamous socializing statism, to be followed by the abyss of uncontrolled inflation, public deficit, nationalizations, and chaos. The triumph of democratic forces was thus portrayed as incompatible with the maintenance of economic freedoms. The continuity of Pinochet and military intervention was, in their view, the necessary condition for Chilean capitalism. Behind this dramatic message was something other than the regime economists' ideological aversion to politicians, to political parties and – to be more exact – towards the democratic economists who would take charge of running the economy after President Aylwin had assumed office. They were deeply suspicious of, and rejected, democratic decision-making processes and the consequences of democracy as a social system of political organization. They demonstrated their aversion to politics in general and, in particular, to the return of a decision-making process that would require extra-economic variables to be taken into account or which – put in terms of their own ideology – would mean the "revaluation of non-market situations."

The switch to democracy produced a stabilization of economic policy, due mainly to political consensus over the type of overall economic structure and the nature of democratic government. At the same time, after initial adjustment and anti-inflation measures during the first year of democratic government, the favorable rates of growth and the adoption of social policies legitimized and stabilized an open and free economic structure. A factor that affected the way in which public opinion perceived this change was the replacement of the neo-liberal economists in government with a "new model" of economist. The latter was characterized by a discourse capable of blending economic rigor with a generous dose of social conscience. The new economists were prepared to prove that, in a democratic context, persuasion and the search for consensus via joint efforts with political and social actors would give better economic results than the dogmatic application of theoretical principles in an authoritarian political framework.

Soon after the change in government, in a generalized and occasionally somewhat surprising fashion, the Chilean elites indicated, not just in their discourse, but also through their actions, conformity with and even enthusiasm for the main facets of the liberal economic model. In general, they supported the need to dedicate greater efforts to the solution of social problems, inherited largely from the Chicago experience, and ruled out dogmatic approaches. The most influential social and political actors, including those on the left, made a rapid and pragmatic conversion to the new virtues. Such virtues included the control of inflation; the maintenance of balanced budgets; increased exports; the opening up of the economy to international competition; and the central role of the private sector in the economy. Added to this was the not overly trumpeted decision to revise the privatization processes which had been accelerated by the outgoing administration. Beyond the simple recognition of the virtues of past economic efforts, this ideological homogenization sought to introduce stable rules that would facilitate the necessary investor confidence and the growing ability of the Chilean economy to break into international markets.

The legitimacy of the new "Chilean" market economy model and the commitment (of the government) to social change led, however, to a paradox. Through the relegation of à la Chicago economists to the role of mere articulators or academic gurus, and the triumph of the economist "with a social conscience," Chilean society saw a great spread in neo-liberalism to new social and political arenas. In a general framework marked by the dissolution of ideologies, the basic factors behind the economic individualism underlying the neo-liberal theses have helped to establish cultural models that are reproduced on the wider social plane.

A final point on the economists, democracy, and the Chilean transition

During the seventeen years of authoritarianism in Chile, anti-communism and the logic of an anti-subversive war combined with a rationality that proclaimed the predominance of economic science and elevated the economist to an unassailable position of intellectual and political privilege within society. The period was brief and, in a certain sense, somewhat exceptional. However, it is worth wondering whether it has not been a situation that many economists, in both developed and developing countries, have secretly envied to some degree; a social context in which many economists over the past decade would have wished to work. The fact that, since the fall of the Berlin Wall, absolute power has become ideologically indefensible, should not allow us to lose sight of the fact that few have desired such power more intensely and with apparently more altruistic motives than certain economists. The suppression of "political externalities" greatly facilitates the scientific task in hand, and allows market forces to be fully harnessed. This is what Lord Bauer, for example, alludes to when commenting upon the "appropriate political arrangements for economic achievement." He recommends the situation in Hong Kong, whereby "the absence of election promises, together with an open economy and limited government, have much reduced the prizes of political activity and hence the interest in organizing pressure groups."[24] It only remains to conclude that, according to this view, as Manor says, "Citizens' voluntary associations and an open political system which responds to them must not, it seems, be permitted to retard the free play of market forces."[25]

These economists, who are increasingly labeled neo-Liberals, see themselves as driven to seek an exceptional degree of power on the assumption, present in all authoritarian frameworks, that common people have difficulties in recognizing their own interests and in understanding the significance of their actions. This issue is, today, universal. What this book began by describing as "the Chicago doctrine" has multiplied and developed far beyond that particular school; it has acquired, if not predominance, then at least a powerful presence in international organizations and, in general, a strong influence over economic thinking among the international community of economists. We define as neo-Liberals those economists who – by dint of the scientific qualities they allot to monetarist principles and of their idea that the market embodies most, if not all, human activities – demand for their science and their profession an *instructive predominance* in society. It is to the fading away of the power of this type of economist in Chile, and yet to the extension at the same time of his ideas in society, that we wish to dedicate the closing remarks of this book.

What have been the dogmatic elements characterizing the neo-liberal economist, and which have not survived the onset of debate under democratic conditions? The first is undoubtedly the scientists' claim to possess a vision of a singular economy, valid in all places and at all historical moments and resistant to any ideological contagion or passion alien to science.

It is, in fact, characteristic of the neo-Liberals to claim that there is a *single* economic science, understood as the set of principles and methodology of the monetarist economy. However, everyday practical experience shows that any one situation is subject to various interpretations, combinations of orthodox and heterodox ideas, as well as notions of what should be considered the correct methodological path in the analysis of a particular case. In fact, such occurrences are too frequent to pass unnoticed, even among ordinary citizens. Everyone knows, for example, that – as Tobin stated – a neo-Keynesian "seems to be more concerned about employment, jobs, and producing goods than people who have a great faith in market processes."[26] In other words, there are preferences based on personal criteria which derive, in turn, from the political and social background of the economist, as well as from his education, the orientation that his scientific research will take, and on his identification with one or other "school" of economists. Moreover, he will quickly be affected by events and ideological trends in the outside world. It is unimaginable, in fact, that economists can be immune to the "ideological fashions" set by some of the more cohesive academic groups – fashions which somehow invade university campuses before going on to penetrate the newspapers and the mass media. For these reasons, personal elements and external influences cannot be seen as a factor of discredit on the economic profession, but rather as an element to be borne in mind and to recognize in the recommendations and proposals that this profession makes. Many economists accept that their disagreements are rooted in ideology. Alan Blinder, for example, commenting on debates between economists, recognizes openly that "a lot of disagreement is ideologically based ... certain people have a capacity for ignoring facts which are patently obvious, but are counter to their view of the world; so they just ignore them."[27] And Klamer is right when he says that "economists generally do not like the term 'passion,' but surely it underlies much of what they do. I would even contend that an argument is effective only if it succeeds in appealing to one passion or another."[28] That "strong and perhaps overwhelming feeling that a particular idea is right"[29] is in truth a concept that can be used to describe, for example, the way in which Friedman and Tobin debate the theme of elasticity of demand for money. Passion is also present in the manner in which Tobin describes the stance taken by his opponent over his arguments: "I believe that Friedman had a crusade that he was pushing all over the world, not just in the profession. He saw the big picture, and the big picture was right for him. He didn't really want to be bothered by these little technical problems."[30]

The Chilean elites, and specifically those with influence on economic decision-taking, came thereby to recognize the existence of several criteria and focuses, to posit the existence of different worlds: the world of the neo-Keynesian, the world of the new classical economists, the world of the monetarists, etc. It was recognized that "the contrast between the worlds is quite sharp; it concerns not only substantive ideas but also values and ways of arguing."[31] And this recognition also revealed the practical risks of dogmatism in the decision-making process.

Economists who recognize the existence of these ideological viewpoints in conducting their scientific work, who are conscious of holding such views, logically possess a great capacity for separating their personal preferences from rigorous and scientific research. The neo-liberal economist, on the other hand, refuses to consider the ideological factor. He is therefore much more prone to his own ideology, which can easily lead to dogmatism. He will continue to insist that there is but one economic science, giving as his reasons not only the belief that the principles derived from the classical school are permanently and universally valid, but also that the methodology of positive economics is fundamentally sound, and that price theory is all-encompassing. Suffice it to recall, like Leonard Rapping, that "it is in the nature of human beings, and the Chicago students prove this point, to forget after a time that the assumption may be false. You start thinking that it describes reality. Repetition not only makes perfect, it makes believers. Many Chicago people would argue that the world is, in fact, competitive. They tend to believe their own pragmatic myth."[32]

The criticism of dogmatism included, by the way, the end of the discourse which extended price theory to social analysis, and which attempted to reduce all social interactions to the ambit of the market. Therein lay the pretension to scientific superiority of the entire edifice constructed by the neo-liberal economists. Let us recall, for example, how Brunner, arguing with the neo-Keynesians, expressed his belief that price theory would eventually replace sociology and even politics. His view of the role of politics is the key to understanding why a perspective of this nature seems, at least initially, incompatible with a transition to democracy such as occurred in Chile.

We reject ... an escape into sociology which offers no relevant analytic framework. We maintain that socio-political institutions are the proper subject of economic analysis. This entails an entirely different view of political institutions and their operation. The sociological view typically supports a goodwill theory of government and yields conclusions favoring a large and essentially unlimited government. An application of economic analysis, in contrast, alerts us to the fact that politicians and bureaucrats are entrepreneurs in the political market. They pursue their own interests and try to find optimal strategies attending to their interests. And what is optimal for them is hardly ever optimal for the "public interest."[33]

Brunner
u. Klamer

This view is notable for its radical simplicity and dogmatism. However it is particularly appropriate in instances of political degradation and corruption such as that recently seen in Italy. It is, in reality, the image of politics in a situation in which the market has become the only valid paradigm for regulating social relations. In effect, as Alain Touraine has written, "when society becomes comparable to a market in which the ideological and even political issues seem to have disappeared, only the fight for money and the search for identity survive; social problems have been replaced by non-social problems, both those of the individual and of the planet, which overwhelm the social and political field from above and below, stripping it of all content."[34] It is true that Brunner and other like-minded economists are totally unaware of the difference between the public and private domains, as well as between the *polis* and the market. Hence, he and his ilk are, in reality, ignorant of the existence of politics itself, and anyway evidence a manifestly contemptuous view of democracy. As John Toye has said, this view is so cynical that it is difficult to discuss it without dismissing it as a theoretical pathology. "It is shocking because it denies and disparages all the norms and values of political life no less dramatically than those ancient philosophers who pretended they were dogs in order to demonstrate their scorn for the ideals of the Greek *polis*. However one defines the public interest, and however much scope one grants to the protection of private interests as part of the definition of the public interest, the unbridled pursuit of self-interest by rulers belongs to the pathology of politics – to tyranny or dictatorship or, ultimately, to anarchy."[35] One should be careful, however, not to mystify the state and civil society to the same extent as the neo-Liberals mystified the market. The degradation of politics could lead to a notion of public activity and of politicians such as that suggested by the neo-Liberals, especially if they are successful in diffusing cultural models of economic individualism in society as a whole, able to destroy any semblance of altruism and social solidarity.

An additional implication of this view has been scorn for the capacity of the state, and for possible peculiarities in the economic policies of developing countries. The neo-liberal economist scorns the historical, social, and political complexity of developing nations. He regards differences between political systems, and the historical context of collective attitudes in society, as irrelevant to the drawing up of a program to totally reform the way in which society functions. Isaiah Berlin has correctly observed that some forms of liberalism are not pluralist.[36] Behind this neo-liberal reductionism – limiting social analysis to a conflict between economic growth and populism, efficiency and demagoguery, and realism and ideology – lies a basic dichotomy that they regard as unbridgeable: namely, between a market (seen as a creative and liberating instrument) and the state (regarded as an archaic and oppressive, institutionalized bureaucracy). The concept of uncompromising state opposition to the market is not simply a dogmatic stance, but rather an error of diagnosis that can lead to political catastrophe. As Manor has observed in referring to the case of China since 1978, the process:

has not entailed a simple shrinkage of the state and an equal and opposite expansion of the private sector. This is no zero sum game. The state and party as coercive instruments have certainly contracted, but the state has had to grow quite markedly in other respects ... A new corpus of contract law has had to be created, and since a legal system barely existed before 1978, a set of new judicial institutions has had to be generated to administer new laws. As new enterprises arose and economic growth gathered momentum the state also developed new instruments to regulate and, more especially, to abet market forces.[37]

We have seen how something similar occurred in Chile, a country where in spite of the high degree of state intervention, a capitalist system was already in existence and where the judicial system was comparable to that of any western democracy. The 1982 crisis forced an increase in state regulation over the previously liberalized financial system. Shock treatment and the aversion to any form of state intervention led to concentrations of ownership, disorder, and financial speculation, which then necessitated the return of a strongly interventionist state to the economic arena. In reality, the obsession with setting the state and the market against one another is the final factor in explaining why Chile failed to stabilize its economic reforms for over seventeen years. The crucial point is that capitalism requires the presence and the assistance of the state, and this is something that the neo-liberal economists fail to recognize. In doing so, they also show up a contradiction that it is worthwhile underlining. While the neo-Liberals view the state as necessarily a poor administrator and believe that state intervention in the economy constitutes an attack on economic liberty, their confidence in the state is absolute when it comes to carrying out structural adjustments or greater processes of liberalization.[38] Chile's is a model case in this regard. Those who most vehemently berated the state installed themselves at the controls of the state apparatus, and used it to administer the complex process of economic transformation.

The economists in Chile's democratic government have made efforts to distance themselves from the set of theoretical limitations and ideological reductionism that had so vividly characterized the Chicago Boys' experience under the authoritarian regime. It was no accident that those who organized the 1988 plebiscite campaign against General Pinochet and, subsequently,

President Aylwin's election campaign, gave priority to the aim of denouncing the dogmatism and social and ethical indifference of the regime's economists. The new government took great care to highlight the profile of the new economists who, in addition to professional rigor and technical quality (accompanied by postgraduate studies at several US universities, including Chicago), also had compassion for poverty and indicated that they were prepared to share responsibility for leading society in a framework of social justice that permitted the consolidation of democratic politics. The performance of the economic team led by Alejandro Foxley has largely fulfilled this role. In this sense, the current perception of the economists and of their public service role constitutes an excellent element of distinction between the democratic and authoritarian governments. In reality, as far as public opinion is concerned, the social action undertaken by the Aylwin administration, which government economists have always identified as their chief achievement, has clearly separated these economists from their predecessors. Foxley has become the most highly rated public figure after President Aylwin in the opinion polls.

The model of economist that has been promoted, and successfully so, has very little in common with the old, 1973 socialist and statist economist. His commitment to the market economy, and his intransigence on the need for rigorous control over macro-economic variables, is no less than that of a neo-Liberal. He is equally enthusiastic about policies on economic openness. But he is, at the same time, a very different economist from the neo-Liberal. He seeks to sustain a discourse and a pattern of decision-making that reflects an economic vision in which the market is a freedom subordinated to the common good. He favors consensus and agreements and prefers to prevent and correct the effects that his measures have on the poorest sectors of society. He participates actively in the preparation and development of social policies, and understands that the state must intervene to correct a market that fails either to conform to ideal models of perfect competition, or to provide social services to the most needy. He stresses the education of citizens as a fundamental factor in people's ability to choose between options and, therefore, to make use of their liberty, as well as to understand and accept that the state has a role to play in the social arena. Finally, and above all, the economist of democratic times revives and values the role of politics as the creation of a social consensus and good government. He does not regard politics as an obstacle to the economic process, but rather as an essential requirement for the efficient functioning of society and, hence, especially for the decision-making process (public and private) in the economy. Thus, the behavior of political leaders and citizens is a variable that helps to determine whether economic measures are effective or not. And we return, in this way, to the notion of "citizen," as being beyond the idea of a mere participant in the market. Moreover, one accepts the idea's most essential definition: that citizens may enjoy approximately the same political resources despite their differing degrees of fortune in the market.

The adoption of this "model" of economist by the democratic economic teams in Chile is due mainly to the change in the political circumstances of society; a society that can no longer combine economic growth, from which only a minority benefit, with an authoritarian regime that excludes the majority. Nor can society renounce its incorporation into an increasingly internationalized economy. The economists are led to tackle in a consensual fashion the tension between economic growth and the social aspirations that it generates. They must also recognize that the new, liberalized economic structure allows Chile to break into international markets and that this necessitates the maintenance of an internally sound economy, able to generate and attract private investment.

The change in the "model" of economist with the transition to democracy has not meant, however, any reduction in the importance of the role played by economists, or in the notion of the economy in the functioning of society. Neo-liberal logic has spread among the relevant social and political actors, while alternative arguments are weak. Such developments are demonstrated by a certain sense that the poorest sectors will inevitably be positively affected by economic rigor and that, therefore, the main assumptions underlying economic decisions are excluded from public debate. The normalization of a liberal economy in a democratic political system means that Chile's social values are similar to the patterns characteristic of contemporary, developed societies. The penetration of neo-liberal individualistic and economic fundamentals in civil society does not, therefore, simply reflect the continuity of the ideology that characterized the Chicago Boys' transformation of Chile's economic structure. Rather, it indicates the conformity of a small and relatively developed society with the currently dominant international ideological trends. But, in sum, these factors indicate that the Chicago revolution has left an indelible stamp on Chilean society's complex route towards modernity.

Notes

Introduction

1 For a discussion on adjustment policies in Latin America see Nelson, Joan M. (ed.), *Economic Crisis and Policy Choice: The Politics of Adjustment in the Third World*, Princeton: Princeton University Press (1990); also Vial, Joaquín (ed.), *Adónde va América Latina? Balance de las Reformas Económicas*, Santiago de Chile: CIEPLAN (1992); and Agosin, Manuel R., "Las Experiencias de Liberalización en América Latina: Lecciones y Perspectivas," *Pensamiento Iberoamericano* 21, Enero–Junio de 1992, "Comercio, Apertura y Desarrollo, Casos Seleccionados," Volumen Especial no.10 Aniversario, pp. 13–29.

2 In January 1991, *The Economist*, commenting on the situation in the Soviet Union, declared, "if Mr. Gorbachov chooses the smack of firm government, it could turn out to be as lethal to reform as martial law was in Poland. But it might, just might be the Soviet Union's turn for what could be called the Pinochet approach to liberal economics." See "Order, can Mikhail Gorbachov deliver the Soviet Union from chaos without restoring centralized autocracy?," leader in *The Economist*, 22 December–4 January 1991, vol. 317, no. 7686/7 pp. 12–13.

3 See Williamson, John, "What Washington Means by Policy Reform," in Williamson, J., *Latin American Adjustment. How Much has Happened?* Washington DC: Institute for International Economics (1990): pp. 5–20. By "Washington consensus," Williamson is referring to the US Congress, the upper echelons of the US administration, and technocratic Washington – the international financial institutions, economic centers linked to the White House, the Federal Reserve Board and think-tanks.

4 See Larraín, Felipe and Meller, Patricio, "La Experiencia Socialista–Populista Chilena: La Unidad Popular, 1970–73," *Colección Estudios CIEPLAN* 30, December 1990, Santiago de Chile, p. 194.

5 *Ibid.*, p. 165.

6 De Castro, Sergio, *Exposición sobre el Estado de la Hacienda Pública*, Ministerio de Hacienda, January 1978, Santiago de Chile, p. 381.

7 The expression is taken from the economist J. Ramos. See Ramos, J., *Chile: Una Economía en Transición?* Santiago de Chile: CESA, Editorial Universitaria (1972); quoted in Larrain, F. and Meller, P., "La Experiencia Socialista-Populista Chilena," p. 156.

8 This concept is taken from Brunner, José Joaquín, *La Cultura Autoritaria en Chile*, Santiago de Chile: FLACSO (1981).

1 Authoritarians without a project

1 For a discussion of this period, see Vergara, Pilar, *Auge y Caída del Neoliberalismo en Chile*, Santiago de Chile: Facultad Latinoamericana de Ciencias Sociales (FLACSO) (1985); also Tironi, Ernesto, "El Modelo Neoliberal Chileno y su Implantación," *Documentos de Trabajo* 1, Santiago: Centro de Estudios del Desarrollo (CED), Diciembre de 1982; Moulian, Tomás and Vergara, Pilar, "Estado, Ideología y Políticas Económicas en Chile, 1973–1978," *Colección Estudios CIEPLAN* 3, Santiago de Chile: FLACSO, 1983. CIEPLAN provides the best critical analysis of the Chicago Boys' economic policy, and the evolution of the economy during the seventeen-year Pinochet regime, mostly contained in the Institute's magazine. Many of these studies are to be found in CIEPLAN, *El Modelo Económico Chileno: Trayectoria de una Crítica*, Santiago de Chile: Editorial Aconcagua (1982). Outstanding among later studies are Foxley, Alejandro, *Latin American Experiments in Neo-Conservative Economics*, California: University of California Press (1982); Ffrench-Davis, Ricardo, "El Experimento Monetarista en Chile: Una Síntesis Crítica," *Colección Estudios CIEPLAN* 9, Santiago de Chile, Diciembre de 1982; Meller, Patricio, "Los Chicago Boys y el Modelo Económico Chileno: 1973–1983," *Apuntes CIEPLAN* 43, Santiago de Chile: CIEPLAN, Enero de 1984; and Muñoz, Oscar, "Chile: El Colapso de un Experimento Económico y sus Efectos Políticos," *Colección Estudios CIEPLAN* 16, Santiago de Chile: CIEPLAN, Junio de 1985. For a thorough analysis on the whole period, see Edwards, Sebastián and Cox, A., *Monetarism and Liberalization: The Chilean Experiment*, Massachusetts: Ballinger (1987).

2 See Garreton, Manuel Antonio, *El Proceso Político Chileno*, Santiago de Chile: FLACSO (1983), p. 101.

3 Personal interview with Sergio Molina, Santiago de Chile, 30 September 1983. Molina was in Buenos Aires at the time and Gotuzzo offered him the position by phone. When Molina refused to discuss the subject over the phone, the admiral despatched an aircraft to bring him to Santiago. During their interview, however, it became clear that the navy no longer wanted experts linked to the PDC. Molina recommended Victoria Arellano for Undersecretary and Juan Villarzú for Budget Director. The latter, a Christian Democrat, was an economist who had studied at Chicago.

4 For an analysis of these concepts and more detailed description of the initial tensions between the groups that formed the insurrectional coalition, see Vergara, Pilar, *Auge y Caída del Neoliberalismo en Chile*, Santiago de Chile: FLACSO (1985), p. 17 onwards.

5 See *Declaración de Principios del Gobierno Chileno*, Santiago de Chile, 11 March 1974. Reprinted in *La Nación*, 11 March 1983, p. 58.

6 See *Revista Hoy* 374, Santiago de Chile, 17–23 September 1984, p. 28.

7 For a description of the plan, see chapter 10.

8 The CIA origin of these funds was well known among Chilean businessmen at the time and was acknowledged to me by Orlando Sáenz, then president of the Sociedad de Fomento Fabril, the main business association (personal interview, Santiago de Chile, 27 July 1985). CIA funding of a group of Chilean economists for the specific task of preparing an alternative economic program for Chile was also mentioned by the US Senate Investigative Committee on CIA Activities. See *Covert Action in Chile*, 1963 Staff Report of the Select Committe to Study Governmental Operations with Respect to

Intelligence Activities, United States Senate, Washington DC: US Government Printing Office (1975), pp. 35 and 40.

9 Ibanez Ojeda, Pedro and Luders, Rolf, *Una Economía para Chile*, mimeo, Santiago de Chile, June 1983. See also (especially in the first section) Bardón, Alvaro, Carrasco, Camilo, and Vial, Alvaro G., *Una Década de Cambios Económicos. La Experiencia Chilena 1973–1983*, Santiago de Chile: Editorial Andrés Bello, p. 19.

10 Vergara, Pilar, *Auge y Caída del Neoliberalismo*, p. 28.

11 Vergara, Pilar, *Auge y Caída del Neoliberalismo*, p. 30.

12 Quoted in Vergara, Pilar, *Auge y Caída del Neoliberalismo*, p. 33.

13 Tironi, Ernesto, "El Modelo Neoliberal Chileno y su Implantación," *Documento de Trabajo* 1, Santiago de Chile: Centro de Estudios del Desarrollo (CED), December 1982.

14 Harberger, Arnold C., "The Chilean Economy since 1973," article prepared for *Die Welt* (Hamburg) and *Die Presse* (Vienna), December 1976, mimeo, p. 5. I thank Professor Harberger for this document.

15 "La Semana Política," in *El Mercurio*, 28 March 1983.

16 Meller, Patricio, "Revisión del Proceso de Ajuste Chileno de la Década del 80," *Colección Estudios CIEPLAN* 30, Santiago de Chile, December 1990, p. 7.

17 'La Semana Política," in *El Mercurio*, 28 March 1983.

18 See Meller, Patricio, "Los Chicago Boys y el Modelo Económico Chileno 1973–1983," *Apuntes CIEPLAN* 43, January 1984, p. 1.

19 See Moulian, Tomás and Vergara, Pilar, "Estado, Ideología y Políticas Económicas en Chile, 1973–1978," *Colección Estudios CIEPLAN* 3, Santiago de Chile: CIEPLAN, June 1980, p. 88.

20 *Ibid.*, same page.

21 For a detailed analysis, see Ffrench-Davis, Ricardo, "Liberalización de las Importaciones: La Experiencia Chilena en 1973–1979," *Colección Estudios CIEPLAN* 5, July 1980, Section 1.

22 See Tomic, Esteban, "El Retiro de Chile del Pacto Andino," *Apuntes de CIEPLAN* 58, November 1985.

23 Tironi, E., "El Modelo Neoliberal," p. 16. Also Vignolo, Carlos, "La Inversión Extranjera en Chile 1974–1979," *Revista Mensaje* 286, January 1980.

24 See Ffrench-Davis, Ricardo and Arellano, J.P., "Apertura Financiera Externa: La Experiencia Chilena 1973–1980," *Colección Estudios CIEPLAN* 5, July 1981.

25 Tironi, Ernesto, *El Modelo Neoliberal*, p. 16. Specifically, see Foxley, Alejandro, "Hacia una Economía de Libre Mercado," *Colección de Estudios CIEPLAN* 4, Santiago de Chile: CIEPLAN, November 1980.

26 Tironi, Ernesto, *El Modelo Neoliberal*, p. 20.

27 Tironi, Ernesto, *El Modelo Neoliberal*, pp. 16–17.

28 See Vergara, Pilar, *Auge y Caída del Neoliberalismo*, p. 81.

29 De Castro, Sergio, *Qué Pasa*, 1–7 June 1978, pp. 19–20.

30 According to official figures, "social expenditures" increased from 27 percent to over 50 percent from 1973 to 1979. This calculation was rejected by opposition economists who held that the official data were not strictly comparable to prior levels of spending, since the statistics included "social" items not considered as such by previous governments. See Marshall, J., "El Gasto Público en Chile, 1960–1979," *Colección Estudios CIEPLAN* 5, Santiago de Chile: CIEPLAN, July 1981.

31 See Meller, Patricio, "Los Chicago Boys y el Modelo Económico Chileno 1973–1983," p. 19.

32 See Pinto, Aníbal, "Chile: El Modelo Ortodoxo y el Desarrollo Nacional," *El Trimestre Económico* 192, October–December 1981.

33 See Meller, Patricio," Los Chicago Boys y el Modelo Económico Chileno 1973– 1983," p. 10.

34 Foxley, Alejandro, "Experimentos Neoliberales en América Latina," *Colección Estudios CIEPLAN* 7, Santiago de Chile, March 1982.

35 See Tironi, Ernesto, *El Modelo Neoliberal*, p. 1.

36 See Ffrench-Davis, Ricardo, "Desarrollo Económico y Equidad en Chile: Herencias y Desafíos en el Retorno a la Democracia," *Colección Estudios CIEPLAN* 31, Santiago de Chile: CIEPLAN, March 1991, pp. 31–51.

37 See Muñoz, Oscar G. and Schamis, Héctor E., "Las Transformaciones del Estado en Chile y la Privatización," in Vial, Joaquín (ed.) *Adónde va América Latina?* Santiago de Chile: CIEPLAN (1992), pp. 277–300.

38 See Foxley, Alejandro, "Experimentos Neoliberales en América Latina," *Colección Estudios CIEPLAN* 7, Santiago de Chile: CIEPLAN, March 1982. Quoted in Muñoz and Schamis, "Las Transformaciones," p. 287.

39 Meller, Patricio, "Los Chicago Boys," p. 1.

40 See Meller, Patricio, "Los Chicago Boys," p. 2.

41 See Meller, Patricio, "Revisión del Proceso de Ajuste Chileno en la Década de los 80," p. 8.

42 Meller, Patricio, "Revisión del Proceso," p. 17.

43 In March 1975, *El Mercurio* still did not refer to a "revolution" in listing the objectives of the "economic de-intoxication plan." It spoke of the need to "eliminate inflationary foci, reallocate resources to improve their profitability, promote new initiatives for production, and emancipate Chilean society from fiscal paternalism." See "La Semana Política" in *El Mercurio*, 23 March 1975.

44 As J. J. Brunner has written: 'Through its descriptions, journalism contributed to making a monument out of these Boys. They were always presented as the product of a special class of men: slightly imposing, with exceptional educational curricula, assertive in their ways, very direct in conversation, simple, but extraordinarily coherent." See *Entrevistas, Discursos, Identidades*, Santiago de Chile: FLACSO (1984).

45 *El Mercurio*, "La Semana Política," 21 September 1980.

46 De Castro, Sergio, *Dirección de Presupuesto*, 1978, p. 361. Quoted by Vergara, Pilar, *Auge y Caída del Neoliberalismo*, p. 79.

47 *El Mercurio*, "La Semana Política," 23 July 1978.

48 Baraona, Pablo, "Economía y Nueva Institucionalidad," paper presented at the Universidad Católica de Chile, also in *Dirección de Presupuesto*, 1978, p. 389.

49 Bardón, Alvaro, "En Chile no hay todavía verdaderos demócratas," *Qué Pasa*, Santiago de Chile, 31 May–6 June 1979, pp. 30–1.

50 *El Mercurio*, "Semana Política," 18 June 1976.

51 *El Mercurio*, "Temas Económicos," 11 November 1978.

52 *El Mercurio*, "Semana Política," 25 September 1977.

53 Baraona, Pablo, *Revista Ercilla* 2161, 2 January 1977. Quoted in Vergara, Pilar, *Auge y Caída del Neoliberalismo en Chile*, p. 98.

54 De Castro, Sergio (15 February 1976), quoted in Vergara, Pilar, *ibid.*, pp. 98–9.

55 Baraona, Pablo, *Qué Pasa*, 29 June–5 July 1978, p. 25.

56 Bardón, Alvaro, *Qué Pasa*, 31 May–6 June 1979, p. 31.

57 Chile's Counter-Revolution: A Survey," *The Economist*, 2 February 1980, p. 17.

58 *El Mercurio*, "Temas Económicos," 24 July 1976. Quoted in Brunner, J., *La Cultura Autoritaria en Chile*, Santiago de Chile: FLACSO (1981), p. 70.
59 Bardón, Alvaro, 1978. Quoted in Vergara, Pilar, *Auge y Caída del Neoliberalismo*, p. 132.
60 "Chile's Counter-Revolution: A Survey," *The Economist*, 2 February 1980, p. 17.
61 Sanfuentes, Emilio, "Responsabilidad en el Debate Público," in *Qué Pasa*, 31 May–6 June 1979.
62 *El Mercurio*, "Temas Económicos," 17 July 1976. Quoted in Brunner, J., *La Cultura Autoritaria en Chile*, p. 156.
63 *El Mercurio*, "Temas Económicos," 17 July 1976. Quoted in Brunner, J., *ibid.*, p. 132.
64 "De la Libertad Económica a la Libertad Política," *Qué Pasa*, 4–10 January 1979.
65 See Vergara, Pilar, *Auge y Caída del Neoliberalismo en Chile*, p. 132.
66 Baraona, Pablo, *Qué Pasa*, 29 June–5 July 1978, p. 24.
67 Piñera, José E., *Qué Pasa*, 27 December 1979.
68 Baraona, Pablo, *Dirección de Presupuesto*, 1978, p. 305; underlined in the original and quoted in Vergara, Pilar, *Auge y Caída del Neoliberalismo*, p. 156.
69 For a discussion of the political development of the process during this period, see Baño, Rodrigo and Canales, Manuel, "De la Dictadura a la Democracia," in *Chile: Evolución Macroeconómica, Financiación Externa y Cambio Político en la Década de los 80*, CEDEAL Situación Latinoamericana, Madrid : Serie Estudios (1982), pp. 97–185.
70 See "Los Secretos del Terremoto Financiero," chapter 1, *Qué Pasa*, 16 January 1993, p. 32.
71 Brunner, J., *Entrevistas, Discursos, Identidades*, p. 82.
72 Quoted anonymously in Brunner, J., *ibid.*, p. 83 (interview G-141).
73 Quoted anonymously in Brunner, J., *ibid.*, p. 84 (interview L-107).
74 One of the main points stressed by the academic members of this "school of thought" is the transfer of all government activities to the private sector. See Tullock, Gordon, *Towards a Mathematics of Politics*, Ann Arbor: University of Michigan Press (1967).
75 Quoted in *El Mercurio*, Part D, "Por qué atacar la economía chilena?" 6 July 1987.

2 Ideological transfer

1 This reference was taken from C. D. W. Goodwin and I. B. Holley jr., 'Toward a Theory of the Intercultural Transfer of Ideas," in *The Transfer of Ideas: Historical Essays*, edited by C. D. W. Goodwin and I. B. Holley, jr., *The South Atlantic Quarterly*, Durham, N.C.: Duke University Press (1968), pp. 171–9.
2 Karl Deutsch had pointed out, twenty years ago, the importance of communications in politics and had used cybernetic models to explain the functions of the state in political analyses in his work on *The Nerves of Government: Models of Political Communication and Control*, New York: Free Press (1966).
3 C. D. W. Goodwin and I. B. Holley jr., "Toward a Theory of the Intercultural Transfer of Ideas," p. 173.
4 See Clifford Geertz, *The Interpretation of Cultures*, New York: Basic Books Inc., Harper Torchbooks (1973). As we shall see later on, Geertz' work provides the conceptual basis for using the concepts of culture and ideology.
5 We have not referred to "mass media" studies, their development, or research

methods. They all have "resources" that make it possible to design competent, although insufficient, approaches for studying the subject that concerns us here.

6 C. D. W. Goodwin and I. B. Holley jr., "Toward a Theory of the Intercultural Transfer of Ideas," pp. 176-7.

7 See Clifford Geertz, "Thick Description: Toward an Interpretative Theory of Culture," in Geertz, *The Interpretation of Cultures*, p. 14.

8 Evidently, these last two possibilities depend on the characteristics of the emitter and the receiver. A course on J.-J. Rousseau's political philosophy would not normally engender a task orientation, but a course on J.-J. Rousseau's political philosophy by H. Marcuse during the 1960s might have done so.

9 Max Weber refers to this problem when he states that "however important the significance even of the purely logically persuasive force of ideas . . . nonetheless empirical–historical events occurring in men's minds must be understood as *primarily psychologically* and not logically conditioned" (Weber's own emphasis). See *The Methodology of the Social Sciences*, translated and edited by Edward A. Shils and Henry A. Finch, New York: The Free Press (1949), p. 96.

10 For a discussion on the interdependency between societies and the process of transnationalization, see Robert Keohane and Joseph S. Nye, *Power and Interdependence: World Politics in Transition*, Boston: Little, Brown and Co. (1977).

11 We say "apparently" because, as we shall see, some approaches on modernization also acquire certain structuralist overtones.

12 See J. Samuel Valenzuela and Arturo Valenzuela, "Modernization and Dependency: Alternative Perspectives in the Study of Latin American Underdevelopment," in Heraldo Muñoz, (ed.), *From Dependency to Development: Strategies to Overcome Underdevelopment and Inequality*, Boulder, Colo.: Westview Press (1981).

13 A good discussion on dependency theories can be found in Peter Evans, *Dependent Development. The Alliance of Multinational, State and Local Capital in Brazil*, Princeton: Princeton University Press (1979), chapters 1 and 2.

14 Aníbal Quijano Obregón's work represents a typical study from this perspective. Ruy Mauro Marini is also a typical representative of this line of dependency studies. Evidently, not all the literature on the subject falls into this type of reductionism. This is the case with the now famous study by F. H. Cardoso and Enzo Faletto, *Dependencia y Desarrollo en América Latina*, Mexico: Siglo XXI Editores (1969). Their study expresses the whole wealth of an approach that was definitive for the sociological understanding of Latin American development.

15 See, for example, Karl W. Deutsch, "Social Mobilization and Political Development," *American Political Science Review* 55, September 1961, p. 493.

16 See, especially, *The Politics of the Developing Areas*, edited by Gabriel A. Almond and James S. Coleman, Princeton, N.J.: Princeton University Press (1960); and *Elites in Latin America*, edited by Seymour Martin Lipset and Aldo Solari, New York: Oxford University Press (1967).

17 David Apter, *The Politics of Modernization*, Chicago: The University of Chicago Press (1965) p. 9.

18 David Apter, *ibid.*, p. 78.

19 *Ibid.*, p. 165.

20 *Ibid.*, same page.

21 *Ibid.*, p. 173.

22 See chapter 5 of this study.

23 The majority of scholars who theorized on modernization were experts on South East Asia (Lucian W. Pye) and Africa (James Coleman, David Apter).

24 Gabriel Almond, "Introduction" in *The Politics of the Developing Areas*, edited by Gabriel A. Almond and James S. Coleman, Princeton, N.J.: Princeton University Press (1960), p. 53.

25 Talcott Parsons, "The Social System" quoted in Seymour Martin Lipset, "Values, Education and Entrepreneurship," in *Elites in Latin America*, p. 7.

26 Reinhard Bendix, "Tradition and Modernity Reconsidered," *Comparative Studies in Society and History* 9 (1967), pp. 292–313. Quoted in Theda Skocpol, *States and Social Revolutions. A Comparative Analysis of France, Russia and China*, Cambridge University Press (1979), p. 19.

27 Theda Skocpol, *ibid.*, pp. 19–20.

28 Actually scholars searching for a definition and a way to systematize the concept of "political modernization" of political development did in fact include the concept of "modernizing oligarchies" – like Shils did – in their classifications. However, they were referring to the concentration of power by military bureaucracies or by civilians that thrust democracy upon agrarian and primitive populations. The examples provided by Shils with regard to this category include Sudan, the Turkey of Ataturk, and Pakistan. See the Introduction to G. Almond's *The Politics of the Developing Areas*, p. 53.

29 Parsons, quoted in S. M. Lipset, "Values, Education and Entrepreneurship," p. 7.

30 In one of his many studies on Latin America, Kalman H. Silvert posed the problem with his usual clarity: "What else is one to do other than define development by the selection of certain characteristics of the already developed states?" See Kalman H. Silvert, 'The Politics of Social and Economic Change in Latin America," in Howard J. Wiarda (ed.) *Politics and Social Change in Latin America: The Distinct Tradition*, Amherst, Mass. (1974).

31 We are referring especially to historical views on modernization such as those proposed by Cyril Black's study on *The Dynamics of Modernization: A Study in Comparative History*, New York: Harper and Row (1966); and Marion Levy's study on *Modernization: Latecomers and Survivors*, New York: Basic Books (1972), p. 3.

32 F. H. Cardoso and Enzo Faletto, *Dependencia y Desarrollo en América Latina*, quoted in Peter Evans, *Dependent Development*, p. 27.

33 See Octavio Ianni, "Imperialism and Diplomacy in Interamerican Relations," and "Commentary on Ianni" by Marcos Kaplan in Julio Cotler and Richard R. Fagen (eds.), *Latin America and the United States. The Changing Political Realities*, Stanford University Press (1974), pp. 2351 and 2352.

34 Rosenau defines linkages as "any recurrent sequence of behavior that originates in one system and is reacted to in another." The concept of "linkage" was taken from Karl Deutsch's essay on "External Influences on the Internal Behavior of the States," in R. Barry Farrel (ed.), *Approaches to Comparative and International Politics*, Evanston, Ill.: Northwestern University Press (1966). Regarding Rosenau's work, see "Toward the study of National-International Linkages," in James A. Rosenau (ed.), *Linkage Politics, Essays on the Convergence of National and International Systems*, New York: The Free Press (1969), pp. 44–63.

35 *Ibid.*, same page.

36 James N. Rosenau, *Linkage Politics*, p. 45.

37 See Douglas A. Chalmers, "Developing on the Periphery: External Factors in Latin American Politics," in James N. Rosenau, *Linkage Politics*, pp. 67–93. It is worth noting that this article by Chalmers preceded the publication of the famous work by F. H. Cardoso and Enzo Faletto on the subject of dependency.

38 Rosenau, *Linkage Politics*, p. 54.

39 An evident example of the existence of manifold linkages is the contrast between ideas transferred on the basis of an official policy, such as the Alliance for Progress, and those that continued to be transferred at the same time through missions such as the IMF, or even through the training of Latin American economists in Chicago.

3 The Chicago School of Economics

1 See Milton Friedman, "Schools at Chicago," *University of Chicago Magazine,* August 1974, pp. 11–16.
2 See H. Lawrence Miller, jr., "On the Chicago School of Economics," *Journal of Political Economy* 70, February 1962, no. 1, p. 64. Also George J. Stigler, "Comment," in *ibid.,* p. 70, and M. Bronfenbrenner, "Observations on the Chicago School," *ibid.,* p. 72.
3 See A. W. Coats, "The Origins of the Chicago School(s)," *Journal of Political Economy* 71, February–December 1963.
4 See Barry D. Karl, "The Power of Intellect and the Politics of Ideas," in Philosophers and Kings: Studies in Leadership, *Daedalus,* summer 1968, p. 1003.
5 Coats, "The Origins of the Chicago School(s)," p. 489.
6 At the university Strauss stood "alone among eminent refugee intellectuals in attracting a brilliant galaxy of disciples who created an academic cult around his teaching": Lewis A. Coser, quoted in M. F. Burnyeat, "Sphinx Without a Secret," *The New York Review of Books* 32, 30 May 1985, p. 30.
7 See George J. Stigler, *The Economist as a Preacher,* Chicago: University of Chicago Press (1982), p. 170.
8 See Melvin W. Reder, "Chicago Economics: Permanence and Change," *Journal of Economic Literature* 20, March 1982, p. 5.
9 See Don Patinkin, *Essays On and In the Chicago Tradition,* Durham, N.C.: Durham University Press (1981), p. 47.
10 See George J. Stigler, *The Economist as a Preacher,* p. 168.
11 *Ibid.*
12 D. Patinkin, *Essays,* p. 5.
13 *Ibid.,* p. 28.
14 M. Reder, "Chicago Economics," p. 10.
15 At Chicago Friedman had done course work in statistics under Henry Schultz and in political economy under Frank Knight, Henry Simons, and Jacob Viner. He left Chicago for Columbia, where he studied mathematical statistics and mathematical economics under Harold Hotelling, monetary economics under James Angell, and history of thought and business cycles with Wesley Mitchell. From 1937 to 1940 he developed empirical work at Mitchell's National Bureau of Economic Research. Upon his return to Chicago, he met Rudolf Carnap and Frederick Hayek, who taught in the philosophy department. During the 1960s he would also establish close intellectual contacts with Karl Popper, the philosopher. See William J. Frazer, jr. and Lawrence A. Boland, "An Essay on the Foundations of Friedman's Methodology," *American Economic Review* 73, no. 1, March 1983, pp. 133–4.
16 M. Reder, "Chicago Economics," p. 10.
17 D. Patinkin, *Essays,* p. 265.
18 See George J. Stigler, "Comment," and M. Bronfenbrenner, "Observations on the Chicago School(s)," pp. 70 and 72, respectively.
19 See Daniel Bell, "Models and Reality in Economic Discourse," in D. Bell and

Irving Kristol (eds.), *The Crisis in Economic Theory*, New York: Basic Books (1981), pp. 57-8.

20 See Daniel Bell, *ibid.*, p. 58.

21 See Henry Johnson, *On Economics and Society*, Chicago: The University of Chicago Press (1975), p. 94.

22 *Ibid.*, p. 164.

23 *Ibid.*, p. 103.

24 See Milton Friedman, *Capitalism and Freedom*, Chicago: The University of Chicago Press (1982), p. vi.

25 See Warren J. Samuels, "A Constructive Critique," in W. J. Samuels (ed.), *The Chicago School of Political Economy*, published jointly by the Association of Evolutionary Economics and the Division of Research, Graduate School of Business Administration, Michigan State University, East Lansing (1976).

26 G. J. Stigler, "Comment," p. 70.

27 Johnson, *On Economics and Society*, p. 223.

28 M. Friedman, *Capitalism and Freedom*, p. xi.

29 For a discussion of the economist's role as apologist, see Joan Robinson, *Economic Philosophy*, New York: Penguin Books (1974).

30 See Clifford Geertz, "Ideology as a Cultural System," in David Apter (ed.), *Ideology and Discontent*, New York: The Free Press of Glencoe (1964).

31 See Warren J. Samuels (ed.), *The Chicago School of Political Economy*, pp. 9-10.

32 The most important exception is, of course, George Stigler's reply to Henry L. Miller on the existence of the Chicago School of Economics. Stigler's differences with M. Friedman will be described in the next section. See George J. Stigler, "Comment," pp. 70–1.

33 Quoted in Gunnar Myrdal, *The Political Element in the Development of Economic Theory*, New York: Simon and Schuster (1963), p. 3. We express our indebtedness to Myrdal's analysis in the development of most of this section.

34 Gunnar Myrdal, *The Political Element*, p.4.

35 The similarities with the physiocrats seem to be particularly noticeable. As Schumpeter describes them, they were particularly aware of the importance of economic propaganda and their work was oriented toward influencing individuals holding important political positions. The physiocrats were characterized by strong convictions, a talent for polemics, an inability to look at things from any other angle except the orthodox, resentment against their critics, and a total absence of self-criticism. See Joseph A. Schumpeter, *Historia del Pensamiento Económico*, Mexico, D.F.: Fondo de Cultura Económica (1971), pp. 213–14.

36 Gunnar Myrdal, *The Political Element*, p.8.

37 Obviously, this is not a closed subject and the discussion about it continues to develop. During the last decades, it has usually utilized Lionel Robbins, *An Essay on the Nature and Significance of Economic Science*, New York (1935), as its starting point. See Paul Streeten, "Recent Controversies," appendix in Gunnar Myrdal, *The Political Element*, p. 208 and Johnson, *On Economics and Society*, p. 17.

38 Myrdal has focused on this last point from a similar perspective, although he defines the number of logical steps between premises and conclusions as a sign of the degree of "conscientiousness" of the writer. See Gunnar Myrdal, *The Political Element*, p. 14.

39 See Milton Friedman, "Schools at Chicago," pp. 11–16.

40 See George Stigler, "Comment," pp. 70–1.

41 See H. Laurence Miller, "On the Chicago School of Economics," pp. 64-9.

42 See Warren J. Samuels, "A Constructive Critique," in W. J. Samuels (ed.), *The Chicago School*, pp. 3–4.

43 David Wall (ed.), *Chicago Essays in Economic Development*, Chicago: University of Chicago Press (1972), p. vii.

44 It is not precisely in its polar position with respect to some notions that Chicago could be seen as departing from an "orthodox" neo-classical view by means of exaggeration. See Samuels, *The Chicago School*, p. 418.

45 William Breit and Roger Ramson, quoted in Daniel Bell and Irving Kristol (eds.), *The Crisis in Economic Theory*, p. 50.

46 George Stigler, *The Economist as a Preacher*, p. 26.

47 Milton Friedman, *Capitalism and Freedom*, p. 13.

48 George Stigler, *The Economist as a Preacher*, p. 22.

49 We shall discuss Pareto optimality in more detail in the following sections.

50 Milton Friedman, *Capitalism and Freedom*, p. 13.

51 *Ibid.*, p. 35.

52 Warren J. Samuels, *The Chicago School*, p. 418. For an extensive critical discussion of Chicago views on the rationality assumption and the market, see "Further Limits to Chicago School Doctrine," in Warren J. Samuels, *The Chicago School*, pp. 397–457.

53 Frank Knight, quoted by Warren J. Samuels, "Further Limits to Chicago School Doctrine," in Warren J. Samuels (ed.), *The Chicago School*, p. 404.

54 See John McKinney, "Frank H. Knight and Chicago Libertarianism," in Warren J. Samuels (ed.), *The Chicago School*, pp. 191–213.

55 See Ezra J. Mishan, "The Folklore of the Market: An Inquiry into the Economic Doctrine of the Chicago School," in W. J. Samuels (ed.), *The Chicago School*, pp. 95–7.

56 Milton Friedman, *Capitalism and Freedom*, pp. 14–15.

57 Milton Friedman, *ibid.*, p. 15.

58 *Ibid.*, same page.

59 The possibility that market mechanisms could be enforced through the use of coercion and the exercise of political and military authority does not seem to have been contemplated by Knight.

60 Milton Friedman, *Capitalism and Freedom*, p. 28.

61 Frank H. Knight, quoted by John McKinney, "Frank H. Knight and Chicago Libertarianism," p. 193.

62 Henry Simons, quoted by George Stigler, *The Economist as a Preacher*, p. 43.

63 Gary Becker, quoted by Melvin Reder, "Chicago Economics: Permanence and Change," p. 122.

64 Milton Friedman, *Capitalism and Freedom*, p. 28.

65 *Ibid.*, p. 25.

66 *Ibid.*, p. 27.

67 *Ibid.*, p. 27.

68 Melvin Reder, "Chicago Economics: Permanence and Change," p. 25.

69 See George Macesich, *Monetarism, Theory and Policy*, New York: Praeger Special Studies (1983), p. 3.

70 For a historical discussion of the idea, see James W. Dean, "The Dissolution of the Keynesian Consensus," in Daniel Bell and Irving Kristol (eds.), *The Crisis in Economic Theory*, p. 38.

71 The quotation comes from the initial statement of a Friedman conference on inflation. See Milton Friedman, *Inflation: Causes and Consequences*, New York: Asia Publishing House (1963).

72 George Macesich, *Monetarism*, p. 4.
73 James M. Buchanan, quoted in W. J. Samuels, "Chicago Doctrine as Explanation and Justification," in *The Chicago School*, p. 375.
74 Communication from James Buchanan to Warren J. Samuels, dated 30 June 1975. Quoted in Samuels, *ibid*.
75 W. J. Samuels, "Chicago Doctrine as Explanation and Justification," in *The Chicago School*, p. 375. In this paragraph, Samuels includes a quotation from Joel Jalladeau, "Restrained or Enlarged Scope of Political Economy?" *The Journal of Economic Issues*, 9 May 1975, pp. 1–13.
76 Melvin Reder, "Chicago Economics".
77 See Melvin Reder, "Chicago Economics," p. 12.
78 See Daniel Bell, "Models and Reality in Economic Discourse," in Daniel Bell and Irving Kristol (eds.), *The Crisis in Economic Theory*, pp. 57–8.
79 *Ibid.*, p. 53.
80 M. Reder, "Chicago Economics," p. 12.
81 *Ibid.*, p. 13.
82 M. Friedman, "Schools at Chicago," pp. 11–16. My emphasis.
83 Published by the University of Chicago Press (1953).
84 Laurence A. Boland, "A Critique of Friedman's Critics," *The Journal of Economic Literature* 17, June 1979, pp. 503–22.
85 See William J. Frazer jr., and Lawrence A. Boland, "An Essay on the Foundation of Friedman's Methodology," *American Economic Journal* 173, no. 1, March 1983, p. 129.
86 Milton Friedman, *Essays in Positive Economics*, Chicago: University of Chicago Press, (1953), p. 15.
87 W. J. Frazer and L. A. Boland, "An Essay on the Foundation of Friedman's Methodology," p. 131.
88 *Ibid*.
89 Quoted in Frazer and Boland, "An Essay," p. 139.
90 See "Ideology as a Culture System," in David Apter (ed.), *Ideology and Discontent*, p. 71.
91 See Klamer Arjo, *Conversations with Economists*, Totowa, N.J.: Rowman and Allanheld Publishers (1984), p. 227.
92 See Klamer, *Conversations with Economists*, p. 183.
93 *Ibid.*, p. 185.
94 Frank H. Knight, "The Ethic of Competition," quoted in John McKinney "Frank H. Knight and Chicago Libertarianism," p. 196.
95 Frank H. Knight, quoted by W. J. Samuels, *Chicago Doctrine as Explanation and Justification*, pp. 365–6.
96 Frank H. Knight, quoted by W. J. Samuels, *Chicago Doctrine as Explanation and Justification*, p. 365.
97 Frank Knight, *Freedom and Reform*, New York: Harper (1947), p. 336.
98 Frank Knight, quoted in W. J. Samuels, *Chicago Doctrine*, p. 367.
99 *Ibid*.
100 *Ibid.*, pp. 372–3.
101 See Gunnar Myrdal, *The Political Element*, p. 5.
102 Henry C. Simons, quoted by Warren J. Samuels, *Chicago Doctrine*, p. 382.
103 W. J. Samuels, "Further Limits to the Chicago Doctrine," in W. J. Samuels (ed.), *The Chicago School*, p. 499.

4 The actors of ideological transfer

1 See Philip Glick, *The Administration of Technical Assistance: Growth in the Americas*, Chicago: University of Chicago Press (1957), p. 14. See also Williard L. Thorp, *The Reality of Foreign Aid*, New York: Praeger Publishers (1971).
2 Quoted in Philip Glick, *The Administration of Technical Assistance*, pp. 7–10.
3 See "The Servicio in Theory and Practice," by Kenneth R. Iverson, president of the Institute of Inter-American Affairs. Reprinted from *Public Administration Review* 11, no. 4, autumn 1951.
4 See Thorp, *The Reality of Foreign Aid*.
5 Quoted in Robert A. Packenham, *Liberal America and the Third World, Political Development Ideas on Foreign Aid and Social Science*, Princeton, N.J.: Princeton University Press (1973), p. 43.
6 Thorp, *The Reality of Foreign Aid*, p. 50.
7 Packenham, *Liberal America and the Third World*, p. 44. For a discussion about the frustrations in the expectations that accompanied US foreign aid, see Edward C. Banfield, "American Foreign Aid Doctrines," in Robert A. Goldwin (ed.), *Why Foreign Aid?* Chicago: Rand McNally (1962). For an exhaustive discussion of the American motivations behind the cooperation programs, see Joan M. Nelson, *Aid, Influence and Foreign Policy*, New York: Macmillan (1968).
8 The quotation from Tocqueville appears in Carl N. Degler, "The American Past: An Unsuspected Obstacle in Foreign Affairs," *The American Scholar* 32, no. 2, spring 1963, p. 205.
9 See Robert A. Packenham, *Liberal America and the Third World*, p. 98.
10 For a discussion of American missionary expansion and the role of education as an international enterprise, see Frank Bowles, "American Responsibilities in International Education," *The International Record* 45, no. 1, winter 1964.
11 See Michael Kent O'Leary, *The Politics of American Foreign Aid*, New York: Atherton Press (1967).
12 Glick, *The Administration of Technical Assistance*, p. 108.
13 Simon Rottenberg, *The International Transfer of Technology and US Firms in Latin America*, Washington DC: National Planning Association Pamphlet Series (1957).
14 Michael Kent O'Leary, *The Politics of American Foreign Aid*, p. 15.
15 This parceled view of development problems is similar to the attitude of evaluation teams which has been laughingly, but adequately, described as the "Aha! approach." "The visiting team of experts arrives, talks generally and pleasantly about the program until a soft spot is suspected, shouts 'Aha!,' and targets thenceforth on the questionable item." In this case, "the Aha! approach" was applied to societies, choosing a problem for which a solution was sought without giving consideration to the effect produced in other areas of the same society. I thank Richard Moore for this comment. See Robert A. Packenham, *Liberal America and the Third World*, p. 118.
16 See Joan Nelson, "Aid, Influence and Foreign Policy," in Paul Y. Hammond and Nelson W. Polsby (eds.), *Government in the Modern World*, New York: Macmillan (1968), pp. 11–12. Nelson also indicates other lines of American interest in the assistance programs: protection of the economic initiative of American citizens abroad and trade and investment conditions; certain specific interests linked to military and political factors of the cold war; and other interests that, although linked to the cold war, have the broader motivation of generating a responsible international community, promoting peace and international cooperation.

17 See R. Packenham , *Liberal American and the Third World*, pp. 109–10.

18 Bowles, "American Responsibilities," pp. 19–20.

19 The discussion about the subject of elites in US academic and political perspectives on development and maturation is extensive and we cannot address it here. Although we will return to this point later, it would be wise to remember, however, an important current of thought, situated in those segments of the elite that were able to "split off" and endorse modern values at the center of the development process. Talcott Parsons, for example, affirmed that "within the existing elites, such people are most likely to be found among intellectuals, especially those who have had direct contacts with the west, particularly through education abroad or under western auspices at home." See S. M. Lipset, "Values, Education and Entrepreneurship," in S. M. Lipset and Aldo Solari (eds.), *Elites in Latin America*, New York: Oxford University Press (1967). See also Talcott Parsons, *Structure and Process in Modern Society*, New York: The Free Press (1960), pp. 116–29; and David E. Apter, *The Politics of Modernization*, Chicago: University of Chicago Press (1965), pp. 145–6.

20 P. Glick, *The Administration of Technical Assistance*, p. 17.

21 *Ibid.*, p. 19.

22 See Clarence Herdeshot, *Politics, Polemics and Pedagogs*, Chicago University Press: Chicago (1966), p. 51.

23 See Senator William Benton, *The Voice of Latin America*, New York: Encyclopaedia Britannica (1961), p. 169. Our emphasis.

24 *Ibid.*

25 The National Public Association brings together businessmen, academics, and former officials with the purpose of promoting US interests and international cooperation. See the pamphlet *Technical Cooperation, a Statement by the NPA Special Policy Committee on Technical Cooperation*, July 1955, p. 6. Our emphasis.

26 *Ibid.*, p. 3.

27 *Ibid.*, p. 7.

28 *Ibid.*, p. 10.

29 See T. W. Schultz, *The Economic Test in Latin America*, New York State School of Industrial and Labor Relations, Cornell University, Bulletin 35, August 1956, p. 1. Our emphasis.

30 See Mutual Security Program, Vol. II, Fiscal Year 1955, p. 479.

31 See Mutual Security Program, Vol. II, Part 2. Estimates Fiscal Year 1956 Regional and Country Program Detail, Latin America, Non-Regional Programs, Section III, Washington DC, p. 387.

32 *Ibid.*

33 See Mutual Security Program, Vol. IV. Program Estimates Fiscal Year 1957, Regional and Country Program Detail, Latin America, Non-Regional (Unclassified). Section IV, Washington, DC, p. 46. My emphasis.

34 *MSP*, Section IV, p. 47.

35 See Mutual Security Program, Fiscal Year 1959. Estimates for Latin America, p. 126. Our emphasis.

36 See "United States Technical Assistance and Related Activities in Latin America" (hearings before a Subcommittee on Government Operations, House of Representatives, Eighty-fourth Congress, First Session, 10, 11, 13, 14, 17, 18, 20, 22, 24, 26 and 28 October 1955), Washington, DC: United States Government Printing Office (1956), pp. 354–5. Our emphasis.

37 *Ibid.*, p. 367. Our emphasis.

38 See International Cooperation Administration, List of F.Y. 1961 Major Active Projects, MSP Congressional presentation and financial status. Country: Chile. Table E-IV-A. Our emphasis.

39 The interest in US government financing, reception of fresh, new corps of students with good intellectual abilities and, finally, the personal interest in Latin America and Chile in particular by some members of the School can be included with this reason. We will approach these aspects further on.

40 See *El Pensamiento de la CEPAL*, Santiago de Chile: Editorial Universitaria (1969), pp. 13–14. See also David Cameron Bruce, "The United Nations ECLA and National Development Policies: A Study of Non-Coercive Influence," PhD dissertation, University of Michigan (1977). The summary above comes from David H. Pollock's excellent discussion of US reactions to ECLA proposals: "La Actitud de los Estados Unidos hacia la CEPAL. Algunos cambios en los últimos años," *Revista de CEPAL*, second semester 1978, pp. 59-86.

41 Among others, H. W. Singer, Paul Rosenstein Rodan, Gunnar Myrdal, Juan Tinbergen, and Arthur Lewis. See Albert O. Hirschman, "Ideologies of Economic Development in Latin America," in Albert Hirschman (ed.), *Latin American Issues*, New York: The Twentieth Century Fund (1961), p. 37.

42 See David H. Pollock, "La Actitud de los Estados Unidos hacia la CEPAL," p. 67.

43 See Paul W. Strassman, "Development Economics from a Chicago Perspective," in Warren J. Samuels (ed.), *The Chicago School of Political Economy*, East Lansing: Michigan State University Press (1976), pp. 277–94. Among the contributors to the discussion were: Jacob Viner, Milton Friedman, Arnold Harberger, Harry Johnson, Theodore Schultz, Larry Sjaastad, and George Stigler. Obviously, the "psychic spur" was not limited to the Chicagoans. Other distinguished economists, such as Peter Bauer from the London School of Economics and Gottfried Harberler from Harvard, decided to mobilize against the new theories.

44 See John Maynard Keynes, "National Self-Sufficiency," *The Yale Review* 22, summer 1933, pp. 761–2.

45 Quoted in Paul W. Strassman, "Development Economics," p. 279. See Gunnar Myrdal, *Economic Theory and Underdeveloped Regions*, London: Duckworth (1957), p. 90.

46 The quotation is from Paul Streeten, "Social Science Research on Development. Some Problems in the Use and Transfer of an Intellectual Technology," *Journal of Economic Literature* 12, no. 4, December 1974.

47 Strassman, "Development Economics," p. 278.

48 Jacob Viner, *International Trade and Economic Development*, quoted in Strassman, "Development Economics," p. 279.

49 See Harry G. Johnson, "The Ideology of Economic Policy in the New States," in David Wall (ed.), *Chicago Essays in Economic Development*, Chicago: University of Chicago Press (1972), p. 23.

50 Milton Friedman, "Foreign Economic Aid: Means and Objectives," in *The Yale Review*, summer 1958, p. 509.

51 Viner's criticism of Prebisch has been rebutted by Fernando H. Cardoso, who affirmed that Viner simply did not understand Prebisch's point. Prebisch was referring to agriculture – Cardoso says – in order to underline the fact that, in general in Latin America, agriculture productivity was low in comparison to the urban industrial sector and, therefore, poverty was more widespread in the countryside. "Being well versed in the Argentinian economy, Prebisch always

affirmed that greater agricultural productivity constituted a good instrument to increase living standards." See Fernando H. Cardoso, "La Originalidad de la Copia: La CEPAL y la Idea del Desarrollo," *Revista de la CEPAL*, second semester 1977, p. 19.

52 See Theodore W. Schultz, "The Economic Test in Latin America," New York State School of Industrial and Labor Relations, Cornell University, Bulletin 35, August 1956, p. 16.

53 Milton Friedman, "The Reduction of Fluctuations in the Income of Primary Producers," quoted in Strassman, "Development Economics," p. 282.

54 Strassman, "Development Economics," pp. 282–3.

55 *Ibid.*, pp. 284–5.

56 This quotation comes from an unpublished memo that Friedman directed to ICA, written during the same period in which the contracts between his department and the Universidad Católica de Chile were being discussed. Quoted in Strassman, "Development Economics," p. 280.

57 P. T. Bauer quoted by Strassman, "Development Economics," p. 280.

58 Some of these findings were reported in Abramowitz's article "Resources and Output Trends in the United States since 1870," *American Economic Review, Proceedings* 46, May 1956, pp. 5–23.

59 See T. W. Schultz, "The Economic Test in Latin America," p. 20.

60 See T. W. Schultz, "Human Wealth and Economic Growth," in *The Humanists*, 19, no. 2, March–April 1959, pp. 71–81. See also "Education and Economic Growth," in *Social Forces influencing American Education*, the Sixtieth Yearbook of the National Society for the Study of Education, Part II. Also Nelson B. Henry (ed.), *The Economic Value of Education*, New York: Columbia University Press (1953).

61 T. W. Schultz, "Human Wealth and Economic Growth."

62 Schultz, "The Economic Test," p. 20.

63 T. W. Schultz, "Human Wealth and Economic Growth," p. 76.

64 Jerome Karabel and A. H. Halsey, *Power and Ideology in Education*, New York: Oxford University Press (1977), p. 14.

65 This list of inadequacies in Latin America belongs to Arnold C. Harberger. See his "Issues concerning Capital Assistance to Less Developed Countries," in David Wall, *Chicago Essays in Economic Development*, p. 354.

66 Schultz, "The Economic Test of Latin America," p. 20. Our emphasis.

67 Schultz's article, "The Economic Test in Latin America," previously quoted, constitutes an excellent example of how these views were articulated. He begins by distinguishing between development – which includes "social, cultural and political arrangements plus the economic system" – and economic growth – "a subset of activities in development." He then proposes characteristically to "take the social, cultural and political arrangements as parts of the conditions that are given and proceed to an analysis of the functioning of the economic system." "If, however, the growth in output, where it exceeds the additional inputs of labor, land and reproducible goods (i.e., investment in education and productive techniques), were a consequence of development (i.e., social, cultural, or political arrangements plus the economic system), our narrowing of the study would take us astray," he confesses. But this is not the case, he says, since "the persistent long rise in per capita output since the Civil War argues against changes in social, cultural and political arrangements having played the big roles." It is hard to see how the levels of education of a particular country – "the quality of its people as producers" – could not be directly related to the factors that Schultz includes as

parts of development. But even if this were acceptable for the United States, Schultz does not seem to visualize the possibility that this might not have been the case for the Latin American countries, which were the main object of this analysis in this article. See "The Economic Test," p. 18.

68 We have deliberately excluded from our analysis the discussion about the role performed in Chicago by Arnold Harberger in the development of these subjects. The importance of the Chicago mission in Latin America requires a separate treatment aside from Harberger himself and his ideas. Furthermore, Harberger did not have, in the period prior to the agreements to which we refer here, a role comparable to that of Schultz.

69 Personal interview with Dr. Albert Rees, former chairman of the Department of Economics of the University of Chicago (1960–64), Princeton, New Jersey, 10 November 1985.

70 This expression was often used by the late brilliant Bolivian political scientist, René Zavaleta, to describe Chile.

71 Born from military power in the colonial period, the state consolidated its authority over society during the nineteenth century, first with the "República Portaliana" and then with the War of the Pacific and the nitrate boom, which increased its power and autonomy, announcing the central role it would acquire in economic activities during the twentieth century. See Mario Góngora, *Ensayo Histórico sobre la Noción de Estado en Chile*, Siglos XIX y XX, Santiago de Chile: Ediciones La Ciudad (1981). See also Gonzalo Vial, *Historia de Chile, 1881–1973*, Santiago de Chile: Editorial Santillana (1981).

72 Of all the countries of Latin America, Chile was the one most affected by the depression. Its impact was catastrophic. As a consequence, "the model of outward development," based on the export of primary products, which had characterized the country's economic development during the nineteenth century was closed. The demand from different sectors in society to build a new economic structure capable of providing jobs for the millions of unemployed and of recovering the levels of economic activity was an obvious result of this process. The depression also put an end to the dominance of "laissez faire" doctrines which had oriented the economic policy of the country during the last decades of the nineteenth century. See Eduardo Ortiz, "La Gran Depresión y su impacto en Chile, 1929–1933," *Estudios VECTOR*, Santiago, Chile, 1982. Also Oscar Muñoz and Ana María Arriagada, "Orígenes Políticos y Económicos del Estado Empresarial en Chile," *Estudios CIEPLAN* 16, Septiembre 1977.

73 CORFO was the first institution in Latin America specifically in charge of actual planning and promotion of overall economic development. It succeeded in channeling a high proportion of those resources that the Chilean government decided to spend in the fostering of economic growth. As an indicator of its impact, it should be mentioned that during its first twenty years of existence (1938–58), "the institution, among other achievements: (a) was co-founder of eighty corporations; (b) was the senior founding partner of three of the ten most important industrial corporations of the country, including the major one, a steel-manufacturing complex; (c) built and administered the country's biggest dams and power plants." See Marcelo Cavarozzi, "The Government and the Industrial Bourgeoisie in Chile, 1939–1964," PhD thesis, University of California (1977).

74 See Aníbal Pinto, "Estado y Gran Empresa: De la Pre-Crisis hasta el Gobierno de J. Alessandri," *CIEPLAN*, mimeo, August 1985. Other recent studies on the

relationship between the state and private enterprise in Chile are, besides the Cavarozzi study previously mentioned, Oscar Muñoz and Ana María Arriagada, "Orígenes Políticos"; Ricardo Ffrench-Davis, *Políticas Económicas en Chile, 1952–1970*, Santiago, Chile: Ediciones Nueva Universidad (1983). Aníbal Pinto's classical works continue to be a necessary guide for the analysis of the period. See, in particular, his *Chile, un Caso de Desarrollo Frustrado*, Santiago, Chile: Editorial Universitaria (1958); and *Chile, una Economía Difícil*, Mexico: Fondo de Cultura Económica (1964). Also see his *Ni Estabilidad ni Desarrollo, la Política del Fondo Monetario en Chile*, Santiago, Chile: Editorial Universitaria (1958). See also Albert O. Hirschman, *Journeys toward Progress*, New York: Twentieth Century Fund (1963).

75 See Muñoz and Arriagada, "Orígenes Políticos," p. 6.

76 Consensus with regard to industrialization is shown by the fact that, when the Corporación de Fomento was proposed to Congress, the organized groups supporting it included the professional associations, working-class organizations, and the industrialist and agricultural societies. See Muñoz and Arriagada, "Orígenes Políticos," pp. 13–24. Also, M. Cavarozzi, "The Government and the Industrial Bourgeoisie," p. 13.

77 The fact that this ideology was predominant does not mean, of course, that the "liberal" classical approach to economic policy had no advocates in Chilean society. As we shall see later, these ideas returned in waves, depending on the level of inflation or the degree of state intervention.

78 In the following pages, we will discuss the Klein Saks mission's attempts at stabilization and the attitudes of industrialists in response to them.

79 Cavarozzi, "The Government and the Industrial Bourgeoisie," p. 114.

80 Muñoz and Arriagada, "Orígenes Políticos," pp. 14–15. The depression and the decline of the traditional agrarian and mining sectors favored the ascent of a small group of entrepreneurs, who, in 1934, organized into the Confederación de la Producción y el Comercio, produced a series of documents which constitute true "manifestos" of the industrialists. Their main argument was that industry was the only source of a permanent increase in national wealth and living standards and that the state should protect it without intervening, however, in the internal market.

81 The role of these *técnicos* in the launching of the state industrialization drive cannot be overemphasized. Most of them were engineers and taught at the School of Engineering at the Universidad de Chile. Some of them, such as Guillermo del Pedregal, who was the organizer of CORFO, participated in the founding of the School of Economics at the Universidad de Chile. As Pinto describes them, they were people who socially and ideologically were closer to the right than to the left, but whose attitudes differed from the pattern of attitudes of the traditional oligarchic groups. They were actually more convinced about the need for industrialization than the industrialists themselves and, as such, helped to dilute initial entrepreneurial suspicions against public enterprises. See Cavarozzi, 'The Government and the Industrial Bourgeoisie"; Pinto, "Estado y Gran Empresa"; and Muñoz and Arriagada, "Orígenes Políticos."

82 Cavarozzi, "The Government and the Industrial Bourgeoisie," p. 131.

83 Muñoz and Arriagada, "Orígenes Políticos," p. 43.

84 Tomás Moulian and Isabel Torres D., *La Derecha en Chile: Evolución Histórica y Proyección a Futuro*, Centro de Estudios del Desarrollo, July 1985, p. 11.

85 These coalition governments existed from 1938 to 1946. The Communist Party

participated as a full member during the first year of the administration of Gabriel González Videla (1946). In 1947 they were not only expelled from the government, but also outlawed. See Robert Stevenson, *The Chilean Popular Front*, Pennsylvania: Greenwood Press (1942) and Paul Drake, *Socialism and Populism in Chile, 1932–1952*, University of Illinois Press (1978).

86 The Central Unica de Trabajadores (CUT) was capable of organizing national strikes even during the period of the illegality of the Communist Party. In 1955 CUT organized two strikes: the first was very successful and the second, though a partial failure, led to the unity of Communists and Socialists and the creation of the Frente de Acción Popular (FRAP). See Moulian and Torres, *La Derecha en Chile, Evolución Histórica y Proyección a Futuro*, p. 18.

87 See Ernesto Tironi, "Evolución Socio-Económica de Chile antes del Neoliberalismo: Una Reintegración," *Documento de Trabajo* 19, Centro de Estudios del Desarrollo, Santiago, Chile, Octubre de 1984.

88 See Enzo Faletto, *Génesis Histórica del Proceso Político Chileno*, Santiago, Chile: Editorial Quimantú (1971).

89 One of the main effects of this class alliance was that, until the Frei government, it prevented the implementation of agrarian reform, a task which was considered urgent for the economic modernization of the country.

90 Tomás Moulian and Isabel Torres, *La Derecha en Chile*, p. 22.

91 Electoral figures for both parties in percentage of total votes were as follows: 1937, 42.0; 1941, 30.7; 1945, 43.7; 1949, 40.5; 1953, 25.0; 1957, 33.0; 1961, 30.4; 1965, 12.5; 1969, 20.0; and 1973, 21.3. Figures for 1969 and 1973 represent the vote of the National Party. See Moulian and Torres, *La Derecha en Chile*, appendix.

92 The notion is taken from Roberto Swartz's analysis of positivism in Brazil. See "As ideias fora do lugar," *Cadernos de CEBRAP*, August 1973. The situation of rightwing ideology in Chile was reproduced also in the left. The Communist Party maintained an ideological discourse, where concepts such as "dictatorship of the proletariat," "international workers movement," or "socialist revolution" were in common use. For a party which was a respectful participant of parliamentary democracy, these principles could not be practiced, but at the same time were indispensable.

93 Nobody expressed better than Jorge Alessandri the ideological characteristics of the Chilean entrepreneurial and business sectors. During his long career as an industrialist, senator, and then president of Chile, Alessandri maintained his prestige as *nulli secundus*, leader, and guide of the right and the propertied classes in the country. This quotation is from his speech before the "Reunión de Importadores de Chile," 4 May 1955. See *El Mercurio*, Santiago, Chile, 5 May 1955, p. 19.

94 *Ibid.* Our emphasis.

95 See "Semana Política,"*El Mercurio*, 2 December 1956, p. 7.

96 Pinto, "Estado y Gran Empresa," p. 45.

97 See "Comentario Editoriales: De vuelta a Courcelle Seneuil?" *Panorama Económico* 174, 30 August 1957.

98 For a discussion of the Klein Saks mission and the arguments favoring and opposing it, see Joseph Grunwald, "The 'Structuralist' School of Price Stabilization and Economic Development: The Chilean Case," in Alberto O Hirschman, *Journeys towards Progress*, p. 99.

99 The Central Unica de Trabajadores organized, in 1955 and 1956, two national

strikes, the first very successful, the second with only relative success. This was achieved in spite of the fact that, at the time, the Communist Party, which held a large representation in the workers union, was outlawed.

100 The journal *Panorama Económico* recorded a number of interesting opinions about the mission and its results. See "Balance de la Gestión Klein Saks y sus Perspectivas," in *Panorama Económico* 192, 4 July 1958.

101 Arturo Fontaine A., former director of *El Mercurio*, says that the newspaper was always a persistent and untiring defender of liberal economic thought. During the 1950s, however, only a handful of businessmen with intellectual interests were conversant with the theories or names in orthodox economics. Among them, besides Edwards and Urenda, were Jorge Errázuriz and Pedro Ibáñez Ojeda, a prestigious lawyer, the first linked to American enterprises and a businessman, the second the founder of a business school in Valparaiso, the Escuela de Negocios Adolfo Ibáñez. Personal interview with Arturo Fontaine A., Buenos Aires, 28 May 1984.

102 See "La Semana Políitica," *El Mercurio*, 2 December 1956.

103 Personal interview with Flavián Levine, former professor at the Economics Institute of the Universidad de Chile, Santiago, 3 October 1984.

104 See Grunwald, "The 'Structuralist School' of Price Stabilization and Economic Development: The Chilean Case," p. 96.

105 The first imported "expert" to visit Chile was the French economist, Gustave Courcelle Seneuil, who organized, in 1860, the political economy studies of the Universidad de Chile, and generated a "school" of followers in the strictest adherence to Manchester classical economics. More recently, in 1925, the government of Chile invited the Kemmerer mission, which organized the Banco Central; later, in 1950, the government received a mission of experts from the UN, presided over by professors Karl Iversen from the University of Copenhagen, Simon B. Lenan from the University of Illinois, and Erick Lindahn from the University of Stockholm. In 1950 and 1953, two missions from the International Monetary Fund visited Chile and in 1955 the Klein Saks mission made its visit.

106 See Luis Correa Prieto, *Aspectos Negativos de la Intervención Económica: Fracasos de una Experiencia*, Santiago, Chile: Empresa Editora Zig-Zag (1955), p. 192.

107 See "Ayuda de Expertos," *El Mercurio*, 3 July 1955, p. 3. For the opposite viewpoint, see "Una Misión," *Panorama Económico* 26, 15 July 1955.

5 The contracts between ICA, Chicago, and the Universidad Católica

1 See Philip Glick, *The Administration of Technical Assistance: Growth in the Americas*, Chicago: University of Chicago Press (1957), p. 168.

2 This part of the research would not have been possible without the generous cooperation of Ronald Hellman. Due to his assistance, we were able to learn the role played by A. W. Patterson in the agreements. Hellman gave us access to the text of the interviews that he and his research assistant, David Flood, carried out first in Chile and then in the United States, during 1979, for a research project on the development of the studies of economics in Chile. Among these interviews there were important conversations with A. W. Patterson and T. W. Schultz, which have been extremely useful. We also appreciate the assistance of D. Flood in meeting with Patterson. We had the opportunity to interview him by phone in two extensive sessions. The information included in this and other chapters comes from both sources. However, from here on, each reference to an interview with Hellman or Flood will be indicated separately.

3 Telephone interview with Albion W. Patterson, 5 May 1984.
4 Quoted in Philip Glick, *The Administration of Technical Assistance: Growth in the Americas*, p. 23.
5 Albion Patterson interview with David Flood, July 1979.
6 Patterson's passion for education and his conviction that cultural transfer was the essential element behind modernization led him, in the 1960s, while serving in Argentina, to write to the administrator of the Agency for International Development to propose "a massive program to make English the second language of the Argentine middle classes, from which the future leaders of the economic transformation of Argentina will emerge." In his letter, addressed to Fowler Hamilton and dated 25 October 1961, Patterson explained his proposal, saying: "What Argentina is talking about will require a whole transformation of the economy, in the ways of thinking and acting of the Argentine people. It will require an intimate acquaintance with the vast scientific, technical, industrial and managerial literature of the twentieth century. Most of this literature is in English." Patterson accompanied his report to the AID administrator with a series of pamphlets of his own writings, whose titles were: *Let's Make Argentina our Partner in Education*; *Education: Science and the Strategic Subjects have Highest Priority*; *Can Science Temper the Latin American Mind?* and *Project to Build Up Latin American Universities in the Strategic Fields*.
7 This was aggravated by the awkward situation in the health program in Chile created by its director, an American, who besides settling down (marrying a Chilean, buying land and building a house), had provoked a certain uproar in Washington as a result of his excessive cooperation with *carabineros*, the national police force, to whom he granted funding for a hospital. Telephone interview with A. W. Patterson, 5 May 1984.
8 For a complete description and discussion of the *Plan Chillán* by Albion Patterson, see *United States Technical Assistance and Related Activities in Latin America* (hearings before a Subcommittee of the Committee on Government Operations, House of Representatives, Eighty-Fourth Congress, First Session; 10, 11, 13, 14, 17, 18, 20, 22, 24, 26 and 28 October 1955). Washington, DC: US Government Printing Office (1956), pp. 28–34.
9 Albion Patterson interview with David Flood, July 1979.
10 The NPA mission produced a series of studies and pamphlets. See particularly Simon Rottenberg, *The International Transfer of Technology and US Firms in Latin America*, Washington DC.: NPA Pamphlet Series (1957), p. 22.
11 Letter from Theodore W. Schultz to David Flood, 9 June 1979.
12 Telephone interview with Albion W. Patterson, 5 May 1984. Patterson's plan was approved in principle by the Organization of American States, but was never applied in its original form. On this matter, see US Senator William Benton, *The Voice of Latin America*, New York: Encyclopaedia Britannica (1961), especially pp. 170–3.
13 Personal interview with Juan Gómez Millas, 5 July 1984.
14 *Ibid*.
15 Joseph Grunwald told this author that his thought was: "If all Chileans are like this one, that is a country I ought to know." Personal interview with Joseph Grunwald, Washington DC, 12 March 1984.
16 Gómez Millas gave this author a detailed account of these initiatives, of which the most important was the organization, promoted by the Universidad de Chile, of a Society of Latin American and North American Rectors, that was to convene to discuss cooperation plans once a year from 1954 onward.

17 Telephone interview with Albion W. Patterson, 5 May 1984.

18 The details of the UC perspective of the deal are discussed in the next section.

19 Personal interview with Albion Patterson, 15 May 1984.

20 William Benton, *The Voice of Latin America*, p. 171.

21 Albion W. Patterson interview with David Flood, July 1979. Ambassador Willard Beaulac wrote later on the value of education as "the enemy of demagogy" and told the story of the contract in the following terms: "In the United States, the aid director (Albion Patterson) sought the one educator he considered most qualified to head up the American end of the project, and that person agreed to give his cooperation and his university's cooperation only after he had made more than one trip to Santiago and had his own conversations with the persons and groups he considered important. Finally, when the project was agreed to, only the most carefully selected professors from the United States and professors and graduate students from Chile were permitted to take part. Success, in those circumstances, was substantially assured before the project was undertaken." From Willard L. Beaulac, *A Diplomat Looks at Aid to Latin America*, London: Feffer and Simons (1965), pp. 132–3.

22 Personal interview with Dr. Joseph Grunwald, 12 March 1984. David Flood interview with Dr. Grunwald, Washington, DC, 3 July 1979.

23 Ronald Hellman interview with Mario Corbo, 7 June 1971.

24 The discussion of the conference is based on the complete report made about it in the article, "Conferencia de Facultades de Ciencias Económicas alcanzó relieve americano," *Panorama Económico* 92, 18 December 1953, pp. 831–43.

25 See Luis Escobar Cerda, "Necesidad de una Interpretación Nacional del Desarrollo Económico," *El Trimestre Económico* 27, no. 108, October–December 1960, pp. 606–15.

26 See Raúl Prebisch, *Towards a Dynamic Development Policy for Latin America*, New York: United Nations (1963), p. 14.

27 See "Principales Aspectos de la Educación Económica Universitaria," speech presented by Rafael Correa Fuenzalida, dean of the Facultad de Economía, Universidad de Chile, in the opening session of the Conferencia de Facultades de Ciencias Económicas Latinoamericanas. *Panorama Económico* 92, 18 December 1953, pp. 833–4.

28 *Ibid.*

29 See Luis Escobar Cerda, Director of the School of Economy of the Universidad de Chile, "El Desarrollo de la Enseñanza de la Economía," *Panorama Económico* 92, 18 December 1953, p. 385.

30 See "Acuerdos adoptados por las tres sub-comisiones," *Panorama Económico* 92, 18 December 1953, p. 840.

31 *Ibid.*

32 The motion was presented by Carlos Martínez and Guillermo Coto Conde of the Unión de Universidades Latinoamericanas. See *Panorama Económico* 92, 18 December 1953, p. 831.

33 Personal interview with Julio Chaná C., Santiago, 31 May 1984.

34 See *El Mercurio*, 14 April 1955.

35 Personal interview with Julio Chaná, 31 May 1984.

36 Personal interviews with Washington Cañas on 13 June 1985, and Patricio Ugarte on 14 May 1985.

37 Chaná's reluctance has been confirmed to this author by Hugo Hanisch, at that time secretary of the faculty, and by Washington Cañas, aside from Ugarte.

According to the letter, Chaná was so mad at feeling forced to accept the interview that he threatened Ugarte with expelling him from the faculty if the meeting failed.

38 See "Reunión sobre Economía en la Universidad Católica," *El Diario Ilustrado*, 7 January 1955.

39 The letter signed by Julio Chaná Cariola, dean, was sent to Albion Patterson, director of technical cooperation, Institute of Inter-American Affairs, Santiago, 27 January 1955.

40 The mentioning of MIT was a *ballon dessai* – as Ugarte indicated – presented to measure Patterson's flexibility on the subject. It was not even discussed. Personal interview with Ugarte, 14 May 1985.

41 Letter from Julio Chaná C. to Albion Patterson, 27 January 1955.

42 These names were mentioned to the author by Julio Chaná. Carlos Vial did not remember exactly what his position was at the time, but thought that it was most probable that he opposed it. Personal interview with Carlos Vial Espantoso, 22 August 1984.

43 Personal interview with Julio Chaná, 31 May 1984.

44 Personal interview with Professor Gregg Lewis, 15 May 1984.

45 Julio Chaná, 31 May 1984.

46 The details of this meeting were disclosed in the interviews with Julio Chaná and Albion Patterson.

47 Files from the Ministry of Foreign Relations of Chile: letter to Osvaldo Koch, Minister of Foreign Relations from Rector Alfredo Silva Santiago, Santiago, April 19, 1955; official communication no. 3905 of the Political Direction of the Department of International Organizations to His Excellency Monsignor Alfredo Silva Santiago; official communication no. 4328 from the same source, dated 6 May and directed to the rector which accompanied Note 117 of the Embassy of the United States.

48 *Ibid.*

49 Report on the Centro de Investigaciones Económicas, Faculty of Economic Sciences, Universidad Católica de Chile, Santiago, 15 June 1957, 11 pages.

6 The Chile Project and the birth of the Chicago Boys

1 The training aspects of the project were completed in June 1963. The "modernization of teaching and research" under the project lasted until the middle of 1964.

2 For a discussion of this point, see chapter 3.

3 For a discussion of this perspective with respect to educational projects, see Keith Lewin and Angela Little, "Examination Reform and Educational Change in Sri Lanka, 1972–1982: Modernization of Dependent Underdevelopment," in Keith Watson (ed.), *Dependence and Interdependence in Education: International Perspectives*, London: Croom Helm (1984), p. 56.

4 This point is well made by Neely Sanchetti in her study of the Harvard Business School experience in India. The recipient, in her case study, appears to have behaved in an altogether different way. See Neely Sanchetti, "Institutional Transfer and Educational Dependency: An Indian Case Study," in Watson, *Dependence and Interdependence*, pp. 108–18.

5 See *The Chile Project*. Third report to the Catholic University of Chile and the International Cooperation Administration, August 1957. Signed by Gregg Lewis, University of Chicago, p. 3.

6 See Frank Bowles, "American Responsibilities in International Education," *The Educational Record* 45, no. 51, winter 1964, pp. 19–20.

7 T. W. Schultz interview by Montague Yudelman, 29 November 1956. Economic Research Center, Rockefeller Foundation Archives, Box 40, R.G.1.2. Series 309 S.

8 See Bowles, "American Responsibilities," pp. 30–1.

9. *The Chile Project.* First report to the Catholic University of Chile and the International Cooperation Administration, 20 July 1956. Signed by Gregg Lewis, University of Chicago.

10 *The Chile Project.* First report, p. 2.

11 Professor Hoselitz was also a member of the Economics Department. This is the only time the reports mention his name, and his designation seems to have been only formal. It is interesting, though, because it is the only indication of the awareness by the Chicago economists of the social and cultural elements involved in the project. Besides Hoselitz's name, we could find no indication that works by authors like Edward Shils and Mary Matossian on "intellectuals" in "modernizing countries" had been important in the shaping of the project's development. However, their works were very influential at the time and were published in Hoselitz's review, *Economic Development and Cultural Change*, printed by the University of Chicago. Furthermore, this could be an indication of a fact mentioned in various personal interviews with Chicago professors, namely that communications were very scarce between the social sciences departments at Chicago.

12 This was the first instance of the Foundation's participation in the project, which would become quite substantial in the following years.

13 Personal interview with Dr. Joseph Grunwald, The Brookings Institution, Washington, DC, 12 March 1984. Alfonso Santa Cruz, an economist who was at the Economic Commission for Latin America at the time of the project's initiation, remembers a meeting with Simon Rottenberg at ECLA headquarters in Santiago, at which time the general lines of the project were presented. He characterizes the meeting as formal and as the last time he heard about the initiative.

14 *The Chile Project.* Second report to the Catholic University of Chile and to the International Cooperation Administration, May 1957.

15 The "Chilean group" also included Herta Castro, a graduate of the Universidad de Chile studying in Chicago with a Fulbright scholarship.

16 *The Chile Project.* Ninth report, July 1960.

17 At the moment when the contracts were signed, three Chilean students were already at Chicago with ICA scholarships. They were Víctor Ochsenius, Carlos Clavel, and Florencio Fellay. The first two named continued in the program after 1956.

18 Personal interview with Ricardo Ffrench-Davis, 16 August 1984.

19 Personal interview with Carlos Massad, 13 September 1984.

20 "The Instruction of Chilean Participant Trainees at the University of Chicago," *The Chile Project.* Ninth report to the Catholic University of Chile and the International Cooperation Administration, July 1960.

21 Harberger's expression is included in a Rockefeller Foundation report. Montague Yudelman to Leland C. DeVinney, 23 December 1958. Rockefeller Foundation Archives, Box 40, R.G.1.2. Series 309 S.

22 See *The Chile Project.* Second report to the Catholic University of Chile and the International Cooperation Administration, May 1957, pp. 3–4.

23 Sectarianism is, of course, one of the recurrent themes of critics of the Chicago Boys in Chile and the point was brought up in most of the interviews conducted with "non-Chicagoan" economists, a category which includes both non-Chicagoan and Chicago-trained economists, who do not consider themselves "Chicagoans," as the Chicago Boys are known. The tendency to look for other postgraduate alternatives is well illustrated by the cases of Ernesto Tironi and José Piñera, two students with the best qualifications, who, by the end of the 1960s, rejected Chicago, preferring instead MIT and Harvard, respectively. Piñera, who later became Labor Minister for the Pinochet regime and was widely identified with the Chicago Boys, constantly declared his Harvard origin.

24 On the Rockefeller Foundation contribution, see *The Chile Project:* second report. Of the total amount, $15,000 was used for projects under the direction of the Chicago staff and $400 for the appointment of new research assistance in Santiago.

25 First report, pp. 9–10.

26 Third report, p. 3.

27 First report, p. 11.

28 Second report, p. 6.

29 The reports do not specify the reasons for the suspension of the initiative. It was probably due to the discussion on the usefulness and quality of these papers, a discussion which became acrimonious, as some documents seem to show. "One has to learn in Chile to keep his trap shut until he knows something," James O. Bray commented to Clifford M. Hardin from the Rockefeller Foundation in reference to the "popular papers." Excerpt from diary of Clifford M. Hardin, 9–14 May 1961. Rockefeller Foundation Archives, Box 40, R.G.1.2. Series 309 S.

30 We are using the concept of "organic elite" in the Gramscian sense of "organic intellectual."

31 Personal interview with Washington Cañas, 13 June 1985. Cañas was appointed the first president of the Foundation. See also, *Fundación Facultad de Ciencias Económicas Universidad Católica de Chile. 1982 Memoria Anual,* Santiago: Alfabeta Impresores (1982).

32 *The Chile Project.* Seventh report to the Catholic University and the International Cooperation Administration, July 1959, p. 2.

33 Second report, p. 10.

34 Second report, p. 10.

35 Consequently, this decision diminished the number of people to be trained under the financial restrictions defined in the initial contract. Chicago requested ICA permission to amend the contract in order to allow the training of a few more students from 1958 on. This expansion, which was granted, was financed by savings from elsewhere in the contract.

36 Second report, p. 10.

37 Ninth report, p. 5.

38 These are curious statements, given the fact that, from the Chicago Department of Economics viewpoint, the mastering of "principles" is a requisite for *any* economist and that the same emphasis attributed here to an "underdevelopment necessity" was present in the general course program of the department: ninth report, p. 5.

39 *Ibid.*, pp. 5–6.

40 In 1959, at the request of Dean Chaná, who felt that "the economic side" of the faculty activities was being disproportionately emphasized to the detriment of

business administration, Chicago moved several of the Chilean students to that field. The ninth report informs that "they devote all of their first quarter in residence and part of their second quarter to courses in economics and they are then transferred to the university's Graduate School of Business." The students were prepared for teaching accounting and finance, production and quality control, marketing, etc. See ninth report, pp. 6–7.

41 "The Instruction of Chilean Participant Trainees," ninth report, p. 7.

42 Melvin W. Reder, "Chicago Economics: Permanence and Change," *Journal of Economic Literature* 20, March 1982, pp. 8–9.

43 Second report, p. 11.

44 Among them were Hans Peter Picker and Benito Vignolo, who had ICA scholarships at Northwestern University. Alvaro Marfán, an economist who was later in charge of Eduardo Frei's presidential campaign, is also mentioned as having visited the workshop for a certain period. During that time, Albion Patterson made an emotional visit to one of the meetings and was presented to the students as the father of the initiative.

45 Third report, p. 8.

46 *Ibid.*

47 First report, p. 12.

48 The first report makes a point of the fact that research plans had been made "well before the arrival of the Senior Economist in Santiago . . . indeed even before the contracts and agreements had been signed." This was in spite of the fact that, as Professor Lewis told this author, the Chicago professors "knew nothing" about Chile at that period. First report, p. 12.

49 The nineteen Chilean students scored an average of 2.82, compared to 3.06 of forty randomly selected students from the US and Canada, and 2.62 of thirty randomly selected foreign students (except Canadians and Chileans). The comparative grade averages were constructed on a numerical equivalency scale of 4-3-2-1-0 for A-B-C-D-F. If the three Chilean students, who did not stay for a second year, were excluded, the grade average of the remaining sixteen was 2.97.

50 Second report, p. 10.

51 Although grades are not mentioned for the individual students, the ninth report indicates the comparative grade averages of Chileans. The first listed receives 3.93, followed by 3.52 and 3.36.

52 The fourth report indicates: "each will be asked, before he is appointed for a third year, to commit himself, after completion of training at Chicago, to take a full-time post at the Catholic University."

53 Of the first group, Massad, who obtained a Fulbright fellowship, was well advanced in his PhD dissertation when he returned to Chile. Fontaine, de Castro, Fuenzalida, and Jeftanovic left Chicago without having started their theses, but Fontaine completed his at a later date. Sergio de Castro, who, along with Fontaine and Fuenzalida, became a full-time professor at the Universidad Católica upon returning and was elected dean of the faculty in 1965, went back to Chicago in the early 1970s to finish his dissertation and was granted his degree in 1972. That was nearly two years before he became Finance Minister of the Pinochet regime.

54 *The Chile Project.* Fifth report, p. 8; seventh report, p. 2; ninth report, p. 12.

55 Economics 301, the first course in the graduate price theory sequence, had been traditionally taught by the "big guns" of the department – Viner, Friedman, and then Becker. It combined "well organized presentation, seriousness of purpose

and strictness of standards": also toughness ("inappropriate questions or erroneous answers are exposed without concern for the feelings of the inept offender"). Reder's language reflects, consciously or unconsciously, the dogmatic framework of knowledge ordering these courses. See Melvin W. Reder, "Chicago Economics, Permanence and Change," pp. 8–9.

56 *Ibid.* Our emphasis.

57 The students' attitude towards the program and the project, in general, will be discussed in the next pages.

58 The curriculum changes introduced at the Faculty of Economics, as well as the "climate" created by the return of the Chicago Boys, is one of the subjects of the next chapter.

59 Second report, p. 11.

60 Rottenberg's research on entrepreneurial behavior concentrated on Levantine immigrants, Syrians and Lebanese, who were "breaking the crust of custom," and by "behaving like rational gain maximizers," were "compelling similar behavior by entrepreneurs outside their own communities." *The Chile Project*, third report, p. 16.

61 Second report, p. 11.

62 See "Memorandum sobre Chile," by Arnold Harberger, University of Chicago, *El Mercurio*, Santiago, 26 December 1956.

63 Seventh report, p. 1.

64 Fourth report, p. 3.

65 Fourth report, p. 3.

66 These references are scattered throughout the fifth and seventh reports.

67 Fourth report, p. 3. Our emphasis.

68 *Ibid.* Our emphasis.

69 The two exceptions were Carlos Massad and Ricardo Ffrench-Davis, who were linked to the Christian Democratic Party.

70 The first "ideological" elections at the Faculty of Economics were in 1957. Ricardo Ffrench-Davis, who was one of the organizers of the Christian Democratic youth at the faculty, recalls that the PDC was defeated by a two-to-one margin by a rightwing ticket (Conservative–Liberal), headed by Pablo Baraona, who would later become one of the most important members of the Chicago group. Personal interview with Ricardo Ffrench-Davis, 16 August 1984.

71 This characterization of the ideological outlook of the students was emphasized by most of the interviews of students and professors of the faculty. These features correspond, moreover, to the fact that economics was, at the time, a "new career," appealing to "modernizing" sectors of the middle class.

72 Ernesto Fontaine thinks that the school was very important in the constitution of the initial group. It gave them a sense of team and a tradition of "fair play," which allowed them later – he says – to confront, as a group in the Faculty of Economics, the practice of inherited privileges characterizing admission and promotion at the Universidad Católica. What would be even more relevant, perhaps, in our opinion, is that the school might have transmitted to these students two other typical features of its education: a cultural remoteness from Chilean politics and from Chilean society in general, and a strong sense of competitiveness. It should be added that this author was a student at the Grange School and thus has first-hand knowledge of these characteristics.

73 See Kalman H. Silvert and Joel M. Jutkowitz, "Education, Values and the Possibilities for Social Change in Chile," *ISHI Occasional Papers in Social Change*, Philadelphia: Institute for the Study of Human Issues (1971).

74 Carlos Massad remembers that the strong friendship among the other three students in the first group – de Castro, Fontaine and Jeftanovic – and their relationship with the Universidad Católica, made him feel somewhat isolated at the beginning of their studies. Personal interview with Carlos Massad, 13 September 1984.

75 Sergio de Castro told Ronald Hellman that they had "an awful time during the first months in Chicago." Hellman interview with Sergio de Castro, 13 August 1971.

76 Letter to Dr. William D. Carmichael from Professor Arnold Harberger, 19 January 1972, Ford Foundation Archives, P.A. 65-190. While Harberger was referring in this letter to Latin American students in general, this attention began only with the arrival of the first group of Chileans at Chicago in 1957.

77 The former dean of the Faculty of Economics of the Universidad Católica, Julio Chaná, explaining in a recent interview why the Chicago Boys were, in his words, "men of only one book, inflexible in the application of the model," argues that "Arnold Harberger developed a great friendship with a group of students and had a great influence on them. Precisely, he was an excellent man from the human point of view, but he had a very defined tendency in economic doctrine. And from there stems a great part – although not all – of the economic thought of the Chicago Boys." Interview with Julio Chaná C., *Revista Gestión*, October 1983, p. 16.

78 Although developed in most of the interviews, the point was particularly underlined by Juan Andrés Fontaine, who was a student at Chicago during the 1978–80 period. Personal interview with Juan Andrés Fontaine, 5 September 1985, Santiago.

79 This notion of economics colored his opinions with regard to this student. In conversations with Rockefeller Foundation officials, he made the following comments in relation to Ricardo Ffrench-Davis: "very good but also an ardent Freísta and sometimes allows his political persuasion to interfere with sound economic analysis." Rondo Cameron interview with Professor A. C. Harberger, 14 May 1965. Rockefeller Foundation Archives, Box 40, R.G.1.2. Series 309 S. This observation of Ffrench-Davis's political persuasion was considered important in spite of the student's remarkable performance, which Harberger recognized enthusiastically elsewhere: "I have a special respect for [Ffrench's] abilities because he received the highest grades that I have ever given to any student in my Monetary and Fiscal Policy Course." Letter to Robert L. West from A. C. Harberger, 22 March 1965. Rockefeller Foundation Archives, Box 40, R.G.1.2. Series 309 S.

80 All quotations from A. C. Harberger found on these pages originate from a personal interview with him, Chicago, 5 April 1984.

81 See W. Paul Strassman, "Development Economics from a Chicago Perspective" in Warren J. Samuels (ed.), *The Chicago School of Political Economy*, published jointly by the Association of Evolutionary Economics and the Division of Research Graduate School of Business Administration, East Lansing: Michigan State University Press (1976).

82 See Arnold C. Harberger, *Economic Science and Economic Policy*. Department of Economics, University of Chicago, mimeo, 1984.

83 Strassman, "Development Economics," p. 290.

84 Harberger, *Economic Science and Economic Policy*.

85 *Ibid.*

86 Kalman Silvert added to his comment, "If he is managing to get the two together, then we should know about it." He was referring to one of Harberger's reports to the Ford Foundation about PhD dissertations written in his Latin American program at Chicago, in which – according to him – a majority of the topics were macro-economic in orientation. We shall examine more thoroughly the Ford Foundation reaction to the Chicago programs for Latin American students in the next chapter. Memo to Dr. William D. Carmichael from Kalman H. Silvert, 7 January 1972, Ford Foundation Archives, P.A. 65–190.

87 The program was financed by the Ford Foundation. We will refer more extensively to it and to Harberger's role in the next chapter.

88 The Universidad Católica program oriented toward undergraduates was also financed by the Ford Foundation.

89 Personal interview with Ernesto Fontaine, 9 August 1985, Santiago.

90 Personal interview with Ernesto Fontaine, 9 August 1985, Santiago.

7 The implantation of the Chicago School in Chile

1 University of Chicago report, *The Chile Project Under Contract AID/w-74 Between the Agency for International Development and the University of Chicago*, 1 January 1963 to 15 June 1963, pp. 2–3.

2 *A Report on the Development of the Faculty and the Curriculum in Economics under the Chile Project of the University of Chicago and the Agency for International Development.* Contract AID/w-74, July 1963. Prepared by Richard H. Leftwich, 9 August 1963.

3 *Ibid.*, p. 17.

4 University of Chicago report, 1 January to 15 June 1963. Degrees are in Spanish in the original.

5 *Ibid.*, pp. 2–3.

6 Ronald Hellman's interview with Sergio de Castro, former dean (1965–8) of the Faculty of Economics and Social Sciences, the Catholic University, Santiago, 13 August 1971.

7 We shall refer in detail later in this chapter to Davis and Bray's views on the project's development.

8 Both letters were published by the magazine *Panorama Económico*. For Levine's letter see no. 159, 28 December 1956, p. 816. For Bailey's answer see no. 160, January 1957, p. 24.

9 The paper was entitled "Reflexiones sobre la industrialización y el desarrollo económico." It was delivered as a conference at the Catholic University and published in the Catholic University magazine *Finis Terrae*, 10, segundo trimestre, 1956.

10 Quoted in Aníbal Pinto, "La industriaización y el profesor Rottenberg," *Panorama Económico* 180, 22 November 1957, pp. 734–5.

11 *Ibid.*, same pages. Pinto began his assault with his characteristic trenchant style: "Let us suppose that all the productive assets of the country are occupied . . . let us suppose that they are employed in such a way as to guarantee a maximum productivity . . . let us suppose that they can be mobilized from one point to another according to the most favorable combination and variation in demand . . . Then . . . then, my dear reader, you can be sure that you will deduce some stupidity."

12 Pinto recognized that: "from the Institute they [the Chicago professors] direct and feed, some studies of considerable interest have been issued; also some of less interest and some that make you wonder why so many dollars were spent on the

trip and on the accommodation of their authors." By that time another attack on the Rottenberg paper was reproduced in the socialist newspaper *Ultima Hora*. The article, an editorial, was probably written by Pinto himself, who was a member of the editorial board.

13 See *The Chile Project*, fourth report to the International Cooperation Administration and the Catholic University, February 1958. The report does not mention the publicity of the discussion or the impact it had on the students.

14 CMH (Clifford Morris Hardin) diary excerpt, 12 May 1961, p. 1. Rockefeller Foundation Archives, Universidad Católica, Santiago de Chile, Tom Davis, Box 40, R.G.1.2. Series 309 S, Box 40.

15 CMH (Clifford Morris Hardin) diary excerpts, 9 May, 14 May 1961, p. 2. Rockefeller Foundation Archives, Catholic University Economics, Santiago de Chile, James Bray. Box 40, R.G.1.2. Series 309 S.

16 *Ibid.* Underlined in the original.

17 *Ibid.*, p. 4, our emphasis. Hardin reports that Davis has also changed his mind with respect to policy measures: "When Davis came here he believed strongly against land reform helping alleviate misery, etc. All these seemed palliatives to him. Now Davis thinks that the United States should try to help Chile move on land reform and on public housing, while increasing social security. (Some of these things from the standpoint of economic theory he still doesn't like, but he believes this may be the necessary price of maintaining democracy in Chile.)"

18 CMH (Clifford Morris Hardin) diary excerpts, 9 May, 14 May 1961, p. 2, our emphasis. Bray distributed criticisms to Gregg Lewis who answered him "bland and indecisive" letters; to T. W. Schultz who "tried to shove all of the relationships to Lewis"; and to Harberger who "seemed to think he was running the Chilean Project, that Schultz had devolved its control to him." He was also very critical of the way in which S. Rottenberg, his predecessor, has handled the program. According to Hardin's notes, Bray said that Rottenberg "suffered with the comparison with Grunwald. The latter pushed out, expanded and did a lot of research. The Chicago group did very little research and concentrated on training students." Bray also distributed criticisms to Svi Goriliches and Reuben Kessel whom he calls "barbarians" and whose behavior he describes as "obstreperous" and to M. Ballesteros whom he saw as uninterested.

19 *Ibid,,* p. 3.

20 Julio Chaná, letter to the director of the Social Science Division, the Rockefeller Foundation, 31 December 1958. Attached document: "A Request to the Rockefeller Foundation for Financial Support of Research in the Economic Research Center, Catholic University of Chile." Rockefeller Foundation Archives, Box 40, R.G.1.2, Series 309 S.

21 "Sketch of Crucial Problems in Chilean Economy," document attached to "A Request to the Rockefeller Foundation."

22 During his year as a minister, Chaná continued formally to be dean of the faculty. Professor Hugo Hanisch became acting dean.

23 See Aníbal Pinto S. C. "Estado y Gran Empresa: De la pre-crisis hasta el Gobierno de J. Alessandri," mimeo, CIEPLAN (1985), pp. 47–9.

24 See "La política económica de Chile en el decenio 1954–63," *Estudio Económico*, CEPAL, 1964, p. 314ff. Quoted by A. Pinto in "Estado y Gran Empresa," pp. 77–80.

25 Personal interview with Ernesto Fontaine, director of the School of Economics of the Catholic University, Santiago, 9 August 1985.

26 See Rubén Corvalán, "La UC tercia en Polémica del Dólar," *Ercilla* 1421, 15 August 1962, pp. 22–3. The arguments around the rate of exchange and its impact on the economic structure of the country are of course identical to those given some years before by Arnold Harberger in his "Memorandum on Chile" which we commented on in the previous chapter.

27 Sergio de Castro commented to Ronald Hellman with respect to the article: "Although its effect was political, the major purpose of the article was not at all intended to be in this direction. It was not criticizing the government in the political sense but rather the article was showing the effects of the policy being used and examining possible policies which might have been better." Interview with Sergio de Castro, former dean (1965–8) of the Faculty of Economic and Social Sciences, the Catholic University, 13 August 1971. Ronald Hellman Papers on the Development of Economic Science in Chile.

28 *The Chile Project under contract AID/w-74, Between the US Agency for International Development and the University of Chicago,* 20 June to 31 December 1962, pp.13–16.

29 Arnold Harberger spent some time in the Center in August and again in December of that year. Chicago report, 20 June to 31 December 1962, p. 11.

30 Chicago report, *The Chile Project under Contract AID/w-74, Between the US Agency for International Development and the University of Chicago,* 1 January to 15 June 1963, pp. 15–16.

31 Chaná said to this author that the Chicago Boys accused him of not being "pure enough" as a dean. They considered him "excessively pluralistic." He related the following anecdote. When he invited Paul Baran to visit the School in 1959, Sergio de Castro offered himself to translate his talk. According to the ex-dean, it was soon evident that de Castro was not being fair in his translation and that most concepts and arguments became, in de Castro's Spanish, a mere caricature of Baran's ideas. Suddenly Baran interrupted his translator and said: "My young friend, some translations are as dangerous as some women: when they are too beautiful they can be very unfaithful." And he proceeded with his talk in correct Spanish. According to Chaná the new professors rejected this sort of invitation to the School. Personal interview with Julio Chaná, Santiago, 31 May 1984.

32 Personal interview with Sergio Undurraga who attended some of these meetings. 8 August 1985.

33 Veckemans' efforts in this direction are discussed below.

34 See the Chicago report, *The Chile Project under contract AID/w-74. Between the US Agency for International Development and the University of Chicago,* 1 January to 15 June 1963, pp. 6–10.

35 The Center had two research contracts. The first was with the United States Department of Agriculture "to study Chilean agriculture with the objective of making projections of Chilean import demand for various agricultural products for the years 1965, 1970 and 1975." The other was a contract with the Departamento de Programación de Ferrocarriles del Estado de Chile, to study the costs of the State Railway System in Chile. There were two research grants: one from the Braden Copper Co. of $25,000 to support studies in connection with the Latin American Free Trade Zone, and another grant of $15,000 was given by the Rockefeller Foundation for research assistants and calculating equipment. The Rockefeller Grant covered the period from 1 July 1962 to 31 December 1964. See Chicago report, *ibid.,* pp. 10–12.

36 *Ibid.*

37 *Ibid.,* p. 17.

38 *Ibid.*

39 Personal interview with Carmen Tessada, 15 July 1985. Ms. Tessada, at the time a student who attended the meetings with the new professors, later became subdirector of the School of Economics at the Catholic University.

40 Among those asking for support for the strike were two students who would later become famous as "Chicago Boys": Manuel Cruzat, who is at present the head of the main economic group in Chile; and Pablo Baraona, who was then the president of FEUC, the student body. Personal interview with Cristián Ossa, former student at the School of Economics of the Catholic University. New York City, 5 November 1985.

41 Personal interview with Cristián Ossa. Personal interview with Ernesto Fontaine, Santiago, 9 August 1985. This was, naturally enough a confused episode, mixing up different sorts of grievances. It is clear, however, that the new orientation of the School was heatedly debated in the multiple meetings that went along with the strike. Pedro Lizana, the expelled student, who is at present the vice-president of the SOFOFA, the industrialists' organization, was a good student and the most open critic of the Chicago approach among the students. His preoccupation, and that of the other students who left, with the difference between the Chicago theories and Chilean reality, seems to have been genuine. It is interesting to note, at the same time, that the Chicago Boys were divided with respect to the strike: while Fontaine thought that the hair cut incident had been magnified by the authorities, de Castro supported the expulsion of Lizana, upholding the principle of authority.

42 Personal interview with Rolf Luders, Santiago, 4 October 1984.

43 The Chicago report, *The Chile Project under contract AID/w-74, Between The US Agency for International Development and the University of Chicago*, 1 January 1963 to 15 June 1963, pp. 17–18.

44 The Chicago report, *The Chile Project at the Catholic University of Chile under Contract AID/w-74 and the Agency for International Development*. Report for the period 1 January 1964 to 30 June 1964.

45 Personal interview with Julio Chaná, 31 May 1984.

46 Personal interview with Ernesto Fontaine, 9 August 1985. Sergio de Castro, personal interview with Ronald Hellman, 13 August 1971.

47 The Chicago report, *The Chile Project at the Catholic University of Chile under Contract AID/w-74 and the Agency for International Development*. Report for the period 1 January 1964 to 30 June 1964, p. 3.

48 *Ibid.*, pp. 5–6.

49 *Ibid.*, pp. 7–8, our emphasis.

50 The Chicago report, *Participant Training in the Chile Project of the University of Chicago and the Agency for International Development under Contract AID/w-74*, 1964, pp. 11–13. Emphasis in the original.

51 *Ibid.*, p. 12.

8 The export of the Chicago tradition

1 There are seventeen reports entitled *The Cuyo Project of the National University of Cuyo, the Catholic University of Chile, the University of Chicago and the US Agency for International Development in Mendoza, Argentina under contract N° AID/1a-1 (Argentina)*. These reports cover the period from 30 December 1960 to 31 March 1967, with a final report without date. For a history of the initiative, see *Preliminary Report to the International Cooperation Administration on the Projected Program in Economics at the National University of*

Cuyo in Mendoza, Argentina, p. 1. These reports were prepared by Professors Arnold Harberger and Gregg Lewis.

2 *The Cuyo Project*, final report, p. 3.

3 *Ibid.*, p. 4.

4 *Ibid.*, p. 5.

5 See *The Cuyo Project*, final report.

6 See Universidad del Valle, Cali, Colombia: grant $15,000, 28 May 1965. Rockefeller Foundation Archives, Universidad del Valle Economic Research Center (CIDEVAL), Box 40, Series 311 S.

7 For a document confirming the extraordinary role of Harberger as promoter of his students, see Ralph Kirby Davidson, interview with Arnold Harberger, Wednesday, 24 February 1965. Rockefeller Foundation Archives, Universidad del Valle Economic Research Center (CIDEVAL), Box 40, Record 1.2. Series 311 S.

8 Arnold Harberger letter to RKD (Ralph Kirby Davidson), 5 March 1965. Rockefeller Foundation Archives, Universidad del Valle Economic Research Center (CIDEVAL), Box 40, Record 1.2. Series 311 S. In another document Harberger describes Nuñez as "a solid good econometrist, in many respects the equal to de Castro." RKD interview with Arnold Harberger, Wednesday, 24 February 1965. In a letter from RKD to Laurence de Rycke dated in Cali, Colombia, 25 February 1964, referring to Rockefeller Foundation activities in Panama, Davidson reports that "Harberger was one of the group who examined the Panamanian plans and it became very clear, according to Al, that the only one who really knew . . . what economics was all about was Nuñez."

9 Letter from Rondo Cameron to RKD (Ralph Kirby Davidson). Visit to Del Valle, 25 November 1965. Rockefeller Foundation Archives, Box 40, Record 1.2. Series 309 S.

10 Interview CMH (Clifford M. Hardin) dated 27 December 1962, New York City, with Professor A. Harberger, Department of Economics, University of Chicago. Rockefeller Foundation Archives, Box 40, Record 1.2. Series 308 S.

11 Memorandum to Mr. William D. Carmichael, via Mr. Jeffrey M. Puryear, from James W. Trowbridge, 24 October 1984, "Final Evaluation: The University of Chicago, Program of Latin American Economic Research and Training." The Ford Foundation Archives, PA 64–190.

12 Grants to Chile 1960–1973. Query ARNP-100T, The Ford Foundation Archives.

13 Post-1960 institutions include the University of Chile Center of Planning (CEPL 1960); the Center of Socio Economic Studies (CESO 1965); and the Center of Statistical and Mathematical Studies (CEDEM 1965). At the Catholic University they include the Institute of Economics (1961); the Department of Agricultural Economics (1968); and the Center of National Planning Studies (CEPLAN 1970). Ronald G. Hellman papers on the development of economic science in Chile, notes on the Ford Foundation, "The Impact of a Decade Long Assistance Program on Teaching and Research. Some observations on the Impact of the Foundation on the Discipline over the Last Decade." Unpublished manuscript, 1967.

14 Ronald G. Hellman, *ibid.*, pp. 6–7.

15 The Escolatina program was directed by Joseph Grunwald and Carlos Massad, a fact that greatly contributed to the Foundation's support. Hellman notes that "Carlos Massad was also trained at Chicago but never became a follower of Friedman's economics." *Ibid.*, p. 7.

16 Ronald G. Hellman, *ibid.*, p. 8.
17 One of the reasons for this was the decay of the *Instituto* of the University of Chile and of Escolatina after the loss of personnel to the Frei government and the ideological divisions which followed the university reform of 1968. Hellman, *ibid.*, p. 7.
18 Request for Grant Action, 7 January 1965, Pontifical University of Chile, Development of a Latin American Teaching Program in Economics and a Center for Educational Research, p. 1. The Ford Foundation Archives, PA 65–96.
19 Memo to Mr. Peter Bell from John Strasma, 10 September 1971. Ford Foundation Archives, PA 65–96.
20 "The Faculty of Economics and Social Sciences, UC. Proposal for an Undergraduate Latin American Economic Program," mimeo. Ronald G. Hellman papers on the development of economic science in Chile, notes on the Ford Foundation, p. 25.
21 "Proposal for an Undergraduate Program in Economics for Latin American Students," Catholic University of Chile, June 1964, p. 6. The Ford Foundation Archives, PA 65–96.
22 Memo to Peter D. Bell from John Strasma, "Terminal Reports, Catholic University Economics Grant (65-96)," 10 September 1971, p. 11. Ford Foundation Archives, PA 65–96.
23 "First Report Grant by the Ford Foundation to the Catholic University of Chile for the Development of Economic and Sociological Research on Education in Chile," March 1966. The Ford Foundation Archives, PA 65–96.
24 Request for Grant Action, 7 January 1965, Pontifical University of Chile, p. 1. The Ford Foundation Archives, PA 65–96.
25 A proposal for the establishment of a Center of Instruction and Research at the University of Chicago. Program of Latin American Research and Training. The Ford Foundation Archives, PA 65–190.
26 *Ibid.*
27 Harberger makes, as usual, enthusiastic comments about his students. He distinguishes this time Adolfo Diz, an Argentinian economist, of whom he says: "he returned from the University of Chicago to the University of Tucuman, where he has almost single-handedly revitalized the program of training and research in economics. He is the key economist in the University of Tucuman." Diz became, during the 1970s, under the Argentinian military dictatorship, president of the Central Bank and the key ideologue behind Minister Martínez de Hoz.
28 Memorandum to Mr. William D. Carmichael, via Mr. Jeffrey Puryear, from James W. Trowbridge, 24 October 1984, "Final Evaluation: The University of Chicago, Program of Latin American Economic Research and Training." The Ford Foundation Archives, PA 650–0190.
29 Seven from Argentina, five from Bolivia, one from Brazil, seven from Colombia; four from Ecuador, five from Mexico, two from Panama, one from Paraguay, twenty-seven from Peru, and one from Uruguay. Memo to Mr. Peter Bell from John Strasma, 10 September 1971, pp. 7-9.
30 *Ibid.*
31 *Ibid.*
32 *Ibid.*
33 John Strasma reports that the supplement proposed by the project from 1968 to 1969 wanted to concentrate on students coming from the "Andean Pact"

nations: Bolivia, Ecuador, and Peru, plus Paraguay. "Unfortunately," he says, "three of those countries were served by the Lima office, which had interim leadership and no economic program advisor in early 1969. When New York ruled that the respective field office should decide whether Foundation money would be used to upgrade economics in each country and if so, where and how, the supplemental grant project was abandoned." Memorandum to Mr. Peter D. Bell from John Strasma, 10 September 1971, p. 12. The Ford Foundation Archives, PA 65–96. That there were also some recriminations between the Santiago and the New York offices of the Foundation and some doubts about the usefulness of the program itself is proven by a memo from Kalman Silvert to Nita Manitzas and Harry Wilhelm dated 29 April 1969. "It is not true that New York does not like the Catholic University," Silvert says. "What happens," he argues, "is that Santiago [the Foundation office] was never able to explain if the Catholic University has or has not a good program for the needs of Colombians, Bolivians and Peruvians." The Ford Foundation Archives, PA 65–92. Silvert was obviously not a neo-classical economist. If he had been one he would have considered the whole question superfluous. What else could Colombians, Bolivians, or Peruvians need besides the basic principles and their repeated application to their own economies?

34 Memorandum to Mr. Peter Bell from John Strasma, 10 September 1971. The Ford Foundation Archives, PA 65–190.

35 *Ibid.*

36 "The University of Chicago. Center for Latin American Economic Studies," Final report on Grant N° 650–0190, 1 October 1965–30 September 1973. The Ford Foundation Archives, PA 65–190.

37 *Ibid.*, p. 1.

38 *Ibid.*, p. 2, our emphasis.

39 *Ibid.*, pp. 3–4, our emphasis.

40 Memorandum to Mr. Bruce L. Gibb from Eduardo Venezian, 27 May 1970, Chicago, "Review of Grant to the University of Chicago, Economics" (PA 65–190), p. 2. The Ford Foundation Archives, PA 65–190.

41 Memorandum to Mr. Bruce L. Gibb from Eduardo Venezian, 27 May 1970, p. 5.

42 *Ibid.*

43 In a memo to Richard W. Dye, 10 May 1978, "Recommendation for Closing – Institute of Economics – Catholic University of Chile (PA 72–107 and A)," Jeffrey Puryear indicated that "the military coup of 1973 generated conditions in Chilean universities which caused the Foundation to ban any new support for programs involving incountry graduate training, and to nearly eliminate research assistance to universities. While the Institute [of Economics of the Catholic University] was virtually unaffected by the coup, overall restrictions on the Chilean university system plus a lack of dynamic leadership and the continued inability of the Institute to maintain top-quality staff members, led the Foundation to reject proposals for supplementary assistance." The Ford Foundation Archives, PA 72–107. We shall refer in more detail to this period in the following chapter.

44 Mr. Hertford, quoted in a memorandum to Mr. William D. Carmichael, via Mr. Jeffrey M. Puryear, from James W. Trowbridge, 24 October 1984, "Final Evaluation: The University of Chicago, Program of Latin American economic research and training (PA 65–190)," p. 3. The Ford Foundation Archives, PA 65–190.

45 John Strasma, quoted in memo to William Carmichael, 24 October 1984, p. 3.
46 Ronald G. Hellman papers on the development of the social sciences in Chile, notes on the Ford Foundation, "Some Observations on the Impact of the Foundation on the Discipline over the Last Decade," p. 7.
47 *Ibid.*, p. 6.
48 Memorandum to Mr. William D. Carmichael, via Mr. Jeffrey M. Puryear, from James W. Trowbridge, 24 October 1984, p. 4.
49 Memorandum to Dr. William D. Carmichael from Kalman H. Silvert dated 12 February 1972, "Renewed Support for Center for Latin American Economic Studies – The University of Chicago (PA 65–190)," p. 2. The Ford Foundation Archives, PA 65–190.
50 *Ibid.*
51 Memorandum to Mr. Peter D. Bell from John Strasma dated 16 March 1972, "University of Chicago Request for Supplemental Grant," p. 6. The Ford Foundation Archives, PA 65–190.
52 Memorandum to Dr. William Carmichael and Dr. Kalman H. Silvert from Reynold E. Carlson from the Ford Foundation office in Buenos Aires, dated 7 March 1972. The Ford Foundation Archives, PA 65–190.
53 The University of Chicago Center for Latin American Economic Studies. Report on Grant no. 650-0190, September 1971, p. 22. The Ford Foundation Archives, PA 65–190.
54 Memorandum to Mr. Peter Hakim from John Strasma, dated 15 October 1971. Copy to Mrs. Nita Manitzas. "Background memo to support request for 'A' Status: Institute of Economics, Catholic University of Chile," p. 14. The Ford Foundation Archives, PA 72–107.
55 "The Impact of a Decade Long Assistance Program on Teaching and Research," Ronald G. Hellman papers on the development of economic science in Chile, notes on the Ford Foundation, p. 18.
56 Memorandum to Mr. Peter Hakim from John Strasma, 15 October 1971.
57 Memorandum to Mr. Bruce Gibb from Eduardo Venezian dated 27 May 1970 in Chicago, "Review of Grant to the University of Chicago, Economics (PA 65-190)." The Ford Foundation Archives, PA 65–190.
58 Memorandum to Mr. Peter Hakim from John Strasma, 15 October 1971, pp. 10–12.
59 Interviews with RLW (Robert L. West, associate director), Pablo Baraona, Mario Albornoz, Sergio de Castro, School of Economics, Catholic University of Chile, 21 and 23 July 1964. The Rockefeller Foundation Archives, Box 40, R.G. 1.2. Series 309 S.
60 Tom Davis thought that this was the reason why Sergio de Castro was trying to postpone his scholarship in 1961. Clifford M. Hardin interview with Tom Davis, Santiago de Chile, 12 May 1961. The Rockefeller Foundation Archives, Box 40, R.G. 1.2. Series 309 S.
61 Memorandum to Mr. Peter D. Bell from John Strasma, 16 March 1972, "University of Chicago Request for Supplemental Grant.," pp. 3–4. The Ford Foundation Archives, PA 65–190.

9 In search of politics

1 Given its "pontifical" character, the ultimate authority of the university is the Pope himself. It was the Vatican therefore who appointed Cardinal Silva

Henríquez, investing him with the authority to decide the conflict. The cardinal decided in favor of the students.

2 "La Facultad de Ciencias Económicas y Sociales e la Universidad Católica de Chile, reunida en pleno, acordó hacer pública la siguiente declaración ..." Las Condes, Santiago, 14 August 1967, mimeo. Another identical document contains in handwritten form the changes that three members of the faculty council attempted to introduce, softening or altogether changing the de Castro version. The stronger version was approved, however, and published in *El Mercurio*. Out of a number of around sixty professors the opposition was reduced to three: Mario Zañartu for both copies of this document.

3 Jaime Guzmán was later to become one of the most articulate politicians supporting the military dictatorship and the main ideologue of the Pinochet constitution of 1980. The convergence between de Castro and Guzmán personifies the original reunion between Catholic corporatism and neo-liberalism. This combination would characterize the declaration of principles of the military junta written in 1974. See the last chapter of this work.

4 "Chilean, *El Mercurio* lies."

5 Letter from Del Fitchett to Dr. Ralph K. Davidson, Santiago, 21 September 1967. The Rockefeller Foundation Archives, Catholic University of Chile Economics, Box 40, Series 309 S.

6 We shall refer in the next chapter to the importance of this independent campus in the Chicago Boys' plan for their faculty's development.

7 Personal interview with Cristián Ossa, New York City, 5 November 1985.

8 "Nuestra Visión de la Universidad Católica de Chile," Escuela de Economía y Administración, September 1967, p. 15. Our translation.

9 Mario Zañartu, SJ, professor of the School, "Comentarios de la 'Visión Crítica de la Universidad Católica de Chile' del actual cuerpo docente (de dedicación completa y de media jornada) de la Escuela de Economía y Administración." Undated mimeo, p. 1.

10 *Ibid.*, pp. 1–2.

11 Ronald M. Hellman, personal interview with Mario Zañartu, Santiago, 27 May 1971.

12 On 24 October 1967, Dieter Benecke, Ricardo Morán, and Raúl E. Yver sent a letter to Sergio de Castro declaring that Zañartu "charges" "affect directly" the body of full- and half-time professors of the School of which they were members and demanded that Zañartu be brought to a general meeting to "personally substantiate its charges." I thank Father Mario Zañartu for showing me a copy of this letter.

13 Letter from Ernesto R. Fontaine, director *ad interim*, to Dr. Mario Zañartu SJ, 17 October 1967.

14 Letter from Pablo Baraona Urzúa to Mario Zañartu SJ, Santiago, 16 October 1967.

15 See "The Chicago tradition" in chapter 3 of this work.

16 Letter from Pablo Baraona to Mario Zañartu SJ, p. 4.

17 Letter from Mario Zañartu SJ, professor of the School, to Ernesto Fontaine, director *ad interim*, School of Economics and Administration, Santiago, 20 October 1967.

18 See Tomás Moulian and Isabel Torres Dujisin, *La Derecha en Chile: Evolución Histórica y Proyecciones a Futuro*, Centro de Estudios del Desarrollo, July 1985, p. 30.

19 Personal interview with Rolf Luders, 4 October 1984.

20 José M. Piñera, *Reflexiones sobre orientación de la Universidad y de la Escuela de Economía*. Undated mimeo, 2 pages. Mario Zañartu SJ archives. Besides their interest as an example of the values and ideology of Christian Democratic students, these paragraphs are a curiosity in view of who wrote them. José M. Piñera is the same José Piñera Echenique who, as Minister of Labour of the Pinochet regime, contributed to the organization of the "seven modernizations" blowing up the Chicago economic model to a total society view. See chapter 1.

21 *Ibid.*, p. 2.

22 *Ibid.*

23 Universidad Católica de Chile, Escuela de Economía y Administración. *Orientación Escuela de Economía y Administración*. Report prepared by Alejandro Gutiérrez, Gabriel Palma, José M. Cortínez, Hugo Vera, Nicolás Flaño, in representation of the 11th of August Movement. Undated. Mario Zañartu SJ archives.

24 Roger Veckemans SJ, "Estructura de la Universidad," *Nuestra Visión de la Universidad Católica de Chile*, Escuela de Economía y Administracón, Comando Pro-Nerva Universidad, pp. 1–3.

25 R. Veckemans SJ and Mario Zañartu SJ, *Nuestra Visión*, Part II, "Juicios de hecho y juicios de valor en la Ciencia," pp. 3–7.

26 Mario Zañartu SJ, *Nuestra Visión*, Part III, "Problemas Específicos de las Ciencias Sociales," p. 7.

27 Ricardo Ffrench-Davis, Franz Himkelammert, Roberto Maldonado, Cristián Ossa, Mario Zañartu SJ, *Nuestra Visión*, Part IV, "La Escuela de Economía y Administración," p. 9.

28 *Ibid.*

29 Pablo Baraona Urzúa, *Comentarios: "Nuestra Visión de la Universidad Católica de Chile,"* 24 October 1967, p. 1.

30 *Ibid.*, p. 3.

31 *Ibid.*, pp. 1–2.

32 *Ibid.*, p. 7.

33 *Ibid.*

34 *Ibid.*

35 Personal interview with Cristián Ossa, former faculty member, New York City, 5 November 1985.

36 Rolf Luders, personal interview, Santiago, 4 October 1984.

37 *Ibid.*

38 Eduardo García, personal interview, 29 July 1986.

39 It was determined that only those professors who had been faculty members for more than six months were entitled to vote. Consequently, all the faculty members associated with the reform were left out and the Chicago group, even though reduced in numbers, recovered its control of the Institute.

10 The elusive hegemony

1 The best analysis of the movement initiated by entrepreneurs in Chile can be found in David P. Cusack, "The Politics of Chilean Private Enterprise under Christian Democracy," PhD dissertation, University of Denver (1970); Ann Arbor, Michigan: University Microfilms (1972).

2 See Tomás Moulian and Isabel Torres D., *La Derecha en Chile: Evolución Histórica y Proyección a Futuro*, Centro de Estudios del Desarrollo, July 1985, p. 30.

3 See Tomás Moulian, "Estabilidad Democrática en Chile: Una Mirada His-

tórica," in Ignacio Walker, Juan Gabriel Valdés *et al.*, *La Democracia en Chile*, CIEPLAN (1986).

4 Moulian and Torres, *La Derecha en Chile*, p. 31.

5 Hugo Zepeda, president of the Sociedad Nacional de Agricultura, as quoted by David F. Cusack, *The Politics of Chilean Private Enterprise*, p. 363.

6 The CPC was created in 1935 as a reaction to the political crisis that involved situations such as the fall of General Ibáñez, the Socialist Republic, and the unification of the labor movement in 1934.

7 On this mater, see Cusack, *The Politics of Chilean Private Enterprise*, p. 69.

8 *Ibid.*

9 *Ibid.*, p. 70.

10 *Ibid.*, p. 75.

11 *Ibid.*, p. 75.

12 *Ibid.*, pp. 363–4.

13 Hernán Errázuriz T., open letter to Eugenio Heiremans, president of the Sociedad de Fomento Fabril, Santiago, August 1969. Quoted in Cusack, *The Politics of Chilean Private Enterprise*, pp. 359–60.

14 *Ibid.*,m p. 359.

15 *Ibid.*, p. 366.

16 Carlos Hurtado, economic advisor to the president of the CPC. Personal interview, Santiago, 3 September 1985.

17 Quoted by Cusack, *The Politics of Chilean Private Enterprise*, pp. 81–2.

18 Orlando Sáenz, former president of the Sociedad de Fomento Fabril. Personal interview, Santiago, 27 July 1985.

19 Orlando Sáenz, personal interview.

20 Cusack, *The Politics of Chilean Private Enterprise*. The phrase in brackets is ours.

21 *Ibid.*, p. 86.

22 *Ibid.*, p. 87.

23 Carlos Urenda Zegers, president of the National Convention of Productions and Trade in 1968. Personal interview, Santiago, 23 October 1984.

24 Carlos Hurtado, personal interview.

25 Orlando Sáenz, personal interview.

26 Arturo Fontaine Aldunate, former director of *El Mercurio*. Personal interview, Buenos Aires, 1 July 1984.

27 Sergio Undurraga, former professor at the School of Economics, Universidad Católica de Chile. Personal interview, Santiago, 8 August 1985.

28 Carlos Urenda Zegers, personal interview.

29 Sergio Undurraga, personal interview.

30 Adelio Pipino, former CESEC member. Personal interview, Santiago, 5 June 1989.

31 Cusack, *The Politics of Chilean Private Enterprise*, p. 80.

32 Adelio Pipino, one of CESEC's most outstanding members, states that, when he returned from Chicago in 1966, he was immediately contacted by Pablo Baraona, who said: "You must join CESEC." Pipino had already been offered a job in the Sociedad de Fomento Fabril by Juan Ramón Samaniego but, as he puts it, "as a good soldier" he immediately decided to join CESEC. A. Pipino, personal interview.

33 Grant files memorandum to Mr. Peter D. Bell from John Strasma, 10 September 1971. Ford Foundation Archives, PA 65–96, p. 2.

34 Cristián Ossa, former student at the School of Economics, Universidad Católica. Personal interview, New York, 5 November 1985.

35 Ernesto Fontaine, director of the School of Economics, Universidad Católica. Personal interview, Santiago, 9 August 1985.

36 *Ibid.*

37 See "The Rise and Fall of Javier Vial," *Institutional Investor*, August 1983, pp. 84–90.

38 Ernesto Tironi. Personal interview, Santiago, 23 March 1985.

39 Raúl Devés, former dean (1960–70) of the Faculty of Engineering, Universidad Católica, personal interview, 15 May 1985. According to Devés, the isolationism of the School of Economics in relation to the rest of the university was quite obvious. It was clearly evident in Sergio de Castro's indifferent attitude to the collective problems discussed at the university's Higher Council. De Castro expressed "total contempt for anything that did not concern him personally" (*sic*).

40 Carlos Urenda Zegers, personal interview.

41 See Guillermo Sunkel, "El Mercurio como medio de educación político-ideológica (1969–1973)," in Fernando Reyes Matta, Carlos Ruiz, and Guillermo Sunkel (eds.), *Investigación sobre la Prensa en Chile (1974–1984)*, Santiago de Chile: CERC-ILET (1986).

42 *Ibid.*

43 Adelio Pipino, personal interview.

44 We refer to articles by members of the Chicago group in the PEC magazine, which we shall examine later.

45 Pipino, personal interview.

46 *El Mercurio*, 8 June 1968, p. 5.

47 See *El Mercurio*, 16 March 1968, p. 5.

48 See *El Mercurio*, 9 November 1968, p. 2.

49 Personal interview with Adelio Pipino.

50 *Ibid.*

51 See *PEC* 187, Santiago, 26 June 1966.

52 Wilhelm Roepke "Social-Cristianismo y Neo-Liberalismo," *PEC* 67, Santiago, 13 April 1964.

53 See, for example, "El inteligente y los tontos," *PEC* 320, Santiago, 14 February 1969.

54 See Coriolano, "Reprivatización," *PEC* 332, Santiago, 9 May 1969. Our emphasis.

55 "¿Existió el Milagro Alemán?" *PEC* 332, Santiago, 9 May 1969. Our emphasis.

56 Carlos Urenda Zegers, personal interview.

57 Indeed, the GNP rate of growth was 6.2 percent per year and the per capita growth was 3.7 percent. The latter rate was the highest in South America and it was more than double the mean growth rate of 1.3 percent estimated by ECLA for Latin American countries. See documents of the CPC Convention "La Empresa Privada y su Participación en el Desarrollo Económico," p. 17.

58 *Ibid.*, pp. 17 and 19.

59 Section IV, "La Descentralización de las Decisiones Económicas y el Mejoramiento de la Eficiencia," pp. 26–8.

60 *Ibid.*, pp. 26–7.

61 The first meeting was attended by: Jorge Ross, Ernesto Pinto Lagarrigue, Carlos Hurtado, Julio Philippi, Jorge Fontaine, Pierre Lehman, Jaime Guzmán, and Gisela Silva. Carlos Hurtado, personal interview, Santiago, 3 September 1985.

62 Carlos Hurtado, personal interview.

63 Carlos Urenda, personal interview.

64 *Ibid.*

11 Under the *Unidad Popular*

1 Seminar: "The Last Dope from Chile." Mimeo signed "Al H.," dated Santiago, 7 September 1970, 6 pages. I would like to express my appreciation to Manuel Antonio Garretón for making this document available.

2 *Ibid.*, p. 2. Our emphasis.

3 *Ibid.*, p. 3.

4 *Ibid.*, p. 4.

5 See Bitar, Sergio, *Transición, Socialismo y Democracia*, Mexico City: Siglo XXI (1979), p. 53.

6 Carlos Urenda Zegers, personal interview, 23 October 1984.

7 Arturo Fontaine Aldunate's book, *La Historia no contada de los Economistas y el Presidente Pinochet*, Santiago, Chile: Empresa Editora Zig-Zag (1988), written from a defensive viewpoint regarding the Chicago economists, is the best narration published to date about the period. See also Philip O'Brien " 'The New Leviathan': The Chicago School and the Chilean Regime, 1973–1980," *Bulletin of the Institute of Development Studies*, 13, no. 1, 1981, Institute of Development Studies, Sussex, England, pp. 38–50.

8 Orlando Sáenz, an entrepreneur in the sector of metallurgy, was thirty-five years old when he was offered – in April, 1971 – the directorship of SOFOFA. He was a small businessman, with a dynamic and energetic personality, who was not linked economically to big business and, in social terms, was not connected to the more powerful clans. He was viewed by these groups as the ideal leader for the confrontation against the Allende administration.

9 Orlando Sáenz, personal interview. Santiago, 27 July 1985, p. 4.

10 Sergio Undurraga, personal interview. Santiago, August 1985, p. 5.

11 See Larraín, Felipe and Meller, Patricio, "La Experiencia Populista Chilena: La Unidad Popular 1970–1973," *Colección Estudios CIEPLAN* 30, December 1990, pp. 173–4.

12 *Portada* began to be published in 1968. *Qué Pasa* was founded in 1971 as a more pugnacious magazine.

13 Orlando Sáenz, personal interview, p. 5.

14 Arturo Fontaine A., *La Historia no contada de los Economistas y el Presidente Pinochet*, p. 34.

15 See *ibid.*, pp. 18–19. Juan Braun, also considered an "honorary Chicago Boy" by his friends was an executive officer with the Cruzat group. See Philip O'Brien, " 'The New Leviathan,' " p. 40ff.

16 *Ibid.*, p. 19.

17 According to Sáenz, this subject was discussed during a dinner party to which he, as President of SOFOFA, had invited the main political leaders of the opposition to Allende, at which Frei was also present. On that occasion, Sáenz explained SOFOFA's need for alternative economic programs representing the viewpoints held by economists from the various political parties, not only from the conservative ones. According to Andrés Sanfuentes, however, Frei never had any contact with the economic team led by Andrés Sanfuentes and Alvaro Bardón. Their main link with the Christian Democrats was through Senator José Musalem.

18 Orlando Sáenz, personal interview.

19 Orlando Sáenz, "Las Fuerzas Armadas no gobiernan, ocupan Chile." Interview by Mónica González, *Cauce* 20, 28 August–3 September 1984, Santiago, Chile, p. 11.

20 Orlando Sáenz insisted on referring to the money received as "international," claiming that the "priority at the time was not the origin of the funds so much as the use to which they were put." He accepted that all business leaders assumed the CIA to be among the donors.

21 Roberto Kelly and José Radic managed a poultry farm that belonged to Agustín Edwards. The farm was located in the town of San Bernado.

22 Quoted in Arturo Fontaine Aldunate, *La Historia no contada*, p. 18.

23 Arturo Fontaine A., *La Historia no contada*, pp. 19–20.

Conclusion

1 For figures on the period of military rule and of President Aylwin's administration, see Meller, Patricio, Lehman, Sergio, and Cifuentes, Rodrigo, "Los Gobiernos de Aylwin y Pinochet: Comparación de Indicadores Económicos y Sociales," *Apuntes CIEPLAN* 18, September 1993.

2 For a discussion of the figures covering the crisis period, see Meller, Patricio, "Revisión del Ajuste Chileno de la Década de los 80," *Colección Estudios CIEPLAN* 30, December 1990.

3 Fontaine, Juan Andrés, "Transición Económica y Política en Chile: 1970–1990," *Revista de Estudios Públicos* 50, Autumn 1993, pp. 250–1. Fontaine's article provides probably the most coherent defense of the Chicago Boys' experience. Its weakness lies precisely in attributing *a posteriori* excessive political astuteness and coherence to a period plagued by confusion and setbacks as much as by achievement.

4 See Meller, "Revisión del Ajuste Chileno," p. 19.

5 *Ibid.*

6 *Ibid.*, p. 42. Also Ffrench-Davis, Ricardo, "Desarrollo Económico y Equidad en Chile: Herencias y Desafios en el Retorno a la Democracia," *Colección Estudios CIEPLAN* 31, March 1991, p. 44.

7 See Meller, Patricio and Romaguera, Pilar, "Chile: Evolución Macroeconómica, Financiación Externa y Cambio Político en la Década de los 80," in Meller, Patricio *et al. Situación Latinoamericana*, Madrid: CEDEAL (1992).

8 See Méndez, Juan Carlos *et al.*, "Por qué ganó el 'No,'" *Estudios Públicos* 33, Santiago de Chile, 1989.

9 Ffrench-Davis, "Desarrollo Económico y Equidad," p. 33.

10 *Ibid.*, p. 34.

11 *Ibid.*, p. 37.

12 See Foxley, Alejandro, *Latin American Experiments in Neo-Conservative Economics*, University of California Press (1983), pp. 16–17.

13 Fontaine, "Transición Económica y Política en Chile," p. 252.

14 *Ibid.*, same page.

15 *Ibid.*, p. 262.

16 *Ibid.*, p. 252.

17 See, for example, Patricio Meller's work on the period, especially "Los Chicago Boys y el Modelo Económico Chileno 1973–1983," *Apuntes CIEPLAN* 43, January 1984, p. 1.

18 Fontaine, "Transición Económica y Política en Chile," p. 252.

19 *Ibid.*, p. 258.

20 *Ibid.*, p. 259.

21 For a recent contribution on this theme, see "Los Secretos del Terremoto Financiero," *Qué Pasa*, 16 January 1993.

22 Ffrench-Davis, "Desarrollo Económico y Equidad," p. 42.

23 The expression is found in Foxley, Alejandro, *Economía Política de la Transición*, Santiago de Chile: Ediciones Dolment (1993), p. 8.

24 Bauer, P. T., *Equality, the Third World and Economic Delusion*, London: Weidenfeld & Nicolson (1981). Quoted in James Manor, "Politics and the Neo-Liberals," in Colclough, Christopher and Manor, James (eds.), *States or Markets? Neo-Liberalism and the Development Policy Debate*, Oxford: Clarendon Press (1991), p. 314.

25 Manor, 'Politics and the Neo-Liberals," p. 314.

26 See Klamer, Arjo, *Conversations with Economists*, Totowa, N.J.: Rowman and Allanheld Publishers (1984), chapter 5, "James Tobin," p. 101.

27 *Ibid.*, chapter 8, "Alan S. Blinder," p. 159.

28 *Ibid.*, chapter 13, "An Interpretation of the Conversations," p. 252.

29 *Ibid.*, same page.

30 *Ibid.*, chapter 5, "James Tobin," p. 106.

31 *Ibid.*, chapter 13, p. 253.

32 *Ibid.*, chapter 12, "Leonard A. Rapping."

33 *Ibid.*, chapter 10, "Karl Brunner," pp. 185–6.

34 Touraine, Alain, *Critique de la Modernité*, Paris: Fayard (1992).

35 Toye, John, "A New Political Economy of Development?" in Colclough, C. and Manor, J. (eds.), *States or Markets? Neo-Liberalism and the Development Policy Debate*, p. 322.

36 See "Isaiah Berlin: En Toutes Libertés," *Entretiens avec Ramin Jahanbegloo*, Paris: Editions du Felin (1990), p. 65 onwards.

37 Manor, "Politics and the Neo-Liberals," p. 309.

38 *Ibid.*, pp. 312–13.

Index